Introduction to
TECHNICAL SERVICES
for
LIBRARY TECHNICIANS

LIBRARY SCIENCE TEXT SERIES

Introduction to
TECHNICAL SERVICES
for
LIBRARY TECHNICIANS

Fifth Edition

Marty Bloomberg
Associate Director of the Library
California State University
San Bernardino

G. Edward Evans
Associate Dean
Graduate School of Librarianship
and Information Management
University of Denver
Denver

1985

LIBRARIES UNLIMITED, INC.
Littleton, Colorado

LIBRARIES UNLIMITED, INC.
P.O. Box 263
Littleton, Colorado 80160-0263

Library of Congress Cataloging in Publication Data

Bloomberg, Marty.
    Introduction to technical services for library
technicians.

    (Library science text series)
    Bibliography: p. 375
    Includes index.
    1. Processing (Libraries) 2. Library technicians.
I. Evans, G. Edward, 1937-   . II. Title. III. Series.
Z688.B5 1985   025'.02   85-10332
ISBN 0-87287-486-9
ISBN 0-87287-497-4 (pbk.)

CONTENTS

LIST OF ILLUSTRATIONS

PREFACE TO THE FIFTH EDITION

In the fifteen years since the first edition of this text, library paraprofessionals have continued to play an increasingly important role in most libraries. The growing use of automation in technical services has further enhanced the importance of trained paraprofessional staff. In fact, automation seems to expand the duties of paraprofessionals beyond what is possible in a nonautomated system. The creation of new levels of paraprofessionals and the corresponding increase in responsibilities continue to free librarians from clerical duties to perform professional work.

This text presents materials appropriate for an introduction to technical services and is suitable for a one-semester course. The authors stress library skills that can be developed through work experience, in-service training, classroom instruction, or a combination of these methods. The text is not intended as a handbook for establishing a technical services department, nor will reading it provide sufficient background for an inexperienced person to assume major responsibilities. However, the text should make work experience more meaningful, thereby allowing a more rapid acceptance of responsibility.

The publication of this edition allows the authors to add new materials and to update information. Some of the major revisions in this edition are (1) addition of a new chapter on acquisitions automation, (2) inclusion of new information on automation throughout the text, (3) expanded coverage of serials cataloging, (4) revision and expansion of the glossary, and (5) a completely revised and updated bibliography.

The authors wish to thank those librarians who continue to make valuable suggestions for improving the text. Special thanks go to the organizations and publishers who cooperated in supplying materials and granting permissions to use those materials.

Throughout the text the authors have used examples of various products and services. This should not be construed as an endorsement of any product or service, but merely as a reflection of widespread use and availability.

Library services are normally discussed in terms of two broad categories—public and technical. Any operation that involves direct contact with the library patron is considered a public service; all other operations are technical services. This is a very general definition, but it does provide a point of reference. Activities usually considered as technical services are acquisition work, cataloging, bindery preparation, gifts and exchange, and serials. These activities may be combined in various ways into departments or administrative units, but most libraries usually have at least an acquisition and a cataloging department.

Technical service activities require the efforts of a large portion of library staff; in some large libraries, more than 60% of the staff is assigned to such work. Because of the number of individuals involved, and because a large percentage of any library's budget is spent on technical service units, work efficiency becomes a real concern.

When the first edition of this book was published in 1971, most technical services work was done manually. Libraries were experimenting with automating some aspects of library work, and a few cooperative efforts in library automation were underway. Today, many medium-sized and large libraries are using computers for at least one activity (circulation, cataloging, serials control, bookkeeping, interlibrary loan, acquisitions, or online searching). The major changes in this fifth edition relate to automation issues. As the variety of available systems increases and the cost of these systems decreases, even small libraries will have an opportunity to make use of technology to improve the efficiency of their operations.

Despite the increased use of technology to improve operational efficiency, there has been no significant decrease in the number of persons working in technical services. In fact, there are probably more library technicians employed in technical services today than there were in 1971. The functional responsibilities that are performed have not changed that much in the last 15 years, and for that reason, the topics covered in this edition are basically the same as in the first edition. However, the activities, the way the person discharges his or her responsibilities, have changed in content and form; thus each edition has focused on those changes in order to keep pace with the "real world."

TECHNICAL SERVICES—OVERVIEW

Technical service operations are concerned with securing and processing materials for patron use. While this work must be performed for all libraries, it need not be done in the same building as public services. Some libraries have found it convenient to place all technical service functions under the direction of one person. Yet, in many small and some large libraries, there is no "technical service" administrative unit. Instead, there are independent departments such as acquisitions, cataloging, and serials, and the work in each of these areas depends greatly upon the work performed in the other areas. Therefore, as a library grows, the coordination and effective use of its staff may present problems in the absence of an overall supervisor.

Centralized, Cooperative, and Commercial Processing

Technical service work is repetitive when viewed from outside the library. That is, in the past, each time each library acquired an item for its collection, all the activities described in the following pages had to be carried out. When a neighboring library acquired the same item, all the activities were repeated. With more than 100,000 libraries in the United States, a single popular item could require the same process to be carried out several thousand times. In 1983 B. Turlock estimated that less than 5% of all public libraries were using "major bibliographic utilities" ("Public Library in the Age of Electronic Information," *Public Library Quarterly* 4 [Summer 1983]: 3-11). If processing information and activities could be shared among libraries, there would be significant savings in the cost of technical service. During the 1960s and early 1970s, many projects and systems for sharing were tried, and a few proved to be very successful. Three basic variations for sharing technical services are still in use today.

First, one library system may serve an entire county, municipality, or school system. Normally, in such cases, a *central* library handles the technical processing operations for all of the sub-units within the system. In this situation, it is most unusual for a branch library to handle any part of technical services.

A second variation is cooperative systems. These systems are similar to the one library system described above. The basic differences are:

1) the system is composed of several independent library systems, perhaps with branches of their own, and

2) only a portion of each library's total technical service work is handled by the cooperative.

Obviously, such a system makes more effective use of resources, personnel, and equipment; it also results in higher discounts on bulk purchases. This type of arrangement requires some degree of standardization in cataloging, processing, ordering, and other set procedures. Otherwise, no library would benefit from the system as far as technical services are concerned. The most important factor to remember is that, except for the very smallest library, the cooperative system does not do all of the technical service work for its members.

A third variation is the use of commercial services now being offered by a number of firms. These services, however, do not relieve the library of all technical service work, since most commercial firms limit their services to certain types of material or to certain aspects of technical services. In most cases, these firms will only supply and process in-print English-language books, and some firms have further restrictions, such as handling only certain titles (popular items) or charging an additional service fee for items not in stock. While most of the savings here are in the cataloging and processing procedures, some savings are realized in acquisition work because of simplified order procedures.

Each of these alternatives now makes increasing use of automation to improve efficiency. In later chapters, we will explore some of the more common systems available to libraries for handling various technical service activities.

One other variation has come into use in the last five years, especially in U.S. government libraries. With this variation a commercial firm enters into a contractual agreement to provide technical services for the library. It is similar to the commercial processing in that the people who do the processing are not employees of the library. It differs from such services in that the technical services are provided and customized for that library. In addition, very often the company personnel do the work in the library. One such firm is the Maxima Corporation. Technical assistants with science or technology backgrounds may be interested in contacting it or similar organizations that provide information services.

Basic Functions of Technical Services

A library, media center, learning resource center, or information center exists only to provide service to the patron. The kind and degree of service will vary from library to library, but even the "archive-museum" library provides a research and preservation service. Nevertheless, while service to the patron is the objective, in a very real sense the origin of this service lies within technical services. Without the work performed by this unit, the library would find it impossible to provide any real service. Technical service activities revolve around three basic functions:

1) purchasing library materials (primarily for the collection rather than office supplies or equipment)—acquisition department;

2) organizing and processing materials so patrons may use them—catalog department; and

3) maintaining the collection and the records (primarily the public catalog and shelflist) that provide access to the library's collection—bindery and catalog departments.

Some technical services departments combine all three of these functions, while others perform only one or two.

The two major administrative departments in technical services are acquisition and cataloging. Acquisition work involves purchasing materials for the library's collections; it includes ordering, bookkeeping, and receiving procedures. Cataloging work consists of informing the library user of the types of information available in the library. This work has two components: descriptive cataloging (describing an item as a physical object) and subject cataloging (determining what subject or subjects the item deals with and assigning it a classification number).

The maintenance aspect of technical services is often neglected. This work may be considered in two parts: maintaining the public record of the library's holdings, and caring for and repairing items in the collection. In addition to the general public catalog, a number of other public records must be kept up to date by technical service personnel. Examples of such records are a serials holding list, government documents catalog, phonograph record catalog, or special collections catalogs. Not only must the necessary entries be made for new materials, but effective records will also reflect any change in the location of materials and will contain a record of lost or discarded items. Another aspect of the maintenance problem is the need to shift catalog cards in the public file in order to make room for new material. As the collection grows, the catalog also grows. But some sections of the alphabet grow more rapidly than others, which requires shifts and eventually the purchase of additional catalog units. If a card catalog is in use, then worn or damaged cards must be replaced.

One of the great advantages of an online catalog is that much of the maintenance work is performed by a computer. Each year more and more libraries have online or computer-generated catalogs; however, this does not mean the traditional card catalog has disappeared, even in libraries with computer-based catalogs. Most computer-based catalogs include materials acquired and processed after a specific date, for example, items published after 1985. Very rarely do libraries have enough money to perform "retrospective conversion," in other words, to convert the cards in the card catalog to machine readable form. Thus, most libraries will continue to have a card catalog; although the maintenance problems will decrease with each passing year, card catalogs will remain.

Most libraries do little repair work on books, except for minor problems such as torn pages. Almost all repairs are handled by the book binder. The exception is pamphlets, which are usually protected by commercially available "pam" binders of stiff cardboard. If a library has a power stapling machine, some of the smaller paperback books (usually under 100 pages) may be given an additional protective cover. In a medium-sized library, the cost of maintaining the collection may represent a significant expenditure of time, effort, and money.

Several other departments are often considered part of technical services: serials, government documents, binding, and gifts and exchange. (All but government documents will be discussed in later sections of this book.) Serials control is a universal problem in all types of libraries; government documents control, however, is a much less common problem, since fewer libraries acquire these materials in large numbers and since fewer libraries catalog government documents and use the U.S. Superintendent of Documents system to organize these items.

DEPARTMENTAL FUNCTIONS

Acquisition Department

Although an acquisition department rarely has responsibility for the selection of materials, a few do carry out this function for the library. Usually, the department's involvement in selection is limited to helping the unit responsible for selection to develop an acquisition policy. Regardless of which unit handles the process, however, professional librarians are responsible for the work. Library Media Technical Assistants (LMTAs) need a knowledge of the selection process to understand how a library operates and how book request forms are filled out. Selection work is a decision-making process: this item will be useful to the library, therefore we should acquire it—this one is not needed and we will not buy it.

Selection work determines what is needed, and the acquisition department then secures that material.

Acquiring an item is often more difficult than it might seem. For various reasons, even verifying an item's existence may be a problem. The first step in the acquisition procedure is to verify existence, determine price, and identify the publisher or supplier. An order is then placed with the appropriate supplier (publisher, wholesaler, bookstore, or other source).

Another major duty of the acquisition department is to maintain the fiscal records for the library. In many libraries, because of budget size, this becomes a full-time job for one or more persons. While all aspects of bookkeeping are important, one of the most critical and difficult tasks is keeping the book budget up to date. The last task of the acquisition department is receiving. Although this particular operation might seem undemanding, if it is not carried out with care, it can waste a great deal of the library's time and money.

Cataloging Department

Like acquisitions, the catalog department has three basic functions to perform. The first is cataloging and classification, which includes determination of authorship, description of the item, and assignment of subject headings and classification number. The determination of authorship is important not only in cataloging but also in acquisitions. (As readers will discover, this can be a complicated task.) Subject headings help the patron locate materials on given topics. The number of subject headings that can be assigned is limited, however, by the amount of time that can practically and economically be spent on this task. Unlike subject headings, only one classification number can be assigned to an item. It serves two purposes: 1) to place together on the shelves materials on similar subjects (class number), and 2) to give each item a definite physical location that allows the library patron and staff to locate the item easily (call number).

The catalog department's second basic function is the physical preparation of material for use. One such task involves making labels that display the call number. An item that can be removed from the library may need to have a book pocket and date due card inserted. (The exact nature of the pocket and date due card depend, of course, on the type of circulation system being used.) Other routines of physical preparation include shellacking the label to prevent fading and smearing, and covering the book jacket with a plastic cover or adding a pamphlet binding. If a card catalog system is used, a set of catalog cards for the public catalogs, shelflist, and any other catalogs must be prepared.

The third basic function of the catalog department is to maintain catalog records in the library. The maintenance of a card catalog involves filing cards, replacing worn cards, correcting cards if errors are found, and removing cards for items discarded or lost. Each of these areas requires great care, particularly in filing. A misfiled card, especially an author card, is like a lost book. If the library user is to have maximum use of a library and to locate items easily, a well-maintained catalog is essential.

Serials Department

While most libraries separate their catalog and acquisition departments, libraries often combine other technical service functions in one or two units. Serials is the one unit most likely to be found as a separate department. Even the smallest library subscribes to a few periodicals, and as the library grows, the number of subscriptions increases and the daily routines of handling these items require the full-time attention of one or more people. If a library is to be an information center, it must be capable of responding to patron needs for the latest information. Such media as books, films, and phonograph records, because of their nature, cannot or at least do not disseminate information at the rate desired by some people. Because the monthly or weekly news magazine and the daily newspaper are a more rapid form of information dissemination, libraries also subscribe to these. In addition, libraries subscribe to serials whose primary function is to communicate ideas and commentaries without regard for speed of information transfer. A medium-sized library may receive as many as 100 different newspapers and magazines each day.

Bindery Department

Although separate binderies are found only in a few of the largest libraries, all libraries are concerned with bindery preparation. In medium-sized libraries, bindery work is often under the control of the serials department, the unit that requires the most bindery preparation. In most cases, books and serials to be bound are sent to a commercial bindery. Thus, bindery work is briefly discussed in the chapter on serials.

Gifts and Exchange Department

Separate gifts and exchange units are rather common in libraries that have reached medium size. Although all libraries become involved in this work, in smaller libraries, this function is usually handled by the acquisition department. Even the smallest library will receive gifts from time to time from its patrons, and a sizeable portion of these gifts will be items that the library cannot use for a number of reasons (duplicates, too elementary, too dated, too scholarly, no patron interest in the topic). Libraries spend a good deal of time and energy handling gift items, but the value to public relations often far exceeds the staff time and energy devoted to doing the job. Since most libraries are tax-supported institutions, rejecting offers of donated materials may create public relations problems. Therefore, libraries usually accept gifts and develop a policy for their processing. There are two aspects of working with gifts: 1) disposing of unwanted gifts and duplicate titles, and 2) examining lists of duplicate materials from other libraries with the idea of arranging a barter with other institutions to secure otherwise unobtainable materials.

WHAT IS A LIBRARY MEDIA
TECHNICAL ASSISTANT?

Before exploring the role of the LMTA, we need to know something about what an LMTA is and what education is required to become one. In 1968 the Office for Library Education of the American Library Association (ALA) defined several library personnel classes, with the training requirements included. Although the ALA list was subject to modification, it did provide a framework within which to work. Since the ALA attempt, many other groups and individuals have published definitions of library personnel and their educational requirements, but these have been neither more nor less satisfactory than the ALA definitions. In this book, we are concerned with the work usually done by the library assistant, the technical assistant, and the library clerk. Many people have recently started using the term Library Media Technical Assistant, or LMTA, a title that reflects the expanded role of assistants in library work, especially in community college, public, and school libraries.

In 1976 ALA revised its statement, and the title was changed to *Library Education and Personnel Utilization* (*see* below). It remains ALA's official position on library education and training as well as on the types of work that should be performed by each worker's level.

One of the most comprehensive studies of LMTA requirements was funded by the U.S. Office of Education. It defines the types of positions that LMTAs may expect to fill and the basic activities and duties that they might perform. Because it is a comprehensive national report, we quote extensively from it:

Graduates of this program can expect to find employment in many types and sizes of libraries requiring a variety of responsibilities. Most graduates will further develop their abilities by continued study on a part-time basis to keep pace with new developments in their fields. The following listing shows a sampling of only a few of the job opportunities for library technical assistants, as described by employers. Some are beginning positions, others are attained through work experience or further study, or both....

1. *Library Technical Assistant I*—May perform one or more of the following: assist readers in locating books and using the public catalog; supervise shelving and other tasks performed by student assistants and clerks; supervise the maintenance and distribution of special collections and equipment; assist in the cataloging department; and, may be responsible for the reproduction of media materials.

2. *Library Technical Assistant II*—May perform all of the duties of the Library Technical Assistant I, as well as one or more of the following: supervise the work of Library Technical Assistant I; assist in the preparation of bibliographies; develop displays; supervise multiple book stack areas; and, be responsible for the production of media materials.

3. *Library Technical Assistant III*—May perform all duties of the Library Technical Assistant II, as well as one or more of the following: be responsible for supervision of all other library technical assistants and clerical staff; prepare special bibliographies; do basic uncomplicated cataloging; provide reference services on information desks and answer reference questions of an uncomplicated nature;

Categories of Library Personnel — Professional*

Title For Positions Requiring:		Basic Requirements	Nature of Responsibility
Library-Related Qualifications	Nonlibrary-Related Qualifications		
Senior Librarian	Senior Specialist	In addition to relevant experience, education beyond the M.A. [i.e., a master's degree in any of its variant designations: M.A., M.L.S., M.S.L.S., M.Ed., etc.] as: post-master's degree; Ph.D.; relevant continuing education in many forms	Top-level responsibilities, including but not limited to administration; superior knowledge of some aspect of librarianship, or of other subject fields of value to the library
Librarian	Specialist	Master's degree	Professional responsibilities including those of management, which require independent judgment, interpretation of rules and procedures, analysis of library problems, and formulation of original and creative solutions for them (normally utilizing knowledge of the subject field represented by the academic degree)

Categories of Library Personnel — Supportive

Title		Basic Requirements	Nature of Responsibility
Library Associate	Associate Specialist	Bachelor's degree (with or without course work in library science); OR bachelor's degree, plus additional academic work short of the master's degree (in librarianship for the Library Associate; in other relevant subject fields for the Associate Specialist)	Supportive responsibilities at a high level, normally working within the established procedures and techniques, and with some supervision by a professional, but requiring judgment, and subject knowledge such as is represented by a full, four-year college education culminating in the bachelor's degree
Library Technical Assistant	Technical Assistant	At least two years of college-level study; OR A.A. degree, with or without Library Technical Assistant training; OR post-secondary school training in relevant skills	Tasks performed as supportive staff to Associates and higher ranks, following established rules and procedures, and including, at the top level, supervision of such tasks
	Clerk	Business school or commercial courses, supplemented by in-service training or on-the-job experience	Clerical assignments as required by the individual library

*Reprinted by permission of the American Library Association from *Library Education and Personnel Utilization*, A Statement of Policy Adopted by the Council of the American Library Association, June 30, 1970; revised 1976 by the Office for Library Personnel Resources Advisory Committee.

supervise circulation, interlibrary loan or periodical services; and, assist with special community projects and services.

The classifications and degrees of responsibility may vary somewhat depending on the objectives and size of the particular library, and the clientele it serves. Library technical assistants work in a great variety of libraries. These include public and private school libraries, academic libraries, public libraries and special libraries such as medical, business and governmental.

Besides technical skills, some of the positions in a particular library may demand other traits and related skills. For example, a knowledge of medical terminology or a strong background in science and mathematics may be required for effective employment in a special library. A wider background in general education, literature, humanities and communications may be necessary to be an effective employee in a small public library system or a school library. A course in young adult and children's literature would benefit the student who is interested in working with young people.

In addition to the technical courses, general education courses and related technical courses which comprise the suggested two-year curriculum, it is desirable that the library technical assistant have some basic clerical skills. For example, typing skills, while not a prerequisite for entry into a program, should be acquired by the student, either through additional course work or self-study before he enters his internship and graduates from the program. Although typing is a clerical skill, the student may find himself in a position where he has limited clerical assistance or none at all. It is not uncommon for small libraries to have only one to three full-time staff members. This necessitates the acquisition of skills at all operative levels below the technician level, including clerical skills. A minimum typing speed of 35 words per minute is recommended.

Skilled technical assistants must have both technical competence and the ability to react positively to a variety of situations encountered in their working associations with librarians, other technical assistants, clerical employees and, most important, the clientele of the library.

Technician education programs must provide students with opportunities to gain knowledge of the hardware, processes, procedures, techniques, materials, and tools of the library. It must provide educational experiences that will develop a person with the ability to communicate with professionals and to serve as delegates or assistants to them. Some indication of the special nature of technical programs may be obtained from detailed analysis of what technical assistants must know, what special abilities they must possess and what they must be able to do in their daily work.

Special Abilities Required
of Technical Assistants

Technical assistants must have the following special abilities:
1. A thorough understanding of and facility in the use of the materials, processes, apparatus, procedures, equipment, methods and techniques commonly used in the technology.

2. A broad base of general education courses to include communications, social sciences, humanities, physical sciences and mathematics.
3. An expanded knowledge in a specialized area such as medical terminology, special libraries, children's work, art, literature or science to provide students with an individualized program consistent with their career objectives.
4. Business skills, especially typing competency, are advisable, but are not included in the curriculum.
5. Personal qualifications which include an aptitude for library work; ability to communicate clearly and to understand and follow written and oral directions; and, the ability to effectively supervise the work of others.

Activities Performed by Technical Assistants

Generally speaking a technician bridges the gap between the clerk or aide and the professional. He is part of a team. His skills vary widely with training and experience, but some generalizations can be made about the level at which he works. The main thing which separates the technical assistant from professionals — the level above him — and clerks — the level below him — is the way in which he approaches his work. The clerk receives very explicit instructions and has a definite work pattern set up for him. The professional has very vague instructions for work and must often create his own procedures to solve a problem. The technical assistant falls between these two extremes. His output is specified in general terms and he has a set of procedures to choose from to produce this output. He may choose a procedure, modify it somewhat, or synthesize two procedures into one to reach his goal. But the basic emphasis is the same at the technical assistant level: a stated goal with a number of routines to reach that goal with enough discretion given for him to choose his own work pattern to meet the goal. Research in job analysis tends to confirm this distinction between clerk or aide, technical assistant and professional and the distinction holds true from one work field to another.

Technical assistant duties are related to a variety of library functions. Depending upon the size, type and service philosophy of the library, these functions may be very general or very specialized and departmentalized, or both.

1. *Administrative Services.* Assists in administrative duties such as recommending new supplies and equipment; preparing specifications for the purchase of equipment; handling inventory responsibilities for the library collection, supplies, and equipment; compiling and tabulating data for statistical reports; training clerical staff, student aides and volunteers; assigning work distribution to the clerical and student staff; preparing reports on work programs; and, applying libraries' policies, rules and instructions.

2. *Technical Services.* Assists in technical services doing bibliographic work in the preparation of entries for acquisition. This would include verifying data, searching trade journals, catalogs and other reference tools; supervising the preparation of orders and the maintenance of order files; supervising the maintenance of records of serial publications; initial checking and revision of printed cards, and

either temporary or preliminary cataloging and original cataloging in brief form; cataloging duplicate titles, and supervising preparation of additional catalog cards; supervising filing of catalog cards; removing catalog cards for material which has been withdrawn from the collection; supervising the replacement of damaged catalog cards; and, assisting with interlibrary loan of materials.

3. *Public Services.* Assists in public services including supervising circulation routines and controls, and applying the circulation policies of the library; maintaining special and reserve collections; and, assisting in compiling reading lists, bibliographies and other selective lists of materials.

4. *Data Processing Services.* Assists with or supervises data processing operations.

5. *Related Media Services.* Supervising the maintenance and operation of audiovisual equipment, and processing, shelving and filing microforms, tapes and recordings, films and filmstrips, slides, prints and photographs.

6. *Media Production Services.* May be involved in media production services of the library which might encompass photographic production and reproduction, audio recording and duplication, and graphic design and illustration.

7. *Publicity and Public Relations Services.* Responsibility for publicity functions such as compiling and distributing acquisitions lists, and developing and preparing bulletin boards, displays, posters and special reading lists.

8. *Information Services.* May be responsible for answering directional or factual questions, explaining use of bibliographic tools to patrons and answering basic reference questions.

9. *Housekeeping Services.* Has the supervisory responsibility for shelving and filing functions; inventory; shelf reading; transfer of materials to storage; and, discarding of obsolete materials.

10. *Implementing Clerical Services.* Compiling statistics; assisting in the development of procedures manuals; handling the supervision of mail and routing correspondence; maintaining vertical and correspondence files; handling reproduction services; and, preparing purchase orders for library supplies and equipment.

A two-year program to educate library technical assistants must concentrate on primary or fundamental needs if it is to prepare students for responsible technical positions in the modern library. It must be realistic and pragmatic. The program suggested in this guide has been designed to provide maximum technical instruction coupled with a broad general education background in the time allotted.

To those who are not familiar with this type of educational service (or with the goals and interests of students who elect it), the technical program often appears to be inordinately rigid and restrictive. While modifications may be necessary in certain individual institutions, the basic structure and content of this program should be maintained as closely as possible in order to develop the highest level of skill, both operative and cognitive, in the time that is available in a two-year program.

The specialized technical courses in the program are laboratory and field-oriented. They provide time for the application of principles, methods and skills concurrently being taught in the courses in the technical field. The general education courses must be coordinated carefully with technical courses at all stages of the program. This coordination is accomplished by scheduling the communications, humanities, and science courses concurrently with technical courses during the first three semesters. In the third and fourth semesters the student is permitted to select appropriate career electives to prepare him for further specialization in the library service of his choice. Although general education courses and career options are relatively unique to technical programs, the heavy concentration of these courses is justified on the basis of the peculiarities of this program. Since the program is library centered, the student who is to assist in the acquisition and dissemination of knowledge, in a service capacity, must be familiar with the various disciplines of modern society. He must not only be able to help others attain knowledge, but also must be able and anxious to seek and find the answers himself. Although the student may have a general education background when he enters the program, this base must be extended if he is to be an effective agent in disseminating knowledge to others.*

ROLE OF LMTAs IN TECHNICAL SERVICES

Figures 1.1, 4.1, and 15.5, which indicate the role of LMTAs in technical service, were developed on the basis of our experience as working librarians and as teachers. Dr. G. Edward Evans, who has studied the problems of defining job activities and personnel assignment in both American and European libraries, has served on the Library/Media Technicians Articulation Committee of the Community College Conference. This group was concerned, among other things, with the problem of defining appropriate levels of education and "real world" work activities for librarians and paraprofessionals.

Based on data from formal studies and committee work, it is clear that a great deal of work remains in the area of reaching a universal agreement on the roles and activities of all persons working in a library. However, one of the most satisfying results of writing this book has been the positive response of readers to the charts (Figures 1.1, 4.1, and 15.5) in which we identified basic activities. In each edition, we modified and refined the charts. Much of this revision was based upon Dr. Evans' study of methods that Scandinavian library systems use in employing technicians; these methods are some of the most rational in the world of librarianship. Reader input on this topic, which also assisted in the previous editions, indicates that the charts have filled a real need for both librarians and library/media technicians and are as close as we shall come to a universal definition of levels for some time.

Details concerning most of the activities listed in the chart are given in the remainder of the book. Remember, however, that this text is intended as an introduction to technical service work for the LMTA. There will be only limited discussions of the responsibilities of other personnel — enough to provide an overview, but no details. In essence, this book can provide only a background to the

*U.S. Office of Education, Manpower Development and Training Program, *A Suggested Two-Year Post High School Curriculum: Library Technical Assistant* (Washington, D.C.: GPO, 1973), pp. 5-9.

Fig. 1.1
Technical Service Activities

TECHNICAL SERVICE ACTIVITIES	PERSONNEL			
	Librarian	Library Technician	Library Clerk	Part Time Help (Students)
General Activities				
1. Policy Matters	X			
2. Assignment of personnel to all duties	X			
3. Public Relations	X	X	X	X
4. Book Selection	X			
Acquisition Department				
5. Receiving book requests and sorting for verification		X		
6. Verification		X	X	
7. Order preparation		X		
8. Bookkeeping		X or	X	
9. Receiving activities			X	X
Gift and Exchange				
10. Securing gifts	X			
11. Selection of items to retain from gifts	X			
12. Checking selected gifts against holdings		X	X	
13. Preparing exchange lists		X		
14. Typing exchange lists			X	
Catalog Department				
15. Ordering and receiving catalog cards		X	X	
16. Cataloging and classifying without catalog copy	X	X		
17. Cataloging and classifying with catalog copy		X		
18. Book preparation		X	X	X
19. Filing catalog cards		X	X	
Serials Department				
20. Selection of serials	X			
21. Preparing serial orders		X		
22. Receiving serials		X	X	
23. Serial claiming		X		
Bindery Department				
24. Maintain bindery records		X		
25. Bindery preparation		X	X	
26. Typing bindery orders			X	
27. Receiving bindery shipments		X	X	X

actual functions, purposes, and objectives of technical service work. But this background will make the variations and details of an LMTA's first library position more understandable and so will facilitate the task of learning the routines.

The LMTA's role can be significant, as the table shows. Many of the activities suggested as duties for the LMTA were handled, just a few years ago, by beginning librarians. Yet, since the trend toward a more realistic appraisal of technical service work and the training needed for it will no doubt continue, the library technician position can and should become a regular part of a library's personnel program.

Almost every issue of the major library journals has articles or notices about library technician matters—an indication that the role and importance of the technician are steadily increasing. One of the best sources of current information about the field is the *COLT Newsletter*, published by the Council on Library/Media Technical Assistants. COLT publishes a directory of LMTA programs as well.

TERMS

We use the term "LMTA" to mean a person who has completed at least two years of college, with some training in library science. The term "librarian" is used to denote a college graduate who holds a master's degree in library science. Whenever the word "library" is used and not specifically modified as to size and type (school, special, public, or academic), assume that reference is to a medium-sized public or academic library. (By medium-sized, we mean a library with a collection of 100,000-500,000 volumes and a staff of 15 to 50 employees.) The fact that this range is large simply reinforces the view that there is no average or typical library. Because each library combines a number of different objectives, functions, and services, it is impossible to identify any given library as typical.

NEED FOR LMTAs IN TECHNICAL SERVICES

The lack of trained personnel has been a major incentive in the search for cooperative methods. Greater use of non-professional personnel having training in library service should improve total staff efficiency, making it possible to provide full cataloging for pamphlets, pictures, and nonbook materials of all types, which now may only be handled in a cursory manner. Cataloging backlogs—i.e., books not yet cataloged and so generally not available to the public—could be reduced or cleared up entirely with the help of non-professionals. More efficient use of the whole library staff would result in greater depth of cataloging (in terms of subject and added entries), thus providing the user with additional points of access to the library's collection. Employing non-professionals in acquisition work might provide time for more careful selection of materials, and selectors could consider some of the newer information media that previously might have been ignored. In all these areas, the LMTA can contribute significantly to improving library service for the community.

Library assistants, or LMTAs, have a significant role to play in library operations. As more emphasis is placed on efficient operations, the role of the assistant must expand. Use of the assistant is becoming an accepted practice in the United States just as it has in Europe. It is hoped that in the near future, work rationalization studies of the type undertaken in the Scandinavian libraries will be done in the United States. The Nordic libraries have formalized the technician/assistant's role and function in a very logical manner.

The assistant is particularly important in technical services. Much of the work in acquisition and cataloging requires special library skills and knowledge but not graduate training in librarianship. Properly trained technical assistants can be uniquely qualified to perform this type of work.

REVIEW QUESTIONS

1. Define library technician.

2. Identify the categories of library personnel and give three examples of typical tasks each performs.

3. Name one professional association primarily concerned with library technician activities.

4. What types of technical processing methods exist in American libraries?

5. Describe the major reason(s) for employing LMTAs in technical service.

6. What are the basic functions of technical service departments?

7. The two most common administrative departments in technical services are:
   1)   2)

8. Name at least two other departments often found in medium-sized technical service units.

9. What maintenance functions are performed by technical services?

10. What is the first step in the acquisition procedure?

11. What are the three basic functions of the acquisition department?

12. Describe the basic functions of the catalog department.

13. How do most libraries handle the binding of their books and other materials?

14. Describe two reasons for having a gifts and exchange program.

2
AUTOMATION AND LIBRARIES

After reading the library literature of the past 25 years, a person might reasonably expect to find every library fully automated—computer quietly running, lights blinking, and display screens aglow. At least, a large portion of library literature suggests that this is the case. The facts, however, are rather different. Certainly most large libraries and many medium-sized libraries use automation in some manner in their day-to-day operation, but the majority of small libraries still cannot justify the cost of automation. Over the years, the cost of purchasing equipment has dropped from a seven-digit figure to a six-digit one; and now, with microcomputers, it is down to five digits. Some electronics firms even offer a home computer, for under $1,000, that could have limited use in a small library.

As will be discussed, the number of vendors offering some automated technical service packages has increased. One problem with the low-cost home computer is that there are (as of 1985) few library software programs for these units. Creating one's own programs can be very time-consuming; even modifying packaged programs takes time and skill that many small libraries simply do not have. In the last few years, some books have been published that can help speed up the process. One such book is Janet Naumer's *Media Center Management with an Apple II*® (Littleton, Colo.: Libraries Unlimited, 1984). Another factor that will increase the percentage of automated libraries is that many school media centers are becoming the student access point to computers. In 1983/84, for example, the Jefferson County (Colorado) school district placed 15 computers in each school media center. The equipment was also made available for library operations, if the staff had the time to develop suitable programs.

In spite of the fact that less than half of current libraries are automated, most LMTAs will work in libraries that have some form of automation because large- and medium-sized libraries employ most of the persons working in libraries. With the above in mind, we prepared this chapter to give both a few very basic facts about computers and library automation and an overview of how the computer affects technical services.

It is not our purpose in this chapter to provide an in-depth description of computer technology or library automation or of how and when one should consider using a computer in technical services. Such topics are subjects for entire courses and textbooks. We do feel, however, that some very *brief* background information should be available for the reader who knows little or nothing about library automation. (Readers with previous course work or background in computers and automation may wish to skip this section and move on to the section on "Automation and Technical Services.")

LIBRARY AUTOMATION

Computer technology has gone through several stages in a relatively short period of time (30-35 years). In the 1950s, computers were large and, by today's standards, slow vacuum tube units that generated heat and required air conditioning and a great deal of money to buy. By the early 1960s transistor ("second generation") computers came on the scene. This made them smaller, faster, and more reliable as well as making them somewhat less expensive. As a result, more and more organizations began to use them, including some of the larger libraries. "Third generation" computers using something called integrated circuits began to replace the second generation units in the late 1960s. What is important about these technological developments, from the library point of view, is that integrated data systems could become a reality and computers and telecommunications could be used at a cost that many organizations could afford.

The equipment (hardware), as noted earlier, is available and is steadily declining in cost. What has been and continues to be a major problem is the program (software) of instructions that make the computer useful for various functions. People quickly found it was rather easy to program a computer to replicate physical activities (for example, placing the data from a handwritten check—date, name of payee, amount paid—and a code for the account to be charged, in the appropriate places in a bookkeeping system). What has proven much more difficult is to replicate mental/judgment processes. Thus most of the library functions that have been automated and are in general use in libraries are those that are tied to physical activities. In the last few years, significant progress has been made in developing artificial intelligence (AI) computers, which replicate basic human thinking and reasoning. When the AI generation of computers become commercially available, there will be major changes in library automation.

In essence, automation is used to reduce the amount of staff time devoted to repetitive (and often less challenging) activities that must be done in any properly functioning library. One fact must be kept in mind: various *library processes are automated, not the library as such*; a fact many lay people fail to recognize. Automation has many definitions, but for our purposes, one from Martin Weik's *Standard Dictionary of Computers and Information Processing* (New York: Hayden Books, 1969) is satisfactory:

> Automation—The entire field of investigation devoted to the design, development, and application of methods and techniques for rendering a process or group of machines self-actuating, self-moving, or self-controlling. Automation pertains to the theory, art, or technique of making a machine, a process, or a device more fully automatic. Simply, the implementation of a process by automatic means. Computers and information-processing equipment play a large role in the automation of a process because of the inherent ability of a computer to develop decisions that will, in effect, control or govern the process from the information received by the computer concerning the status of the process (p. 31).

For libraries, the most common automation device is the electronic digital computer. Library processes that are now being "controlled" by the computer include bookkeeping, materials ordering, cataloging, serials control, circulation, bibliographic data retrieval, and some aspects of interlibrary loan work.

Computers and Automation

How does a computer control library processes? Basically, all computers (maxis, minis, or micros—more about this later) function in the same manner: they can convert ("read"), store ("remember"), do arithmetic, make simple logical choices (processing), and display ("write"). "Reading" is accomplished by means of a device (input) that gives the computer its information (data). A computer "remembers" when data are put into a storage (memory) device at a specific point (storage address). Arithmetic and logical decisions are made in what is called the central processing unit (CPU). And "writing" is done by a device (output) that transforms the CPU's electronic impulses into either letters or digits that people can read. The computer is so useful because it can perform *all* of these functions at incredibly fast speeds, doing in seconds (or less) tasks that would take a person minutes or hours to do. (A very simplified diagram of a computer system is given in Figure 2.1.) The machines do not read, remember, etc., in the same manner as people do; however, the analogy is useful to keep in mind as you first learn about computers.

Fig. 2.1
Computer Model

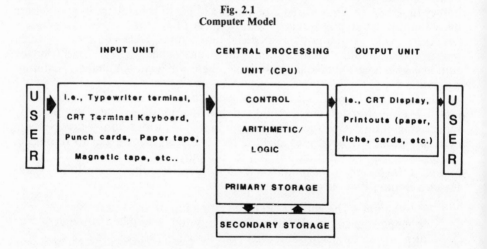

Input devices are units through which words and symbols are converted into the form (usually electrical impulses, positive and negative charges) that computers use in CPU operation. They can take a number of forms—keyboards (like a typewriter), punch cards, or paper or magnetic tape. Another method gaining in popularity is the light pen and OCR (Optical Character Recognition) devices. In retail stores, packages with "zebra stripe" labels are designed to be read by such devices. The light pens and zebra stripes concept is also employed in some library circulation systems. Work has been and is being done to develop effective and fast voice activated input devices, but it will be some time before we see them in regular use in libraries. When they are available it will greatly reduce the amount of training a user will need to utilize a system.

When you prepare information for a computer, you must follow a carefully outlined series of steps and directions. *Computers do not think*; they must be told how to do everything in minute detail (through programs). In the type of computer operations covered in this book, you can assume that the computer has been properly programmed, so that if you accurately follow the directions for inputing the information, the computer will do the rest.

At the heart of the computer is the CPU—central processing unit—which can be thought of as made up of three sections: control, arithmetic/logic, and primary storage. As its name implies, the control section determines what the system does. The entire system is based upon the flow of electrical current, which is a series of controlled impulses (positive and negative), and most computers use a binary number system (base 2, with positive impulses being 1 and negative 0). By means of electronic impulses, the computer converts input letters and symbols (including decimal numbers) into binary numbers; it is then able to perform the adding and subtracting functions and logical functions as required. Although the process sounds complex (and it is), the computer can perform these activities in a thousandth (millisecond) or a millionth (microsecond) of a second. Normally, the CPU's ability to hold and manipulate data is referred to as its capacity. CPU capacity is usually stated in terms of thousands (K) of bytes (pronounced bites)—Kbytes or KBs. Most but not all computers use eight electrical impulses (each called a bit) to make one byte.

A small home computer (a minicomputer) holds between 4 and 8 KB, while the systems most commonly found in libraries have 16 to 64 KB capacity. The largest computers have a capacity of 4 to 8 million bytes. This capacity is stated in terms of primary storage, that is, bytes actually stored in the CPU. It is possible to attach large capacity secondary storage units to the CPU, thus greatly increasing the capability of a small primary CPU. Data then can be moved back and forth between primary and secondary storage sections, but in computer terms, this takes a long time (seconds). Yet, generally for libraries, this "long" time is more than offset by the lower cost of secondary storage.

Output devices are similar to input devices—magnetic tape, punch cards, a typewriter printer, or a cathode ray tube (CRT). Like the input unit, the output is a "conversion" unit. That is, it converts the CPU impulses back into a form people can read (either as words or numbers). The computer printouts that you have heard about and have probably seen result from the output units' conversion of CPU impulses into a form that we all can read. Generally in acquisition, cataloging, or reference work involving a computer, the CRT is the most common; in fact, a terminal (a keyboard and CRT) will be used for both input and output. The CRT lets you see the information on a television-like screen, but if a permanent printed record is needed, the terminal must have a printer unit as well.

Operational Modes

Libraries have available two methods of using the computer—online and batch. When computers were first used in library operations, the batch mode method was common. Batch mode operations were/are less costly because data put into the computer are collected over a period of time (usually at least one day). When sufficient data are collected, the "batch" is fed to a computer input unit (data are collected on punched cards, magnetic tape, magnetic disc, etc.). One advantage is that the library might not need a computer on the premises. A major disadvantage is that the process is slow and information is usually at least 24 hours old.

Batch processing may still be the most common mode when all types of computer processing are considered. Because this method of operation requires collecting data, sending it to the computer center (wherever that may be), and then having the computer output sent back to the library, there is a lapse of time. The most common term used to indicate the time lapse between sending and receiving the data is "turnaround" time. For libraries the shorter the turnaround time the better the system. Most public service staff members who work in circulation or with serials would like a turnaround time of 24 hours or less. Batch processing is generally considered most feasible and satisfactory with routine, highly repetitive functions (especially accounting activities and acquisitions).

The major advantage of the system is in the area of reducing costs. As already noted, it may mean the library will be able to use an existing computer system or commercial service, thereby avoiding, for a while, investing in a computer. Certainly the library will have to pay a service fee and time charges; but if the only use of a computer is to be for functions that are suitable for batch processing, it will be many years before those costs come close to that of buying a computer. Another advantage of the batch process is that so many of the functions/activities using batch processing are very common; thus, there are a number of preexisting software programs that further reduce the cost.

Another example of a library function in which batch processing may provide a cost low enough to start a library moving toward automation of most of its basic functions is circulation. Although it is not a part of technical service, the data from an automated system can be valuable, up-to-date information about topics of current interest (call number data) that can be used by collection department personnel and the acquisition department (the latter for allocating funds to purchase materials).

Online mode (or real time) means an almost immediate input and output—1 to 5 seconds is common. For this mode, the user most often sits at a CRT terminal and inputs the information by means of a keyboard, light pen, or OCR wand. The CPU then processes that information and provides results in an appropriate output form. A term that applies to this process is "interactive"—that is, there is input and feedback by both computer and user. Generally this is done by means of questions and answers—sometimes questions are generated by the computer, and the user indicates the answer; other times the reverse is true. Today, many libraries try to have some online capability if not a totally online system; this is particularly valuable for such activities as bibliographic searching or cataloging.

Earlier, we mentioned maxis, minis, and micros — shortform names for three categories of computers. When computers were first introduced for general use, there was only one type — the large general purpose unit that each cost a million or more dollars (also called mainframe computers). Because of their size and cost, only very well-endowed organizations could afford to have one (few libraries could hope to have one completely at their disposal). More often than not, one unit was shared by a number of organizations, and most early library automation projects were in large academic institutions where there are many other users. All these problems kept library automation at a very low level until the late 1960s. Only when computer systems were capable of time-sharing online operations in the late 1960s was there a large scale move toward automating library operations.

Today, most of the bibliographic data systems you hear about in libraries are based upon a maxi computer being shared by a number of libraries. For example, the OCLC* system provides data to hundreds of libraries across the United States and Canada. Two other systems using a maxi computer are WLN (Washington Library Network) and RLIN (Research Libraries Information Network). RLIN's cataloging system is based on BALLOTS (Bibliographic Automation of Large Library Operations Using a Time-Sharing System), which was developed by Stanford University. (These are discussed in detail in chapter 3.) Similar systems exist for circulation (online — IBM 1030, batch — Checkpoint, etc.), reference (MEDLINE, DIALOG, ORBIT), and serials control (UCLA — UCLA Biomedical Library, CONSER — Library of Congress). Most of these systems are available to libraries on some type of subscription/fee basis, often by simply installing a terminal that is connected to the large computer by means of a telephone line.

One of the major methods for distinguishing between maxi, mini, and micro computers is the size of the CPU's primary storage capability. A mainframe (maxi) computer will have at least a 28 KB and up capacity; mini computers usually range between 12 and 32 KB; and the micro is between 4 and 17 KB. Presently, the distinction between mini and micro is becoming very blurred, as both are now very portable and have overlapping storage capability. One difference with micros is that the electrical power requirement is down to 110v — you can plug a micro in almost anywhere, although some mini computers also operate on 110v power as well. In addition, micros do not have the same almost critical environmental needs as do the larger units. Indeed, there is so much overlap that some manufacturers now call micros minis in their promotional literature.

Another feature is that mini computers are now low enough in cost that it is commercially feasible to sell both the computer and "programming" (instruction to the CPU) to libraries in packages called "turnkey" systems. Many automated library systems are of this type. A vendor supplies the computer equipment (hardware) and the programs (software), installs the system, teaches the staff how to use it, and maintains the equipment. With this approach, a library now no longer needs to worry about having (or hiring) someone on the staff who can program the computer.

---

*OCLC originally was the acronym for the Ohio College Library Center, a technical service cooperative. After becoming a national service center, it changed its name to OCLC, Inc. Pressures from the field that each letter "stand for something" necessitated a change to its present name — Online Computer Library Center, Inc.

AUTOMATION AND TECHNICAL SERVICES

How then can automation directly affect library services – in particular, technical services? In this section we will follow the same order we used in the first chapter to describe technical services – acquisition, cataloging, serials, bindery, and gifts and exchange. The discussion in this chapter will be of a general nature, with specific existing systems being described in later chapters of the book.

Acquisition

Acquisition work will be described more fully in a later chapter. However, Figure 2.2 provides a summary of the process and provides a frame of reference to this discussion. Much of acquisition work involves recording and maintaining files of information about items ordered for the library. Computers are particularly well suited to perform many of the tasks that could easily consume large segments of staff time in the acquisition department. Certainly, a computer will allow a library to handle a significantly larger work load without a major increase in the number of persons required to do that work.

Of the 10 steps shown in Figure 2.2, eight of them can make greater or lesser use of automation. Only steps 1 (request) and 10 (forwarding the item) are unsuitable for automation. This is not to say these steps could not be automated, but just that to do so would be very costly and serve very little purpose.

Bibliographic verification was one of the last steps to benefit from automation, because it had such a large component of mental activity. The key was to have large data bases available and adequate search techniques. One of the major stumbling blocks was/is that many individuals requesting an item fail to give correct and/or complete information (*see* chapters 5 and 6). This problem is still only partially resolved as there is still no good data base for out-of-print (o.p.) searching. With time, as the existing bibliographic data bases that represent current library holdings get older there will be an increasing percentage of out-of-print items in them, which will thus make them useful for o.p. searching.

Order preparation, fund encumbrance, control of records, and fund accounting, because they are primarily physical activities, were among the first acquisition activities to be automated. Bookkeeping functions are easily automated and most large- and medium-sized library acquisition departments have some or all of their bookkeeping activities automated. Typing of orders can be very tedious and can easily be done by computers. Most available commercial automated acquisition systems can perform the order preparation function. With an ever-increasing use of ISBNs and ISSNs (*see* chapter 7) more and more of these activities can be fully automated at a reasonable cost. Other than the bookkeeping activities and the typing of orders none of these steps can be considered to be completely automated even in libraries that make efforts to automate as much as possible.

As far as processing received items is concerned, only a limited amount of automation is currently possible. Most of this is in the area of maintaining records and producing lists of items that require special handling or have not been received. However, checking the physical item and property stamping must be done by people. If an accession record is maintained the computer can be employed to create and maintain the file.

Fig. 2.2
Acquisition Process

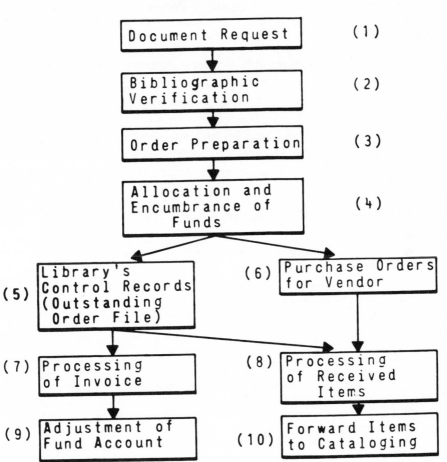

If there can be significant savings in the long run, and if a major portion of the work done in acquisition departments is suitable for computers, why don't more departments use computers? One major reason is that the basis of acquisition work is the bibliographic record of the item to be acquired. Until good (large numbers of items) bibliographic data bases were available, very little meaningful work could be done, beyond automating bookkeeping records. Also, many suppliers of library materials were not ready to handle automated orders, while today, both libraries and vendors (suppliers) are better prepared for this work. Several commercial firms now offer an automated order service, and the cataloging (bibliographic) data bases are sufficiently large that effective searching can be performed.

Both the online and batch mode systems can work effectively for acquisition purposes. Naturally, the interactive potential of the online system is desirable and may save time in the long run, but considerable financial savings can be realized by using the batch mode approach. Any good system will allow you to do all or most of the following:

1) Verify the bibliographic data for a requested item (*see* chapters 5 and 6 for details).

2) Verify that the item is not already on order or in process (*see* chapter 5 for details).

3) Verify price and availability (this was a problem until vendors began to automate their operations; *see* chapter 5 for details).

4) Prepare the purchase order (*see* chapter 11 for details).

5) Encumber the correct amount of money (*see* chapter 10 for details).

6) Handle claims for late or nondelivered orders (*see* chapter 12 for details).

7) Maintain and update the on order/in process file (*see* chapter 12 for details).

8) Record receipts of orders and check for completeness of the order (*see* chapter 12 for details).

9) Prepare payment authorization forms for orders (*see* chapter 10 for details).

10) Prepare the necessary financial and statistical reports for the department (*see* chapter 10 for details).

As can be seen, such a system will touch on almost all aspects of acquisition work (as illustrated in Figure 2.2, page 23).

Currently, several options are available to the library. There are vendor-supplied online and batch mode systems; custom-designed add-on features of an automated circulation system; and add-ons to bibliographic data bases which were developed by libraries. It seems less and less likely that any library will go to the expense of developing its own acquisition system in the future. Most custom systems were developed during the 1970s before vendor systems were available; also, most of these systems are dependent upon easy access to a maxi computer. More details regarding the existing systems for acquisition work can be found in chapter 6.

Cataloging

Cataloging procedures and rules are described more fully in chapters 15-21. However, Figure 2.3 provides a simplified summary of the process and compares a manual and automated approach. The computer is especially helpful in cataloging procedures that require looking for information in large data files. With large files of cataloging information quickly accessible via computer, much

Fig. 2.3
Cataloging Process

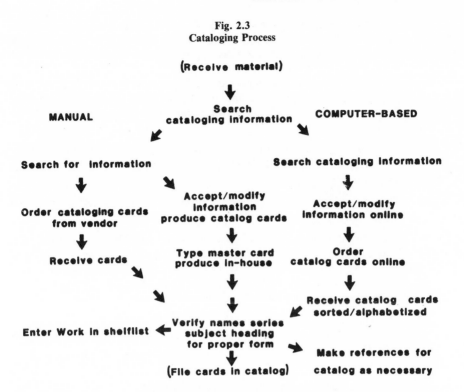

(Receive material)

Search
cataloging information

MANUAL   COMPUTER-BASED

Search for Information   Search cataloging information

Order cataloging cards
from vendor

Accept/modify
information
produce catalog cards

Accept/modify
information online

Receive cards

Type master card
produce in-house

Order
catalog cards online

Receive catalog cards
sorted/alphabetized

Enter Work in shelflist ← Verify names series
subject heading
for proper form

(File cards in catalog)

Make references for
catalog as necessary

staff time can be saved and more work accomplished by the same number of people. As in acquisition work, proper use of a computer can significantly increase the work load without a major increase in staff.

Cataloging was among the first areas in technical processes to receive the attention of librarians interested in computer applications. The vast amount of cataloging data available, the repetitious cataloging of the same work in thousands of libraries, and the desirability of having consistent cataloging information in all libraries combined to make cataloging a natural choice to "tame" with the computer. Unfortunately, the application of computers to cataloging proved more complex than was anticipated because so much of the work requires judgments and not physical process. Only in the late 1970s and early 1980s have successful computer-based cataloging systems become widely available. Even now, however, whether these systems are, in fact, "successful" is being debated by librarians who see much room for improvement in the systems. .

In our opinion computer-based cataloging systems are now among the most successful large-scale applications of computers in libraries. While there is certainly room for improvement, as even the most ardent computer advocate will admit, a major revolution has taken place, so it is just a matter of improving and refining several basic ideas. Keep in mind that many libraries will not be affected immediately by the role of the computer in cataloging. Because of the costs involved, most small libraries and school libraries will have no direct access to computer-based cataloging services.

What should a computer-based cataloging service offer to libraries? While there is no final answer to this question, any service should provide at least the following services or possess the following capabilities:

1) Have a sufficiently large data base to allow most libraries to find a high percentage of titles to be cataloged in the base. (Many medium-sized libraries can locate 90-95% of the items to be cataloged in the OCLC data base.)

2) Provide cataloging products such as catalog cards, computer output microfilm (COM), book catalogs, and catalogs on machine-readable magnetic tape.

3) Provide online access to the data base, indicate whether a particular library has an item, and give the call number.

4) Provide online authority control to ensure that all entries in the data base are consistent in their use of proper forms of names and subject headings. (For example, all works by Mark Twain should be found under Mark Twain with a reference from Samuel Clemens. There should not be works under both names.)

5) Libraries inputting cataloging data should be held to high standards of quality and be required to use the latest cataloging rules (presently *AACR 2*).

6) Have the ability to allow libraries to catalog online and modify the cataloging as necessary for local requirements.

7) Provide catalog cards and other products on a timely basis.

8) Provide all services at a reasonable cost to ensure as broad participation as possible.

These standards are, of course, goals, and no system now available can provide everything suggested here.

The three major computer-based cataloging support services in the United States are OCLC, Research Libraries Information Network (RLIN), and the Washington Library Network (WLN). All three services operate on a nonprofit basis, and at least two—OCLC and RLIN—are rapidly expanding their services. OCLC is by far the largest service. A number of commercial companies sell catalog cards, microform catalogs, processing kits, and book catalogs, but none currently provides online cataloging support. (For a fuller discussion of these and other sources of cataloging data *see* chapter 24.)

Automation of cataloging activities can be of great assistance in the catalog department by reducing the amount of time that must be spent in routine operations. Again we emphasize that almost all successful catalog automation is related to physical rather than mental activities. Locating a catalog record for examination by a cataloger, producing hard copy(ies) of the desired record (printout, card, or microform), and creating an updated listing of library holdings are some examples of what can be done. Such things as deciding main and added entry (*see* chapter 19) or selecting the appropriate subject headings (chapter 20) are still, and for some time to come will be, done by members of the cataloging department.

Serials

Serials work (acquiring and processing magazines and newspapers—*see* chapters 22 and 23), like acquisition work, consists of a number of activities that tend to be very repetitive. Work on some form of automated serials control system has been underway for more than 20 years. Until recently, the existing systems were almost always batch mode and required access to a maxi computer. Like the ones for acquisition and cataloging work, the list of desirable features in an automated serials system is rather long:

1) A system that will allow for ordering, renewing and cancelling subscriptions

2) A system that will allow for cataloging serials and creating a record for the public (like other cataloging a number of forms exist)

3) A system that will allow for check-in and claiming of missing issues

4) A system that will allow for the creation of a binding schedule and a record of what has been sent and is ready to send

5) A system that will allow for fund control or tie into the existing acquisition fund control system

6) A system that will generate serious statistical reports

While a great deal of work with serials is physical—check-in, typing orders, typing claims, and so forth—there are some characteristics that make automation of serials work difficult. Unlike the vast majority of books, serials tend to have a history and in some cases a long history—100 years or more. Even short-lived serials usually have a history of existence of several years. Like people, serials change names from time to time and are often known by a shortened form of the official title—"LRTS" instead of *Library Resources and Technical Services*. This trait, along with a change in the number of issues per volume, makes keeping track of serials a challenge. As with cataloging books the form of entry becomes very important, and, also like cataloging, it presents a problem for automation.

Another factor that may become very important is that more and more indexing services are available for machine searching, and users are more aware of the variety of publications that exist. If computer searching of indexes is increasingly available it is likely there will be greater pressure on serials departments to have an up-to-the-minute record not only of what titles are owned but of what issues have been received. In order to meet the increased work it will be increasingly necessary to have some of the serials work automated.

Bindery and Gifts and Exchange

These two technical service activities are not very suitable for automation. In terms of bindery work, the financial records can and perhaps should be included in an overall automated bookkeeping system. One would expect, as a byproduct of serials automation, a record that indicated the last issue of a title had been received, which would complete the volume, readying it for binding. Typing the binding instructions could also be handled by an automated system. It would seem then that binding should be a "natural" for automation. There are several reasons that this is not the case. Libraries vary a great deal in whether, when, and how they bind their serials and books. Thus, commercial vendors have not found the market big enough to warrant developing programs. Also, many libraries must, for financial reasons, place binding last in the list of expenditures. This may mean binding may be delayed for long periods of time. (Both authors worked in several libraries—even during the high point of library funding in the 1960s—in which serial binding was delayed or drastically cut back for two or three years at a time.) The lack of predictability creates major programming problems which, combined with the other factors, makes automation of bindery work low priority in most libraries.

Gifts and exchange (G&E) work is even more unpredictable. Most of the transactions, if they involve any money, are so low cost in terms of money that there is no point in automating the process. There is no predicting what a library will receive as gifts nor what may be offered by other libraries. If the library's catalog is online, the work of checking gifts against the holdings may be done more quickly, but this is not really an issue of automating G&E functions. Likewise, if there was access to a bibliographic data base that showed which other libraries in the area had or did not have a particular title, decision making regarding a gift might be more effective. But again this is not a matter of automating G&E work, it is rather using existing services in another way.

REVIEW QUESTIONS

1. Define automation.
2. Describe the three basic components of a computer.
3. Name three types of input/output devices.
4. What are the three components of a CPU?
5. Describe the difference between online and batch operation of the computer.
6. What is a CRT?
7. List the functions desirable in a good automated acquisition system.
8. List the functions desirable in a good automated cataloging system.
9. Describe the automated cataloging systems currently available.
10. List the functions desirable in a good automated serials system.
11. What are some of the reasons that bindery and gifts and exchange work are not automated?

3
NETWORKS, COOPERATIVES, AND AUTOMATED SYSTEMS FOR TECHNICAL SERVICES

The previous chapter provided some background on computer systems and how they can help ease work loads in technical services. Such systems have helped eliminate the need for duplicate files. They help streamline the process of library acquisition and cataloging. In time, commercial vendors and/or other bibliographic data base organizations likely will offer total library systems that integrate technical processing, circulation, and other public service subsystems.

Library cooperatives and consortia have been responsible in recent years for organizing networks to aid member libraries in areas like automation, standardization, collection development, interlibrary loans and other services. These groups have had a great influence on the development of the evolving national bibliographic data base, the ultimate goal being the total library system of which technical services is but one part. Before that total system is achieved, however, a total technical services system must be created, and we are fast approaching that goal.

A TOTAL LIBRARY SYSTEM

By a total system we mean one in which all aspects of public and technical services are integrated into one automated system. While librarians have always recognized that these two "services" are interrelated and more often than not exist for administrative purposes rather than for service reasons, artificial barriers do sometimes arise. Such barriers cause staff members to think of "their service" rather than of service as a whole. In part this was/is a function of different staff members' consulting different sources of information (a variety of printed sources) for bibliographic data and creating forms and files for one department's use. Although common elements exist, the differences take on more meaning than perhaps they should and conflicts about duplicated efforts cause problems as well.

An online system can help with these problems. A common data base will result in a higher and more consistent quality of work. Files will be maintained by the computer rather than by people, so conflicts resulting from duplicated efforts will be reduced. Also, because the data can be manipulated so quickly and inexpensively, compared to doing the same thing manually, service ideas can be tried out easily—for example, changing from an author, title, and subject catalog to a dictionary catalog, or even generating a classified catalog. As the data base will be the same for all the activities the interrelated nature of the work will be even more apparent than it is now and better service should be the result, at a lower overall cost.

Figure 3.1 is a simplified model of the technical services aspect of a hypothetical total library system. The figure helps demonstrate how a collection of standard files can be maintained and updated for use by a variety of different functional areas. Libraries of the future will probably adhere to a total systems design in planning automated activities.

Fig. 3.1
A Total Technical Services System

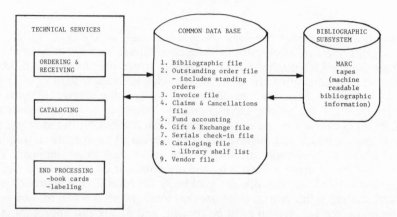

Although the total system is still some distance away, even for technical services some online and batch mode systems do exist and represent steps toward a total system. A number of library organizations exist whose primary purpose is to help achieve a total system. There are four general types of organizations offering packaged computer systems on library technical processing. They are:

1) Library cooperatives and consortia, which provide for the sharing of materials and expertise. These include organizations like the Research Libraries Group (RLG) which organized its membership to provide the capacity to work together to meet mutual needs through inter-institutional planning and cooperation.

2) Nonprofit computerized bibliographic organizations, which provide their services on a fee basis to members. Both the Online Computer Library Center, Inc. (OCLC) and Washington Library Network (WLN) can be included in this group.

3) Commercial vendors with "turnkey" (ready to operate) systems for cataloging, materials control, and acquisition. Biblio-Techniques, Carlyle Systems, Inc., and Midwest Library Service are examples of commercial organizations selling systems that may provide the base for an integrated library system.

4) Broker networks or library service centers that arrange for cooperating institutions to obtain automated services at discounted prices. AMIGOS Bibliographic Council (Dallas), SOLINET (Southeastern Library Network), and SUNY/OCLC (State University of New York and Online Computer Library Center) are examples of this group.

Due to their involvement and increasing networking responsibilities, many of these organizations can now be conceived of as fulfilling a wide variety of roles. Neither significant increases in library purchasing power nor reductions in demand for library services are probable in the near future. Automation is one way for libraries to help themselves resolve these two problems.

Some of the most important developments in automated integrated systems in the last five years have been: 1) the growth in the number of organizations offering services, and 2) the number of subsystems available. In early 1984, some 94 organizations offered turnkey systems, software and/or hardware packages, or library-developed systems. This compares to less than 40 such organizations in early 1980 (many of the 1980 organizations no longer exist or have become part of a larger organization). A major problem is that almost every organization's system will operate with only one computer—for example, IBM or Apple, but not both. Thus, if the library already has or can gain access to a computer, the range of vendors one can select from may not be as large as one might expect or wish for. Another important fact is that by mid-1984, all of the major bibliographic utilities decided to use IBM PCs as their new terminals (J. R. Matthews, "Competition and Change," *Library Journal* 109 [May 1, 1984]: 853-860). This decision will mean that software vendors will develop strong lines for library applications on IBM PCs, as there will be several thousand such terminals in place. What must be and is being developed is a system for linking different automated library systems. Currently the Library of Congress, the RLG, and the WLN—with the assistance of the Council on Library Resources—are testing such a system. When the system is available, we will have achieved a major step toward the ideal integrated system.

Before describing some of the larger systems, a few words explaining some of the basic concepts are in order. For many years, before there was much work done with automated systems, technical service librarians talked about centralized processing and cooperatives. Centralized processing was/is viewed as serving the technical service needs of one library system—a school district, a city, a county, or even a state or nation (for example, much of the technical service work for Veterans Administration libraries and U.S. military post libraries is handled by means of centralized processing). Cooperative processing is usually taken to mean a formal agreement for some or all technical services being performed for a group of independent library systems. Generally what is exchanged is information—reducing duplicate work—and occasionally a service (for example, card production or order placement). "Networks" and "consortia" are terms that tend to be used interchangeably. There are technical differences in their meanings; but, for our purposes, we will consider them both as formal associations of independent libraries often used for aid in technical service activities.

MAJOR ONLINE BIBLIOGRAPHIC SERVICES

Currently there are three major noncommercial online bibliographic networks in the United States: Online Computer Library Center, Inc. (OCLC), Research Libraries Information Network (RLIN), and the Washington Library Network (WLN). Each system started as an online cataloging project but over time has become increasingly technical service oriented with acquisition and serial components. All three also provide an interlibrary loan component. However, the cataloging is still the most widely used aspect of the systems. The three networks were originally established to serve rather different types of libraries. OCLC (whose full name formerly was Ohio College Library Center) was established to serve the needs of colleges and universities in Ohio; RLIN was created to serve the needs of large research libraries; and WLN was primarily for public and private libraries in the state of Washington. Over the years these networks have expanded their memberships, taking in or at least serving new members that do not fit the original group profile; however, the original purpose and group did cause a data base to be created that even today strongly reflects the initial orientation of each.

OCLC

OCLC offers computer support services for cataloging, acquisition, interlibrary loan, and serials control. The cataloging support system is the largest segment of these services and the one used by most libraries. By late 1984, OCLC served 3,800 libraries. The data base contained over 11.1 million records, including MARC records. (About 78% of the cataloging data are contributed by member libraries.) Approximately 23,000 bibliographic records were being added to the data base each week, with some 2.5 million catalog cards being produced and sent to libraries. Fees for services are based on use of the data base, original cataloging contributed to the data base, and the number of cards ordered. OCLC also offers accession lists and magnetic tapes of each member library's holdings as cataloged in OCLC.

Until recently the primary function of OCLC was to provide online cataloging information. Now they also provide acquisition and serials services, as well as interlibrary loan work. Each library using OCLC constructs a profile of its cataloging needs, including the type of cataloging information required, the number of catalog cards needed for each item cataloged, and any special information required on the card. Searching of the bibliographic data base is done by using a CRT terminal with a keyboard (see chapters 6 and 24 for more on searching techniques). The information displayed on the CRT can be modified to satisfy local needs or to reflect cataloging for different editions of a work. A typical modification is to change the call number to conform to local needs. The training needed to catalog on OCLC is beyond the scope of this text, and OCLC and various service centers conduct their own training programs for users. When the cataloging information on the display meets the library's requirements, the user pushes a "produce" key on the keyboard, telling the computer to produce a set of cards for the library. The cards are produced, filed in alphabetical order, and mailed to the requesting library.

The careful reader will notice that computer-based cataloging is an intellectual task eliminating some redundant searching and verification. The ability to analyze the data displayed on the CRT and to make required changes calls for a knowledge of cataloging rules and the special requirements of OCLC. Eliminated is the time-consuming task of manually searching for cataloging information.

Over the years library literature has been filled with articles on the various weaknesses of OCLC. OCLC, however, has stood the test of time and, in the opinion of the authors, is one of the most successful applications of library computerization. Nonetheless, some valid criticisms that may affect daily work are: 1) duplicate entries for the same item are in the data base, sometimes with significantly different information; 2) the quality of some contributed cataloging is poor, and some libraries only accept cataloging contributed by the Library of Congress and major libraries known for quality cataloging; and 3) presently, there is no authority control for the form of a name or subject heading. These criticisms, however, are made primarily by large research libraries, and the high "hit" rate (large number of items found) and overall quality of the data base counterbalance any weaknesses for most libraries. Another problem is that the service center is located in the eastern time zone, so hours of operation are in eastern standard time (Monday-Friday, 6:00 A.M. to 10:00 P.M., and Saturday, 8:00 A.M. to 8:00 P.M. — as of January 1984).

RLIN

The second major national computer-based cataloging service, RLIN, is a service offered by the Research Libraries Group, an affiliation of major research libraries in the United States. RLIN was created in 1978 from the BALLOTS cataloging system developed originally to serve Stanford University. BALLOTS is an acronym for Bibliographic Automation of Large Library Operations using a Time-sharing System. RLIN is much smaller than OCLC in the number of libraries served — in 1984, RLIN served about 400 libraries — however, RLIN serves nine of the twelve largest research libraries in the United States. As of 1984, the RLIN data base contained about 12 million items, including 10 million book records that include MARC cataloging from the Library of Congress. The records are divided into seven files: archival control, books, films, maps, recordings, scores, and serials.

Each library develops a profile of its cataloging needs and its requirements for catalog cards. Cataloging records are also available on magnetic tapes. The skills and information required to input and search cataloging information in RLIN are again beyond the scope of this text, and, like OCLC, RLIN conducts training programs for libraries using its services. Basically, information is displayed on a CRT that has a keyboard for communicating with the computer in a manner similar to that used for OCLC (see chapter 24 for more details).

An acquisition and in-process file control system are available along with a name authority file. One hope is that these systems will encourage and aid cooperative collection development, as well as ultimately automate all technical service activities on a cooperative basis.

Special features and services of RLIN that differ from OCLC's are: 1) many academic librarians believe the quality of cataloging information in RLIN is more reliable than in other major data bases, as fewer libraries, and a high proportion of large university libraries, contribute data; 2) the data base can be searched by subject heading and added entries, which is not yet possible with OCLC; 3) because each library has a separate file in RLIN, a library can compare cataloging information from several libraries; 4) in addition to catalog cards and magnetic tapes, "catalog worksheets" that contain information found in searches are available (the worksheets are used in-house to prepare cataloging for input into RLIN).

There are basic philosophical differences between OCLC and RLIN in the way their respective data bases were created and in their standards for entering and retaining bibliographic data. While these differences need not directly concern the paraprofessional, librarians will continue to debate the merits of both systems. The only safe prediction is that these two major services will continue to evolve and change technical service procedures in most libraries in the next five to ten years.

WLN

The newest and smallest of the three bibliographic services is WLN. WLN, like OCLC and RLIN, provides online cataloging information, catalog cards, computer output microfilm (COM), and book catalogs. Originally, membership was limited to the state of Washington, but over the years service has been extended to several western states. In mid-1984, about 140 member libraries were using WLN services. WLN has no plans to expand into a national network. In mid-1984, the data base included about 3.0 million records and was growing by about 300,000 items annually.

In 1984 WLN had two major operational systems: the cataloging system and the acquisitions system. The cataloging or bibliographic system is noted for its emphasis on authority control of names and subjects. Only Library of Congress (LC) MARC formats are used, and WLN conforms to LC's policy in using AACR2 headings with indicated notes and *see* references. The authority control subsystem is interactive, and records can be "called up," edited, or input online.

Perhaps the most complete acquisition subsystem from a noncommercial source can be found in WLN. The system has ordering, claiming, receiving, and payment capabilities for all formats, not just books. Currently, serials are handled through this system, but a separate serials control subsystem is being developed (ordering, check in, claiming, subscription placement, binding, fund accounting). A circulation control subsystem is being used in member libraries.

LMTAs may encounter the WLN system more often in the future since a company by the name of Biblio-Techniques began to market a turnkey system based on WLN software. The package being offered provides indexed access and maintenance for a full MARC data base and authority, acquisition, and accounting functions. Biblio-Techniques also offers a modified version of WLN circulation system. In early 1984, this system was selected for use in the Toronto public library system, which will provide a major test for the package in a large library system environment.

Canadian Networks

We should also note that the University of Toronto Library has been instrumental in starting a Canadian bibliographic network, UTLAS (University of Toronto Library Automation Systems). The library has been involved in MARC work since 1965, and since 1970 it has sold cards produced from MARC tapes to libraries in Canada. The University of Toronto system is tied into a number of other Canadian networks—for example, UNICAT/TELECAT (a consortium of Ontario and Quebec libraries) and TRIUL (Tri-University Libraries). As of early 1984, more than 600 libraries were using some or all of its processing services. It has a data base in excess of 22 million records. The system allows for online editing and for producing printed cards, book catalogs, COM catalogs, acquisition lists, and selective book lists. The major criticism of the system is that until 1977 there was no standard for inputting records; however, since that time, UTLAS has implemented a standardization requirement. The system is beginning to attract American libraries but still is far behind the "Big 3," at least in the United States.

Service Centers/Broker Systems

The systems we have just reviewed are producers of bibliographic data bases and other services. Another type of network exists, one in which the member libraries secure services from a third party. In some instances this is a banding together of many small libraries whose individual needs for such services are small but when combined with a number of other libraries the need is significant. Such a network then contracts for the needed services. For example, when the change to OCLC, Inc., took place, the original Ohio state members formed OHIONET, because only networks could have representation on the new governing board of OCLC, Inc. Some examples of networks that supply various technical service capabilities to member libraries, but do not generate services, are New England Library Information Network (NELINET), California Library Authority for Systems and Services (CLASS), Midwestern Library Network (MIDLNET), and Southeastern Library Network (SOLINET).

Variety in organization and function is the primary characteristic of such networks. Most of them were established in the very late 1960s or early 1970s, often for the purpose of providing member libraries with some type of cooperative technical service processing. Some attempted to develop their own automated system — just as OCLC, WLN, and to a lesser extent BALLOTS and UTLAS were created. Soon it became apparent it was not necessary to "reinvent the wheel," so some networks attempted to use existing data bases, in particular OCLC, and more or less to replicate that system with whatever were felt to be necessary local modifications. Eventually, existing online services like OCLC allowed for sufficient local variation that it was simply more economical to use the services under contract negotiated by the network.

One important service program of these networks is the training of the technical service staff of member libraries in using the online bibliographic data base. This removes the burden of training from the local library and from the staff of the online service. The networks put on workshops to update skills as well as train new staff, or they provide the material for training. Almost all of these systems provide many other cooperative activities.

Another feature, already alluded to, is that there has been a growing concern about how the major online systems are governed. While all of them started off as cooperative ventures with individual libraries as members, growth in membership created problems of representation. There was/is some concern that the systems would be dominated by the large libraries, which are the major users. The arrangement now in operation for OCLC representation on the governing board is through networks, not individual libraries.

As stated earlier in the chapter, one major change has been in the number of organizations that offer software packages or turnkey systems to libraries. Some of these systems were developed by libraries (for example, Biblio-Techniques and WLN, Midwest Library Service and the Tacoma Public Library's Uniface, or Hewlett-Packard and Virginia Tech's UTLS), while others were developed by companies for the library market (for example, Carlyle Systems, Advanced Library Concepts, and Data Phase). Other systems are library developed and are being marketed by the library (for example, the NOTIS system of Northwestern University and Pennsylvania State University library system). At the time this edition was being prepared, all the vendors had only a few customers (25 or less), they offered at least cataloging and acquisition systems, and most included circulation. How many of the present vendors are still in operation by the time the next edition appears would seem to be a major concern for everyone involved in technical services. Problems of compatibility are important, but just as important is the fact that each system requires special training to use it effectively. Staff turnover in libraries using systems that are not widely used will create significant training costs for those libraries, since finding already trained personnel will be very difficult.

FUTURE IMPLICATIONS

What about the future of automated technical services? One does not have to be much of a prophet to predict a trend toward greater and greater growth in the use of online systems. Furthermore, it seems likely that in our lifetimes the technical service aspects of our hypothetical total library system will exist with a national online bibliographic data base. Positive steps are already being taken in that direction, and even some toward an international system.

Undoubtedly hardware and software technology, especially in the area of the small relatively inexpensive mini (even home) computer systems, will make it more and more possible for local variations to exist and yet allow the library to tie into regional and national systems. The idea that homes and offices of the future will all have CRTs that tie into the online catalog of a library is no longer just a daydream. In fact, OCLC experimented in 1980 with a local (Columbus, Ohio) cable television company (in home information service – holdings of the Columbus and Franklin County public libraries), and libraries elsewhere are also exploring the idea of home access to bibliographic data.

Will all this mean there will be less work for the LMTA? If anything, as automation of technical services increases, it should mean an increased role for the trained LMTA. More and more of the work will be handled by the paraprofessional; in fact, it may be that in libraries that acquire standard trade materials and accept online data there will only be two or three professionals in technical services.

REVIEW QUESTIONS

1. What are some of the factors that need to exist to create an automated technical services system?

2. What are the components of a total technical services system?

3. What are the four types of organizations offering packaged automated technical service processing?

4. Name the major online, noncommercial, bibliographic data base services.

5. What are the differences between online services and a service center network?

6. What are some of the major barriers to achieving compatible automated technical service systems?

4
ACQUISITION WORK – OVERVIEW

Each library unit has a particular contribution to make toward providing service for library patrons. When the acquisition department does not have responsibility for selecting materials, then this unit's contribution consists primarily of handling business matters. In smaller libraries, it is concerned with securing materials for the collection, not only by purchase but through gifts and exchange efforts. Frequently, this department is also responsible for bindery preparation work. Each of these aspects of acquisition work will be discussed, but emphasis will be on purchasing materials, the primary method of adding items.

Because of the standardized nature of much of acquisition work, there is little need for a large number of librarians in the department. Nevertheless, most of the work requires a knowledge of special library tools and skills, so library assistants with the necessary education do a large portion of the work in this department. A chart of major acquisition activities and responsibilities is provided at the end of this chapter. The reader might also wish to examine Figure 2.2 (page 23) for an overview of acquisition work.

In libraries, the term "acquisition work" normally applies to the procedures used in buying materials for the collection: books, serials, audiovisual materials, etc. The task of acquiring office supplies and library equipment (typewriters, desks, book trucks, etc.) may or may not be handled by a library's acquisition unit. Should the unit become involved in ordering office supplies and equipment, that work usually only entails typing and mailing orders, keeping financial records of transactions, and receiving the orders. Almost all acquisition work involves a high degree of repetition and lends itself to the development of a series of standard routines. More and more, libraries are receiving funding to support the development and operation of various automated routines, thus reducing the amount of tedious work.

OBJECTIVES OF COLLECTION DEVELOPMENT

A library's basic objective is to serve its patrons. The purpose of collection development is to select materials that serve the educational and recreational needs of the community. Yet, broad objectives such as these are difficult to interpret, since one person's recreation may be another's education. Each type of library – public, school, special, or academic – has a set of specific objectives that either support local community activities with informational materials (public library) or support the present curriculum of an institution (school and academic). Even these objectives are difficult to work with until librarians know the community and its needs, so they must spend a great deal of time getting to know the community or institution they serve as well as learning what materials are available to satisfy a given need. Since few libraries have adequate funds to buy all the materials needed, librarians also must decide which needs and materials are to receive the highest priority.

Book selection policies are developed to reduce the above problems to a manageable size. In all but the smallest library, several individuals normally share responsibility for selecting materials. Naturally, the involvement of several people in the selection process increases the need for coordination and a common understanding of the selection procedure. Policies or programs usually include a number of basic points:

1) who has the authority to select materials,

2) who has the responsibility for selecting materials,

3) a statement of the library's goals and objectives,

4) the criteria to be used in selecting materials,

5) review sources to be used in selecting materials (if any),

6) the procedure for handling problems (complaints about having or not having certain items), and

7) guidelines for allocation of available funds.

Although the technician usually has no responsibility in this area, understanding the policy will provide the background the technician needs in order to see all acquisition activities in the proper perspective.

SELECTION RESPONSIBILITY

Written policies or program guidelines must be specific, yet not so detailed that changing circumstances cannot be handled effectively. In order to operate effectively within the framework of a written policy—and to an even greater extent, in the absence of such a policy—the individual responsible for selecting materials must consider following these guidelines as a primary duty. Librarians are given special training in this area. And since collection development is one of the librarian's primary duties, it is not surprising to find that, whenever possible, librarians retain the authority and responsibility for selection of materials.

Public Library Selection

Public libraries seldom encounter a problem about selection responsibility: librarians have the authority and responsibility for this work. If only one library building serves a community, few problems of coordination arise that cannot be quickly worked out. Often in such situations, one librarian has responsibility for a specific area of the collection: children's books, reference books, fiction, non-fiction, etc.

When the library grows, and branches or bookmobiles are added, problems in coordinating selections increase. At this level, selection committees are usually formed, consisting of two or three people from the main library and the head of each branch or bookmobile. In large systems (10 or more branches), the committee is still used. However, representation of all the units may not be possible due to the numbers involved, so sometimes rotating committee assignments are used. A primary purpose of committee work is to try to get all orders for the same title submitted at the same time, since multiple-copy orders frequently mean a higher discount from the supplier. In any case, it saves the acquisition department time and effort; an order for 10 copies of an item is no more work than an order for one copy.

School and Academic Library Selection

School and academic libraries share a dilemma in the selection process: to what extent should teaching faculty share responsibility for collection development? In a school system, the problem is usually handled on a system-wide basis—a committee composed of librarians and teachers makes up lists of recommended items. The list is to encourage ordering similar items at the same time, again so that the acquisition unit can easily buy multiple copies.

Academic libraries cannot handle the problem so easily. In small institutions, or institutions having very limited budgets, each academic department tries to ensure that its instructional program is adequately covered. Usually a specified amount of money is allocated to each department, which then has the responsibility for expending the funds. Whenever funds are allocated to departments, to branch libraries (public or academic), or to divisions within a library, the work of the acquisition department becomes more complex (*see* the chapters on order procedures and bookkeeping for details). Departmental funds are usually supervised by one faculty member. However, if there are 20 departments on the campus, the acquisition department will be dealing with at least 20 book selectors, each of whom has his or her own idiosyncrasies.

If a library has enough money to be able to honor almost any request for current English-language materials, then responsibility for collection development is usually transferred to librarians. This is primarily because librarians have more time to devote to selecting materials as well as ready access to the necessary bibliographic tools. A major disadvantage, of course, is that librarians usually lack the subject expertise of the faculty members.

Special Library Selection

Defining collection development goals is easier for special libraries than for any other kind of library. Almost all special libraries serve a clearly defined set of needs—such as the research and development needs of a business or industry. A special library may serve as the repository for rare books or may collect all available items on some specific topic or geographical area. Whatever the specific purpose, its needs are more limited and so more easily identified than those of other types of libraries. This does not imply that the work is simple, but clearly defined goals limit the range of problems. In a non-business or industrial special library, the librarian usually has full responsibility for developing the collection. Industrial and business librarians usually share selection duties with the group of individuals served. In some cases, all requests are generated or approved by the users.

Approval of Selections

If selection responsibility lies with individuals not on the library staff, these requests usually must be approved by someone with final authority. For example, in an academic situation, any faculty member may request an item, but the staff member who supervises the department's library expenditures must approve the request. Most request cards provide space for the required signature, so when the book requests are first sorted, the technician or clerk must check for the required approval. This is very important, because funds will be drawn from various allocated amounts on the basis of the approving signature.

In libraries that require such signatures, a request lacking approval is sent back immediately. The entire matter of approval signatures and departmental unit allocation of funds creates many problems and makes public relations difficult for the acquisition department. Therefore, the entire departmental staff—librarians, technicians, clerks, and part-time help—should be aware of the difficulties and do all they can to keep problems to a minimum.

Other Sources of Requests

Although libraries assign collection development responsibility to a relatively small number of individuals, almost every library is happy to receive suggestions from any patron or staff member. These requests usually take longer to process, however, because they still must be approved by the person normally responsible for selecting items of the type requested.

Clearly, a large number of people may participate in the selection process. Requests may be derived from almost any source, and the request (or "order") cards arriving in the acquisition department may be filled out by individuals unaware that certain information is needed before the material can be ordered. This means that all the information supplied on those cards should be viewed with a certain amount of skepticism. With time, though, you will learn which individuals take the time to supply accurate information.

The above discussion only summarizes how selection and collection development work is handled in various types of libraries. Each library has its unique way of handling the process. Nevertheless, technicians and clerks assigned to the acquisition department always should be aware of how the request cards arrive.

PUBLISHING – GENERAL

Because the bulk of a library's acquisition work deals with books and other printed materials, acquisition librarians and all selectors must know a great deal about publishing and the book trade. Quite simply, persons who have studied publishers may be able to determine something about the quality of a book under consideration just by knowing the name of its publisher. Actually, though, anyone working in acquisition departments needs to know about publishers and publishing. One reason is the business factor, because librarians often enter into direct business transactions with publishers. Beyond such direct dealings, however, other factors must be understood: how and why publishers produce the items they do, what economic factors go into determining a book's price, and how publishers market their products. This last information may help determine the source of supply to consult first when seeing a specific item. The librarian must have this knowledge in order to operate effectively; the LMTA and clerk can operate without it, but they will probably operate more effectively when they do know something about publishing.

What Is a Publisher?

Many people equate the publishing business with the printing business, which is no longer valid for most major publishing firms. (Most publishers in the United States and Europe now have their printing done by independent firms.) In general, printers are concerned only with the physical manufacturing of a book: a) composing the type, b) doing the presswork, c) binding the book, and d) shipping the finished product to the publisher. Printers are seldom involved in the risks of publishing, as they usually sign a contract to provide a fixed number of copies of a finished product for a specific price. Thus, they normally receive their money regardless of how many copies of the item are sold.

On the other hand, publishers, along with the author, carry the risks involved in producing a book. Most publishers carry out the following functions:

1) They tap sources of materials, using manuscript scouts, literary agents, editorial staff, and reviewing unsolicited manuscripts.

2) They raise and control the capital necessary to produce the item.

3) They help develop materials to be published (editorial function), ranging from a few comments to the author to a very close working relationship.

4) They draw up contracts and other legal paper work necessary to produce the item (contract with author, printer, advertising agency, etc.).

5) They oversee all production details.

6) They handle the distribution of the finished product to wholesalers, retailers, and individual customers.

7) They maintain records of sales, contracts, correspondence, etc.

Publishers take a number of risks. Employees, printers, freight costs, advertising costs, etc., must be paid even if no copies of an item are sold. The author is usually compensated in terms of the number of copies sold (royalty), but publishers and authors may or may not receive enough income from the sales to recover their costs.

Publishing Today

Until the 1950s, most publishing firms were private partnerships. Very often, a company was controlled by only three or four families throughout its entire history. Family pride and a feeling of personal involvement with each title published were characteristic of such companies. Although they did not set out deliberately to lose money, many such firms passed up manuscripts they knew would make a profit simply because they felt that the material did not merit carrying their company's name.

Beginning in the 1950s, when there was a great increase in the demand for educational materials, the nature of publishing began to change. These changes are still going on, and the final result can not be predicted. Private publishing firms lacked the capital to expand fast enough to meet their growing needs; one method of securing the necessary money was to "go public"—i.e., to sell stock in the firm on an open market. Selling stock to an investor can change the nature of a firm's business, since the firm then is committed to attempt to return a maximum profit to the investor. A family or firm's reputation is still a factor in deciding what to publish, but now many other people are involved. The result is that the primary concern becomes profit, not quality.

As publishing grew more and more profitable, especially in terms of educational items, some larger non-publishing businesses decided that the field was a worthwhile area of investment and expansion. Major electronic, computer, and other communication media companies began to buy up publishing firms. Indeed, some companies of this type now control seven or eight publishing firms, each using its old name but now under the actual control of non-publishing interests. If individual investors caused a change in the nature of publishing, it is not difficult to imagine the long-term effects of corporate investment. Already profitability and the corporate well-being are seen more often as the primary factors in selecting materials to be published. We hope both that the number of small independent publishers will grow and that the gloomy predictions of the results of large corporate ownership will be wrong.

In the 1980s, there is a movement toward electronic publishing. Electronic publishing is a term that is used in a number of ways; however, it generally means that information that, in the past, was printed in multiple copies and distributed for sale is input into a computer and sold to individual users on demand. There is a question as to what the implications are for libraries if electronic publishing becomes the typical mode of publishing. At the present time, this type of publishing seems most appropriate for fact-oriented, rather than recreational or educational, material. It does seem likely that the trend will continue and that it will increase the need for persons who understand information technologies (computers, telecommunication systems, and videosystems) in the library. By the next edition, the direction and nature of this trend should be more apparent; but for now, one needs to be aware that there is such a trend and try to keep up to date with what is taking place.

This text can cover only a few of the major types of publishing houses. (Audiovisual producers are briefly discussed in chapter 8.) Readers who wish to pursue publishing further may find useful historical background reading in D. G. McMurtrie's *The Book*, S. H. Steinberg's *Five Hundred Years of Printing*, John Tebbel's *History of Book Publishing in the United States*, a four-volume set that should be termed "monumental," and C. B. Grannis' *What Happens in Book Publishing*.

Trade Publishers

Trade books are books intended for a very wide general audience. They are sold through bookstores and book clubs—an example is "best sellers." A bookstore's basic stock comprises trade items, best-sellers, and other titles that large numbers of people are likely to buy. Publishers in this category are the companies whose names almost any reader will know: Harper & Row; Doubleday; Macmillan; Random House; Little, Brown; and many, many others. Such publishers often have specialized divisions, but they started with and still concentrate on producing trade titles. Trade books naturally represent a major segment of books acquired by a library. Although a great deal of acquisition work involves them, an acquisition department seldom deals directly with trade publishers, except in very large library systems. This is because trade books from many publishers are handled by wholesalers, and it is usually easier to deal with one source of supply—a wholesaler—than with 50 or 60 individual publishers.

Special Commercial Publishers

Sometimes the term "trade publisher" is used broadly to include specialized houses. Such usage is not really correct. Technically, special publishers produce and sell books in only one or two fields, and usually for a small and clearly identifiable audience. Because the potential market can be pinpointed, a specialized publisher is able to gear the selection-production process, advertising, and marketing to specific needs, and can thus reduce risks. The most common types of special publishers include 1) scientific-technical, 2) medical, 3) legal, 4) textbooks (for schools and colleges), 5) religious, 6) music, 7) maps, and 8) paperbacks. Acquisition departments are more likely to deal directly with such publishers, and LMTAs should learn the names of the leading specialty houses. Examples include Pergamon, well known as a science and technology publisher; Saunders, for the medical field; West, for law books; Scott Foresman, for textbooks; and Dover, for specialty paperbacks. Direct contacts are more likely with these firms since very few wholesalers or retail stores handle specialty items. Small discounts (of 25% or less—also called "short" discounts) and limited sales appeal keep many wholesalers and retailers from stocking these materials. Quality paperbacks are the exception to this pattern, since they are stocked in most bookstores. Recognizing publishers of this type will save time for the acquisition department staff. If special items are requested from a dealer who supplies trade items but does not stock specialty material, the order may be returned. The department will then have to order directly, or from another source, and time and effort will have been wasted. Thus, an understanding of the total picture could save that time and effort.

University Presses

University press operations might be considered a subtype of the special publishers category. They do specialize in scholarly titles whose market may not be more than 1,000 copies. There are, however, two features of university presses that set them apart from other large-scale publishing ventures. Their publication lists normally cover a wider range of subjects than do those of most specialty publishers. Also, most university presses receive financial support from the institution itself and do not pay taxes. No one really expects these operations to show a profit; in fact, a consistent record of breaking even year after year is viewed with some surprise. By the very nature of their objectives, the library market is their best customer. Due to extremely limited sales appeal, many wholesalers and retailers do not stock university press titles. Very likely, LMTAs and clerks will order directly from these publishers, especially if they work in an academic or large public library.

Vanity and Private Presses

Although these two types of publisher are not related, they will be discussed together because libraries acquire very few publications from either source. Of the two, vanity press items are least often sought by libraries. In a sense, they should not be even considered as publishers, since most operate only as printer-advisors. Each author assumes all the risk by paying to have a manuscript manufactured into a book; and in most cases, disposal of the printed copies is also the author's responsibility. Often the author simply gives away copies, so any library in the vicinity of such a new author is likely to receive a free copy. Books that arrive in the mailroom without an invoice, packing slip, or some other identification can and do cause problems. If staff members learn the names of some of the vanity presses, they can avoid looking for a copy of the "original order"—which does not exist. As might be expected, the quality of vanity press items is often highly suspect.

Private presses, on the other hand, often publish original material of high quality. It is not much of an oversimplification to say that most private press operators are more interested in the physical appearance of a book than in its actual content. (Thus, they often reprint "classics" in the public domain.) Many private presses are hand-operated and are owned by one or two individuals who work at fine printing as a hobby. Improvements in type design, format, and printing techniques often originate in the basement or garage of a private press operator. Most large libraries (other than school or special) have at least a small collection of rare and fine books, and many of these titles are from private presses. Some libraries have active programs for the acquisition of private press publications. Those that acquire either vanity or private press publications almost always do so on a direct purchase basis, so the LMTA should learn the names of such publishers.

Government Publications

Almost all major governmental bodies (international, national, state, county, or municipal) carry on some type of publications program—but the quality and range of topics vary a great deal. However, this is one source of up-to-date information available to a library at little or no cost beyond staff time and effort. The U.S. Government Printing Office (GPO) is one of the largest publishing houses in the world. Without question, government publishing on a worldwide basis is greater than all other publishing combined. Although government publications used to be considered hard to read, dry narratives about obscure subjects, some attention is now being paid to the wants of the public marketplace. As the public's buying interest has increased, a number of GPO bookstores have been opened in major U.S. cities. Government documents, like other specialized materials, are almost always purchased directly.

Serial Publishers

Another special publishing activity is issuing a newspaper, magazine, or other serial item (a publication that is published on a regular or irregular basis with no planned date for ceasing to publish). Because people need up-to-date information, some publishers have specialized in producing material to meet these needs. Commercial serial publishers generally have a staff of writers working on the forthcoming material rather than depending on writers outside the firm.

Libraries are expected to acquire all types of serials. Most commercial ones can be secured through a vendor, which saves the library staff time and trouble. Some professional groups and societies will only sell directly. Again, learning the names of such groups can save time and effort.

A number of other publishing organizations exist, of course, but we have covered the major types of book publishers. Subtypes and slight variations exist almost without number. As mentioned earlier, anyone planning a career in acquisition work needs to become familiar with *all* of the variations. Reading the books suggested earlier will help and will also provide guidance for further reading.

TYPES OF MATERIALS PURCHASED

Any library's collection must be built to achieve certain objectives: education, information, aesthetic appreciation, recreation, and research. Each of these may be met by employing a number of different media, which, when combined, usually complement one another. Aesthetic appreciation can be achieved by using recorded music and dramatic recordings to complement music scores and literary works. Photographs, prints, reproductions of famous paintings, and slides may be used to complement art history books. The acquisition of these materials takes a great deal of knowledge about the materials—appropriate items need to be selected from suitable sources of supply.

Printed Materials

As noted earlier, books and printed materials represent the bulk of library purchases. More than 26,000 new titles are produced each year in the United States, and over 10,000 new editions. Even if they devoted all their acquisition money to buying books, most libraries could buy only a fraction of the total output. Some larger jobbers, dealing only in books in the English language, have well over 100,000 titles available. In terms of out-of-print materials, it has been estimated that (as of 1985) over 36 million titles have been produced in western Europe and the United States. Any of these titles could be of interest to a library. (Further, this figure excludes a vast quantity of other printed materials, since it encompasses only monographs of 49 pages or more.)

In addition to books, thousands of periodical and serial titles are produced every year. Government documents—national, state, local, and international—represent another category of printed material being acquired by libraries of all sizes. There are also scholarly publications, dissertations, theses, and publications of learned societies (of primary interest to academic libraries, although some public libraries do acquire them—such items are not usually considered trade books). Atlases are heavily used in libraries; sheet maps (topographic maps; county highway maps; maps of national parks, forests, and recreation areas; aviation charts, and navigational charts), folded maps (highway maps), raised relief maps, and globes are to be found in many libraries, too.

Printed music is still another category of material that should be familiar to acquisition department personnel. Piano-vocal scores, miniature scores, and monumental sets may be found in larger libraries. Pamphlets and ephemera of all types (broadsides, house organs, personal papers, and documents) are also handled by the acquisition department.

Non-Print Materials

Microfilm and microfiche are two different aspects of the non-print medium called "microforms"—films that carry copies of printed matter. Many out-of-print books are now being reproduced in microform because the cost of reprinting is very high. Making a microfilm copy and reproducing it is much less expensive, so all or part of a book may be reproduced on demand from a master negative at a reasonable price. To order microforms, one must know something about how the material in question is to be used, why it is needed, and what methods of reproduction are available. Sometimes, 35mm microfilm is not satisfactory; a hard copy reproduced in the same size as the original could be needed. The order department must be aware of such factors before an intelligent order can be placed.

Other popular audiovisual materials are phonograph records, audio tapes, and 16mm and 8mm films. Most libraries (medium-sized or larger) have at least a small record collection. Public and school libraries tend to have larger nonbook collections than do academic libraries. In the last five years, there has been increased demand for and use of videocassettes loaned by libraries. Some libraries, generally public libraries, have been circulating software packages for home computers. A great many problems are involved in acquiring these items, but many of the steps used to order a book apply to these other media as well. (Details about working with nonbook media will be found in chapters 8 and 18.)

GENERAL ORGANIZATION AND PROCEDURES OF ACQUISITION DEPARTMENTS

Staffing patterns vary in acquisition departments, but a librarian is almost always the unit's immediate supervisor. As the work load increases, it may be divided into sub-units, and other individuals may be assigned supervisory responsibility. A very large library might have separate units for verification, ordering, bookkeeping, receiving, bindery preparation, and gifts and exchange. The head supervisor of each of these units need not be (and often is not) a librarian. LMTAs could reasonably expect to supervise, in time, a verification, bookkeeping, or receiving unit. And it would not be surprising to find a technician in charge of an order or a bindery preparation unit. Figure 4.1 lists the activities carried out in an acquisition department and indicates responsibilities for the activities. Details concerning the major activities will be found in the following chapters.

Fig. 4.1
Acquisition Department Activities

ACQUISITION DEPARTMENT				
Activities	Librarian	Library Technician	Library Clerk	Part Time Help (Students)
Preliminary				
1. Receive book requests			X	
2. Sort requests for duplications			X	
3. Sort requests by type for verification		X		
Verification				
4. Verify current imprint requests		X	X	X
5. Verify out-of-print requests	X	X		
6. Verify foreign imprints	X	X		
Order Preparation				
7. Check problem requests	X	X		
8. Assign order numbers		X		
9. Assign dealers	X	X		
10. Type orders			X	X
11. Revise typing		X		
12. Prepare purchase authorization	X			
13. Mail orders			X	X
14. File copies of orders		X	X	
Bookkeeping Procedures				
15. Prepare budget	X			
16. Allocate funds	X			
17. Set up records of allocations		X	X	
18. Encumber funds to cover outstanding orders		X	X	

(Fig. 4.1 continues on page 48.)

Fig. 4.1 (cont'd)

ACQUISITION DEPARTMENT				
Activities	Librarian	Library Technician	Library Clerk	Part Time Help (Students)
Bookkeeping Procedures (cont'd)				
19. Check invoices		X	X	
20. Approve invoice for payment	X			
21. Prepare monthly balance statements		X	X	
22. Annually balance records	X	X	X	
Receiving Procedures				
23. Unpack boxes				X
24. Check packing slips and invoices		X	X	X
25. Return errors in shipments		X	X	
26. Claim missing items		X		
27. Accession (if done)				X
28. Property mark items				X
29. Pull copy of order from file		X	X	
30. Forward items to catalog department				X
Gifts and Exchange				
31. Secure gifts	X			
32. Evaluate gifts	X			
33. Check selected gifts, exchange lists, etc. against holdings		X		
34. Prepare exchange lists		X	X	
35. Type exchange lists			X	
36. Handle exchange list requests			X	X
Other Activities				
37. Assign duties to all personnel	X			
38. Maintain relations with dealers	X			
39. Determine policies and work procedures	X			
40. Public Relations	X	X	X	X

REVIEW QUESTIONS

1. Identify the major purpose(s) of library collections.

2. Discuss the basic elements and purposes of book selection policies.

3. How is materials selection handled in public libraries? How does this differ from educational institution libraries?

4. In what ways does selection for special libraries differ from that for other types of libraries?

5. What is final approval of selection? Why is it important?

6. In what ways do publishers differ from printers?

7. Describe the three types of publishers that supply the majority of library books.

8. What are some of the differences between book and serial (magazine/newspaper) publishers?

9. Identify five of the most commonly acquired non-print formats.

10. List the 15 duties of librarians in the acquisition department.

5

BIBLIOGRAPHIC VERIFICATION —
GENERAL PRINCIPLES AND MANUAL SYSTEMS

Bibliographic verification, the first step in the acquisition procedure, is perhaps the most interesting and challenging duty in this department. The attempt to establish an item's existence when there is very little information is similar to detective work. (Note: Anyone who wishes to engage in bibliographic work must study with great care the section on rules of entry in the cataloging chapter, for they are as basic to bibliographic verification as they are to cataloging.)

There are two major phases to bibliographic verification. The first establishes a particular work's existence, which includes determining the exact name of the author (person or organization responsible for the intellectual content), the title, when it was produced, who produced it, how much it costs, and where it may be acquired. The second phase consists of determining whether the library wants or needs a copy of the work. If the library already has a copy, for example, the verifier must determine whether an additional copy is desired or whether the request is an error.

Painstaking care is essential, since carelessness in verification work can be extremely costly to the library. For example, two editions of a book may exist; but if the checker is not careful, a perfectly "correct" order could be sent out — for the wrong book. (It would be correct in the sense that all the information would agree with an existing book, but it would not agree with what the selector requested.) Such an error might not be found until the book was cataloged and ready to be used, and all the time and effort would have been wasted. Discrepancies between the material requested and the information verified might be significant; time taken at the beginning to determine which is correct can save time and trouble in the long run.

Most verification activities are carried out by library technicians, clerks, or occasionally (when the work load is heavy) by part-time help. The librarian's role in the process should be limited. Normally, librarians work only on special verification problems or requests in foreign languages. As staff size increases, technicians are very likely to gain some supervisory responsibility in this area.

More and more frequently, libraries have access to machine-readable data bases that can be used in the verification process. Some specific differences between manual and machine searching will be discussed in the next chapter. However, the most important factor to bear in mind is that there is no difference between the two approaches insofar as the principles and purposes of verification are concerned. Therefore, much of what is discussed in this chapter on manual searching applies to both manual and machine searches.

REQUEST CARDS

In almost all libraries, a request card for a specific title may be submitted to the acquisition department by a librarian, a patron, or a staff member. These cards must be sorted so that duplicate requests can be removed. For efficient searching, one should collect a number of request cards before beginning any search sequence. In a large library system, several hundred cards can accumulate during a day, and they should be sorted and alphabetized to make the search as productive as possible and to eliminate any duplication.

Many individuals may request items, yet the accuracy of the information supplied by these persons may vary a great deal. Experience in working with each selector's requests will soon teach a verifier which requests need to be examined very carefully. Requests from individuals who are inexperienced or uninformed about acquisition operations will, of course, need to be critically examined. Requests from librarians, faculty members who are charged with selection responsibility, or selection committees ought to be reasonably accurate. Nevertheless, the LMTA should *never assume* such accuracy; it can lead to costly mistakes.

Requests for books are usually submitted on printed cards purchased from a commercial library supply house. The format standardizes the necessary order information, providing space for recording some or all of the following information: author, title, publisher or producer, date of publication, and price. When necessary, other information must be provided—the edition, the volume if it is part of a series or is a serial, the fund to be charged, the name of the requestor, and the supplier to be used. There may be a list of standard bibliographies to be checked off as an indication of the source used to verify a particular piece of information (author's name, title, publisher, price, and so forth). Figure 5.1 provides an example of a book request card.

Fig. 5.1
Book Request Card

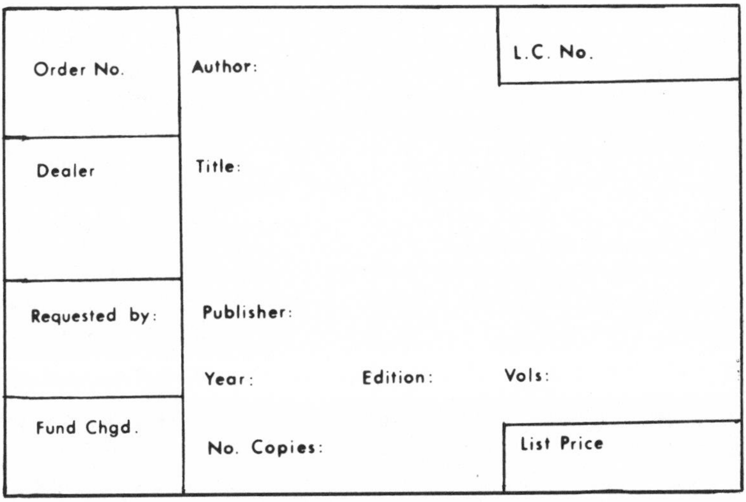

Order No.	Author:	L.C. No.
Dealer	Title:	
Requested by:	Publisher:	
	Year: Edition: Vols:	
Fund Chgd.	No. Copies:	List Price

Note: Examples of order forms are in chapter 9.

The verifier will be confronted with many problems. Some will result from inadequate or incomplete information: no date of publication, no publisher, no author. Other problems result from the requestor's incomplete understanding of the information needed. In the space marked "year," for example, the requestor may supply the current year rather than the year of publication. Probably the primary source of the verifier's difficulty is misinformation: a subtitle is given rather than the title, the wrong author is listed, the second edition is requested when the third was desired, and so forth. A few of these problems can be solved at the first sorting; cards lacking information can be set aside, and the requestor can be asked to supply additional data.

Book requests are usually divided into three groups: current imprint, out of print, and foreign. There is no problem in determining the foreign-language requests; but errors are bound to occur in sorting current and out-of-print requests, since requestors sometimes give incorrect imprint dates. This sorting can be handled by an experienced technician, if adequate guidelines are established by the librarian. Sorting by type obviously serves to make verification more efficient. Current imprints can be verified more quickly in trade bibliographies, while retrospective bibliographies are used for out-of-print materials. Searching the national bibliography of a particular country improves the chances of finding the necessary information for foreign imprints. Grouping requests by type and selecting the proper starting point will allow verifiers to concentrate their efforts most productively.

BIBLIOGRAPHIC SEARCH PROCEDURES

The question of where to begin the search routine is always valid. Does one establish a work's existence and then determine whether the library wants a copy of it, or does one first determine whether the library already has a copy and then verify the item's existence? The order of these verification procedures depends on the library. To some degree, this problem is reduced when doing machine searches, if the library is using an online acquisition system.

The author-main entry arrangement (*see* chapter 19) is the best method of arranging request cards for verification, because all bibliographies provide for this approach. Using the author entry approach, a technician should be able to verify approximately 80% of all items. Others will have to be verified under the title or another author entry because of an error made by the requestor. If the author-title method fails to achieve results, then a subject approach must be attempted. A very few items will defy verification. When sorting request cards, it is also useful to sort on the basis of difficulty, so that the difficult search items become the responsibility of the librarian or one of the senior bibliographic searchers. It is pointless to give difficult or complex search problems to a beginner who lacks the experience and the knowledge needed to solve the problems. This, of course, is one of the reasons that bibliographic searchers need some formal training in bibliographic-library work. Such training allows searchers to do more of the exciting and challenging verification work much sooner than if they had to learn it entirely on the job.

Establishing a Search Sequence

Because of the high repetition rate and the relative ease of verifying most titles, a searching sequence makes the work more efficient and allows titles to be verified more quickly. This sequence is normally established by the head of the acquisition department. In the absence of such a routine, however, the efficient searcher will establish a personal sequence, simply as part of the normal work schedule. As an example, take a set of cards to be verified and check them in the sources normally used, noting how many items were verified in each source and how much time was spent on each. Say that you searched 100 titles on a given day, and you verified all but two of the items. You record that 25 titles were verified in Source A; in Source B, only 75 titles were searched, since 25 titles had already been verified in Source A. Of these 75 titles, 15 were verified in Source B. Source C verified 30 of the remaining 60 titles; in Source D you located 18 titles, and in Source E, 12 titles. The next time you have 100 titles to be verified, vary the search sequence on the basis of the previous performance—i.e., you start with Source C, the one that produced 30 verifications. After checking the 100 titles through this tool, you find that you have verified 45 of the 100 items. You then go to Source A, the one that produced 25 verifications in the previous search, and find that you verify only 10 of the remaining 55 items. You then search the remaining sources in an order based on the number of verifications produced in the first search.

Repeating this process over the course of a month will give a fairly clear idea of which sources provide the greatest number of verifications in the shortest possible time. While the methodology outlined above is not scientific, it is workable and useful. A scientific approach would take a random sample of titles over a long period of time. This formal approach would produce a more accurate picture and could be the basis for establishing a standard sequence for everyone.

The main entry is critical as it gives the searcher some idea of how a work may be entered in a bibliography. Briefly, the searcher is concerned with three types of entry: the personal author entry, the corporate entry, and the title entry. A work that apparently has no personal author entry might be entered under a corporate entry or under the title. It is very important for a searcher to understand the rules of entry as well as the filing rules that libraries employ. The time spent learning these rules will be compensated for by more efficient verifications.

As the library's size increases, searchers' problems increase in complexity. A small, non-technical library will enter almost all items under personal author entries, and most of these items will be in English and in print. Out-of-print materials in the small library are usually replacement copies of items that have been lost, damaged, or worn out. The larger library presents a slightly different pattern: more material will be entered under a corporate or title entry, and it will be more difficult to determine what the entry might be. English-language, current, in-print materials still represent a high percentage of the items acquired, but out-of-print acquisitions become increasingly important. Large public and academic libraries maintain substantial collections of foreign-language material. In general, the larger the library, the greater its out-of-print and foreign-language acquisitions.

Verifying a Work's Existence

After completing the sorting procedure, removing the duplicate requests, and arranging the remaining requests in alphabetical order by author entry, a searcher should begin to search in the most productive bibliography according to the established sequence. If the author-entry search procedure does not verify between 60% and 90% of the items, examine the procedure very closely. Probably either the request cards are inaccurate or the wrong bibliographies are being used for the search. For the remaining items, the title approach should be the next step in the procedure. Most bibliographies provide both author and title access to their contents, and a title search should verify most of the remaining items. Occasionally, an item cannot be located in any standard source; when this happens, the requestor is usually contacted to verify or provide the source of information.

If the requestor cannot give any further information, the searcher may try a subject approach, but the success ratio is generally low because of a number of factors. First, not all bibliographies provide a subject approach, so it is impossible to use this method consistently in the more commonly used bibliographies. The second, more critical factor is that subject assignment is quite arbitrary. Even with a work in hand, two individuals may very well provide two different subject categories for the same book. Thus, the searcher must look under as many subjects as can be thought of but still can never be certain that all appropriate headings have been searched. Because of its low success ratio, the subject method of verification should be used only as a last resort for urgently needed items about which the requestor can provide no further information.

Clearly, the more information that can be verified in a single source, the more efficient the search procedure will be. In determining the sequence of bibliographies to be used in the search pattern, some consideration should be given to the number of items of information that can be established in each. Bibliographies commonly used in the acquisition department will be discussed in the next chapter.

Occasionally, you must examine three or four sources in order to verify all required order information. One may quickly find the author, title, publisher, date of publication, and price; but it is sometimes difficult, for instance, to determine whether the item is in a series. Even if one checks all the sources that should provide this information, it is sometimes unavailable.

In order to reduce the amount of duplicated effort, the sources in which the information is verified should be recorded on the back of the request card. This will save time and confusion within the acquisition department; anyone looking at the card will be able to determine quickly that it has been verified and where the information was found. This procedure also saves time in the cataloging department, since often the request card, along with other slips, is placed in the book when it arrives, to be forwarded to cataloging. Sometimes the entry under which an item was verified is not the one that catalog department wishes to use, but the decision can be made more efficiently if the department knows the sources used by the acquisition department in its own choice of main entry. Figure 5.2 is an example of the verso of a request card.

Many different types of sources are used to verify and search out the information needed for ordering an item. The basic tools used are bibliographies, which are discussed later in Chapter 7. Dealers' catalogs are another helpful source. These catalogs may or may not use standard rules of entry, and the information contained in the entry may or may not be complete for a library's

Fig. 5.2
Verso of Request Card Showing a Record
of Sources Checked by Verifiers

____Public Catalog	____Series Treatment	____Shelflist
____Process File	____Serials Record	PRL:
____Proof File		Publisher's Address
____L. C. Catalog		

SFVSC LIBRARY ORDER REQUEST CARD

	____UCB	
____BM	____UCLA	
____Publisher	____O P	
____CBI		
	____PTLA	
____BIP	____LEV	
____PW	____Lit. Kat.	
____PBIP	____DB	
____BNB		
____BBIP		
____Whitaker		
____Biblio.		

REQUESTED BY_____   REQUEST RECD
APPROVED_____
SOURCE_____

purposes. Some of the catalogs, however — and especially those produced by antiquarian or rare book dealers — are so thorough and comprehensive that they serve as retrospective bibliographies and can be consulted not only by librarians and booksellers, but by scholars who want information about rare books.

Another source is announcements and catalogs from publishers. Book publishers' catalogs usually are annual publications that list all books in stock, and announcements of new publications are issued at various intervals. A searcher should remember that the catalog represents everything a producer has in stock, while the announcement represents only new items being produced.

Library Requirements for an Item

Upon establishing the main entry and other order information, the searcher must determine whether the library actually needs the item. Does it already have a copy; if it does, was the request submitted because an additional copy or a replacement was needed? Such information is usually supplied by the requestor. Otherwise, if the library already has a copy of the requested item, assume that the request is an unintentional duplication.

If a requested item is found to be in the collection already, return the request card with an indication that the library has a copy. The requestor must then make it clear that a second copy is needed and why. Another consideration must be whether the book is "in process." This means that the item has already been ordered but is not yet represented in the public catalog.

Several files must be checked to establish the library's need for a requested item. The most obvious file for beginning the search is the public catalog. A searcher first checks under the assumed main entry; if results are negative but some doubt exists as to the main entry's validity, a title search should also be made. (For an explanation of main entry variations, see chapter 19.) Some librarians suggest that searchers begin with the title rather than the author because there are fewer variations in titles. Some libraries use separate catalogs to list phonograph records, government documents, series, and collections in special libraries or subject areas. These must be checked if the requested material falls into one of these categories and if the public catalog does not list all such collections. In some cases (very expensive items, large sets, etc.), you may have to check the special catalogs even if the main catalog does include all entries. Other public service files to examine are those for lost and missing books or damaged books (replacement file). The searcher does not examine all of these files for all items, but merely for those popular duplicate items not marked "added copy" or "replacement." If the requestor has simply forgotten to indicate "replacement," this procedure will save time on popular works.

The technical services department maintains several files that must be checked to determine whether an item is in-process, but the fewer files to examine, the lower the rate of unintentional duplication. Multiple files may have varying entries, which makes a search very difficult and often causes unavoidable errors. At least three basic files must be examined: the in-process file, the file of verified requests, and the standing order file. The in-process file represents books on order, books received but not yet sent to cataloging, and books in the cataloging department. The verified request file contains those items waiting to be typed on order forms. The standing order file represents those items to be received automatically from the supplier. Usually these items are in publishers' series, so the searcher examines the standing order file only when an item has been established as part of a series. Most files in technical services are arranged by main entry. Some, however, have begun to use a title approach, which speeds up the search procedure, because the title is a much less variable factor than main entry.

The above discussion applies in principle to all formats the library may purchase—periodicals, newspapers, other serials, audiovisual materials, pamphlets, etc. The sources one uses to verify the necessary ordering information are different, but the steps are the same.

Summary of Verification Procedures

1) Receive order-request forms.

2) Sort for duplication.

3) Sort by type (current, out-of-print, foreign, etc.).

4) Establish bibliographic data (e.g., author, title, publisher, date, price, etc.).

5) Establish library's need for item (e.g., check public catalog, on order, in-process file, series file, etc.).

REVIEW QUESTIONS

1. What are the purposes of verification work?

2. What are the first three steps in verification work?

3. What should be done with duplicate requests?

4. Identify the usual elements found on a request form.
5. Describe the advantages of establishing a standard search sequence.
6. Describe the method for establishing a personal search sequence.
7. Why record the sources searched and the information verified?
8. When should a subject search be conducted?
9. What is the major problem in using dealer catalogs to verify information?
10. What library files are searched during the verification process?

6
MACHINE-AIDED VERIFICATION

As noted in chapter 2, most online acquisition systems provide more than verification capability, but this alone would be desirable for many libraries. A 1977 study was a test of the OCLC system simply as a verification tool.[1] At that time, OCLC did not have an acquisition subsystem, so the study was just one library's attempt to assess the value of an online bibliographic data base for searching order requests.

The study compared OCLC's data base with Library of Congress' depository cards (LCD), *National Union Catalog* (*NUC*), *American Book Publishing Record* (*BPR*) and *Weekly Record* (*WR*) as one service, and *Cumulative Book Index* (*CBI*).* Using a sample of 534 titles (somewhat like the technique for establishing a search sequence) each of the identified search tools was checked to determine 1) how many items could be verified, and 2) how long it took to finish the search. All titles were expected to be in print and would be ordered from an American book jobber.

The result was that OCLC searching located 495 or 92.7% of the sample titles. The other sources were, in order of their "success" rate: LCD—73.2%, BPR—69.9%, NUC—44.6%, and CBI—32.8%. Thus, OCLC proved to be the most complete searching source. Yet, completeness alone would not be sufficient reason for shifting the search pattern, if the most complete source took a significantly longer period of time to use. This is why the study also checked on the time factor. Here, the results were as follows: LCD—.699 minutes per title found, OCLC—.758, NUC—1.123, CBI—1.123, and BPR—1.586. One reason that the time for BPR was longer was that the *Weekly Record* was included (thus there were more sequences to examine). The conclusion was that OCLC was the most productive source for searching—both in terms of "hits" (items found) and in time spent per search. This is especially true now, as not many libraries still subscribe to LC's depository cards program.

NUC, BPR, WR, and *CBI* are all discussed in detail in chapter 7.

MACHINE SEARCHING

Several things are different about machine searching. Since OCLC is probably the most widely used online bibliographic data base, and the Acquisition Subsystem became available in 1981 (and, as of 1984, has 170 users), we will use it as our example system.*

One of the first differences is that the LMTA may have to alter the time of day for searching. National online systems are fine, but even the largest maxi can be faced with too many requests at once. The situation might be thought of in terms of going to the public catalog of a medium-sized library only to find several hundred persons already using it. Although theoretically there may be enough points of access (drawers of cards) to accommodate everyone, there is not enough physical space to get into the "system." In the same way, a computer can only handle so many requests for information at one time. Because of this limitation, most national online systems have arranged for different times of access; libraries in the eastern, midwestern, and far western United States are given prescribed periods of time during the normal working day when they can use the system, or at least certain subsystems. For example, while a library may be able to do a title search at any time, it may only be allowed certain hours for corporate author searching (*see* the cataloging chapters for an explanation of authorship).

Another factor that will seem to be a problem at first is that information is presented in a specified sequence and appears line by line. This means that the searcher may have to wait for information for a long time, especially with a CRT. When you do a manual search and you know the tool you are using very well, your eye quickly moves to the correct point on the page. In comparison, the print-out, whether on paper or a screen, seems to take a long time. Also, when you go to do your machine searching you may find the computer is "down" (not operating). In spite of all of these "problems," research results show that machine searching still is faster than manual searching.

Time spent in searching, even with the above factors, is very productive, since most systems allow order preparation once information has been verified (usually by merely pushing a button). According to Earl Kunz, assistant head of the order department of the Buffalo and Erie (NY) County Public Library:

> We're online as much as we can staff the terminals, which usually means 8:30 to 5:00 five days a week. Ten percent of time is spent in searching; the other 90% in ordering. We're printing up about 1,000 order forms a week, pushing orders through the system at the rate of 30 to 35 an hour. From initial search to printed form it takes us less than 120 seconds to process an order.[2]

While this rate refers to the Brodart online system, most systems claim a rate between 30 and 50 items per hour, which includes the order preparation.

---

*This should *not* be construed as an endorsement of that system, but merely as a reflection of its widespread use and availability.

You have nine options for locating a title in the OCLC bibliographic data base. For most verification activities, however, you really have only three choices (author, title, and author/title). The other methods require your knowing an identification number; the Library of Congress catalog card number (LCCN); the International Standard Book Number (ISBN)*; International Standard Serials Number (ISSN)*; OCLC control number, or by CODEN number. All of these approaches will immediately display the desired item, as these are unique numbers for the item, but generally, you do not have this information when going to verify an order request. Therefore, you go with the author and/or title search. In the OCLC system, author and title searching can be done using four approaches: search by personal name, search by corporate name, search by title, or search by author and title. Having the option of searching both author and title at the same time is very useful for persons with less than common names and for titles that are somewhat unusual.

The following is a hypothetical situation—although the book is real, as are the printouts. You are to verify a request slip containing the following information: author—Charles Collins, title—*Public Administration*, year—1975, publisher—left blank (as is the rest of the slip). As is so often the case when order requests are taken from patrons (or even trained bibliographers who are in a hurry), the information provided is not complete. The item actually desired is Charles H. Collins's *Public Administration in Hong Kong* (New York: AMS, 1975), a reprint of the 1952 edition that was published by the Royal Institute of International Affairs in London. Is it possible to locate the correct item given the information in hand by using an online system?

The first step in using the system is to "log-on," start the equipment and establish your authority to use the system (Fig. 6.1). After "log-on," you are ready to start the search. Which of four possible approaches should you start with? What are some guidelines for deciding where to start? Personal authors with very common names (such as John or Jane Smith) ought not be searched under author name for the first attempt; either title or author/title should be used first. (We can eliminate the corporate author search for this search.) If the title is short and distinctive, a title search will probably give you the best results. If both the author and title are fairly common, you may have a problem. Most online systems have limits on how many entries will be displayed. With OCLC, if your search code will generate more than 50 possible "correct" entries, the system will indicate this and ask if you want to continue to search. Should the total of potential "right" entries exceed 200 or 250, most systems will not continue the search, so you will need to use a different approach.

The log-on procedure can be acquisitions-specific. If searching in Acquisitions, if the library has already placed an order for the title, the order record itself displays. Also, with search qualifiers, the entire search can be streamlined by specifying the type of material and date or range of years. For example, a search could be qualified with the characters "bks" for books, or with "1970-5/bks" for year and format. In the first instance, the search would include only books; in the second, only books published between 1970 and 1975. Such qualifiers can speed up the search by limiting the scope. In our search example, however, the author's name and most of the title words are fairly common,

---

*See page 77 for discussion of these numbers.

making it less likely the qualifiers will be of assistance in reducing search time.

Another important consideration is what information you can use in the search. When doing an author search in OCLC, type the first four letters of the last name, the first three letters of the first name, and the first letter of the middle. By looking in a large telephone directory using Smith, John J. as an example, you would encounter a number of possible "correct" entries (that is, entries that match the letters used). For a title search, type the first three letters of the first word (other than an article), the first two letters of both the second and third words, and the first letter of the fourth word. As long as the words are fairly uncommon this approach can be rather effective, but something like *Short Stories for a Long Night* would not be as effective (Sho St fo a). Author/title searches use a combination of the first four letters of an author's last name and the first four letters of the first word in the title.

Fig. 6.1*
OCLC – "Logging on" the System

```
THE OCLC ON-LINE SYSTEM
PLEASE LOG ON
2-32-305746\)+
4
PLEASE LOG ON.
2-32-305746+
4
HELLO STUDENT.
YOU WILL BE USING THE CATALOGING SYSTEM IN THE TRAINING MODE.

THE SAVE FILE IS NOW AVAILABLE FOR USE.   NO RECORDS WILL BE PURGED
UNTIL SHUTDOWN TUESDAY 1980 FEBRUARY 19.   RECORDS SAVED DURING THE
EARLY MORNING HOURS EST OF 1980 FEB. 15 SHOULD BE CHECKED.

CHANGES TO "SERIALS:  A MARC FORMAT, LC ADDENDUM NO. 13 (791205) ARE NOW VALID.

CATALOG CARDS FOR FEBRUARY 4,5 AND 6 HAVE BEEN SHIPPED.
```

Author/Title Searching

Let us now see how these factors would come into play in our search for Charles Collins, *Public Administration in Hong Kong*, 1975. Assuming we start with the author/title search, we would type COLL, PUBL. The results of that search are shown in Figure 6.2 (page 62). Examining the 13 entries displayed, nothing matches what we are looking for; however, entry 5 indicates 16 entries for authors whose names start COLL and who also wrote a book that starts with a word spelled PUBL. We request that those 16 entries be displayed (Figure 6.3, page 62). In this display, we see entries for Collins, Charl with titles that start with PUBL, so we have *those* entries displayed (Figure 6.4, page 62). Here we find two entries (3 and 4) that match the information given on the request slip. Asking that first entry 3 and then entry 4 be displayed, we find further that they are apparently for the same item (Figure 6.5, page 63). At this point, we have gone as far as we can—we have matched all the information supplied to us. Now, check with the person who requested the book to ensure that this is the book desired. Thus, using an author/title search took a minimum of four displays to

---

Fig. 6.2
Author/Title Search — First Display

```
COLL,PUBL\+
TO SEE TITLE FOR A COLLECTIVE ENTRY, TYPE LINE#, DEPRESS DISPLAY RECD,
SEND.

   1  AMERICAN  (6)
   2  ARIZONA. UNIVERSITY. COLLEGE OF LIBERAL ARTS.   PUBLICATIONS OF
THE FACULTY.   TUCSON.
   3  ASSOCIATION OF COLLEG (4)
   4  CALIFORNIA. STATE COLLEGE, SAN DIEGO. PUBLIC AFFAIRS RESEARCH
INSTITUTE.   PUBLIC ADMINISTRATION AND THE WAR ON POVERTY. JAMES M.
ELDEN AND HAINES B. REMMEY, EDITORS.   SAN DIEGO,   1966
   5  COLL (16)
   6  COLLVER, ANDREW.   PUBLIC IMAGES AND COASTAL ZONE MANAGEMENT /
[ALBANY?  :   1974
   7  COLORADO COLLEGE   PUBLICATION (4)
   8  GEORGIA  (4)
   9  MINNESOTA  (3)
  10  NATIONAL COLLEG (2)
  11  NEW YORK STATE STATE UNIVERSITY COLLEGE BUFFALO PROGRAM IN  (3)
  12  PENNSYLVANIA. STATE UNIVERSITY. COLLEGE OF MINERAL INDUSTRIES.
PUBLICATIONS OF THE SCHOOL OF MINERAL INDUSTRIES.   UNIVERSITY PARK,
PENNSYLVANIA.   19UU
  13  UNIVERSITY OF  (3)
```

Fig. 6.3
Author/Title Search — Second Display

```
5\+
TO SEE TITLE FOR A COLLECTIVE ENTRY, TYPE LINE#, DEPRESS DISPLAY RECD,
SEND.

   1  COLLAZO, DEBRA P   PUBLIC SERVICE DIRECTORY : UNIVERSITY OF
ARIZONA /   TUCSON :   1979
   2  COLLEGE  (3)
   3  COLLINS BARRY E   PUBLIC AND PRIVATE CONFORMITY COMPETING
EXPLANATIONS BY IMPROVISATION COGNITIVE DISSONANCE AND ATTRIBUTION
THEORIES (2)
   4  COLLINS CHARL (5)
   5  COLLINS PHILIP ARTHUR WILLIAM  PUBLIC READINGS (2)
   6  [COLLINS, WILLIAM LUCAS]   THE PUBLIC SCHOOLS; WINCHESTER--
WESTMINSTER--SHREWSBURY--HARROW--RUGBY; NOTES OF THEIR HISTORY AND
TRADITIONS,   EDINBURGH, LONDON,   1867
   7  COLLISON, ROBERT LEWIS.   PUBLISHED LIBRARY CATALOGUES; AN
INTRODUCTION TO THEIR CONTENTS AND USE   LONDON,   1973
   8  COLLOQUE FRANCO-ALLEMAND SUR "LA PUBLICATION DE MANUSCRITS
IN'EDITS," PARIS, 1977.   PUBLICATION DE MANUSCRITS IN'EDITS.   BERN :
LAS VEGAS :   1979
```

Fig. 6.4
Author/Title Search — Third Display

```
4\+
   1  COLLINS, CHARLES HENRY, SIR,   PUBLIC ADMINISTRATION IN CEYLON.
LONDON, NEW YORK,   1951  DLC
   2  COLLINS, CHARLES HENRY, SIR,   PUBLIC ADMINISTRATION IN HONG KONG.
LONDON, NEW YORK,   1952
   3  COLLINS, CHARLES HENRY, SIR,   PUBLIC ADMINISTRATION IN HONG KONG
/   NEW YORK :   1975  DLC
   4  COLLINS, CHARLES HENRY, SIR,   PUBLIC ADMINISTRATION IN HONG KONG
/   NEW YORK :   1975  DLC
   5  COLLINS, CHARLOTTE ANNA HAHNE,   PUBLIC SCHOOL CERTIFICATION IN
HISTORICAL PERSPECTIVE.   [ANN ARBOR, MICH.]   1970  [MICROFORM]
```

Fig. 6.5
Author/Title Search—Fourth and Fifth Displays*

```
3\+
NO HOLDINGS IN CUG -  FOR HOLDINGS ENTER DH DEPRESS  DISPLAY RECD SEND
OCLC: 1174691        REC STAT: N ENTRD: 750106      USED: 791124
TYPE: A BIB LVL: M GOVT PUB:     LANG:  ENG SOURCE:    ILLUS:
REPR:     ENC LVL: J CONF PUB: 0 CTRY:   NYU DAT TP: R M/F/B: 10
INDX: 1 MOD REC:     FESTSCHR: 0 CONT: B
DESC: I INT LVL:     DATES: 1975,1952
    1 010       74-34411
    2 040       DLC $C DLC
    3 043       A-HK---
    4 050 0     JQ675 $B .C6 1975
    5 082       354/.51/250009
    6 090        $B
    7 049       CUGA
    8 100 10    COLLINS, CHARLES HENRY, $C SIR, $D 1887-
    9 245 10    PUBLIC ADMINISTRATION IN HONG KONG / $C BY CHARLES COLLINS.
   10 260 0     NEW YORK : $B AMS PRESS, $C [1975]
   11 300        P. CM.
   12 500        REPRINT OF THE 1952 ED. PUBLISHED BY THE ROYAL INSTITUTE OF
INTERNATIONAL AFFAIRS, LONDON.
   13 504       BIBLIOGRAPHY: P.
   14 500       INCLUDES INDEX.
   15 651   0   HONGKONG $X POLITICS AND GOVERNMENT.

4\+
SCREEN 1 OF 2
NO HOLDINGS IN CUG -  FOR HOLDINGS ENTER DH DEPRESS  DISPLAY RECD SEND
OCLC: 2616476        REC STAT: P ENTRD: 750224      USED: 791208
TYPE: A BIB LVL: M GOVT PUB:     LANG:  ENG SOURCE:    ILLUS:
REPR:     ENC LVL:   CONF PUB: 0 CTRY:   NYU DAT TP: R M/F/B: 10
INDX: 1 MOD REC:     FESTSCHR: 0 CONT: B
DESC: I INT LVL:     DATES: 1975,1952
    1 010       70-179180
    2 040       DLC $C DLC
    3 020       0404548105
    4 043       A-HK---
    5 050 0     JQ675 $B .C6 1975
    6 082       354/.51/250009
    7 090        $B
    8 049       CUGA
    9 100 10    COLLINS, CHARLES HENRY, $C SIR, $D 1887-
   10 245 10    PUBLIC ADMINISTRATION IN HONG KONG / $C BY SIR CHARLES
COLLINS.
   11 260 0     NEW YORK : $B AMS PRESS, $C 1975.
   12 300       IX, 189 P. ; $C 19 CM.
   13 500       REPRINT OF THE 1952 ED. PUBLISHED BY THE ROYAL INSTITUTE OF
INTERNATIONAL AFFAIRS, LONDON.
   14 504       BIBLIOGRAPHY: P. 182-184.

NS\+
SCREEN 2 OF 2
   15 500       INCLUDES INDEX.
   16 651   0   HONGKONG $X POLITICS AND GOVERNMENT.
```

---

*For a full explanation of all the items in this figure, see pages 323-327.

find an exact match. Checking back with the person requesting the book is something that has to be done whether using a manual or machine search method. With the name of the publisher, we would actually be able to place the order, but that information would not have affected the verification process. This example reinforces the recommendation that requests be screened before starting any search and that you attempt to secure the maximum amount of information from the requestor.

Author Searching

What would have happened had we chosen to start by using just the author's name? Having only a first and last name, we would type COLL, CHA, which results in the display shown in Figure 6.6. That display shows that entry 7 is the one we should look at next; Figure 6.7 illustrates the result of that request. This display gives (entry #4) 43 possible correct items under Collins, Charles; therefore, we have this information displayed (Figure 6.8).

Fig. 6.6
Author Search – First and Second Displays

```
COLL,CHA, \+
 YES OR  NO
COLL,CHA, PRODUCES MORE THAN FIFTY ENTRIES.
DO YOU WISH TO CONTINUE THIS SEARCH?

YES+
TO SEE TITLE FOR A COLLECTIVE ENTRY, TYPE LINE#, DEPRESS DISPLAY RECD,
SEND.

    1   COLL CHARLES J    (4)
    2   COLLA (6)
    3   COLLE (17)
    4   COLLETT (7)
    5   COLLEY CHARLES   (5)
    6   COLLIER CHARLES   (14)
    7   COLLIN (104)
    8   COLLIS (4)
    9   COLLMAN CHARLES ALBERT    (4)
   10   COLLODI, CHARLES, PSEUD.   WALT DISNEY'S PINOCCHIO.   1977
   11   COLLON, CHANTAL,   CHANGEMENT SOCIO-PROFESSIONNEL ET FORMATION:
'ETUDE D'UNE SITUATION DE CRISE DANS LE BASSIN DE BRIEY.   NANCY,   1971
   12   COLLUM CHARLES   (4)
   13   COLLYNS CHARLES PALK   NOTES ON THE CHASE OF THE WILD RED DEER IN
THE COUNTIES OF DEVON AND SOMERSET WITH AN APPENDIX DESCRIPTIVE OF
REMARKABLE RUNS AND INCIDENTS CONNECTED WITH THE CHASE FROM THE YEAR
1780 TO THE YEAR 1860 (2)
7\+
```

Fig. 6.7
Author Search – Third Display

```
TO SEE TITLE FOR A COLLECTIVE ENTRY, TYPE LINE#, DEPRESS DISPLAY RECD,
SEND.

    1  COLLINGSWOOD, CHARLES.   ISRAEL.   1970
    2  COLLINGWOOD CHARLES    (8)
    3  COLLINS, CHARLENE RENEE,    A HISTORICAL AND DESCRIPTIVE STUDY OF
ADULT COOPERATIVE VOCATIONAL EDUCATION PROGRAMS IN COLORADO
POSTSECONDARY INSTITUTIONS /   GREELEY :    1977
    4  COLLINS CHARLES  (43)
    5  COLLINS, CHARLES, POET.   GREEN LEAVES : OR, LAYS OF BOYHOOD /
LONDON :   1844
    6  COLLINS CHARLES T (4)
    7  COLLINS CHARLES W (21)
    8  COLLINS, CHARLOTTE ANNA HAHNE,    PUBLIC SCHOOL CERTIFICATION IN
HISTORICAL PERSPECTIVE.   [ANN ARBOR, MICH.]   1970
    9  COLLINS, CHASE.   THE COUNTRY GUIDE FOR CITY PEOPLE.   NEW YORK,
1973
   10  COLLINSON CHARLES   (20)
   11  COLLINSTRELAWNY CHARLES TRELAWNY  PERRANZABULOE THE LOST CHURCH
FOUND OR THE CHURCH OF ENGLAND NOT A NEW CHURCH BUT ANCIENT APOSTOLICAL
AND INDEPENDENT AND A PROTESTING CHURCH NINE HUNDRED YEARS BEFORE THE
REFORMA (3)
```

Fig. 6.8
Author Search – Fourth Display

```
4\+
TO SEE TITLE FOR A COLLECTIVE ENTRY, TYPE LINE#, DEPRESS DISPLAY RECD,
SEND.

    1  COLLINS CHARLES    (3)
    2  COLLINS CHARLES A (5)
    3  COLLINS CHARLES B   (3)
    4  COLLINS CHARLES C   (9)
    5  COLLINS CHARLES D (2)
    6  COLLINS CHARLES H (7)
    7  COLLINS, CHARLES J.,   MANAGEMENT OF AMENORRHEA   SPRINGFIELD,
ILL.,   1966
    8  COLLINS, CHARLES JOSEPH,   FORTUNE'S BEFORE YOU! TODAY'S
INVESTMENT OPPORTUNITIES.   NEW YORK,   1937
    9  COLLINS CHARLES M   (8)
   10  COLLINS, CHARLES MICHAEL.   MEMBRANE TRANSPORT MECHANISMS AND
HEMODIALYSIS OF LIPOPHILIC COMPOUNDS /   1977
   11  COLLINS, CHARLES NATHANIAL.   AN INVESTIGATION OF THE SOCIO-
ECONOMIC CHARACTER AND THE DEGREE OF SELF-MOTIVATION POSSESSED BY
STUDENTS IN THE DEPARTMENT OF DESIGN AND INDUSTRY /   SAN FRANCISCO :
1972
   12  COLLINS CHARLES O  POLITICAL GEOGRAPHY OF NATIONBUILDING THE CASE
OF BELIZE  (2)
```

We are now confronted with a problem. Previous displays showed only one obvious choice to make. Now, since the request slip has only a first and last name, any of the first six lines could be the one we want. Certainly the other items which do not display the right title can be rejected. One way is to start with the first one, then follow in sequence until the match is found.

Another approach is to look at the author(s) with the most entries (#4), because this has the best probability of being correct. So we have that one displayed (Fig. 6.9, page 66) but find it does not contain what we need. Therefore, we recall the previous display (Figure 6.8) and decide to try #6 (Figure 6.10, page 66).

Fig. 6.9
Author Search — Fifth Display

```
4\+
   1   COLLINS, CHARLES C.   BLUEPRINT FOR A CLUSTER COLLEGE.   LOS
ANGELES, CALIF.,   1975
   2   COLLINS, CHARLES C.   COLLEGE ORIENTATION: EDUCATION FOR RELEVANCE
BOSTON,   1969   DLC
   3   COLLINS, CHARLES C.   EVERYMAN COMMUNITY COLLEGE : A CLUSTER MODEL
/   WASHINGTON, D.C. :   1973
   4   COLLINS, CHARLES C.   FINANCING HIGHER EDUCATION: A PROPOSAL   LOS
ANGELES,   1970   DLC
   5   COLLINS, CHARLES C   GENERAL EDUCATION : A COMMUNITY COLLEGE MODEL
/   [S. L.] :   1976
   6   COLLINS, CHARLES C.   GOVERNANCE : A COMMUNITY COLLEGE MODEL /
[S.L.] :   1977
   7   COLLINS, CHARLES C   JUNIOR COLLEGE STUDENT PERSONNEL PROGRAMS:
WHAT THEY ARE AND WHAT THEY SHOULD BE.   WASHINGTON,   1967
   8   COLLINS, CHARLES C.   THE PEOPLES' COMMUNITY COLLEGE : A CLUSTER
MODEL /   [S.L. :   1977   DLC
   9   COLLINS, CHARLES C.   PREMISES: PLANNING STUDENT PERSONNEL
FACILITIES,   [WASHINGTON,   1967
```

Fig. 6.10
Author Search — Sixth Display

```
6\+
   1   COLLINS, CHARLES H   DEMOBILIZATION OF MAN POWER IN THE UNITED
STATES ARMY 1918-1919 /   [WASHINGTON] :   1942
   2   COLLINS, CHARLES H   FROM HIGHLAND HILLS TO AN EMPEROR'S TOMB.
(EPISODICAL, REFLECTIVE, AND DESCRIPTIVE.)   CINCINNATI,   1886   DLC
   3   COLLINS, CHARLES H.   THE NEW YEAR COMES, MY LADY,   BUFFALO,
1895   DLC
   4   COLLINS, CHARLES HENRY, SIR,   PUBLIC ADMINISTRATION IN CEYLON.
LONDON, NEW YORK,   1951   DLC
   5   COLLINS, CHARLES HENRY, SIR,   PUBLIC ADMINISTRATION IN HONG KONG.
LONDON, NEW YORK,   1952
   6   COLLINS, CHARLES HENRY, SIR,   PUBLIC ADMINISTRATION IN HONG KONG
/   NEW YORK :   1975   DLC
   7   COLLINS, CHARLES HENRY, SIR,   PUBLIC ADMINISTRATION IN HONG KONG
/   NEW YORK :   1975   DLC
```

At last, we have a complete match with numbers 6 and 7. If those two items are displayed, we see the information shown in Figure 6.5. Thus we end this search with the same records as in an author/title search, but it took longer (seven displays, counting the need to answer the question about continuing and to recall a previous screen). Had we chosen to conduct the search from display three on, in terms of sequential searching, it would have taken a minimum of 12 displays. And if we had to return to the third display after each unsuccessful search, it would have been 18 displays to get to the proper record. Clearly, in most instances, starting with the entries with the most potential "correct" records saves search time.

Title Searching

Here we would type PUB, AD, as this is all the title information we have. This would result in the information in Figure 6.11. Again, several possible choices are right. Since we have only *Public Administration* as the title, and there are 60 records under that heading, we have number 5 displayed (Figure 6.12). From this display, we see two possible choices — number 1 or 5. We try 5 (Figure 6.13), but discover that none of the items match what we have on the request slip. Because numbers 9, 10, and 11 have no publication dates, we might try these (if

Fig. 6.11
Title Search—First and Second Displays

```
PUB.AD,  ,  \+
YES OR  NO
PUB.AD,, PRODUCES MORE THAN FIFTY ENTRIES.
DO YOU WISH TO CONTINUE THIS SEARCH?
YES+
```

```
TO SEE TITLE FOR A COLLECTIVE ENTRY, TYPE LINE#, DEPRESS DISPLAY RECD,
SEND.

    1  PUBLIC ADDRESS /   EYRE, FLOYED G.   [SALT LAKE CITY] :   1935
    2  PUBLIC ADDRESS.   FLORIDA. DEPARTMENT OF COMMERCE. DIVISION OF
LABOR AND EMPLOYMENT OPPORTUNITIES.
    3  PUBLIC ADDRESSES  BRIGHT JOHN (2)
    4  PUBLIC ADDRESSES.   PADILLA, AMBROSIO.   [MANILA?]   1958
    5  PUBLIC ADMINISTRATION   (60)
    6  PUBLIC ADMINISTRATION  P (11)
    7  PUBLIC ADMINISTRATION  RI (2)
    8  PUBLIC ADMINISTRATION  S (8)
    9  PUBLIC ADMINISTRATION  WHITE LEONARD DUPEE (3)
   10  PUBLIC ADMINISTRATOR /   NATIONAL LEARNING CORPORATION. CIVIL
SERVICE DIVISION.   SYOSSET, N. Y. :   1975
   11  PUBLIC ADVERTISER.   NEW YORK,   1807
   12  PUBLIC ADVISORY  US INTERSTATE COMMERCE COMMISSION (13)
   13  PUBLISHERS' ADVERTISING : BEING THE REACTIONS OF A PRACTISING
PUBLISHER-ADVERTISER TO THE EXHORTATIONS OF NON-PUBLISHER THEORISTS.
SADLEIR, MICHAEL,   LONDON :   1930
```

Fig. 6.12
Title Search—Third Display

```
5\+
TO SEE TITLE FOR A COLLECTIVE ENTRY, TYPE LINE#, DEPRESS DISPLAY RECD,
SEND.

    1  PUBLIC ADMINISTRATION   (3)
    2  PUBLIC ADMINISTRATION.    LONDON [ETC.]   1926
    3  PUBLIC ADMINISTRATION.    LONDON [ETC.]   1926
    4  PUBLIC ADMINISTRATION.    SYDNEY,   1939
    5  PUBLIC ADMINISTRATION   (11)
    6  PUBLIC ADMINISTRATION  AVASTHI, AMRESHWAR.   AGRA,   1966
    7  PUBLIC ADMINISTRATION  B (9)
    8  PUBLIC ADMINISTRATION ;   CONNORS, BRENDAN.   MILTON KEYNES :
1974
    9  PUBLIC ADMINISTRATION  DIMOCK MARSHALL EDWARD (6)
   10  PUBLIC ADMINISTRATION : THEORY AND PRACTICE /   FESLER, JAMES
WILLIAM,   ENGLEWOOD CLIFFS, N.J. :   1980
   11  PUBLIC ADMINISTRATION  G (14)
   12  PUBLIC ADMINISTRATION  H (3)
   13  PUBLIC ADMINISTRATION /   LORCH, ROBERT STUART,   ST. PAUL :
1978
   14  PUBLIC ADMINISTRATION  M (6)
   15  PUBLIC ADMINISTRATION ;   NEGRO, JOSEPHINE.   MILTON KEYNES :
1974
```

Fig. 6.13
Title Search—Fourth Display

```
5\+
    1  PUBLIC ADMINISTRATION    WELLINGTON,   1949  S  DLC
    2  PUBLIC ADMINISTRATION ;    MILTON KEYNES [ENG.] :   1974  DLC
    3  PUBLIC ADMINISTRATION.    MILTON KEYNES [ENG.] :   1974  DLC
    4  PUBLIC ADMINISTRATION    [SYDNEY,   1976  S  DLC
    5  PUBLIC ADMINISTRATION : CONCEPTS AND CASES /     BOSTON :   1976
DLC
    6  PUBLIC ADMINISTRATION : CONCEPTS AND CASES /     BOSTON :   1976
    7  PUBLIC ADMINISTRATION.    [WELLINGTON]   1978  S  DLC
    8  PUBLIC ADMINISTRATION    [WELLINGTON]   1979  S
    9  PUBLIC ADMINISTRATION.    LONDON [ETC.]   S
   10  PUBLIC ADMINISTRATION -A DIRECTORY OF UNOFFICIAL ORGANIZATIONS IN
THE FIELD OF PUBLIC ADMINISTRATION IN THE UNITED STATES AND CANADA      S
   11  PUBLIC ADMINISTRATION    LONDON   S
```

we did we would find none of them were matches). Going back to the third display, we might decide to try number 1. The result would be equally unsatisfactory, as all three items would have the wrong publication date. Even if you searched all items listed in the third display (we did), the result would be the same: it is not possible to verify our example request using the title approach, because we do not have enough information. With the full title, we could immediately locate the item in question (Figure 6.14).

Fig. 6.14
Title Search with Full Title — First and Second Displays

```
PUB,AD,IN,H\+
    1  PUBLIC ADMINISTRATION IN HONG KONG.    COLLINS, CHARLES HENRY, SIR,
LONDON, NEW YORK,   1952
    2  PUBLIC ADMINISTRATION IN HONG KONG /    COLLINS, CHARLES HENRY,
SIR,   NEW YORK :   1975  DLC
    3  PUBLIC ADMINISTRATION IN HONG KONG /    COLLINS, CHARLES HENRY,
SIR,   NEW YORK :   1975  DLC


2\+
 SCREEN 1 OF 2
 NO HOLDINGS IN CUG -  FOR HOLDINGS ENTER DH DEPRESS  DISPLAY RECD SEND
 OCLC: 2616476      REC STAT: P ENTRD: 750224        USED: 791208
 TYPE: A BIB LVL: M GOVT PUB:   LANG:  ENG SOURCE:    ILLUS:
 REPR:    ENC LVL:    CONF PUB: 0 CTRY: NYU DAT TP: R M/F/B: 10
 INDX: 1 MOD REC:    FESTSCHR: 0 CONT: B
 DESC: I INT LVL:    DATES: 1975,1952
    1 010      70-179180
    2 040      DLC $C DLC
    3 020      0404548105
    4 043      A-HK---
    5 050 0    JQ675 $B .C6 1975
    6 082      354/.51/250009
    7 090       $B
    8 049      CUGA
    9 100 10   COLLINS, CHARLES HENRY, $C SIR, $D 1887-
   10 245 10   PUBLIC ADMINISTRATION IN HONG KONG / $C BY SIR CHARLES
COLLINS.
   11 260 0    NEW YORK : $B AMS PRESS, $C 1975.
   12 300      IX, 189 P. ; $C 19 CM.
   13 500      REPRINT OF THE 1952 ED. PUBLISHED BY THE ROYAL INSTITUTE OF
INTERNATIONAL AFFAIRS, LONDON.
   14 504      BIBLIOGRAPHY: P. 182-184.
NS\+
 SCREEN 2 OF 2
   15 500      INCLUDES INDEX.
   16 651  0   HONGKONG $X POLITICS AND GOVERNMENT.
```

While this example is based on OCLC, other online systems follow the same basic principles. If the library's system is a full acquisition system, you will also be able to check whether your library has already ordered the item. Should you need to order it, you can then generate the order form or, in some cases, actually transmit the order directly to a vendor that either supplied or shares the system you are using.

We wish to reemphasize that this discussion has been an *overview* of how machine verification can work. It is *not* a detailed explanation of how the total OCLC acquisition system operates; a detailed description of any such system is beyond the scope of this book. However, further information about the OCLC acquisition system can be found in chapter 13.

NOTES

[1]Marion Reid, "Effectiveness of the OCLC Data Base for Acquisitions Verification," *Journal of Academic Librarianship* 2 (January 1977): 303-306.

[2]Earl Kunz, *Meeting the Challenge* (Williamsport, Pa.: Brodart Inc., n.d.), unpaged.

REVIEW QUESTIONS

1. In what ways do manual and machine searching differ?

2. What are some of the ways one can call up an online bibliographic record?

3. Which methods will be most frequently employed in machine-aided verification?

4. What are some factors to consider when deciding which method to start with in machine-aided verification?

5. What are the major advantages of conducting online searching?

7
VERIFICATION AND SOURCES: BOOKS

Since bibliographies are the primary sources for establishing the existence of an item, we will discuss some of the most frequently used bibliographies for printed materials. A bibliography is a publication that lists and describes informational materials of all types. The term is generally applied to lists of books, but in its broadest sense, it includes a much wider range of material (printed or nonprint).

Among the types of bibliographies most frequently used in searching are national, trade, and general bibliographies. A "national bibliography" attempts to list all works about (or produced in) a given country, or works written in a language common to several countries (e.g., *British National Bibliography*). A "trade bibliography" lists current, in-print books judged to be of interest to the general book-buying public (e.g., *Weekly Record*). A "general bibliography" lists all books or items that exist in the collection of a particular library or on a particular subject (e.g., *Library of Congress Catalog*).

Other types of bibliographies are retrospective, current, and comprehensive. A "retrospective bibliography" lists older items not generally available (e.g., *Books Relating to America from Its Discovery to the Present Time*). One must avoid assuming, however, that even if the items are several hundred years old they are not available. The activity of reprint publishers has brought many older works back into print. In practice, the terms "retrospective bibliography," "out-of-print bibliography," and "out-of-print catalog" are almost synonymous, although the latter two imply that the items listed are not generally available. A "current bibliography" lists items that are presently available or that will be published commercially (e.g., *Books in Print*). This is the type most frequently used in bibliographic verification work. The final type is the "comprehensive bibliography," which lists both retrospective and current items (e.g., *National Union Catalog*, a frequently consulted, very useful tool).

Actually, a bibliography may be a combination of several of the above types. For example, one source that is commonly used for verification purposes is the series of Library of Congress catalogs. These are general bibliographies because they include only the books acquired and cataloged by the Library of Congress. Nevertheless, they also serve as a major segment of the American national bibliography series, because they include a very high percentage of all the books published in the United States. In yet another sense, LC's catalogs are general, comprehensive bibliographies because they are not confined to either current or retrospective materials. The *British Museum Catalog of Printed Books* would be another example of a general comprehensive catalog. Therefore, keep in mind that the inclusion of the name of a country or a library in its title does not necessarily mean that a bibliography is solely national in scope. The catalog of both the British Museum and the Library of Congress represent national bibliographies, but they also are more than that; they should be classified as general *and* national bibliographies. A strictly national bibliography that is also a trade and current bibliography is *Books in Print* (*BIP*), which lists books currently available from a number of American publishers. A national retrospective bibliography that a searcher may encounter is Joseph Sabin's *Dictionary of Books Relating to America from Its Discovery to the Present Time*, which was published in 1892.

SEARCHING

From the searcher's point of view, the existence of more general comprehensive bibliographies means that the searching function can be performed more effectively. Some of the more common sources used in the verification process will be discussed, then, in terms of the type of information they contain and their value to the searcher.

Although the types of information needed to complete the order form will vary, a few items are basic. Entries in each bibliography should be examined to determine how many of these basic items can be verified in each bibliography. The information needed is:

1) author,

2) title,

3) publisher and place of publication,

4) date of publication,

5) price,

6) ISBN, and

7) series note.

The bibliographies should also be examined to see what search approaches are possible and the frequency with which such approaches may be made. Three basic approaches are:

1) author approach,

2) title approach, and

3) subject or classified approach.

The frequency with which a bibliography is published is also important in determining where to begin a search. Bibliographies are published weekly, semimonthly, monthly, quarterly, semiannually, annually, and in other accumulations.

In earlier editions of this text, we checked three book titles through the basic American and British bibliographic tools to illustrate how much variation existed among them. Because of space limitations in this edition, we can only provide a summary of the results (full details can be found in the third edition of this work). We found the following. The characteristics of the books searched (3 books) were:

1) All had personal author entries.

2) All were monographs.

3) Two of them were available in both hardbound and paper covers.

4) Two of the books were American and one was British.

The characteristics of the bibliographies searched (14 titles) were:

1) Although each title was searched through all available approaches to each bibliography (author, title, and sometimes subject), only 2 of the 14 bibliographies searched listed all three books.

2) American titles are slow to appear in British sources.

3) When a title is released in England and the United States at the same time, it appears in the trade bibliographies of both countries.

4) Subject entries vary even within the same bibliography.

5) There is little consistency in the listing of series.

The limitations of an introductory textbook make it impossible to list and discuss all the bibliographies that might be used for verification purposes. We will only briefly cover the basic American and British bibliographies, and for a full listing of sources, the reader should consult the following:

American Reference Books Annual. Littleton, Colo.: Libraries Unlimited, 1970- . (with 3 cumulative 5-year indexes).

Sheehy, Eugene P. *Guide to Reference Books.* 9th ed. Chicago: American Library Association, 1976. (also see supplements—1st, 1980 and 2nd, 1982).

Walford, A. J. *Guide to Reference Material. Vol. 1, Science and Technology.* 4th ed. London: Library Association, 1980.

_____. *Guide to Reference Material. Vol. 2, Social and Historical Sciences.* 4th ed. London: Library Association, 1982.

_____. *Guide to Reference Material. Vol. 3, Generalities, Languages, the Arts and Literature.* 3rd ed. London: Library Association, 1977.

American Sources

The R. R. Bowker Company is the mainstay in the field of American current bibliographies; without their publications, work in the acquisition department would be much more complicated and time consuming. Bowker publishes a series of bibliographies that will list new American titles from a publisher's first announcement of a new title until that title ceases to be available in the current book trade. Although all of their publications are used at various times in acquisition work, some are more frequently used, so we will focus on those most often used. The following are major Bowker bibliographic publications; those with an asterisk (*) are the items we will examine in some detail:

*Forthcoming Books
  Subject Guide to Forthcoming Books
*Weekly Record
*American Book Publishing Record
*Books in Print
  Subject Guide to Books in Print
  Publishers Trade List Annual
  Paperbound Books in Print

All these publications are concerned with book materials (i.e., publications of more than 49 pages).

Forthcoming Books and its subject guide are useful in the acquisition department to check on the status of an announced title. Publishers submit information to Bowker about titles they expect to publish in the near future—anywhere from two to three months to almost a year. *Forthcoming Books*, then, provides current information that is supplementary to *Books in Print*. However, some publishers submit their information even before a manuscript has been received, so occasionally (for this and other reasons) a title announced in *Forthcoming Books* is never published. More frequently, the title changes, which may cause one to think that it was not published. Another problem is that sometimes a main entry is changed sometime between the announcement and the publication of the book. Because of these limitations, and its author-title arrangement, *Forthcoming Books* is of limited value in verification and order work. Still, since each issue lists all newly announced books and previously announced books that have not yet been published, this tool can be employed to check on problem requests or on reports that an ordered title is "NYP" (not yet published). An asterisk indicates items appearing for the first time.

After a book is printed and "released" (made available for purchase), it is listed in the *Weekly Record (WR)*. Until 1974, *WR* was part of *Publishers Weekly (PW)*, which is a professional journal for the American book trade. When *PW* included the "Weekly Record" as the last section, no large- or medium-sized library could do without a subscription. Certainly *PW* is still an important source of information and statistics about the book trade, but many libraries find now that they *must* subscribe only to the *Weekly Record*.

The *Weekly Record* does an excellent job and is reasonably comprehensive, but it does have some major limitations. Some of these limitations are: 1) only books of 49 pages or more are listed, 2) only titles/information about titles submitted to *WR* are included, and 3) no serial publications are included. Changes in its scope do occur, so it is wise periodically to check such statements even if you think you know the work. Several factors make *WR* an essential tool in larger technical service departments. As already indicated, it is the first listing and the most comprehensive listing of a book's availability. Another very important factor is each entry (it is arranged by main entry) usually provides full cataloging information. The information is derived from that supplied by the Library of Congress (MARC records) and a limited amount of cataloging done by Bowker.

Verification through *WR* will likely yield information complete enough for order work; still, using *WR* for verification work is time-consuming because, with very few exceptions, a book only appears once. As its name implies, *WR* is published on a weekly basis, so many issues may have to be searched, unless you are lucky enough to know in what month the book was released.

Fortunately, the *American Book Publishing Record* (*BPR*) helps to bridge the gap until a book is listed in *Books in Print*. *BPR* is a monthly listing of books from the previous month's *Weekly Record* issues, arranged by Dewey Decimal numbers (*see* the chapter on classification systems). The author and title indexes are the primary points of access for verification/order purposes, although a subject search is also possible. *BPR* is the one source that allows a fairly good chance of finding an item when you must attempt to verify by using the subject approach. Monthly issues are cumulated into an annual volume.

For retrospective searching, the *American Book Publishing Record Cumulative: 1950-1977* is most useful. Not only is this a cumulation of *WR* and *BPR*, but the editors attempted to include as many books as possible (American and published between 1950-1977) that were found in the *National Union Catalog* and on MARC records and that were somehow missed in *WR* and *BPR*. Any project that involves several hundred thousand entries from several different sources is bound to have flaws, and this one does; but it still can be a real time saver.

Books in Print (*BIP*) is an annual publication with a mid-year supplement. Thus, in theory, you should only need to consult *Forthcoming Books, Weekly Record,* and *American Book Publishing Record* for the very latest books. But as noted above, this is not the case. Occasionally, books still "disappear" for a few months and then reappear in the listings. Because this tool has become so valuable to booksellers and libraries, almost all major American publishers contribute information to it about all the books they have available for sale ("in print"), even if somehow they were not included in *FB, WR,* or *BPR*. *BIP* is a multiple author-title volume set in which you find the most complete information under the author entry. There is also a subject guide, so you can gain access to information in a variety of ways. Both *Forthcoming Books* and *Books in Print* subject guides are based upon the *Library of Congress Subject Headings* (*see* chapter 20 for a description of the LC headings). *Books in Print* is now available online (see page 137 for more information about this service).

Works to which the Library of Congress does not assign subject headings are not listed in *Subject Guide to Books in Print*: fiction, poetry, drama, and bibles. However, collections and criticism of fiction and poetry are listed, as are individual works of fiction whose subject background seems "extensive enough to warrant mention." Entries are arranged in alphabetical order under Library of Congress subject headings and include the same bibliographic information provided by *BIP*. Juvenile books are sometimes listed separately under subject headings designed for this purpose and sometimes with adult books, but they are always identified by grade range. *Subject Guide* is a valuable tool for locating available titles on specific subjects, but it is obviously not a complete listing of all books in print.

BIP and its companion, *Subject Guide to Books in Print*, are the basic tools for determining both availability and price of a book. With the exception of the 1968 edition, which contains many inaccuracies, these tools are generally reliable in coverage and accuracy of information. Keep in mind that information is supplied by publishers during the spring and early summer, but that *BIP* is not published until the fall (usually in October), a time lag that is particularly significant when using *BIP* to determine the availability and price of a given title. No printed bibliographic tool can be completely accurate and up to date, since changes in price do occur and titles are rescheduled by publishers. *Forthcoming Books* and *Subject Guide to Forthcoming Books* supplement *BIP*, serving as a bimonthly cumulative index to books published after the summer closing date for the current *BIP*, as well as to books yet to be published.

Other Bowker publications include such specialized bibliographies as *Medical Books and Serials in Print, Children's Books in Print,* and *Large Type Books in Print.* Bowker can produce so many specialized tools because the basic bibliographic data is on computer, which means that it is relatively easy to produce a variety of tools, certainly vastly easier and quicker than doing it manually. Another example of such specialized tools is *Paperbound Books in Print.*

Cumulative Book Index (New York: Wilson, 1898-) is one of the basic tools of acquisition departments. (The previously listed Bowker publications are very useful, but they are limited to American trade publications.) *CBI* is one of the most useful verification tools available to the searcher for books in the English language. It attempts to list all books produced in the United States, regardless of language, and all books in the English language regardless of country of publication. When a title is published in both England and America, both items are listed. The information supplied in the author entry is reasonably complete, although series data are not always given. A number of subject entries are made for a title; at the same time, the *see also* references are evidence that there are a great many alternative choices. No clearer indication of the difficulties of a subject search could be found. The major limitation in using *CBI* is that it does not include government documents, periodicals, most paperbound books, maps, pamphlets, or sheet music. It is published quarterly, semiannually, and annually, and author, title, and subject entries are provided in a dictionary arrangement.

The *National Union Catalog* (Washington: Library of Congress, 1956-1982) in print format is one of the most important retrospective verification tools for acquisitions departments. The *NUC* represents the holdings of the Library of Congress and about 1,100 other participating libraries. Supplements list cards issued prior to July 1942 and from 1942 to 1955. The *NUC* starting in 1956 was published quarterly with annual, and quinquennial cumulations. (See page 315 for details.) From 1950 to 1982 *NUC* was supplemented by the *Subject Catalog* which presented a subject heading entry approach.

The LC Catalog and *NUC* have two very important limitations that must be kept in mind. A very high percentage of English-language materials are acquired and cataloged by LC and the cooperating libraries; nevertheless, not everything published and available in the United States will be listed. Second, although most verification data can be found in these sources, the price of an item must always be established from another source.

As of January 1983, five major parts of the *NUC* are issued only in microfiche: 1) *National Union Catalog. Books*, 2) *National Union Catalog. U.S. Books*, 3) *National Union Catalog. Audiovisual Materials*, 4) *National Union Catalog. Cartographic Materials*, and 5) *National Union Catalog. Register of Additional Locations*. Three parts of the *NUC* are issued in print format: 1) *Music, Books on Music, and Sound Recordings*, 2) *National Union Catalog of Manuscript Collections*, and 3) *New Serial Titles*. (For additional information about this series, see pages 281 and 315-320.)

British Sources

Bookseller (J. Whitaker and Sons) performs the same function for Great Britain that *WR* performs for the United States—providing a weekly listing of trade books in an author, title, subject arrangement. These issues are cumulated quarterly and form the basis of *Whitaker's Cumulative Book List*. Several distinctions exist between *Bookseller* and the weekly *British National Bibliography* (*BNB*). First, *Bookseller* lists only trade books, while *BNB* lists everything received for copyright (*see* discussion below). Second, *Bookseller* lists British and U.S. titles, whereas *BNB* covers only British books. It should also be noted that *Bookseller* lists new issues and cheap editions that are sometimes omitted from American publications.

British Books in Print (*BBIP*) (J. Whitaker and Sons) is the equivalent of *BIP* in the United States. An annual publication, it is based on information derived from *Bookseller* and contains no more and no less information than does that publication. Its author, title, and subject approach makes it a very useful searching tool. Its entries provide series information, which can be most valuable, and it is also important to note that the *only* complete entry is for the author.

Whitaker's Cumulative Book List (*CBL*) (J. Whitaker and Sons), based on *Bookseller*, is a classified, alphabetical approach to *Bookseller* entries. It is published on a quarterly and annual basis, with additional five-year cumulations. The five-year cumulations are in an alphabetical author-title arrangement, with only a very few subject entries.

The difference between *CBL* and *BBIP* is that *CBL* lists *all* books published, even after they have gone out of print. Thus, the existence of a title in *CBL* does not mean that it is available. The latest edition of *BBIP* must be checked to determine availability.

British National Bibliography (Council of the British National Bibliography, Limited) is a weekly publication that lists new British books received by "The Agent for the Copyright Libraries." There are monthly and annual cumulations. All the publications allow for an author or title series search. Arranged by Dewey Decimal Classification, entries are cataloged according to the British text of the *Anglo-American Cataloguing Rules*. Because the main entry is determined by the British text, there are occasions when the American and British practices will differ.

British Museum General Catalog (British Museum) is similar to the *Library of Congress Catalog*. Because of the great size of the British Museum collections, however, it is not up to date. In 1979 a significant effort was announced that would be devoted to generating a new complete, up-to-date catalog. This will be a major achievement and of great use in acquisition departments if it is accomplished. Presently, the amount of information one can find varies, depending on when an item was originally cataloged. Most early works have very limited entries, while contemporary titles are fully cataloged. A subject index is also being published, but it is rather slow in appearing. The greatest difficulty in using this catalog stems from the fact that the rules of entry may vary from American practice. This is particularly true of works that might be considered for corporate author entry.

STANDARD BOOK NUMBERS

For some time both publishers and librarians have been attempting to establish standard numbers for books and serials. The purpose is to have a unique number for each title published. In time, it may be possible to order a book or serial simply by using this number. Presently, with some automated order systems, it is possible to order a book with just an International Standard Book Number (see chapter 13). Book publishers have now established such a system, but it applies only to current titles. International Standard Book Number (ISBN) supplies the basic information about an item.

Standard book numbers will become more and more important in acquisition work as jobbers and publishers automate their accounting and inventory procedures. In time, libraries may begin to use these numbers for their internal control purposes, as well. Twenty-two nations presently use the system (1980), and most Western European and English-language publishers now use standard book numbers. Approximately 80% of all book production in participating countries is included.

One important characteristic of ISBN is that each *form* of the same book has a different number. That is, each edition has a unique number, as do the paper and hardbound versions. For example, the number for the first edition of this book was 0-87287-02904; the second edition was 0-87287-125-8; the hardbound version of the number for the fourth edition was 0-87287-228-9; and the paperbound was 0-87287-248-3. From the point of view of the acquisition department, the ISBN is the only information needed for ordering a book from a jobber, since it identifies the specific edition and binding. This could be a major time-saving device, reducing the amount of typing required on orders—no more typing of author, title, publisher, place, date, or price. However, mistakes might arise in typing the ISBN itself (e.g., transposed numbers, errors in copying). If author, title, publisher, etc., are provided, the jobber may be able to provide the desired item despite a typing error. Nevertheless, we think serious consideration should be given to using only the ISBN.

The Library of Congress is investigating the problems and advantages of replacing LC card numbers with ISBNs. The British National Bibliography has already done this; one now orders BNB catalog cards using the ISBN. Using the ISBN in accounting activities could reduce typing required, since invoices could use only the ISBN even if the order form provides additional information. This would save some effort for both suppliers and libraries. Other possible uses of the number are in cataloging, data processing, and public service activities, so it is important to understand the ISBN system and how it works.

The International Standard Serial Number (ISSN) is an eight-digit number that identifies the publisher and title. As with the ISBN, the last digit serves as the control. ISBN and ISSN are both being developed in the expectation of extensive computer use in book distribution.

REVIEW QUESTIONS

1. What is a bibliography?

2. Name the types of bibliographies and give one title.

3. How does *BIP* differ from *CBI*?

4. What are the scope limitations of *WR*?

5. What is the main advantage of using *BPR*?

6. Are British and American cataloging rules for selecting the main entry the same?

7. What are the similarities and differences between *Bookseller* and *PW/WR*?

8. What are the differences between *Bookseller* and *BNB*?

9. What are the differences between *BBIP* and *CBL*?

10. What is an ISBN and how can/could it be used in acquisition work?

8
VERIFICATION AND SOURCES: NON-PRINT

The preceding chapter covered the verification methods used for books and discussed verification sources for most English-language books. (Chapter 9 will discuss order procedures.) Much of the material in both chapters applies not only to books but to other media as well (films, phonograph records, microforms, videotapes, audio tapes, etc.). Nevertheless, some very basic differences between books and audiovisuals must be noted.

DIFFERENCES IN VERIFYING BOOKS AND NON-PRINT MATERIALS

Perhaps the biggest difference is that most nonbook materials are requested on a preview basis.* This is particularly true of films, videotapes, series of audio tapes, 35mm slide-tape series, etc. Because of this difference, identification of the correct supplier is extremely important. But the detailed verification used for books is not essential, since unwanted nonbook materials can be returned. In the case of books, the department issues a purchase order and so legally must buy what has been ordered, even if it turns out to be the wrong edition or the wrong title. A vendor may or may not allow the library to return such items for credit. The use of "preview only" requests places the library under no obligation to purchase the material. Still, nonbook materials must be carefully verified, because errors waste everyone's time; but the cost of an error can be considerably less with nonbook materials than with books.

A second difference is that the verification tools are different. Because books and nonbook materials are very seldom covered in the same source, a search for each medium usually involves a distinct set of sources. This chapter will examine only some of the more common sources for the most frequently purchased items. (Again in the interest of saving space, we will not provide sample entries from the verification tools.) Until rather recently it was unusual to find suppliers that handled all formats, or even a variety of formats. Now, several of the book jobbers handle nonbooks as well as books. In time, this merging of formats may result in fewer verification sources, and from the searcher's point of view, nothing could be more desirable.

---

*Note: This chapter uses producers' terms for media rather than the terms used in cataloging materials after they have been acquired. This is because catalogs and verification tools use the producers' terms.

There are several other differences. It is usually necessary to schedule previews (ask the supplier to send the preview material on certain dates, if possible). Remember to list a number of alternative dates, since the preview material may be booked up several weeks in advance (after all, a number of people will usually preview the same material before purchasing). Films and video materials are almost always previewed by a group; in schools and academic situations, this group includes teachers as well as librarians. Examples of preview request forms are illustrated in Figures 8.1, 8.2, and 8.3.

Fig. 8.1
Form for Requesting Preview Material

Gentlemen:

The _____ County Library is interested in previewing films on _____. At the bottom of this letter are listed those films that we would like you to schedule for us on the dates indicated.

Thank you for your cooperation.

Very truly yours,

Fig. 8.2
Sample Order Form for Nonbook Materials

Gentlemen:

The _____ County Library would like to purchase _____ new (16mm—8mm) technicolor cartridge(s), (sound—silent), (color—black & white), (print—prints) of the following (title—titles):

Sincerely,

Preview material is normally returned to the supplier, *even if the library decides to order that material*. Preview copies are used over and over. For its use, the library always orders new copies, and this statement should always be included on the order form. Suppliers normally include a return shipping label with their preview material, so the acquisition department should save the packaging and the return label when any preview material arrives. In the last five years, there has been a trend among audiovisual producers to either charge for the preview or send a new copy of the material "on approval" with only a short period of time in which to accept or reject the material.

Fig. 8.3
Sample Order Form

ORDER FORM–COUNTY LIBRARY

Requested by: _____ Date: _____

Quantity	Unit	Description of Item	Stock or Catalog No.	Estimated Price	Supplier or name and Number of Catalog

Department Approval _____ Date _____

Charge to:
Fund: 1220 _____ Date Ordered: _____
Department: 7150 0 _____ Requisition No.: _____
Object. No.: _____

9/71

USES OF MULTI-MEDIA IN LIBRARIES

An extended discussion of media, libraries, education, and future trends is neither appropriate nor necessary here. Some understanding of the role of media, however, is required. School libraries are probably more concerned with the multi-media approach than are other libraries, while academic libraries are the least likely to acquire media other than books in any significant quantity. Libraries are slowly recognizing the fact that not all of the population is print oriented, and that if they are to serve the information needs of the *entire* community, multi-media formats are essential.

The list of media that might be included in a library collection is extremely long. A list, but not an exhaustive one, would include:

1) films (8mm and 16mm, including single concept)

2) filmstrips

3) slides (35mm, 4x4, and others)

4) transparencies

5) microforms (all types)

6) opaque projector materials

7) flat pictures (photographs, illustrations, posters, etc.)

8) video formats (including kinescopes)

9) phonograph records (all speeds)

10) audio tapes (single and multiple track)

11) programmed learning materials

12) games (usually limited to educational)

13) globes

14) maps (flat and raised relief)

15) working models

16) realia

17) specimens

18) printed music

19) laser formats (including holograms)

20) mixed media packages

This wide range of formats can be and has been combined in an almost endless variety of kits and packages.

The variety of equipment required to handle "software" is even greater. One problem for libraries entering the multi-media field has been the lack of standardization for either hardware or software. Consequently, ensuring compatibility of formats becomes an important factor in the selection process. This often means that technical data about a particular item must be located, in addition to the information needed to request a preview copy.

The problems encountered can be illustrated using 35mm slides as an example. The slide's size is standardized (2x2-inches); however, the type of mounting used varies. Some slide projectors and slide carriers (tray or carousel) function properly only with cardboard mounts. But slides can be purchased in a number of mounts (plastic, metal, glass, cardboard, and unmounted), but not all suppliers offer a full range. Often, slides are available only in one particular mounting; to be used with available equipment, they may have to be remounted by the library. Every format that must be used with equipment poses similar "minor" problems of standardization. Sound films may have different types of sound tracks (magnetic or optical); audio tapes may have any number of tracks; anything packaged in a cassette form (film, audio, video, etc.) may not be compatible with the available equipment; and microforms are prepared with a number of different reduction ratios. These problems are slowly being overcome, but they still represent an important consideration in any library's selection-acquisition procedure.

Despite the problems of working with other media, more and more libraries are buying and using these materials, so LMTAs should have some knowledge of the field. The methods and tools for acquiring books have been available for a great many years; the multi-media field, on the other hand, is changing daily. What is new and exciting today can easily be obsolete tomorrow. For this reason, books dealing with the field are, at best, only general guides.

VERIFICATION AND ORDER PROCEDURES

An audiovisual department usually combines public and technical service functions, since such materials require special skills and knowledge to be used effectively. Anyone who works in this area must take additional course work in media and then gain practical experience working under the direction of an experienced media specialist. Combining public and technical services usually means that the department carries out its own activities. Occasionally, however, the acquisition department will handle the ordering and paper work for the audiovisual department.

The media department maintains most of the same files as the acquisitions department, with one very important addition—the "preview file" (*see* Figure 8.4, page 84). This file can serve a number of purposes: 1) it should list all items to be previewed and the date they are to arrive; 2) it should indicate how often material was previewed, and who previewed it; and 3) it should list all items previewed, and the decisions on each. This file is usually maintained in title order.

As indicated earlier, most of the basic verifying and ordering procedures used for books apply also to nonbook materials. It is even possible to use the same multiple-copy order form for all formats. The primary difference arises when materials are requested on a preview basis. A rubber stamp with the statement, "This is *not* a firm order. This is only a request for a *preview* copy," should be adequate for most purposes. If not, a form letter can be prepared to cover the specific needs of any library or funding agency.

Fig. 8.4
Film Preview Card

FILM PREVIEW CARD

Title: Review Date:
Time & Color:
Producer:
Distributor:
Copyright date:
Price:
Reviews:
Annotation:

                                              Reviewer/Library
9/72 Serra Regional Library System

VERIFICATION SOURCES

The most reliable source for establishing required bibliographic data is producers' catalogs. Any library buying this type of material *must* maintain an extensive file of producers' catalogs. While most libraries have collections of book publishers' announcements and catalogs, these are not so critical because most books are listed in *BIP* or *CBI*; unfortunately there are no equivalents for nonbook materials. Bibliographic control of this field is improving every day, but it can still be characterized as chaotic. Therefore, the producer's catalog is a most important verification tool. Because there are thousands of producers' catalogs, we will not attempt to illustrate this type of material. We will discuss *some* of the general commercial tools, library catalogs, and one wholesaler catalog (we emphasize *some* because there simply are too many sources in this area to describe in a survey).

AudioVideo Market Place: A Multimedia Guide (New York: Bowker, 1969- . Biennial) is one of the most useful general directories of producers and distributors of A-V software; manufacturers of equipment; companies providing cataloging, film processing, and other services; associations; reference books; and review journals. The main sections are arranged alphabetically by name, followed by indexes classified by media subject or product type. Coverage is good but not comprehensive; and the guide is *not* evaluative.

The Equipment Directory of Audio-Visual, Computer and Video Products (Fairfax, Va.: NAVA, The International Communications Industries Association, 1953- . Annual) is an equipment guide that does not claim to be comprehensive. Most equipment listed is of the type that educational institutions would purchase. The purpose "is to supply all pertinent facts about such items as we could discover" (foreword). There is no evaluation of the equipment.

Blue Book of Audiovisual Materials (Chicago: Educational Screen and Audiovisual Guide, 1922- . Annual) is a guide that covers films, slides, and sound recordings. It includes well-written reviews, which are useful for selection purposes. The major problem is that it is limited to a small number (200 to 300) of educational media producers.

The past two decades have witnessed both a rapid growth in the use of educational film materials and an expansion of the types of non-print media. But lagging far behind these technological and educational advances are the tools needed for locating and verifying the large number of non-print items available. The first large-scale project designed to offer bibliographic control of all forms of non-print media was *Educational Media Index* (New York: McGraw-Hill, 1964. 14 vols.). Its poorly designed, computerized format, combined with serious subject indexing problems, made the index difficult to use. (It never achieved its planned goals, and supplements were never produced.)

The *Educational Media Index* was superseded by a series of separate media indexes planned and published by NICEM (Access Innovation, Albuquerque, N.M.). Each NICEM index covers one non-print form—e.g., 35mm filmstrip, slide sets, or 16mm films. Several multi-media indexes covering broad subject areas such as ecology or vocational education have recently been published. All these indexes are derived from NICEM's data bank, which is claimed to be the largest in the world for educational non-print materials. The NICEM indexes can be searched online through the DIALOG system (an online reference/bibliographic data base).

All NICEM indexes follow the same pattern of arrangement and provide the same types of information. The main sections are: 1) subject heading outline and index to subject headings, then the actual subject guide, listing titles and producer's codes; 2) alphabetical guide, with full entry listings (title, series, release date, technical description, LC card number, producer/distributor code, brief synopsis); and 3) directory of producers/distributors and list of producer's codes.

The NICEM indexes provide no prices or evaluations. They are only comprehensive finding lists that offer some assistance in locating information on non-print educational media. However, the indexes are difficult to use because of the computer format. Also, subject indexing is sometimes inconsistent.

A source for audio materials is the *New Schwann Record & Tape Guide* (Boston: Schwann Publications, 1949-). This monthly guide lists over 75,000 phonorecords, digital compact discs, cassettes, and 8-track cartridges. Monthly issues alternate between listing classical music and pop and jazz music. The December issue combines all listings. This work replaces the *Schwann 1* and *Schwann-2* catalogs issued through December 1985.

A semiannual publication is *Library of Congress Catalog—Music, Books on Music and Sound Recordings* (Washington: Library of Congress, 1973- . Current semiannual issue and annual cumulation). This catalog covers music scores, disc recordings, and (since 1963) librettos and books about music. Main entry is under the name of the composer or author. The *Catalog* includes subject entries as well as added entries. All entries are on the basis of LC's cataloging program. Records from all producers are included, but emphasis is on commercial rather than educational recordings. Classical music, standard repertory of pop and contemporary vocal instrumental music, dramatic readings, motion picture soundtracks, children's records, and sacred music are all included.

The Library of Congress published a catalog entitled *Audiovisual Materials* (1979); this supersedes *Library of Congress Catalog—Films and Other Materials for Projection: A Cumulative List of Works Represented by Library of Congress Printed Cards* (formerly titled *Motion Pictures and Filmstrips*). "The Library of Congress attempts to catalog all motion pictures, video-recordings, filmstrips, sets of transparencies, and slide sets released in the United States or Canada which have educational or instructional value. At present, the kits cataloged are limited to those items added to the collections of the Library of Congress. Data needed for the catalog entries are supplied mainly by producers, manufacturers, film libraries, or distributing agencies. The National Audiovisual Center provides information for United States government materials. In most cases cataloging is done from the information thus provided, without actual viewing of the material itself. *Audiovisual Materials* appears in three quarterly issues (January-March, April-June, July-September), with annual and quinquennial cumulations. For the convenience of users, entries published in an annual cumulation for the first time, without having appeared in any of the three quarterly issues for that year, are identified by an asterisk following the Library of Congress card number" (foreword to first issue). Since 1983, these entries have been available only in microfiche.

Information regarding maps may be found in *NUC*. This source is good, but maps are slow to be entered into the catalog. This is one of the sources that supplies cataloging information. The *National Union Catalog. Cartographic Materials* is a new quarterly publication issued since 1983 in microfiche by the Library of Congress. At this time only maps cataloged by the Library of Congress are included. (See page 320.)

The *National Register of Microform Masters* (Washington: Library of Congress, 1965- . Annual) "has two basic purposes. One is to provide a complete national register of microform masters from which libraries may acquire prints.... The other purpose is to help libraries assure the preservation of our intellectual heritage ..." (introduction). The *Register* covers both monographs and serials, but not newspapers. It includes the holdings of American libraries, associations, and microform publishers.

Guide to Microforms in Print (Westport, Conn.: Meckler, 1961- . Annual) is a guide to currently available microforms published in the United States. All microformat materials are included—real microfilm, micro-opaque cards, microfiche, and ultramicrofiche. The arrangement is alphabetical; books are entered under author; journals, under title. Entries give author and/or title, date of publication in original format, publisher of the microfilm, and price. A directory of publishers gives addresses and phone numbers. A companion set, *Micropublishers Trade List Annual* (Westport, Conn.: Meckler, 1975-) is also a useful tool for lists of publications by publisher.

REVIEW QUESTIONS

1. What are the major differences in the verification of books and non-print materials?

2. What are some considerations in preview planning?

3. What are the most commonly purchased non-print materials by libraries?

4. Discuss some of the "software"/"hardware" problems involved in the use of non-print materials in libraries.

5. In what ways do non-print verification sources differ from book verification sources?

6. In general can you order non-print materials from the same jobber that you use for books?

9
ORDER PROCEDURES

Almost all ordering procedures should be the responsibility of an LMTA, with aid and supervision from the librarian. The librarian's responsibility is to establish the guidelines and policies to be followed in 1) establishing factors for deciding which sources of supply (vendors) to use; 2) establishing overall methods for processing orders; and 3) authorizing expenditures of funds. The LMTA may be given the responsibility for choosing which sources of supply to use (within guidelines established by the librarian). In addition, the LMTA should 1) secure order numbers, 2) supervise typing operations, 3) secure authorization signatures, and 4) supervise the disposition of copies of the order, including filing. As with every acquisition procedure, all four classes of personnel have both responsibilities and contributions to make to the efficient operation of the department. At times, of course, the work load will be so great that everyone must work on a particular activity, regardless of his or her usual assignment or responsibility. But as more and more libraries use online acquisition systems, the processes will tend to be less time consuming.

VENDORS

In selecting the source from which to secure materials, a library needs to consider several factors. One is the speed with which the order will be filled, which is significant because patrons may be waiting to use the material. The longer they must wait for the material, the more unhappy patrons become. In essence, speed is a public relations consideration and, as has been pointed out, public relations is an important aspect in a tax-supported institution. Furthermore, to many people, speed represents better service, and service is the library's primary reason for existence.

Consider, too, the size of discount that the source will give. Clearly, the greater the discount, the more money will be available to buy additional materials. Since very few libraries have enough money to buy everything they could use, stretching funds can contribute greatly to an improved library collection. The question of discounts can occupy a major segment of the librarian's time. Library materials — whether books, films, phonograph records, etc. — are unique in that each item might appeal to different groups of users. The producers of the items are aware of this differing appeal, so they vary their discounts according to appeal (the wider the appeal, the greater the discount). For this reason, very few sources of library materials will ever promise a blanket discount on all items purchased. Because of these variable discounts, no one in an acquisition department ever knows *exactly* how much money is available for spending — except at the beginning and end of a fiscal year. At best, only general guidelines can be established, and the LMTA and the librarian have to work together very closely in deciding the expenditures.

Service is another factor to consider in selecting a source. Does the source correct mistakes quickly and easily, or is there a lot of paperwork involved? Are additional services given with the basic service (such as sets of catalog cards, book processing for a small added fee, paid shipping costs)? These and similar questions need to be asked before deciding on any source. Ease in dealing with a source is perhaps the most important service factor, as a great deal of time and energy might be devoted to handling such matters when another supplier could reduce problems and free staff members for more productive work.

For many items, there will be only one source of supply. In the case of serial or periodical titles, a library might use only one source because of legal restrictions. For most items, however, a selection process must be followed. As with request forms, the order forms are usually sorted into three categories: 1) current materials; 2) out-of-print materials; and 3) foreign materials.

Current materials are reasonably easy to acquire quickly, with a discount and with some degree of added service. English-language out-of-print material will take longer and will carry little, if any, discount, and no extra services. Foreign materials are in the same category as out-of-print materials, if the library uses an American jobber or has excellent connections in foreign countries. If not, then speed, discounts, and service all will be rather poor.

The supplier chart (Figure 9.1) provides an overview of some of the factors involved. A wholesaler or "jobber" provides the library with one source of supply for a number of different publishers, which will reduce the number of invoices and payments to be made, but the discount will be low. The retailer can sometimes supply current popular items immediately, and such speed might be important in some cases, but this will again be at a very low discount. Still, for out-of-print items, a retailer may be the only source of supply. While such firms have only a limited stock of titles, they should be considered as an out-of-print source. Reprint houses—e.g., Kraus, Johnson, Gale—reprint thousands of out-of-print books, but in small quantities and at rather high prices. Buying direct from the publisher will often provide the highest discount, but it will increase the work load. In some cases, the publisher may be the only source; for example, some learned societies will sell only directly to a library. Government documents are complex to handle, inexpensive, and carry no discount, so they are handled by very few dealers.

Since several variables enter the picture, the decision about sources is complex and important. The only generalizations about how libraries *tend* to operate in this area are: 1) for current trade items, libraries use wholesalers; 2) for other current materials, they use the publisher; 3) for very popular current materials with an immediate need, libraries will try retailers; 4) for out-of-print items, retailers; 5) for foreign items and serials, wholesalers. Once decisions as to sources have been reached, the actual ordering procedure is relatively simple.

ORDER FORMS—GENERAL

There are three basic types of order forms. One is the "single card," which is essentially a request card. This is not often used, because most libraries need several copies of their orders. The smaller the number of people involved in the

Fig. 9.1
Chart of Suppliers

	WHOLESALER			RETAILER			PUBLISHER		
	Speed	Discount	Service	Speed	Discount	Service	Speed	Discount	Service
Current Items Trade Publications	excellent	medium	excellent	good	low	excellent	excellent	high-medium	good
Society Publications	slow	low	fair	slow	low	fair	good	low	good
Government Publications	seldom handle			seldom handle			good	none	good
Technical Publications	slow	low	fair	slow	low	fair	good	low	good
Out of Print Items	seldom handle			medium to slow	none	good	(Reprint houses) medium to slow	low	fair
Foreign Items	good	low	good	good	low	good	fair	low	fair
Serials and Periodicals	good	low	excellent to good	seldom handles subscriptions			excellent	low	good

process of selecting, ordering, and processing, the more likely it is that a single card will be sufficient. The most common type of order is the "multiple-copy order form." A third type is the "punched card," which is not very common, except in larger libraries or in cooperative library systems with a high volume of business.

Regardless of the form used, the order slip must supply the dealer with certain basic information to assure shipment of the correct materials: author, title, publisher, date of publication, price, edition (if there are various editions), number of copies, order number, and any special instructions regarding invoicing or methods of payment. All of this information is necessary because items may have similar authors, titles, or dates of publication, and the supplier must be able to differentiate among items in order to supply precisely the ones wanted. The order form also contains a great deal of information pertinent only to the library or the agency that oversees the library's budget. This type of information includes the classification number, the accession number, the date the item was ordered, the date received, the name of the dealer, the fund to which the item's cost is to be charged, and the name of the person making the request. Not all of this information can be filled out at the time the order is sent. However, the multiple-copy order form and the punched card system allow that information to be inserted later on the extra copies, which will serve a number of different functions in the various technical service units. The cataloging department uses some of these slips, adding the classification number and the accession number for each item.

Several times we have made the point that good relations with patrons and suppliers are important, but nowhere are good relations more important than in the ordering process. For some time ALA has recognized this point and has established a Bookdealer-Library Relations Committee with the Resources and Technical Services Division. Over the years, the committee has dealt with many complex issues and often provided recommendations. One of its recent projects was the preparation of the *Guidelines for Handling Library Orders for In-Print Monographic Publications* (2d edition, 1984). Although the overall implementation of the guidelines is a policy matter, *anyone* working in acquisitions should read the pamphlet. It is only 21 pages long. It provides detailed suggestions regarding the content and format of order forms and placement claiming activities, cancellations, returns, and invoicing and payment procedures. It also outlines steps dealers should take to facilitate efficient and effective fulfillment of library orders.

A new element that is recommended and being implemented is SAN (Standard Address Number). The American National Standards Institute (ANSI) Committee 239 is having a unique seven digit number (the SAN) assigned to every address or organization that engages in *transactions* in the book industry. The process is similar to the one using ISBNs; the process is expected to speed up transactions and reduce error, especially in automated systems. Libraries are being assigned numbers by R. R. Bowker through Jaques Cattell Press; these numbers were first listed with the library address in the 33rd edition of *American Library Directory*.

MULTIPLE-COPY ORDER FORMS

As indicated earlier, the multiple-copy or fan-fold order form is most common. The number of copies ranges from four to twelve, all uniform in size — 3x5-inches (standard library file drawer size). Each copy is a different color for easy identification, though no standard dictates a particular color for a certain purpose.

In the sample order forms (Figures 9.2 and 9.3), the front of each slip is basically the same, although occasionally (as in Figure 9.2), information is blotted out by having a section of the form blanked out. This allows the slip to serve a number of specific purposes without unnecessarily conveying all of the library's information to outside sources. The forms should contain all the elements outlined in the *Guidelines*.

Fig. 9.2
Multiple Order Form (Prepared by the Library)

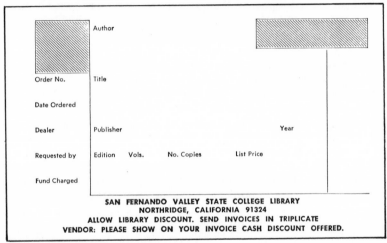

	Author
Order No.	Title
Date Ordered	
Dealer	Publisher Year
Requested by	Edition Vols. No. Copies List Price
Fund Charged	

SAN FERNANDO VALLEY STATE COLLEGE LIBRARY
NORTHRIDGE, CALIFORNIA 91324
ALLOW LIBRARY DISCOUNT. SEND INVOICES IN TRIPLICATE
VENDOR: PLEASE SHOW ON YOUR INVOICE CASH DISCOUNT OFFERED.

Fig. 9.3
Multiple Order Form (Prepared by the Wholesaler)

CLASS NO.		L. C. CARD NO.	
LIST PRICE	AUTHOR		Out / C
DATE ORDERED	TITLE		R / On / Oe
ORDER NO.	PLACE	PUBLISHER	YEAR	Cl / Rd
DEALER	VOLS.	SERIES	EDITION	P / D
NO. OF COPIES	RECOMMENDED BY	FUND CHARGED	COST	Np / NR
DATE REC'D			

No.   Subscriber   Variation in ed.   Order held   No. of cards

USE OF MULTIPLE COPIES

The multiple-copy order slip usually consists of at least the following: the outstanding order copy, the dealer's copy, and a claiming copy. Other copies may serve any number of functions (two slips may be sent to the dealer, three or four slips may be kept in the outstanding order file). Other uses for the slips are for bookkeeping purposes: one for the bookkeeper in acquisitions, one for the agency that supervises the library's budget and expenditures. In larger systems where book requestors do not have close contact with the acquisition department (as in an academic library where faculty members do much of the selecting), a copy is sent to the requestor, so that person knows the order has been placed.

Outstanding Order Copy

The outstanding order slip is one of the most important copies because of its many uses. It is essential that this be a clear, readable copy, so it is usually either the ribbon copy or the second or third copy in the multiple order form. The filing of this slip depends on the particular library, but it is most commonly placed in the outstanding order file (the significance of this file was noted in the section on verification); it is the one place to determine whether an item has already been ordered but not yet received. In some instances, there is only one file—the "in-process" file—which contains all of the slips remaining in the library after an order is placed, from the time an item is ordered until it is put into the collection.

In such a case, when the order is sent, the in-process file might receive five slips. The first represents the on-order status, the next three slips are copies used later in the catalog department for processing purposes, and the final slip remains in the file to indicate that an item is in the catalog department and not yet ready for public use. Once an item is received, the on-order slip and the three cataloging slips are removed, leaving only the in-process slip. When the cataloged item is ready to go to public service, one slip from the catalog department is returned to acquisition to signal the removal of the in-process slip. Presumably at this point, a set of cards will be filed in the public catalog, indicating that the item is now available to the public.

Another method of handling these slips is to keep them by order number, which makes it quite easy to check in an order from a given supplier. This method, however, is not very useful when checking the library's need for a given title, because its *only* approach is by order number. Often, two files are kept—one by order number and one in alphabetical order by main entry.

A third possibility is to file a slip in the public catalog under the main entry, which serves two purposes: it informs both patrons and selectors that an item is on order, and it reduces the number of files that must be searched in the verification procedure. However, since the correct main entry is occasionally difficult to determine until the material is in hand, the result may be a public catalog sprinkled with slips not pulled when an item was received because no catalog cards were made for that heading.

Dealer's Copy

Since dealers find individual 3x5-inch slips easier to use than a long list of books, they also receive a copy of the multiple-order form. A single long list is less likely to get lost, but if only a few of the requested items are available, then individual slips facilitate shipment of partial orders. If the library sends only an order blank, the dealer will usually make up individual slips, for easier stock access. No matter what the arrangement, the copy sent to the dealer must be a clear copy. If only one slip is sent, it must have space for the dealer to report the status of any item that cannot be supplied. It is usual to supply two slips, so if material is out of stock, the dealer retains one and returns the other to the library, indicating that the item will be supplied as soon as it is restocked.

Claiming Copy

A claiming copy is a slip retained by the library for inquiry when an item has been ordered but has not been received. While this copy must be readable, it does not have to be one of the most legible. (As very few of these claiming slips have to be used, most will be thrown away when the order is received.) The claiming slip asks the dealer an order's status and what will be done about filling it. On the slip's verso are printed four or five different status categories (out-of-stock, out-of-print, etc.); the dealer merely checks the appropriate one and returns the slip to the library. Claim slips should also record the date on which a claim was sent, because many libraries have a policy of automatically cancelling any order outstanding and unreported for more than 90 or 120 days.

Catalog Card Order Copy

A catalog card order slip has been important for libraries; they have used it to acquire cataloging copy for items being added to the collection. This use is decreasing, though, since many libraries now secure cards from online catalog systems. Another reason for the declining use of this slip is the availability of processing kits. Very often, a book is ordered with its own processing kit (catalog cards, pockets, labels, etc.) from a single commercial source. One more factor is the Polaroid® camera, with a special attachment that will take a photograph of a single entry in the *National Union Catalog* or the *Library of Congress Catalog* and provide a 3x5-inch enlargement. This copy then may be used as the master from which a library may produce its own cards. If this technique is used, the acquisition department may become involved as part of the verification process. The photograph is retained until the item is received, and all material is forwarded to the catalog department. Some smaller libraries simply produce their own cards because they feel they do not need all of the information contained on the Library of Congress cards.

Other Uses

As indicated earlier, the remaining slips have a wide variety of uses, and all of them require readable copy. An accounting copy is often used by the bookkeeper to encumber funds. Some libraries find it more convenient to maintain their bookkeeping copies in sheets rather than separating them, as is done with other copies. Since libraries usually do not pay invoices until each order is complete, this system works well. When it is possible to make payments on partially filled orders, individual slips make it easier to remove items from a file and forward this information to the accounting office.

COMPLETION OF THE ORDER

After verification, a number of steps must be taken to complete the order procedure. Assignment of the dealer is first, and the question of how to select vendors was discussed at the beginning of this chapter. Remember, though, that the dealer who has had a number of transactions with a given library is more likely to understand and abide by its accounting system and special bookkeeping procedures, while a new dealer might not fully understand some of the variations. This will include the new SAN information.

Assignment of an Order Number

After the dealer has been assigned, either the librarian or the LMTA will assign the order a number and the fund to which the cost of the items is to be charged. Assignment of the order number is the very simple and straightforward matter of checking with the bookkeeper to determine the last order number used and assigning the next number in sequence. Fund assignments, however, are usually handled by a librarian. In a library where funds are assigned on the basis of department (academic library: English, history, chemistry; public library: children's, reference), those items selected by members of each department will be assigned to that department's fund. In other situations, costs are assigned to a subject area, so one must decide which items will be charged to which area. Appropriate assignments must be made and the costs equally distributed.

Typing Orders

When the assignment of the dealer, order number, and fund is completed, the order is ready to be typed, which entails at least two operations. A standard cover letter is typed giving the dealer information and details regarding billing, credit memos, invoicing procedures, and so forth. The body of this letter is duplicated in quantity, so typing becomes simply a matter of inserting the appropriate names, addresses, date, and order number information (see Figure 9.4).

Notice that the letter indicates that the invoice must be sent in triplicate and that titles not received within six months of the date of the list are to be considered cancelled without further notice. Other information concerning invoicing is given on the back of the dealer's copy of the order slip. An "out-of-print" cover letter would be quite similar, again indicating requirements for invoicing, how long an order is to be held, and providing a price limit beyond which the dealer must ask the library's approval before shipping and billing.

The next step in this procedure is typing the multiple-copy order forms or having the punched card generate the necessary copies. Normally, a list is also sent to the dealer, typically an alphabetical author listing. Individual order slips make it easier to pull items out of a dealer's stock, but the single list will be much more convenient in the bookkeeping office.

Naturally, online systems eliminate the need for anyone to type up order slips after an item has been located, which saves time and errors. You must, of course, supply the system you use with all of the appropriate information described above.

Fig. 9.4
Example of Form Letter

Gentlemen:

From your catalog no. ———————.

Please ship to us the items listed on the attached list. Please invoice in triplicate.

All titles not received within six months from the date of this list will be considered cancelled without further notice.

Thank you for your prompt attention to this order.

Very truly yours,

Authorization Signature

Many libraries require that all orders be signed by the person authorized to spend library funds, who may be the director of the library or the head of the acquisition department. Yet, this requirement is something of a nuisance when several hundred orders are sent out, each one requiring a signature. Therefore, orders are usually collected during each day and all signed in the early morning or late afternoon. It is helpful to arrange this signing time so that orders may be sorted and prepared by the time the library's mail is picked up.

Mailing Orders

The final step in the order procedure is the sorting and disposition of the slips. Usually done by clerical personnel, pages, or student help, this is a time-consuming job; yet it must be done carefully and accurately. If a slip is misplaced, an item will be delayed in processing. The dealer will not send an item if there is no slip; the bookkeeper will not encumber funds and will not pay for it; and the in-process file will not show whether it was really ordered. All of these possibilities can generate unfortunate and unnecessary delays. Any slips remaining for other areas are distributed to the individuals or files to which they are assigned at this time.

REVIEW QUESTIONS

1. Describe the factors to consider in selecting a vendor.

2. Is it appropriate to use an out-of-print dealer for new foreign items?

3. What are the most commonly used order forms?

4. What is SAN?

5. Describe some uses for a multiple-copy order form.

10
ACCOUNTING AND BOOKKEEPING

Accounting is "the process of identifying, measuring, and communicating economic information to permit informed judgements and decisions by users of the information" (*A Statement of Basic Accounting Theory*, Evanston, Ill.: American Accounting Association, 1966, p. 1). A library has several groups or individuals that use accounting information (the term "accounting" includes bookkeeping activities): selectors need to know how much money they have to spend; the head of acquisitions needs the information to plan the department's work; the head librarian needs data to maintain control over the library's operation; and the library's business office must have the information to ensure that funds are being properly handled. Usually, accounting activities are handled by a non-professional with training in accounting and bookkeeping. Anyone interested in a career as an LMTA might consider taking course work in accounting, since such work expands the employment opportunities (both in terms of seeking a position and of promotion).

The bookkeeping unit usually handles all of a library's accounting work (payroll records, accounts payable/receivable, purchasing, inventory control, and some cost accounting). Frequently, this unit is part of the acquisition department. When this is not the case, the unit must work very closely with the acquisition department, since a large percentage of the work involves both units. Consequently, everyone must have some basic understanding of accounting and bookkeeping—even those who are not directly involved in this type of work.

The reason for discussing accounting is that business departments follow standard accounting practices, although library bookkeeping requires some variations from standard practice. The library bookkeeper, for example, must reconcile library records with those of the business office. Since the results concern many people, it is important to understand the business office's records and what they represent.

ACCOUNTING

The term "accounting" covers a number of activities that may be thought of as separate fields:

1) *general accounting* deals with the process of recording fiscal data (includes bookkeeping);

2) *cost accounting* is concerned with determining business costs (most frequently, unit costs);

3) *tax accounting* determines liability for taxes, especially income and Social Security taxes;

4) *auditing* is the process of verifying the accuracy of financial records;

5) *budgetary accounting* prepares systematic forecasts of operations in fiscal terms;

6) *system building* is the development and installation of the appropriate financial records in an organization;

7) *governmental accounting* is concerned with maintaining financial records for government units.

A library is primarily concerned with the first four fields and the last field; the fifth and sixth fields have only limited application to library situations.

The difference between accounting and bookkeeping is that accounting emphasizes theory while bookkeeping emphasizes technique. Accounting is comprehensive in scope, whereas bookkeeping is concerned primarily with the methods by which fiscal transactions are recorded.

The Balance Sheet

One of the most important elements in accounting/bookkeeping is the balance sheet, which indicates the institution's financial condition at any given time. The amounts and nature of assets, liabilities, and proprietorship are listed. The balance sheet is the statement of the basic equation of accounting: assets = liabilities + proprietorship. Assets are anything of value owned; liabilities are obligations to pay (money or other assets) or to render service to persons or organizations now or in the future; proprietorship is the difference between assets and liabilities. A library is concerned with proprietorship only when it derives a significant portion of its funds from endowments (usually on an annual basis).

Unfortunately, no uniform format exists for the balance sheet. However, two very common methods of presenting a statement of financial condition have been developed: the "account form" (horizontal form) and the "report form" (vertical form). Account forms list assets on the left-hand side of a page, and liabilities and proprietorship on the right-hand side. The two sides are in vertical parallel columns, and the final totals are equal. In the report form, all assets are listed, then all the liabilities, and finally the proprietorship. A great many variations exist on these basic forms, but the important thing to remember is that the assets must equal the liabilities and proprietorship.

Assets can *never* be greater than liabilities and proprietorship. If the assets are greater, then a mistake has been made in recording or in the assignment of data. Liabilities and proprietorship can be greater than the assets, but this is an indication that the organization or individual is or may soon be in financial difficulty. Libraries should *always* have an equal balance sheet.

Accounts and Ledgers

Every business transaction has dual elements. All financial work in the acquisition department is a business transaction of some type. The dual elements arise from the fact that each transaction is an exchange of values: something of value is given up for something else, presumably of equal value. The bookkeeper must record both elements. As these factors are recorded, they change the value of the assets, liabilities, and proprietorship, so it is important to have a recording system that will show those changes with a minimum of space, effort, and error. A poor system can create a tremendous amount of extra work.

Most systems now in use provide a short accurate method for recording transactions, separating the increases from the decreases for each account. This means balancing asset accounts against liability and proprietorship accounts. *Accounts record the effects of a transaction.* An acquisition department will use as many accounts as necessary to provide adequate detailed information. Usually, there will be one account for each fund in the department, and once a month the data in these accounts are assembled into a balance sheet. The conventional method of handling accounts places additions to assets on the left side of the account, and additions to liabilities and proprietorship on the right.

Two terms used in recording changes in value are debit (Dr.) and credit (Cr.). "Debit" refers to the left side of an account (assets); "credit" refers to the right side (liabilities). Thus, a debit is an entry on the left and a credit an entry on the right. The idea of debits tied to assets and credits to liabilities can be very confusing to beginners and to anyone not acquainted with accounting terminology. Perhaps the best way to keep the relationships in mind, and to remember how the terms affect the balance sheet, is with the aid of the table in Figure 10.1.

Fig. 10.1
Debits and Credits

"Debit" indicates:	"Credit" indicates:
Asset *increase*	Asset *decrease*
Liability decrease	Liability increase
Proprietorship decrease	Proprietorship increase
Income decrease	Income increase
Expense increase	Expense decrease

A basic rule of accounting is that *for every debit there must be a credit.* This does *not* mean that the number of debit and credit entries must be equal, but rather that the debit and credit *amounts* must be equal.

A group of accounts is called the "ledger." This is a derived record presenting in an analytical form the total effect of all transactions. Data are taken from the books in which the original entries were made (called journals; *see* below). Normally, only one account is placed on a single page of the ledger. A looseleaf ledger is very common because it is so flexible. Accounts can be arranged and rearranged in whatever system seems best, and single pages can be removed in order to post entries by machine ("posting" is the transferring of debit and credit information from a journal to the proper account in the ledger).

Once a month, a "trial balance" is prepared. This is a listing of ledger accounts showing debit and credit balances. The object is to determine whether the debits and credits are equal or in balance. A trial balance serves a number of purposes:

1) by proving the equality of total debits and credits, it provides a partial check on the accuracy of bookkeeping;

2) errors can be detected more quickly, as can their sources;

3) it provides a condensed picture of each account as well as a summary of all accounts; and

4) it is often the basis for preparing financial statements.

Trial balancing uses three columns: one column is for the account total, and the other two are for the account debits and credits. Two techniques are used to show the amounts for each account on the trial balance. One technique lists only the balance of each account; this approach reduces the initial amount of work. The other method lists the amounts in the debit and credit columns for each account, which provides more detailed information.

While the trial balance is an essential accounting tool, it is not the only one. It indicates whether debits and credits are equal, but it cannot demonstrate whether the books are without error—compensating errors may have occurred on both sides of the account. An item may be properly posted—that is, the right amounts on the debit and credit sides—but the data may have been posted to the wrong account. A mistake in classifying information in the journal cannot be detected through a trial balance. Of course, if a transaction was never recorded in the ledger, its absence cannot be detected by using a trial balance. Therefore, even if the trial balance appears to be correct, there may be a number of errors in the system. This is one of the reasons that it is necessary to have the books audited.

The Journal

As indicated above, the ledger is not a complete record of transactions. For a number of reasons, it is desirable to have a preliminary record, in which transactions are listed in their chronological order along with an explanation of the nature of each one. In an acquisition department, the sequence of order numbers fills, in part, the need for such a primary record. To some extent, the order file is what accountants used to call the "daybook," an informal record of the day's activity.

Today, most organizations do not use a daybook but make entries directly into the journal. The journal is the book of original entry, where transactions are recorded in chronological order. Entries into the journal are made from whatever system has been substituted for the daybook (invoices, orders, sales slips, cash register tapes, etc.). A journal may be more than just a book with account numbers, debits, credits, and a brief explanation about the transaction. Often associated with it are files of documents, punched cards, tapes, or other media (back-up material for explaining the transaction). The important features of the journal are:

1) It is a day-to-day record of each transaction.

2) It is the point at which the debit and credit aspects of all transactions are analyzed. This very important activity can cause a great many problems if done improperly.

3) It is the point at which a transaction becomes a series of numbers. The explanation of the transaction may not be extensive, but it must be

adequate to direct someone from the journal entry to the proper backup file, where a full explanation may be found.

The term used to indicate recording entries in a journal is "journalizing."

Journals and ledgers are the basic items in what accountants call the "double-entry accounting system." Double-entry simply means that each transaction is recorded both in the journal and in the ledger. The journal is the original chronological record, while the ledger is a secondary analytical record. Perhaps the most important difference between the journal and the ledger is that, because the journal is the first entry, it usually carries greater weight as legal evidence.

The Voucher

Most governmental accounting methods, as well as the methods used by many other organizations, are based on a voucher system. A voucher provides verification of all transactions involving expenditures and the authorization for such expenditures. It is a form that both summarizes an expenditure and that also carries the signatures vouching for its correctness. Further, it authorizes entry into the books and approving payment of charges. The requirement of the librarian's signature on the purchase order and on the invoice is part of the voucher system in the library.

Without a voucher, there will be no payment to a vendor. Because of the length of time it takes for a voucher to make its way through a governmental system, a great deal of correspondence can occur between the acquisition department and vendors over the issuing of vouchers. This points up the need for accurate bookkeeping records and close cooperation between bookkeepers and the acquisition department.

This section has covered only the most elementary aspects of accounting. There are a few key concepts and terms that everyone should be familiar with: accounts, balance sheet, credit, daybook, debit, double-entry accounting system, journalizing, ledger, posting, trial balance, and voucher. All of these terms have been discussed in this section, and each is included in the glossary.

BOOKKEEPING

The primary function of the bookkeeping section is to oversee the library's financial transactions. This requires three basic steps. First, funds must be encumbered at the time the order is placed—that is, charge a fund with the list price of the item ordered (the discount is usually not known until the order is filled). Second, maintain a list of funds that have been encumbered but not yet expended—that is, money being held for the items that are on order but not yet received. Finally, approve payment for these items—that is, the actual expending of funds.

A major problem confronting a bookkeeper in the acquisition department is the number of funds against which items may be charged. In some systems, that number may run as high as 50, 80, or even 100 funds; and only specific types of materials may be charged against each fund. While the bookkeeper's job may be to assign charges to the various funds, that person also must know approximately how much money remains, how much has been committed, and how much has actually been spent from each fund.

The librarian must make certain that the appropriate items are charged against the proper funds. Some libraries allocate funds by subject area: X number of dollars is set aside to buy social science materials, X number of dollars for the sciences, the humanities, and so forth. Again, the allocation of the money available to the various funds is the librarian's responsibility. In academic libraries, funds very often are allocated to each of the major teaching departments: chemistry, English, sociology, education, etc. Each department then spends its money on appropriate materials. In such cases, the bookkeeper easily becomes involved in the assignment of funds, since any request coming from a department member is automatically charged against the departmental funds.

Another method of allocation is on the basis of services (children's service, reference service, general collection, branches, etc.). Very often, separate funds have been set up for such things as phonograph records, serials, motion picture films, and art prints. From the *bookkeeper's* point of view, perhaps the best method is no fund allocation at all, since this reduces the number of running accounts to a minimum and avoids the question of improperly charged items. When many funds exist, a great deal of time is spent preparing statements regarding the status of the fund. An almost equal amount of time is devoted to explaining to those concerned with spending money why their fund is at a certain level.

Order-Invoice Control

The bookkeeper ascertains whether the fiscal regulations of the library's governing agency are being met. For instance, an invoice may be received without some of the required information: a signature, a purchase order number, etc. Figure 10.2 is a sample of a form letter often used in such cases.

Fig. 10.2
Form Letter Requesting Additional Information

Date:

Gentlemen:

Your invoice No. _____ dated _____ is returned for the following reason:

_____ Signature of vendor is required when invoice is not imprinted with firm name.

_____ This invoice was processed for payment on _____.

_____ We cannot match your invoice with one of our orders. Please supply purchase order number if given, date of order, and name of requestor.

_____ We require three copies of freight or express bills covering prepaid transportation.

_____ _____
_____ _____
_____ _____

_____ No invoice received; please supply in triplicate.

Your prompt attention to this request will expedite payment. If you have any questions concerning this matter, please write to the Acquisition Department or call _____, ext. _____.

Yours truly,

Acquisition Department

Occasionally, an invoice simply does not conform to the governing body's fiscal regulations, so the library must provide the vendor with the necessary forms. At times, the items ordered are not delivered, so the order must be cancelled and a refund requested if prepayment was made. As was noted earlier, it is very convenient to deal regularly with the same vendor, who will understand the problems involved in issuing payment vouchers. Since this is not always possible, however, a form letter of some type is used to explain to new dealers why it might take up to three months to receive payment.

Occasionally, mistakes are found in the invoice, in calculating discounts, or even in the addition for final total. Checking *all* the invoice figures is the bookkeeper's responsibility before approving any invoice for payment. If errors are found, the vendor must be informed as well as the agency that supervises the library's fiscal transactions. An example of a form that could be used in such an instance is given in Figure 10.3. In that letter, the blanks can be used to specify any number of problems.

Fig. 10.3
Form Letter for Multiple Purposes

Date:

To:

Concerning the item listed below, please see statement checked.

Order Number and Date	Author	Title	Publisher	Invoice Number and Date

_____	Book not received, but was included on invoice; please send book.
_____	Book received, but not included on invoice; please bill.
_____	Wrong book received and returned herewith; please send correct book.
_____	Wrong book received; we are keeping; send invoice.
_____	Defective copy received and returned herewith; please send replacement.
_____	Book received, but not ordered; returned herewith for credit.
_____	Ordered by mistake; unmarked. May we return for credit?
_____	Invoice not received; please supply.
_____	Please cancel.
_____	
_____	

Yours sincerely,

Reconciliation of Accounts

One difficulty facing the bookkeeper is knowing precisely where the library stands financially. The encumbered funds are always greater than the amount expended, because some items have discounts but not others. How many items are discounted and by how much is known *only* when the bill is received. The average discount will be around 10 to 15%. Some items will have no discount at all; others will have perhaps 33% or even 40%. For all items ordered during a year, the average is well under 20%.

Some monthly routines need to be carried out. One is the reconciliation of the library's estimate of its financial status with that of the supervising agency. The agency that oversees the library's expenditure of funds will probably not list all of the separate funds, but will assign X number of dollars for the acquisition of library materials. How the library has distributed these funds is of no interest to the agency. Its concern is with two categories of funds: expended and unexpended.

The library has still a third category of money—the encumbered funds—which makes bookkeeping complex. As part of the reconciliation process, the bookkeeper normally creates for each library fund a statement of its unencumbered balance, encumbered funds, and liquidated or expended funds. These monthly statements are sent to the individuals concerned so they know how much money is left. The final reconciliation sheet (illustrated in Figure 10.4) records the date an invoice is received, the dealer's invoice number, the gross number of dollars encumbered at the time the order was submitted, and the discount received. The next column indicates the amount actually paid to the dealer for the items; the tax column represents the tax on the monies expended.

The library must also carry out a number of end-of-fiscal-year routines, and the bookkeeper is responsible for many of these. The library is normally on a one-year fiscal basis; and any money granted to the library as part of its budget normally reverts to the granting agency if it is not expended within the fiscal year. Therefore, several months prior to the end of the fiscal year, check with the vendors on outstanding orders to determine whether or not they will make delivery in time. If they are unable to deliver the items, the order is cancelled; then a new order is placed for items that can be delivered by or before the end of the fiscal year.

The bookkeeper's primary duty is to ensure that the library neither overspends nor underspends its budget. Since discounts and cancellations are unknown quantities up until the moment they are received, it becomes quite a challenge to the bookkeeper to make an accurate estimate of just where the library stands financially.

Automation and Bookkeeping

Obviously, any mechanical aid that a bookkeeper receives would improve the system. And this is one area where computerization of library records becomes very important. As the size of the budget and the number of funds increase, it becomes very difficult to keep track of all these things; in large library systems, a computer can do it quickly and accurately.

Bookkeeping functions were one of the very first activities that were automated in business. Since the basic activities of bookkeeping are similar

Fig. 10.4
Final Reconciliation Sheet

FINAL RECONCILIATION

Sub. P. O.
Number ———————
Dated ———————

Date Received	Invoice Number	Gross	Disc.	Net	Tax	Trans.	Sch. Date	Sch. No.	Amount	Balance

Payment Data — Claims Paid

regardless of type of organization, many bookkeeping/accounting software programs were/are available. Once the appropriate codes and fiscal information have been input the computer can handle the mechanical tasks of charging the appropriate fund, encumbering funds, and recording the payments, and is capable of issuing a voucher (although as already noted most libraries do not issue vouchers). The computer can produce all manner of statistical and fiscal statements, including monthly and annual reconciliation of accounts. If it is tied into the order system it can alert the staff to orders that have been outstanding (and funds encumbered) for a specified period of time, usually 60, 90, or 120 days.

One task that the computer could assist with is the rational allocation of funds. If there is circulation data available that the computer can use (naturally an online system would be ideal) it can analyze use of the collection by subject areas, and by using projected cost figures for purchasing and the expected budget level for the coming year, develop an allocation plan.

Automation of the mechanical bookkeeping and accounting activities in an acquisition department will free staff for more challenging activities. It should also reduce the number of errors and time spent in correcting the errors. This does not mean all the problems will disappear, just that less time will be spent on the problems.

REVIEW QUESTIONS

1. Who in the library needs to have accounting information and why?

2. What is the primary function of the bookkeeping section in a library, and what are the three basic steps?

3. Define the following: accounts, balance sheet, credit, debit, journal, ledger, posting, trial balance, and voucher.

4. What is the purpose of the form letters shown in Figures 10.2 and 10.3?

5. Define encumber.

6. Name one monthly routine the bookkeeper performs.

7. Name one yearly routine the bookkeeper performs.

Although receiving orders is not hard work, the procedure must be carefully planned. Most receiving work can be handled by part-time employees, if there is a good plan of operation and if they have been given thorough training in it. Supervision of these activities can and should be handled by LMTAs, while the plan can be developed by the supervisor under the direction of the head of the acquisition department. All of this has cost implications if the library is using an automated system. Mistakes will mean more changes and confusion than in a manual system.

CHECKING THE PACKING SLIP/INVOICE

Careful unpacking of shipments can save everyone in the department a great deal of time, energy, and frustration. One of the first steps in this process is to find the packing slip (simply a list of items sent in a particular shipment) and/or invoice (an itemized bill). The business office must have an invoice before it will issue a voucher/check. Thus, any shipment will include a packing slip, an invoice, or both, since without an itemized list of what was sent, it is impossible to determine whether or not a shipment is complete. Because of the importance of the invoice (no invoice—no money), though, the vendor often mails the invoice to the acquisition department rather than sending it with the merchandise.

Most vendors attach an envelope containing the packing slip to the outside of one of the boxes; this will always be clearly marked "packing slip" or "invoice." Other vendors, or their shipping room staffs, seem to take pleasure in finding new ways to hide the slip. Sometimes the slip is placed inside one of the items—when there are several hundred items, it can take time to find the slip. Another favorite hiding place is under a cardboard liner at the bottom of the box. Occasionally a shipment arrives without any slip. When this happens, keep the items together, along with the shipping label. Then contact the order unit to learn whether an order had been placed with the shipper (and if so, what had been ordered). When unpacking a shipment for which no slip has been found, it is also essential to keep these items separated from other materials in the receiving area. Mixing up two or more shipments can create trouble. Gift items sometimes arrive this way, and it takes time to determine what to do with the material. And while such problems have to be solved outside the receiving unit, careful unpacking will keep the problems to a minimum.

Usually, the packing slip is found quickly and the normal procedures follow. When all items have been unpacked, check them against the packing slip; this will reveal any discrepancies between what the shippers think they sent and what the library received. Boxes go astray in shipment, items are overlooked in packing rooms, and items sometimes disappear from the library before they have been processed. Checking the packing slips against items received protects both parties.

CHECKING THE SHIPMENT

The next step in the receiving process is to examine the physical condition of the items received, and then to compare them with the original order. All of this checking is to ensure: 1) that the correct items have been received, 2) that the correct number of items have been received, 3) that the items received are in good physical condition, 4) that no items were received that were not ordered.

Some typical problems will crop up:

1) The wrong edition was received. [Note: The checker must be aware of the difference between an edition and a printing. A new *edition* indicates that the item has been changed, material added and/or deleted; a new *printing* means that the item was replicated with no changes.]

2) Ordered items were not received.

3) Items not ordered were received.

4) Too many copies of an item were received.

5) Imperfect copies were received.

Imperfections can take many forms. Some of these include missing pages, blank pages, or improperly collated texts. Audio tapes should be checked for gaps or blank tapes, and for proper speed of recording. Film items should be examined for proper developing; often a film will be "fogged," "streaked," or spotted with hypo residue.

Any imperfect item can be returned for replacement. Figure 11.1 illustrates a type of work slip that can be used with problem items.

The vendor must be contacted when items are missing. Figure 11.2 illustrates one type of form letter that can be used once it has been approved by the department; form letters of this kind can be prepared and mailed by the receiving unit's supervisor.

Fig. 11.1
Incorrect Order Receipt

DATE_____   BY_____

PROBLEMS: .

Bk(s) missing_____ Def._____ Not ord._____ W/B____
No invoice_____ No slips_____ No card_____ Dead
file_____ Duplicate_____
Cancelled: W/L_____ Cat. No._____
Looked under:_____

Fig. 11.2
Inquiry Form

Concerning your invoice listed below:

Invoice Number_____ Dated_____ Amount_____

Our Order Number_____ Dated_____

We have not received the material listed on your invoice. Was the material shipped?

Date shipped_____ No. of packages_____
Registered_____

How was the material shipped?

Air Mail_____ Sea Mail_____

When may we expect shipment?

To whom was the material shipped?

_____

_____

Your immediate attention to this matter will be appreciated. Please return this letter with your reply to my attention.

(Acquisition Department)

PROPERTY MARKING

The next step in the process is to "property mark" the items. As noted above, items sometimes disappear from the library. The sooner things are marked, the more difficult it is for items to disappear. Property marking takes many forms. Books are usually stamped both on the fore-edge and on the title page. When a library assigns "accession numbers" to items, each number is recorded on the item, and in the accessions book. (Accessioning is a system of assigning a unique number for everything purchased, for purposes of inventory control. This is one of the few receiving activities that has the potential for being automated.)

Films often have a special leader attached, with the library's name imprinted in the leader. If an accession number is used, perforate the leader with the number. For phonograph records, stamp the record label as well as the record jacket. Cassette items often have a special label attached, or else the library's name and the accession number are engraved on the cassette.

RECORD AND FILE CLEARING

After items have been received and property marked, they will be routed to the appropriate departments, which may be the catalog department, serials, documents, or some other. Before items leave the acquisition department, however, their order slips are pulled from the on-order file and inserted in them for use by other departments. Gifts often arrive unsolicited, so there will be no record of them *anywhere*; the librarian must decide what to do with such material. Often such items are routed to the gifts/exchange units for a final decision. The follow-up work on receipt procedures—e.g., letters regarding items not received, duplicate copies, or errors in invoicing, and checking on vendors' responses to inquiries—accounts for much of the acquisition department's staff time.

The last step in the order receipt routine—approval of the invoice for payment—is usually the head of the department's responsibility (or that responsibility is delegated by that person). Payment is approved only when an order has been fully received (or items that were not supplied have been cancelled, so that the order is complete). After the invoice has been approved, the bookkeeper passes this information to the agency that actually writes the check. Rarely will a library itself write checks or vouchers for the materials it acquires. This is done by its governing agency.

REVIEW QUESTIONS

1. Why is the packing list checked against the invoice on an order received?

2. What are the two most common problems in order receipts?

3. How can the inquiry form in Figure 11.1 be used to correct order problems?

4. How is the incorrect order receipt in Figure 11.2 used?

5. How is an accession number used in the order process?

6. How are unsolicited gifts handled?

7. What is the last step in the order receipt routine?

8. Why is property marking important?

12

RECORDS AND FILES OF THE
ACQUISITION DEPARTMENT

While the acquisition department maintains many files, only the more important ones will be discussed here. Most libraries keep files for unverified requests, in-process or outstanding orders, standing orders, serials check-in, want lists, claims, bibliographic sources, correspondence, and special bookkeeping files.

TYPES OF FILES

All order departments maintain a file of requests to be verified. This contains the book selectors' request cards, which will not be verified until a group of them has been collected. These cards should be arranged in some order especially as the number increases. Arrangement at this stage eliminates one sorting step. Also, the longer the delay between the receipt of the request and the time it is verified, the greater the need for a logical arrangement. A title arrangement is probably most suitable.

The "outstanding order file," as the name implies, holds at least one record for each item that has been ordered but not yet received by the library. This important file greatly reduces the possibility of unintentional duplication. The comprehensive "in-process file," which provides information about the status of an item in technical services from the time it is ordered until it is available for general use, substitutes for the outstanding order file.

There will be a "serials check-in file" if there is no separate serials department. It will contain an entry for each serial title the library receives, a check-in card to record the receipt of each individual issue, a record of the subscription payments, the date the subscription began, special indexes, special handling instructions, and the source from which the item is to be acquired.

The "standing order file's" importance to the acquisition department stems from its recording all the series that automatically come to the library. Books that appear as part of a publisher's series fall into this category. If the verification process does not show that the item in question belongs to a series, the library might receive two copies of the work when only one is wanted. This emphasizes the need for care in the verification process and for the recording of *any* information found regarding series.

If verification shows that a title is part of a series, the standing order file must be checked. Related to the standing order file is the question of approval plans. Most dealers provide some information as to what is going to be sent, either with "advance notice" cards, or by using an annotated bibliography (e.g.,

Publishers Weekly) that indicates the items to be sent. When the library uses an approval plan, the searcher *must* take the time to examine the list of approval items.

Another file maintained by the acquisition department is the "desiderata list" (or "want list"). Such files indicate each title or item that the library wants but has been unable to buy. Many of these items are out of print, but now, with increasing budget constraints, in-print items are also likely to be in the file. The form letter shown in Figure 12.1 indicates how this file may be used.

Fig. 12.1
Form Letter to Order Out-of-Print Materials

Gentlemen:

Enclosed is a list of books that [library name] would like to acquire. Please search for those titles *not* in stock. The list is being sent exclusively to you for a period of at least one year. Please continue to search until you receive our letter of cancellation for the remaining titles.

Books may be shipped at any time. The package should be clearly identified. All items should be shipped with invoice in triplicate, noting the date of our want list. We will endeavor to clear all transactions as rapidly as possible. However, because of budgetary restrictions there may be slight delays during the months of May and June.

If available, we will accept a later, or revised edition of a requested title, unless otherwise noted. Books should be in at least good or better condition, the text of the book should have no underlining or other marks, no readily discernible cover or other stains, and no part of the book should be loose. Ex-library copies will be acceptable when they are clean and in good condition.

We expect to pay no more than the current market price for requested titles. On items costing $XXX or more, we require a quotation price prior to shipment and purchase.

If you prefer not to search for this material, please return our list so that we may place it with someone else.

Thank you for your prompt attention and help in this matter.

Very truly yours,

Acquisition Department

A group of titles is identified, listed, and sent to a dealer who handles out-of-print items; a certain period of time is allowed in which to search for these items. The librarian may take segments of the list or the entire list on visits to second-hand stores in search of wanted items. The list is also used by the gifts and exchange department to determine if any of the wanted items are being offered in exchange by other libraries. If the department is fairly large, it always pays to see whether a needed replacement or duplicate copy is available from their stock.

The "claims file" becomes quite large during the course of a year. Usually maintained by the bookkeeper, it consists of correspondence about such problems as late invoice payments or requests for credit memos on unwanted items that were billed. It may also contain claims for any issues of journals or serials that were not received.

The bookkeeping unit maintains a series of files that should be noted. The "order file" or "requisition file" contains one copy of every outstanding and filled order. The length of time this file must be maintained varies according to the regulations of the library's governing board. Another file consists of "packing slips" for shipments received without an invoice, and the bookkeeper also maintains an "invoice file" to answer inquiries about payments. Naturally, the total number of copies of an invoice that the library will require depends on the number of extra files that are kept. Of course, the bookkeeping records themselves are of primary importance. The books are open to authorized personnel — including the head librarian, the head of the acquisition department, and personnel from the business office or the agency that oversees the library's expenditures. All others who have an interest in the status of funds receive monthly reports. These are kept on file and used to prepare the quarterly and annual reports of the acquisition department.

The acquisition department also maintains bibliographic and correspondence files. The correspondence files contain: 1) letters dealing with ordering problems (such as wrong item, discount, etc.); 2) letters requesting information about new services, materials, or discounts; and 3) letters claiming missing materials. The bibliographic files include: 1) catalogs and announcements of new items, which arrive continuously and are maintained in a temporary file; 2) a more permanent file of secondhand and rare book dealer catalogs; and 3) a file of bibliographic tools and their supplements, such as the *National Union Catalog*. Announcements of new materials must be kept until they are listed in the standard bibliographic sources (usually less than a year). The catalogs of major secondhand book dealers are kept both for their bibliographic information and for secondhand materials pricing guides. The need for maintaining standard bibliographic tools is obvious, and they are kept in the acquisition department because they receive the greatest use there.

One bibliographic tool that used to cause problems was the LC/NUC "proof slips." While proof slips did serve a bibliographic-acquisition purpose, their format was very different from that of other bibliographic tools. For a reasonably small annual sum, a library received one copy of every card that the Library of Congress produced or that would appear for NUC. Since this included *all* materials cataloged, it represented a sizable number of slips. The Proofsheet Service was recently replaced by the CDS Alert Service. This new Library of Congress service allows a library to receive bibliographic records for certain selected subject areas. The records are on 3x5-inch cards and are similar to the older "proof slips." Because a number of bibliographic data bases exist and more large and medium-sized libraries have access to them, fewer and fewer libraries use the service.

The full advantage of the CDS Alert Service is realized only when that slip is attached to the order slip in the outstanding order or in-process file. When an item is received, the catalog copy can then be sent with it to the catalog department. Very frequently, the acquisition department is asked to maintain this file. Because of the number of slips received, filing them usually requires the full-time attention of one person.

PROBLEMS IN ACQUISITIONS

The acquisition department faces a number of perennial problems: cancellations, claims, the gift and exchange problem, out-of-print materials, and the monthly or annual reports. All of these problems have been touched on in the preceding discussions; here we will provide more detail on a few aspects.

Cancellations

Any funds not expended during the fiscal year usually revert to the funding agency, and like everyone else, librarians are loathe to let money go unspent. Many libraries follow a fiscal year beginning July 1 and ending June 30. When this is the case, request the bookkeeper in late March or early April to provide a list of outstanding orders, with special attention to those that are older than 60 days. The acquisition department must determine which ones are likely to be filled, and letters need to be sent to the dealers asking whether they can make delivery. In most cases, dealers say they will; this must be accepted at face value, even though past performance predicts that some of them will not. A few, however, will acknowledge that an order cannot be filled within the time limits. The library must then formally cancel the order and spend the money in question elsewhere.

Some time in early or middle May, another letter must be sent to those dealers who have not yet supplied materials, informing them that delivery must be made by a certain date, or the order will be automatically cancelled. The acquisition department may still face an unexpended balance by the first of June, but this must be spent on items that can be received by the middle of the month, so that invoices can be approved and sent to the business office for voucher issuance *before* June 30.

Claims

The claiming problem is particularly acute with standing orders or serials. However, claims for missing items in an order are just as bothersome and create the same problems. In the larger library, claiming may require the full-time attention of one library technician and a clerk. The work involves a great deal of letter writing about orders, invoices, and credit memos, and the librarian will be involved only in a supervisory capacity. The person responsible for this effort must work very closely with the bookkeeping unit.

Reports

The form illustrated in Figure 12.2 gives some idea of the type of reports expected not only from the librarians, but from all people working in the department. Usually, monthly reports are required from all units, which, in turn, provide the material for an annual summation.

Automation of Records and Files

With the development of both batch and online systems file development and maintenance has been simplified. The daily factor in batch processing can be a minor or major problem depending upon the turnaround time. Turnaround time of 24 to 48 hours should prove to be reasonable for most acquisition department files. Longer times can cause staff and others considerable frustration, especially for bookkeeping records. With the online system, as indicated earlier, titles are immediately updated.

Fig. 12.2
Acquisition Department Work Load Statistics

	Total for Period of _____	Year-to-Date Total
Date: _____		

ORDERING

Titles searched—library has	_____	_____
Titles searched—to be ordered	_____	_____
Request cards prepared	_____	_____
Request cards received for checking	_____	_____
Cards rechecked	_____	_____
Availability request letters sent	_____	_____
Materials request letters sent	_____	_____
Cards filed into LC proof file	_____	_____
Book orders prepared	_____	_____
Non-book orders prepared	_____	_____
Titles wanted listed (includes catalog orders and standing orders)	_____	_____
Titles ordered (book, non-book, and want lists)	_____	_____
Gifts received	_____	_____
Gifts added	_____	_____
Documents received	_____	_____
Letters to vendors	_____	_____
Cancellations	_____	_____

APPROVAL

Regular approval received	_____	_____
Foreign approval received	_____	_____
Form selection (books) received	_____	_____
Bindery returns received	_____	_____

RECEIVING

Volumes received	_____	_____
Volumes returned	_____	_____
Non-book pieces received	_____	_____
Letters to vendors	_____	_____
Query letters	_____	_____

ACCOUNTING

Orders processed and keypunched	_____	_____
Book invoices processed	_____	_____
Non-book invoices processed	_____	_____
Claim schedules prepared	_____	_____
Statements checked	_____	_____

Serial check-in information and even the on-order file (or in-process file) can be made available to the users either by means of printouts, COM (*see* chapter 15), or CRT. This information can save time for the entire staff. Patrons will be able to determine whether an issue of a journal has been received without bothering the staff. Duplicate requests for titles already on order or in process can be greatly reduced, if not eliminated, as result of having these files available for non-technical service personnel and users. Certainly the manual files could be and are examined by nondepartment people, however, such consultation disrupts the work flow. By using some form of automated output located in one or more public service points, this problem is avoided.

A major value of automating technical service files is the time saved in filing. Putting in and taking out slips of paper in files take a lot of time. Errors are bound to occur, and more time must be spent correcting the problems. Library rules for filing tend to be complicated (*see* chapter 25) and rather specialized. This means time must be spent training filers. With an automated system the filing and purging (removing of unwanted records) is done by machine; if the data is input properly the filing will be correct, and the amount of training new staff in library filing rules can be reduced.

Automated acquisition systems are good for controlling many of the acquisition department files, as we shall describe in more detail in the next chapter on these systems. What they cannot handle are the non-routine correspondence records and monthly and annual reports (other than statistical). We are not aware of any automated technical service system that incorporates a strong word processing capability. If "office automation" is incorporated into the library it is as an independent system. Such systems will help control the cost of filing as well as preparing the non-routine correspondence and administrative reports.

REVIEW QUESTIONS

1. List the acquisition files maintained by most libraries.

2. What is a desiderata file?

3. The correspondence file represents _____ .

4. The three types of items in the bibliographic file are _____, _____, _____.

5. The perennial problems of acquisition are _____ .

6. Why is it important to a library to handle claims and cancellations quickly?

7. In what way does "office automation" enter into acquisition work?

13
AUTOMATED ACQUISITION SYSTEMS

In chapters 6 through 12, we have described in some detail the acquisition activities as they are performed in a manual system. With that background, the reader will be better able to understand the advantages that can be gained from an automated system. Within the past five years there has been a rapid increase in the number of automated systems that are generally available to libraries. There are four basic types of systems now on the market. All of the major bibliographic utilities (OCLC, RLIN, WLN, and UTLAS) provide an acquisition subsystem. A few library-developed systems that are marketed by commercial firms are also available (for example, MATSS, handled by Midwest Library Service). Commercial firms that offer automated technical service packages naturally have acquisition modules included (examples are CLSI and DataPhase). Finally, the suppliers of library materials and services provide some automated services (Baker & Taylor, Brodart, R. R. Bowker).

Some comments should be made about the cost of these systems. We have used the words "provided" and "available" in describing the systems and not mentioned price or cost. The systems are expensive to bring into the library and expensive to operate. There are "line charges"—cost of telephone or other telecommunications connections—and just as with long distance telephone calls, there is a charge for every second the line is open. It is very important that staff members be as efficient as possible in their use of such systems. In addition to line charges, some systems have screen charges, dial-up charges, and so forth. Automated systems can be very useful in saving staff time and effort, but with inefficient or ineffective use, their costs may outweigh their value in productivity.

In chapter 2 we outlined ten features that should be found or are desirable in an automated acquisition system. The features were:

1. Verify the bibliographic data for a requested item.

2. Verify that the item is not already on order or in process.

3. Verify price and availability.

4. Prepare purchase orders.

5. Encumber the correct amount of money.

6. Handle claims for late or nondelivered orders.

7. Maintain and update the on order/in process file.

8. Record receipts for orders and check for completeness of the order.

9. Prepare payment authorization forms for orders.

10. Prepare necessary financial and statistical reports for the department.

The remainder of this chapter is devoted to a brief examination of *some* of the automated systems currently in use. Selection was based on the number of libraries using the systems and the amount of information we were supplied about the systems. One system (WLN) is covered in considerable detail to provide an idea of the capabilities of these systems. As with the detailed example from OCLC in the chapter on machine verification, the detailed discussion is *not* intended to be taken as an endorsement of that system.

BIBLIOGRAPHIC UTILITIES SYSTEMS

OCLC's "Acquisitions Subsystem" provides access to the Online Union Catalog from which orders may be generated. There is an online in-process file, automatic transfer of constant data (bibliographic information) to other online files, fund accounting and report generation, as well as receipt and claiming. The multiple purpose "action form" is completed and mailed by OCLC to appropriate sources—vendors and your library. Like most systems, it allows you to verify bibliographic information, the library holdings, and the in-process file in one step.

As of April 1984, there was no direct automatic transmission of orders to vendors. Like most of library-based systems, verification of price and availability is sometimes difficult, since the information may not be in the data base and even if it is, it probably is not current. Overall, with the above limits, the system covers the ten features desirable in an automated system. Naturally, if the library is using other OCLC services, the advantage of having everything integrated may outweigh any inherent system limitations.

RLIN II (the acquisition module) is available to libraries through the California Library Authority for Systems and Services (CLASS). It is intended to be a comprehensive acquisition system from verification to receipt. The fiscal management aspect is not covered as part of the basic system, but is available as an option.

Verification is done online and allows the searcher access not only to the library's own holdings records, but also the holdings of the Library of Congress and the 200 member libraries. As with online systems based on library holdings and/or MARC tapes, the searcher must remember that failure to find an item does not necessarily mean it does not exist, but merely that it is not in the data base searched. (Similarly, failure to find an item in *BIP* does not mean that it is not in print.) Certainly failure to find an item in RLIN or OCLC will mean that verification will be something of a problem, and there is a strong possibility the information is incorrect. Also, remember that generally you will not be able to verify cost information or availability.

One unusual feature of RLIN's system is that a library can maintain, in the acquisition system, not only a record of titles ordered, but also titles considered and rejected. In a large library where many persons are involved in collection development, readily available information about rejected titles can be a time saver. A searcher, by going back and forth between the cataloging and the acquisition data base, can verify very quickly the bibliographic information, the library's holdings, and whether the item is in-process.

Preparing the order is then done in the acquisition system. Orders are printed either in the library or at RLG. No matter which approach is used, however, the orders are still mailed to the appropriate vendor by the library—direct electronic order placement with a vendor/jobber is not possible at this time. When the order is prepared, claim periods, the number of claims to be made, and the cancellation notice preparation time lines are input. The system will automatically produce the claims and cancellation notice at the correct times, unless the field indicating the item has been received is activated. The system, while not perfect, can be of great value in large libraries or research libraries.

Our detailed example of an automated acquisition system is the Washington Library Networks' (WLN) "Acquisition Subsystem." The system consists of four files: in-process, standing orders, name and address, and account status. These files, combined with cataloging files, allow the library to operate and maintain acquisitions records for an item from selection to "on the shelf status." One nice feature is that the system handles both individual and standing order transactions.

As might be expected, the in-process file is the heart of acquisition subsystems and is based on the MARC record. Online access to the file is provided directly by purchase order number, or indirectly through what is termed the "Bibliographic Subsystem," (the cataloging subsystem) using any of the full set of "Inquiry" facility access points (including LCCN, ISBN, ISSN, Title Keywords, author, subject, series, corporate heading [author, subject or series], keywords). The in-process file records can handle all information used in the acquisitions process, such as encumbering, claiming, receiving, as well as basic bibliographic data for all types of library materials. Information in this file can be updated online and is available immediately as the order cycle proceeds. The accounting functions of encumbering, invoicing, liquidating, and disbursing are also provided. Upon completion of the order cycle, a "Receiving Report" can be produced which contains invoice information on materials received from the vendor and acts primarily as a voucher for payment. The actual creation of order records and the screen displays that are used are described later in this section.

The "Standing Orders File" contains information related to subscriptions or to any other orders that are renewed or reordered on a periodic basis. "Standing Orders File" records are maintained in the same format as records in the "In-Process File." At the time an order is to be renewed or reordered, a copy of the record in the "Standing Orders File" is transferred to the "In-Process File" and then processed along with other orders. After the order is received and paid for, payment information is copied back to the "Standing Orders File" so that a payment history can be maintained. Online access to the "Standing Orders File" is provided directly by purchase order number. Indirect access through the "Bibliographic Subsystem" is available using any of the full set of "Inquiry" facility access points. Serials check-in on an issue by issue basis is not provided by the "Acquisitions Subsystem."

The "Name and Address File" contains the names and addresses of vendors, main libraries, branch libraries, and other locations. "Order and Accounting Profile" information is also stored in this file. Online access to the names and addresses of libraries is available by library NUC symbol or identification number. Online access to vendor names and addresses is by vendor identification number or mnemonic.

Libraries can add, update, and delete their own branch location names and addresses. The vendor and main library names and addresses are shared by all "Acquisitions Subsystem" participants and are maintained by WLN staff.

The "Acquisitions Subsystem" provides the capability to maintain up-to-date fund accounting status records in the "Account Status File." Accounting transactions are posted to the "Account Status File" nightly and can be displayed online for each account. Account status records contain seven items (noted in Figure 13.1).

Fig. 13.1*
Account Status File Screen – WLN

```
1 00000012 001 JH 503Y 65S                              REGULAR
                                       2 Periodicals
        FY 81 PD 810406   CD 800926           TAX 00000012
        EB 06 PT 002223   ED 800701           PIH 00000012
                          TD 810630

  3 ALLOC    56,000.00 4 ENC   3,426.39 5 DIS  3,281.29 6 F/B   49,292.32
                     7 JUL        0.00              0.00
                       AUG        0.00              0.00
                       SEP       15.00              0.00
                       OCT      686.00            742.45
                       NOV      143.95            368.34
                       DEC      274.04            399.88
                       JAN    1,002.00            923.48
                       FEB      135.00            259.81
                       MAR      940.40            498.32
                       APR      230.00             89.01
                       MAY        0.00              0.00
                       JUN        0.00              0.00
                       EXT        0.00              0.00
```

Key to Note Items in Figure 13.1

[1]Account number and code

[2]A description of the account

[3]Allocation amount

[4]Outstanding encumbrances

[5]Disbursements

[6]Free balance

[7]Monthly expenditures

---

*Figs. 13.1-13.16 reproduced with the permission of the Washington Library Network.

Each library is responsible for the creation and maintenance of its own accounts. WLN offers password control so that each library has the flexibility to specify which passwords allow particular functions, such as the creation and maintenance of accounts. Accounts can be entered or updated by using formatted screens. Transaction detail can be printed following each posting run, if specified in the library's Accounting Profile.

An "Order Profile" is established for each library. Among the options included in the "Order Profile" are: 1) use of the automatic claiming function, 2) initial and subsequent claim intervals, 3) use of the automatic "p-slip" (processing slip) function, and 4) production time of a notification card. These options can be changed at any time by using the online "Order Profile" update screen. The profile specifies data that will automatically appear in an order record, although it can be changed at the time the order record is created or at any time thereafter. An "Accounting Profile" is also established for each library. Some of the options included are: 1) encumbrance and disbursement begin months, 2) prepayment option, 3) "Receiving Report" options, 4) type of fiscal year extension needed, and 5) choice of transaction report details.

The order cycle generally begins with an online search of the "Bibliographic File" to determine if a full or interim bibliographic record exists. The "Summary Holdings File" can then be checked to determine if the library owns the item. The "In-Process File" can also be queried to determine whether other WLN libraries using the "Acquisitions Subsystem" have the title on order. If the record is found in the "In-Process File," a display such as the one in Figure 13.2 (see page 122) provides brief acquisitions data for each library that has ordered the item. The order records can be displayed three at a time (as shown in Figure 13.2) or six at a time in a more abbreviated display format.

If the item is not in the data base, an interim bibliographic record must be created if the "In-Process File" record is to be linked to the "Bibliographic File." The "Acquisitions Subsystem" also allows orders to be created for items that require formats not currently supported by the Bibliographic Subsystem, such as maps.

CREATION OF THE ORDER

An order is created by entering the order command and a purchase order number, after finding the appropriate bibliographic record in the data base. This automatically links the order to the "Bibliographic File" and causes a formatted order screen to be displayed. It is also possible to create an order record which is not linked to the Bibliographic File, for orders such as GOP depository account payments or non-bibliographic items (e.g., library supplies and furniture).

The order screen (see Figure 13.3, page 122) includes options determined by the Order and Accounting Profiles and bibliographic information automatically transferred to the screen from the bibliographic record. Default values can also be established on a session by session basis for several data elements, including vendor number, account number, and invoice number. Additional order and accounting data can then be added to the order screen. The system will handle many types of orders, such as regular purchases, standing orders, quotations, desiderata items, information requests, membership and depository account items, and exchanges. Once an order record is created, all of the information included in the record can be viewed (see Figure 13.4, page 123).

Fig. 13.2
Verification Screen—WLN

```
|                                                                              |
|                                                                              |
|   00006 ITEMS FOUND                                                          |
|                                                                              |
|   NUC: WaPS      PO# 00-038128F ISBN/ISSN 039526684X RID  78002728 |
|   AU: Sheehan, Susan.                                                        |
|   TI: A prison and a prisoner / Susan Sheehan.                               |
|   PUB: Boston : Houghton Mifflin, 1978.                                      |
|   SER:                                                                       |
|   OI:                                               LIST PRICE 10.95 |
|   VEN: BNA        VCAT#              ORD 800409    RECD 800614 |
|                                                                              |
|   NUC: Wa        PO# 81-000345 ISBN/ISSN 039526684X RID  78002728 |
|   AU: Sheehan, Susan.                                                        |
|   TI: A prison and a prisoner / Susan Sheehan.                               |
|   PUB: Boston : Houghton Mifflin, 1978.                                      |
|   SER:                                                                       |
|   OI:                                               LIST PRICE 10.95 |
|   VEN: BT/W       VCAT#              ORD 800630    RECD 800822 |
|                                                                              |
|   NUC: WaWW      PO# 81-000501 ISBN/ISSN 039526684X  RID 78002728 |
|   AU: Sheehan, Susan.                                                        |
|   TI: A prison and a prisoner / Susan Sheehan.                               |
|   PUB: Boston : Houghton Mifflin, 1978.                                      |
|   SER:                                                                       |
|   OI: Paperback                                     LIST PRICE  3.95 |
|   VEN: BT/W       VCAT#       95737 ORD 801127    RECD 800127 |
|                                                                              |
```

Fig. 13.3
Order Screen—WLN

```
|                                                                              |
|                                                              ORDER SCREEN |
|                                                                              |
|   ORDERSCREEN,  PO# 81-005372  ISBN  a090881907  ISSN                        |
|     AU:  Hogg, Garry.                                                        |
|     Ti:1 Orient Express: the birth, life and death of a great train. |
|     PUB:  London, Hutchinson, 1968.                                          |
|     SER:  The Men in action series                                           |
|                                                                              |
|     OI:                                                                      |
|     VID# 35     QTY 4      FY 81     ACCT# 1340     ENCAMT  48.00 |
|     VNA:                                                                     |
|     VCAT#         APGM  NONE      LISTPR 12.95       CLMINT 090 |
|     REC TYPE LAP  BIBLV MONO      ORD TYPE  REGUL    SOURCE PURCH |
|     RID a75359799 ORD IND:                                                   |
|     CIT:                                                                     |
|     NOT:                                                                     |
|     REMARKS:                                                                 |
|     RES:                                                                     |
|     PIECE CODE    NCOPIES              PLOC        SLOC        SLOC |
|     COPY IND:                         COPY#    CALL# |
|     INV#        INVAMT            LINE#    PAGE#     INV DATE |
|                                                                              |
```

Fig. 13.4
Acquisition Screen—WLN

```
                                    ACQUISITIONS DISPLAY

   STATUS: EDITED  PO-WRITTEN  ALL-PAY-CREATED  AUTO-CLAIM
           NOTIFY-WHEN-ORDERED  CAT-PROD-AT-RECEIPT

   ORDER # 81-004214  CREATED     810207  BY OPER 13
                      LAST UPDATED 810207  BY OPER 13 LAST BATCH UPDATE
   ORDER TYPE      REGUL      VENDOR ID  BT/W      QTY            3
   SOURCE CODE     PURCH      VEN STK#             # PSLIP S      0
   RECORD TYPE     LAP        ACCNT# WITH VEN      #CLAIMS        0
   BIB LEVEL       MONO       LIST PRICE 8.00      I CLM INT     90
   ENCODING LEVEL  0          EFFECTIVE            S CLM INT     90
   PHYSICAL MEDIA             CURRENCY TYPE        CLM INV INT    0
   UNITS RECEIVED  0          COST CENTER  0       CANCEL INT     0
   SERIAL TYPE                PAYMENT FREQ UNSPECI REORDER INT  365
   YEAR PUBL                  APPROVAL     NONE

   ORDERED    810207    LAST CLAIM          HOLD
   RECEIVED             NEXT CLAIM   810507  ORDER NOTIFICATION
   CANCELLED            REORDER             RECD NOTIFICATION
   CAN CONF             RENEW               VENDOR CORRESP

    LCN/01:      73004607
    SBN/01:      0800705963
    AUTHOR/01:   Mumford, Bob.
    Title/01:  10 Living happily ever after.
    PUBLISHER/01: Old Tappan, N.J., F.H. Revell Co. [1973]
```

Locations for copies of a title can be added to the acquisitions record using the Location Screen and will appear on the Processing Slip. Shipping, branch, or other locations can be entered on the screen. If it is necessary to encumber funds against separate accounts belonging to various locations, the Location/Encumbrance Screen shown in Figure 13.5 (see page 124) can be used. Use of this screen creates both an accounting and a location segment for each location.

Once the necessary order information has been added to the "In-Process File" record, a purchase order can be printed, or the order can be routed directly to any one of 12 book and periodical vendors using the WLN On-Line Transmission of Orders facility.* Purchase Orders are printed or routed to

---

*Vendors accepting orders online from WLN as of 8/30/84: Academic Book Center, Oregon; Baker & Taylor, Nevada; Blackwell/NA, Oregon; Book Services International, Connecticut; Bookhouse, Michigan; Bro-Dart, Pennsylvania; Coutts Library Service, New York; Ebsco, California (both Burlingame and Los Angeles); Faxon, Massachusetts; Ingram, Tennessee; Midwest Library Service, Missouri; Mook & Blanchard, California.

Fig. 13.5
Location/Encumbering Screen—WLN

```
|                                                              LOC/ENC SCREEN  |
|                                                                             |
|  LENCADDS,   PO# 81-000878  FY ( 81 )                                       |
|    # OF      PRIMARY     SECONDARY     SECONDARY      ENCUMBRANCE            |
|   COPIES     LOCATION    LOCATION-1    LOCATION-2   ACCOUNT      AMOUNT      |
|                                                                             |
|   ( 1   )  ( Wa     )  ( Ref     )  (          )  ( 1206  ) ( 10.00 )       |
|   ( 1   )  ( Wa-Ec  )  (         )  (          )  ( 104   ) ( 10.00 )       |
|   ( 1   )  ( WaMeH  )  ( Juv     )  ( Ref      )  ( 110   ) ( 10.00 )       |
|   (     )  (        )  (         )  (          )  (       ) (       )       |
|   (     )  (        )  (         )  (          )  (       ) (       )       |
|   (     )  (        )  (         )  (          )  (       ) (       )       |
|   (     )  (        )  (         )  (          )  (       ) (       )       |
```

vendors three times a week. The record can be updated online using individual commands and formatted screens. Bibliographic information can be added, deleted, or altered in "In-Process File" records without affecting the "Bibliographic File." All other information in the order record, such as quantity, order type, source of order, list price, claim intervals, reserves, vendor information, location information, and so forth, can also be added, deleted, or altered.

Automatic claiming intervals can be set in an "In-Process File" record. Claim letters are printed automatically after the interval established in the "Order Profile" has passed. Online commands provide both for overriding previously set claim intervals and for inputting additional information to appear on the claims. Vendor reports can also be added to the record. In addition, an order can be cancelled online at any time. Any cancellation will cause a full liquidation of all encumbrances existing against the record and the appropriate account.

Invoice data can be entered and the order marked, received, and invoiced using a formatted screen or individual commands. Thereafter, receiving reports can be produced that list those items which have completed the order cycle and automatically generate disbursement and liquidation transactions. Figure 13.6 illustrates the payment information for a record that has been received, invoiced, and paid.

After completion of the order cycle, "In-Process File" records are copied to an off-line "History File" which is created for each library using the "Acquisitions Subsystem." The "History File" is stored on magnetic tape as a permanent record of a library's past acquisitions activity and can be used to produce statistical and other reports. The "History File" is also available on microfiche.

Fig. 13.6
Payment Screen—WLN

```
┌────────────────────────────────────────────────────┬─────┐
│                                                     │     │
│                                        ACQUISITIONS DISPLAY │
│                                                     │     │
│  PAYMENT 01:  ORDER # 81-004214  PAY TYPE NORM      │     │
│  RECD=810207    INV=810207     PAID=810314          │     │
│                                                     │     │
│  VENDOR BT/W   ENC DT 810103   ENC$  24.00  LIQ DT 810207 LIQ$  24.00 │
│  INV #  638367 INV DT 810202   INV$   0.00  PG/LN 001/01  GAMT$  0.00 │
│  REF #     204 PIH$    0.00    TAX$   0.00  CODE  NONE  QTY   00 │
│  ACCT# 0000012 PIH A# 0000012  TA# 0000012  FY     81  CURR  │
│  RENEWP        FROM            THRU                  │     │
│                                                     │     │
└────────────────────────────────────────────────────┴─────┘
```

Naturally the "Acquisition Subsystem" generates the appropriate forms and reports. Order products are produced for each order based on its status and includes among many products: Purchase Orders, Vendor Reports, Notify Cards, Claim Letters, Receiving Reports, and Processing Slips. The following are some of the products of the system:

1. *Purchase Order.* Requests are initiated by the library and are produced on a two-part form. Basic bibliographic information (as found in the "In-Process File" record), purchase order number, billing address, and basic vendor information are included. Space is provided for a shipping address if it varies from the billing address. An "Instructions" field allows free text messages, such as "Paperback edition only," to be sent to the vendor. Orders may be routed directly to any one of 12 book and periodical vendors using the WLN Online Transmission of Orders facility (see Figure 13.7, page 126).

2. *Processing Slip.* This 7⅜x3½-inch card can be used as a routing slip for received materials. It can be produced automatically at time of order or receipt, or ordered at other times by using an individual command. Basic bibliographic information, purchase order number, and vendor identification are included. Additional information such as locations, call numbers, and status information can also be included (see Figure 13.8, page 126).

3. *Vendor Report.* This report reflects the response from a vendor concerning original orders or claim letters. Basic bibliographic, claiming, and vendor information is included, in addition to the specific report information from the vendor (see Figure 13.9, page 127).

Fig. 13.7
Purchase Order

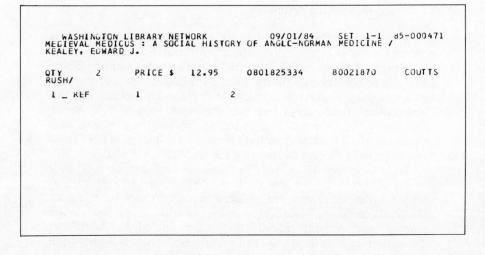

RUSH ORDER

PURCHASE ORDER # 85-000470

DATE 09/01/84

Medieval medicus : a social history of Anglo-Norman medicine /.
Kealey, Edward J..
Baltimore : Johns Hopkins University Press, c1981.

Paperback ed. only.

INSTRUCTIONS

QTY	LIST PRICE	VEN CAT #
2	12.95	JHP-76380B

0801825334   VENDOR ACCT #

BILL TO
Washington Library Network
Library Services Division
Mail Stop AJ-11
Clympia, WA   98503-0000

SHIP TO
          SAME AS ABCVE

COUTTS LIBRARY SERVICE
736 CAYUGA ST
LEWISTON   NY 14092

FORM LIB 37-2 REV 8/79

SIGN

Fig. 13.8
Processing Slip

    WASHINGTON LIBRARY NETWORK   09/01/84   SET 1-1   85-000471
MEDIEVAL MEDICUS : A SOCIAL HISTORY OF ANGLO-NORMAN MEDICINE /
KEALEY, EDWARD J.

QTY   2   PRICE $ 12.95   0801825334   80021870   COUTTS
RUSH/

1 _ REF   1   2

Fig. 13.9
Vendor Report

```
WASHINGTON LIBRARY NETWORK      VENDOR REPORT           W   L   N
                                                        09/04/84

   PURCHASE ORDER: 85-000471
   PURCHASE ORDER DATE: 09/01/84          NEXT CLAIM DATE: 02/28/85

   TITLE: MEDIEVAL MEDICUS : A SOCIAL HISTORY OF ANGLO-NORMAN MEDICINE /

   AUTHOR: KEALEY, EDWARD J.

   SERIES:

   ORDER INFORMATION: PAPERBACK ED. ONLY

   CLAIM INFORMATION: PLEASE REPORT PROMPTLY.  THIS TITLE IS NEEDED FOR A
       CLASS. - BB
   VENDOR NAME: COLTTS LIBRARY SERVICE
   NOTIFY:  PROF. BERWICK HIST. DEPT 459-6539
   VENDOR REPORT: 08/30/84 VENDOR REPORTS THIS TITLE IS OUT OF PRINT.

   ENCUMBERING ACCT:     1     BIB LEV: M      ORDER TYPE: REGULAR
```

4. *Notify Card.* This card records the name and address of an individual who has requested notification about an order's status at a particular time. The card contains basic bibliographic and order information and can be produced at time of order, receipt, and at time of availability, according to the library's profile options (see Figure 13.10).

Fig. 13.10
Notify Card

```
WASHINGTON LIBRARY NETWORK
              NOTIFY REPORT: ITEM ON ORDER              W   L   N
                                                        09/03/84

   PURCHASE ORDER: 85-000471
   DATE ORDERED  : 09/01/84
   DATE RECEIVED :
   DATE AVAILABLE:
   ORDER TYPE: REGULAR

   TITLE: MEDIEVAL MEDICUS : A SOCIAL HISTORY OF ANGLO-NORMAN MEDICINE /

   AUTHOR: KEALEY, EDWARD J.

   SERIES:

   ORDER INFORMATION: PAPERBACK ED. ONLY

   VENDOR NAME: COLTTS LIBRARY SERVICE

   NOTIFY:  PROF. BERWICK HIST. DEPT 459-6539
```

5. *Claim Letter.* These special forms are automatically produced according to the claim intervals established by each library. Claim letters continue to be produced at the designated intervals until the material is received or until the order is cancelled. Appropriate bibliographic information is included as well as a list of possible status indications for the vendor to fill in (see Figure 13.11, page 128).

Fig. 13.11
Claim Letter

WASHINGTON LIBRARY NETWORK

WASHINGTON LIBRARY NETWORK
SEPTEMBER 03, 1984

TO

ACADEMIC BOOK CENTER
2424 NE 52ND AVE
PORTLAND OR 97213

ORDER NO: 25-000001   DATED: 12/29/83

LC CARD NO: 68059464   ISBN/ISSN NO:

KOREA: NEXUS OF EAST ASIA; AN INQUIRY INTO CONTEMPORARY KOREA IN HISTORICAL
PERSPECTIVE,. STEINBERG, DAVID I.. ORDER INFORMATION.
NEW YOR AMERICAN-ASIAN EDUCATIONAL EXCHANGE 1968

THE MATERIAL REFERRED TO ABOVE HAS NOT BEEN RECEIVED. PLEASE REPORT ON ITS
STATUS BY CHECKING THE APPROPRIATE LINE BELOW.

2   25-000001

_____ PUBLICATION SENT, (DATE) _____

_____ PUBLICATION CANCELLED.

_____ NOT YET PUBLISHED. ANTICIPATED PUBLICATION DATE IS _____

_____ PUBLICATION DATE UNKNOWN. ORDER CANCELLED.

_____ PUBLICATION OUT OF PRINT. ORDER CANCELLED.

_____ PUBLICATION OUT OF PRINT. ANOTHER PRINTING EXPECTED (DATE) _____

_____ PUBLICATION OUT OF PRINT. WILL SEARCH AND GIVE QUOTES.

_____ UNEXPECTED DELAY. SHOULD BE SUPPLIED BY (DATE) _____

_____ OUT OF STOCK. SHOULD BE SUPPLIED BY (DATE) _____

_____ CLAIMING. BOOK OR REPORT TO FOLLOW.

PLEASE REPLY TO:

WASHINGTON LIBRARY NETWORK
LIBRARY SERVICES DIVISION
MAIL STOP AJ-11
OLYMPIA, WA 98503-0000

THANK YOU

FORM LIB37-5(2-78)

6. *Title Index.* This index is a list of titles currently in the "In-Process or Standing Orders File" (except desiderata, old standing orders and selection list items). It serves as a quick off-line reference, with up to nine cross-references for each entry. The "Title Index" is sorted by title (the first 50 characters of each title or cross-reference). Purchase order number, vendor, and order status information is included for each title (see Figure 13.12, page 130).

7. *Purchase Order Index.* This index is a quick off-line reference tool for order information regarding "In-Process of Standing Orders File" records. The "Purchase Order Index" is sorted by purchase order number. Brief bibliographic information, vendor mnemonic, list price, record type, and order status is included for each purchase order number (see Figure 13.13, page 131).

8. *Exceptional Conditions Report.* Records in the "In-Process File" are scanned to produce an "Exceptional Conditions Report" with ten categories, including: 1) record created more than 30 days ago but not ordered; 2) order received more than 30 days ago but not invoiced; 3) order on hold; 4) order received 120 days ago but not cleared to "History File"; 5) order cleared for copying to "History File" 45 days ago but not copied. The report contains basic bibliographic information, purchase order number, and the date the order was created for each title.

9. *Journal Account Transaction.* This product generates several reports detailing and summarizing a library's accounting transactions. Some accounting reports list each individual accounting transaction for one day. Other accounting reports list warning and error conditions, account creation and updates, journal voucher transactions, and account balance summaries.

10. *Account Status Cumulative Summary.* This summary is produced on a weekly basis and includes account numbers, account codes, and the allocation, encumbrances, disbursements, and free balance for each of the library's accounts (see Figure 13.14, page 132).

11. *Receiving Report.* This report records invoice information and acts as a voucher for payment to mark items as having been received and paid. It is produced on stock paper until approved by the library, at which time the final Receiving Report is produced. The "Final" liquidates encumbrances and disburses funds. Brief bibliographic information, account code, and tax and invoice information are included for each purchase order number (see Figure 13.15, page 133).

12. *Vendor List.* This list is a vendor "Name and Address File" (over 9000) and is produced semi-annually with supplements between cumulations. It is produced in both alphabetic and numerical order using a WLN-assigned unique identification number.

(Numbered list continues on page 134.)

Fig. 13.12
Title Index

IBM SYSTEM 36 PAGE 1	11-07-83	TITLE INDEX: IN-PROCESS FILE	DIALLP DEMO 2	WASHINGTON LIBRARY NETWORK
84-837035 NON-WLN		A. IBM SYSTEM 360 JCL REFERENCE #GC28-6704. B. MVS UTILITIES #GC26-3902 // 1 COPY EA. OF 2 TITLES, RUSH ASAP		RECEIVED 07/08/83
84-905110 NON-WLN		CALIFORNIA APPAREL NEWS // 1 YR. RENEWAL, STARTS FROM NEXT ISSUE		RECEIVED 07/11/83
84-837091 NON-WLN		AMERICAN HOSPITAL FORMULARY SERVICE: A COLLECTION OF DRUG MONOGRAPHS AND OTHER INFORMATION. // 1984, NEEDED BY 9/1/83 ORDERED BY B. WHITMAN (NC24C2A)		AM ORDERED 08/15/83
84-874905 BH/E		AMERICAN UNIVERSITIES AND COLLEGES. // 12TH ED, 1983		RECEIVED 07/20/83
84-905114 NON-WLN		BOARD REPORT // 1 YR. RENEWAL		RECEIVED 07/11/83
84-875600 0		THE COLLEGE BLUE BOOK. //		AT CRORD 07/19/83
84-875601 NON-WLN		THE COLLEGE BLUE BOOK. // 19TH ED, V.1-5, PREPAY		ORDERED 07/27/83
84-875345 BH/E		DONOVAN, AMERICA'S MASTER SPY / BY RICHARD DUNLOP. // DUNLOP, RICHARD.		RECEIVED 07/20/83
84-871737 8103		ENCYCLOPEDIA OF ASSOCIATIONS. //		PRT RECD
84-875372 UBS		PER ATTACHED LIST (58 TITLES) // CONFIRMING ONLY MATERIALS REC'D, 1 EA. OF 58 TITLES		RECEIVED 06/30/83
84-836953 NON-WLN		TITLES PER ATTACHED LIST //		RECEIVED 07/21/83
84-905109 NON-WLN		FLOWERS & // 2 YRS. RENEWAL		NT ORDRD 07/11/83
84-875593 NON-WLN		ILLUSTRATED LIBRARY OF SACRED IMAGINATION, 10 VOL. SET // PREPAY		PRT RECD
84-837031 NON-WLN		LEADERSHIP DEVELOPMENT THROUGH PLANNED INSTRUCTION IN VOCATIONAL EDUCATION. // NEEDED BY 8/83		RECEIVED 07/08/83
84-871178 BH/E		LIBRARY AUTOMATICA HANDBOOK. / DENNIS REYNOLDS. // REYNOLDS, DENNIS.		ORDERED 07/20/83
84-837029 PH		LIFETIME ENCYCLOPEDIA OF LETTERS / HAROLD E. MEYER. // MEYER, HAROLD E., 1920- PREPAY 07/01/83		RECEIVED 07/01/83
84-836982 NON-WLN		MICROCOMPUTERS FOR LIBRARIES : HOW USEFUL ARE THEY? / EDITED BY JANE BEAUMONT, DONALD KRUEGER. // PREPAY		RECEIVED 07/18/83
84-836982D BH/E		MICROCOMPUTERS FOR LIBRARIES : HOW USEFUL ARE THEY? / EDITED BY JANE BEAUMONT, DONALD KRLEGER. // RUSH		RECEIVED 07/18/83
84-837032 NON-WLN		MODELS FOR THINKING: ACTIVITIES TO ENHANCE MODES OF THOUGHT // EPLEY NEEDED BY 7/29/83		RECEIVED 07/11/83

Fig. 13.13
Purchase Order Index
(Orders In-Progress by Order Number)

84-1	1	PURCHASE ORDER INDEX: IN-PROCESS FILE	DIALUP DEMO 2	
PAGE		11-07-83	WASHINGTON LIBRARY NETWORK	

84-1		PER ATTACHED LIST (A TOTAL OF 10 TITLES) //	$0.00	N M LAP	PRT RECD
BH/E					
84-836938		PUBLIC ACCESS TO ONLINE CATALOGS : A PLANNING GUIDE FOR MANAGERS / // MATTHEWS, JOSEPH R.	$28.50	N P LAP	RECEIVED 07/18/83
BH/E		RUSH ASAP			
84-836938D		PUBLIC ACCESS TO ONLINE CATALOGS : A PLANNING GUIDE FOR MANAGERS / // MATTHEWS, JOSEPH R.	$0.00	N A LAP	RECEIVED 07/18/83
BH/E		RUSH			
84-836953		TITLES PER ATTACHED LIST //	$14.00	N M LAP	RECEIVED 07/21/83
NON-WLN					
84-836982		MICROCOMPUTERS FOR LIBRARIES : HOW USEFUL ARE THEY? / EDITED BY JANE BEAUMONT, DONALD KRUEGER. /	$12.00	A P LAP	RECEIVED 07/18/83
NON-WLN		PREPAY			
84-836982D		MICROCOMPUTERS FOR LIBRARIES : HOW USEFUL ARE THEY? / EDITED BY JANE BEAUMONT, DONALD KRUEGER. /	$12.00	N P LAP	RECEIVED 07/18/83
BH/E		RUSH			
84-837023		TELETEXT AND VIDEOTEX IN THE UNITED STATES // JOHN TYDEMAN	$24.55	A P LAP	RECEIVED 07/19/83
NON-WLN					
84-837029		LIFETIME ENCYCLOPEDIA OF LETTERS / HAROLD E. MEYER. // MEYER, HAROLD E., 1920-	$0.00	N M LAP	RECEIVED 07/01/83
PH		PREPAY 07/01/83			
84-837030		TECHNICIAN EDUCATION YEARBOOK. //	$28.00	N M LAP	RECEIVED 01/07/83
911168		1984 ED			
84-837031		LEADERSHIP DEVELOPMENT THROUGH PLANNED INSTRUCTION IN VOCATIONAL EDUCATION. //	$10.00	N M LAP	RECEIVED 07/08/83
NON-WLN		NEEDED BY 8/83			
84-837032		MODELS FOR THINKING: ACTIVITIES TO ENHANCE MODES OF THOUGHT // EPLEY	$5.25	A P LAP	RECEIVED 07/11/83
NON-WLN		NEEDED BY 7/29/83			
84-837033		1983 SEATTLE DESIGN & ADVERTISING AWARDS CATALOG //	$0.00	N P LAP	RECEIVED 07/19/83
NON-WLN		RUSH, NEEDED BY 6/83			
84-837034		PREPARING FOR HIGH TECHNOLOGY: BOOK 1-3 //	$0.00	A P LAP	RECEIVED 07/19/83
NON-WLN					
84-837035		4. IBM SYSTEM 360 JCL REFERENCE #GC28-6704. 8. WVS UTILITIES #GC26-3902 //	$27.00	N M LAP	RECEIVED 07/08/83
NON-WLN		1 COPY EA. OF 2 TITLES, RUSH ASAP			
84-837091		AMERICAN HOSPITAL FORMULARY SERVICE: A COLLECTION OF DRUG MONOGRAPHS AND OTHER INFORMATION. //	$30.00	A P LAP	ORDERED 08/15/83
NON-WLN		1984, NEEDED BY 6/1/83 ORDERED BY B. WHITMAN (NC240243)		N P LAP	CLAIMED 09/15/83
84-871178		LIBRARY AUTOMATION HANDBOOK. / DENNIS REYNOLDS. // REYNOLDS, DENNIS.	$35.00	N P LAP	ORDERED 07/20/83
BH/E					CLAIMED 10/22/83
84-871737		ENCYCLOPEDIA OF ASSOCIATIONS. //	$0.00	N P LAP	PRT RECD
8103					
84-874905		AMERICAN UNIVERSITIES AND COLLEGES. //	$99.50	N S LAP	RECEIVED 07/20/83
BH/E		12TH ED, 1983			
84-875097		SPECIAL PLACES: IN SEARCH OF SMALL TOWN AMERICA, 1982 //	$12.55	A P LAP	ORDERED 07/20/83
BH/E					CLAIMED 10/22/83

Fig. 13.14
Account Status Cumulative Summary

ACCOUNT STATUS   CUMULATIVE SUMMARY FOR 07-01-80/10-14-80   WASHINGTON LIBRARY NETWORK
WASHINGTON STATE LIBRARY   10-13-80   PAGE 1

ACCOUNT NUMBER *	ACCOUNT CODE	ALLOCATION	NET ENCUMBRANCE	NET DISBURSEMENT	FREE BALANCE
1001	001 01 020 0CC1 JH 0001	0.00	0.00	0.00	0.00
1002	001 02 020 0001 JH 0001	202,406.00	56,090.08	22,341.82	123,974.10
1004	001 02 020 0C01 JH 0001	26,396.00	595.70	11,042.25	14,758.05
1005	001 02 020 0CC1 JH 0001	5,000.00	764.96	54.76	4,180.28
1006	001 01 020 0CC4 JH 0001	127,600.00	1,493.20	3,722.58	122,384.22
1007	001 01 020 0CC5 JH 0001	5,402.00	186.70	512.54	4,702.76
1008	001 01 020 0CC6 JH 0001	4,300.00	183.30	373.02	3,743.68
1009	001 01 020 CCC4 JH 0001	383.00	172.25	412.78	-202.03
1010	001 01 020 0CC5 JH 0001	42.00	5.25	38.70	-1.95
1011	001 01 020 CCC6 JH 0001	0.00	0.00	0.00	0.00
1040	001 01 050 JH 0001	1,156.00	618.80	29.46	507.74
1042	001 01 050 JH 0001	2,177.00	602.78	475.20	1,099.02
1043	001 01 050 JH 0001	3,074.00	537.77	844.18	1,692.05
1044	001 01 050 JH 0001	11,710.00	2,905.40	3,361.17	5,443.43
1045	001 01 050 JH 0001	10,431.00	3,613.67	2,080.73	4,736.60
1046	001 01 050 JH 0001	623.00	10.50	250.95	361.55
1047	001 01 050 JH 0001	1,510.00	58.16	922.35	529.49
1048	001 01 050 JH 0001	0.00	0.00	0.00	0.00
1049	001 01 050 JH 0001	1,264.00	351.20	234.57	678.23
1050	001 01 050 JH 0001	1,000.00	285.55	10.48	703.97
1051	001 01 050 JH 0001	2,780.00	468.54	1,194.74	1,116.72
1052	001 01 050 JH 0001	679.00	67.80	244.62	366.58
1053	001 01 050 JH 0001	2,506.00	531.85	901.05	1,073.10
1054	001 01 050 JH 0001	6,426.00	2,619.94	1,637.60	2,168.46
1055	001 01 050 JH 0001	230.00	0.00	84.84	115.16
1056	001 01 050 JH 0001	11,151.00	2,589.99	3,944.75	4,616.26
1057	001 01 050 JH 0001	6,402.00	1,897.78	2,785.60	1,718.62
1058	001 01 050 JH 0001	1,161.00	244.45	519.51	397.04
1059	001 01 050 JH 0001	5,461.00	1,907.08	2,720.69	833.23
1060	001 01 050 JH 0001	9,457.00	3,244.18	948.94	5,263.88
1061	001 01 050 JH 0001	200.00	84.74	0.00	115.26

* AMOUNTS FOR ACCOUNTS THAT ARE FLAGGED WITH AN ASTERISK ARE NOT INCLUDED IN TOTALS

Fig. 13.15
Receiving Report

RECEIVING REPORT
WASHINGTON LIBRARY NETWORK

WASHINGTON STATE LIBRARY

| AGENCY | 385 | | | | | | | DATE PROCESSED | 790326 | PAGE 1 |

VENDOR NO.	VENDOR NAME & ADDRESS		APPROVED FOR PAYMENT	REFERENCE NO.		VOUCHER NO. 0000000056	
87044	NATL GEOGRAPHIC SOC		RECEIVED			WARRANT NO.	
	17TH & M STS, N.W.						
	WASHINGTON, DC 20036						

DESCRIPTION	ACCOUNT CODE	PURCHASE ORDER	INVOICE NO.	T	INVOICE AMOUNT
		TAX AMOUNT	PIH AMOUNT	C	
ANCIENT EGYPT, DISCOVERING ITS SPLEND	001 02 020 0001 JH 0001	79-003637	030979	C	24.95
5.30% COMPENSATING TAX	001 02 020 0001 JH 0001	1.32	.00		
*** INVOICE TOTALS ***			.00		24.95
		1.32			
*** VENDOR TOTALS ***					
TOTAL NON TAXABLE				N	.00
TOTAL SALES TAX AND PIH		.00	.00	S	.00
TOTAL COMPENSATING TAX		1.32		C	
COMPENSATING TAX	001 02 020 0001 JH 0001	1.32			
* * * * * * * * * * *	* * *	*	*	*	*
*** ACCOUNT DISTRIBUTION ***					
	001 02 020 0001 JH 0001				24.95
TOTAL TO VENDOR					24.95

Form LIB37-4 (2-78)

13. *Costcenter Report.* This report lists records in the "Standing Orders File" sorted by title within costcenter (a three-digit field). Invoice, tax, and postage, insurance, and handling (PIH) amounts are listed for each title and are totaled for each costcenter and for the report as a whole (see Figure 13.16).

14. *Account History Report.* This report lists records in the "History File" sorted by title within account number. Records are selected by a "Paid date" range supplied by the library. Invoice, tax, and PIH amounts are included for each title and are totaled for each account and for the report as a whole.

Fig. 13.16
Costcenter Report

```
                                                        WASHINGTON LIBRARY NETWORK
                                                        10/25/83          PAGE 1
GONZAGA UNIVERSITY LIBRARY
                                      STANDING ORDERS RENEWAL LIST
                                      ITEMS TO BE RENEWED BY 10/31/83
P O NUMBER   RENEWAL    VENDOR NAME          AUTHOR // TITLE // ORDER INFORMATION // SERIES
             DATE

81-0073025   10/01/83   MIDWEST LIBRARY SERV  .//DIRECTORY OF AMERICAN PHILOSOPPERS.//LATEST EDITION AVAILABLE//.

82-0078375   10/01/83   MIDWEST LIBRARY SERV                                          //SHORT-TITLE CATALOGU
                                              WING, DONALD GODDARD, 1904-
                                              E CF BOOKS PRINTED IN ENGLAND, SCOTLAND, IRELAND, WALES, 4//STANDING ORDER TO BE
                                              GIN WITH 2ND. REV. ENL. V. 1        //.

82-0079115   10/01/83   MIDWEST LIBRARY SERV  .//STUDIES IN MEDIEVAL AND RENAISSANCE HISTORY.//STANDING ORDER TO BEGIN WITH NE
                                              W SERIES V. 4//.

*                       MIDWEST LIBRARY SERV   3 ITEMS SELECTED FOR VENDOR

81-0073705   10/01/83   U S GOVERNMENT PRINT  .//CURRENT BUSINESS REPORTS. BR.//.//.

81-0073665   10/01/83   U S GOVERNMENT PRINT  .//DEPARTMENT OF STATE BULLETIN.//.//.

80-0008485   10/01/82   U S GOVERNMENT PRINT  UNITED STATES. BUREAU OF THE CENSUS.//MONTHLY SELECTED SERVICES RECEIPTS.//.//CJ
                                              RRENT BUSINESS REPORTS

80-0088105   09/01/83   U S GOVERNMENT PRINT  .//PROBLEMS OF COMMUNISM.//.//.

81-0072535   10/01/83   U S GOVERNMENT PRINT  .//THE SOCIAL SECURITY ACT AND RELATED LAWS//.//.

*                       U S GOVERNMENT PRINT   5 ITEMS SELECTED FOR VENDOR

81-0040005   12/01/82   ALLYN AND BACON       GEE, ELWOOD GORDON, 1944-//EDUCATION LAW AND THE PUBLIC SCHOOLS : A COMPENDIUM /
                                              //TO BEGIN WITH ALL UPDATES FROM 1978 AND IN CCNTINUATICN//.

*                       ALLYN AND BACON        1 ITEMS SELECTED FOR VENDOR

82-0078015   10/01/83   THOMAS PUBLISHING CO  .//THOMAS REGISTER OF AMERICAN MANUFACTURERS AND THOMAS REGISTER CATALOG FILE.//
                                              ONE SET TO BEGIN WITH THE 1981 EDITION//.

*                       THOMAS PUBLISHING CO   1 ITEMS SELECTED FOR VENDOR

80-0079935   10/17/83   CHRISTIAN SCIENCE PU  CHRISTIAN SCIENCE MONITOR PJBLISHING SOCIETY.//THE CHRISTIAN SCIENCE MONITOR.//.
                                              //.

*                       CHRISTIAN SCIENCE PU   1 ITEMS SELECTED FOR VENDOR

81-0074325   09/01/83   SCHOLARS PRESS        .//SEMEIA.//.//.

*                       SCHOLARS PRESS         1 ITEMS SELECTED FOR VENDOR

80-0089805   10/01/83   BLACKWELL, B H        .//L'ANNEE BALZACIENNE.//.//.

80-0080205   10/01/83   BLACKWELL, B H        .//MUSICA BRITANNICA.//.//.

80-0078395   10/01/83   BLACKWELL, B H        .//THE NEW CAMBRIDGE MODERN HISTORY.//REV. EDS. ONLY//.

*                       BLACKWELL, B H         3 ITEMS SELECTED FOR VENDOR
```

THE UTLAS SYSTEM

The UTLAS system (Online Acquisitions Control System) is similar to the other bibliographic utilities in that the basic functions are covered—verification to payment. What is special about their system and WLN is that, unlike OCLC and RLIN, it is possible to place many orders electronically: "speedier service through electronic communication with vendors holding UTLAS vendor accounts." Another special feature of UTLAS is its international scope; the bibliographic data base for verification covers much more than American publishers' output and publications in the English language. Certainly RLIN with its research library orientation is somewhat international in scope, but it cannot compare to a system that includes—in addition to the Library of Congress, the National Library of Medicine, and the MARC tapes—the National Library of Canada, the British Library, and 600 other academic, public, special, and government libraries (including four Japanese university libraries) around the world. There are more than 15 million bibliographic and authority records in the UTLAS system.

COMMERCIAL SYSTEMS

Innovative Interfaces, Inc. (III), has a system (INNOVACQ) that operates on its own or can be fully integrated into the UTLAS system and other utilities, although they do not publicize that fact as openly as UTLAS does. Anyone who has seen a demonstration of INNOVACQ is impressed by the power of the system including the graphics. Demonstrations of a serials module that they are developing are equally impressive. The major problem from the library's point of view is that the system must be operated on a computer system developed by III. For many libraries the cost is too great despite the quality of the system.

Midwest Library Service has a system (MATSS) that was developed at the Tacoma Public Library. At present the system is compatible and can interface with OCLC and WLN. By means of the interface system a library can verify, order, claim, and handle fund accounting. It can also produce catalog cards and spine labels. Since the system is available through Midwest Library Service (MLS), orders can be placed electronically with MLS. Like most of the major systems, the IBM PC is the system of "Preference" although other intelligent terminal systems can be employed.

DataPhase and CL Systems, Inc. (CLSI) are examples of independent systems available from firms that do not sell library collection material. DataPhase's system operates as a complete package covering most library functions that can be economically automated at the present time: circulation, reserve book room, technical services (cataloging), acquisitions, bookings (audio-visual) and backup security. DataPhase provides for system interface with RLIN, OCLC, and others for bibliographic data.

A special feature of CLSI's system is its routing subsystem. It allows for the tracking of an item and it has a time factor element. This subsystem could be used to route periodicals and other materials to staff members as well as to monitor the length of time the items are held. Very often a person receives an item, does not immediately have time to read or examine it in detail, sets it aside for future use, and then forgets about it. The subsystem, with its time element, could alert the person responsible for routing items that an item has been "forgotten."

BOOK TRADE AND BOOK VENDOR SYSTEMS

R. R. Bowker now offers the Bowker Acquisition System (BAS). Access to BAS is through the Bibliographic Retrieval Services (BRS) that readers may know about as an online retrieval service that the reference department may search from time to time. According to Bowker, the BAS is a simple method for the user to send book orders to the vendor of choice. The simplest order requires only the Standard Address Number (SAN) of the vendor, the International Standard Book Number (ISBN), and the quantity of each book. One can imagine how useful this system would be for bookstores and for acquisition departments, if it interfaced with the automated acquisition system that was in use. It is possible to search Bowker's online version of *BIP* (known as BBIP). The system can be used for inquiries or claims and cancellation routines as well as for ordering. Orders, claims, and cancellations are normally printed at night by Bowker and mailed to the appropriate vendor; for some vendors it is possible to have Bowker transmit transactions electronically the same day and avoid printing and mail delays. A limited amount of fund accounting is possible in the system, but it is not as good as those found in other automatic acquisition systems. The major advantages of using the BAS system are speed in ordering and having the most current pricing and availability information immediately at your terminal.

Baker and Taylor, one of the largest book jobbers in the United States, has several automated acquisition systems available: LIBRIS II^{tm} is a system tied into the Baker and Taylor mainframe computer system, and several variations under Bata SYSTEMS^{tm} are designed to allow libraries to use their computer systems.

LIBRIS II is a more fully developed version of the LIBRIS system described in the fourth edition of this book. Searching is done in the approximately 350,000 title data base created by Baker and Taylor. The data base is updated weekly, much as the Bowker BBIP, to reflect the latest status of a title. Orders can be generated online and electronic order placement to Baker and Taylor is possible. Electronic order placement starts Baker and Taylor fulfillment procedures within 24 hours, saving significant time, especially for rush orders. The system allows for fund accounting and is capable of retaining both the current and previous years' budgets for reconciliation purposes. A warning system is incorporated into accounting systems to protect against overspending a fund. Posting of receipt and back order information is automatically handled for Baker and Taylor orders. (*Note: the system can be used to print orders for other vendors.*)

Three services are available under the Bata SYSTEMS^{tm} program: 1) Title Search and Order; 2) Full Acquisition System; and 3) Title Confirmation Service. Title Search and Order is an online service that allows the library to search Baker and Taylor's data base, order electronically from Baker and Taylor, and print order slips using an asynchronous terminal, a 300 or 1200 baud modem, and a printer. The Full Acquisition System is a combination software package and online service that enables the library to control all ordering, fund accounting, and report functions by using a personal computer. Hardware requirements are a single disk drive computer with a 64-256k RAM and hard disk with a minimum storage capacity of 10 megabytes using either MS/DOS or D/PM operating system (for example, IBM PC/XT, Texas Instrument's Professional, the Tandy 2000, or the Kaypro 10), a 1200-baud modem, and an 80-column printer. The Title Confirmation Service is a software package for personal computers that allows book orders to be keyed in by ISBN and sent on phone lines toll free to Baker and Taylor. Bibliographic data is transmitted back to the library for on-site printing of slips and title confirmation. Unfortunately, at the present time this service will only work with IBM, Apple, or TRS-80 personal computers (single disk drive and 64k RAM). A library must also have a 1200-band modem and an 80-column printer.

One other service (that became available in 1984) from Baker and Taylor is the Bata PHONE[tm]. This device is a hand-held data terminal which allows libraries, that do not own IBM, Apple, or TRS-80 personal computers, to place electronic orders with Baker and Taylor. It is a small battery-powered device that attaches to a telephone using an acoustical coupler. Orders are placed using the ISBN and up to 340 titles per order are possible. Baker and Taylor mails a printed acknowledgment of the order within 24 hours of receipt of the order. It also offers, as an optional feature, to send an individual order slip for each title to the library.

REVIEW QUESTIONS

1. What are the basic types of automated acquisitions now on the market?

2. What are some of the charges that are involved in online acquisition systems?

3. List the ten desirable features of an automated acquisition system.

4. Describe the features that distinguish OCLC, RLIN, and WLN acquisition systems.

5. What are the advantages of using commercial acquisition systems?

14

GIFTS AND EXCHANGE

Very often the acquisition department has a unit to handle the library's gifts and exchange program. This unit checks items received against the library's holdings and against the desiderata list maintained by the acquisition department. If an item is wanted, it will be sent to the catalog department for processing, along with any relevant bibliographic information. Occasionally, gifts and exchange will receive items not on the want list, but that are considered worthwhile additions to the collection. Often, however, gifts are duplicate items or are simply inappropriate for the collection. Since these have to be disposed of in some way, many libraries have set up some type of exchange program.

GIFTS SECTION

The gifts section has a number of responsibilities. A library with a special collections department may actively attempt to secure gifts from various donors (often from an individual's private collection). The ultimate selection of gifts is the responsibility of the librarians, and even the smallest library will receive a few gift items during the course of a year. The primary function of a gifts section is to evaluate any materials donated and to decide what to do with them.

An important tool for this unit is the library's written policy regarding gifts, which provides the framework within which the unit makes its decisions. The same criteria used to select materials for purchase should be applied to gift items. The fact that the library has not paid anything to acquire an item does *not* mean that it is totally cost-free and should be added automatically to the collection. If an item is something the library would not buy on the open market, it probably should not be retained. In addition to establishing criteria for selection, the policy should include information regarding disposal rights, deposit items, memorial gifts, special labeling for gift items, and the acceptance of funds to purchase materials. It is almost impossible to establish an effective gifts unit without a written policy statement.

Checking gift items requires the same verification skills needed for bibliographic checking. The basic difference between checking request slips and checking gifts is that, in the latter case, the actual item is in hand. The gifts unit is thus concerned only with whether the library wants the item. The search procedure to be followed is the same procedure used in bibliographic checking after the existence of the item has been established. Consequently, a sound understanding of the rules of entry can save time and effort in gift checking.

The cost of processing and storage means that no library can afford to add unnecessary items; thus, the checking process is very important. On the other hand, since no library can afford to discard valuable or needed items, it is particularly important to check older books with great care. Variations in printings and editions make all the difference between a valuable item and a worthless one. An item that first seems to be of great value may prove less valuable because it is a second or third rather than the first printing. Because of the problems involved in checking rare items, this work is carried on by persons with extensive training and experience, and under close supervision.

Only a very small percentage of the items given to any library are added to the collection. A large library rejects a high percentage of gifts because they are already in the collection, which means a rather high cost per item added. Careful training and efficient work procedures will help keep this unit cost as low as possible, but it will still be high in comparison to purchased items. Gifts also confront the library with the problem of disposing of a great many unwanted items, but this is usually the exchange unit's responsibility.

EXCHANGE SECTION

There are two basic types of exchange activity: the exchange of unwanted and duplicate materials, and the exchange of new materials between libraries. The latter, the exchange of new materials, usually confined to large university or research libraries, is in essence a trading of the publications of cooperating institutions. For example, the University of California libraries might exchange University of California publications with New York State University libraries for their university publications. This system is sometimes used to acquire materials from countries whose commercial trade operations are limited. Such exchanges are established through formal agreements between the cooperating organizations. The technician's role consists only of maintaining records of what has been sent and received.

All types of libraries engage in the exchange of unwanted and/or duplicate materials. Not all libraries become involved in full-scale exchange programs, but every library is confronted with disposing of unwanted material. Technicians can and should play a major role in the operation of this type of exchange unit.

Frequently, the library prepares a list of unwanted items and sends it to the exchange units in other libraries. The first library to request an item on the list gets it for the shipping cost (normally this is the book rate postage). Lists of this type are produced and sent throughout the year. The basic activities of the exchange unit include, then:

1) organizing unwanted materials into some logical order;

2) preparing and distributing lists of materials available for exchange;

3) checking lists of exchange materials from other libraries; and

4) packing and shipping items requested by other libraries.

All of these activities can be carried out and supervised by technicians under the direction of librarians.

Unwanted material is also sold to secondhand book dealers, usually in blocks of items rather than as individual titles. Normally, no cash is involved, but credit is extended to the library in the amount agreed upon. This credit memo goes to the bookkeeping department for recording in the account book as a credit

Holding a book sale is another method of disposing of unwanted materials, but it is very time-consuming. The exchange staff must choose the materials to be sold, find a suitable location, and staff the area during the sale. Most libraries find this unprofitable, since the amount of staff time involved is not always justified by the returns. Nevertheless, it does clear out a number of items that might not be disposed of by any other method (and having the "friends of the library" group conduct the sale might mitigate some of those costs).

Some libraries have found it useful to join USBE (Universal Serials and Book Exchange, Inc.), a nonprofit organization that helps in handling duplicate and other unwanted materials. USBE has been in existence since 1949 and functions as a clearinghouse for publications from all countries and subject fields. It receives, holds, and distributes publications (within the guidelines established by a governing board of librarians) from and for its more than 1,000 member libraries. As of January 1984, its stock consisted of more than 4 million copies of periodical issues from about 40,000 serial titles and something in excess of 75,000 books and government documents.

Member libraries may deposit, with prior approval, *any* periodical or serial (except newspapers), single issues, and complete volumes (bound or unbound) on any subject in any language. Books and government documents are acceptable on these grounds, except for science and technology items (these should be ten years old or younger unless a classic in the field). A library draws against its deposits by requesting needed items and paying the handling fees. No money is involved, but a good deal of record keeping is required, and there is an annual membership fee.

It is possible to order materials from USBE, Inc., using online through: 1) BRS message switching system, 2) OCLC interlibrary loan subsystem, 3) UTLAS MAIL BOX system, or 4) DIALOG's DIALORDER facility. Rush orders are accepted and are responded to on the same day if received before 11:00 A.M. eastern standard time, or the next day if received after 11:00 A.M.

The final method of disposition is simply to throw the material out and have it destroyed. The exchange section must be *very* certain that the material is of no value to anyone before using this drastic method of disposition.

REVIEW QUESTIONS

1. Describe two methods, other than purchasing, that libraries use to acquire materials.

2. Why must the checking of gifts be done so carefully?

3. What helps in the decision to keep or dispose of a gift item?

4. How does an exchange program differ from a gift program?

5. Describe the common methods for disposing of unwanted gifts.

6. What does USBE stand for?

7. What is USBE's main purpose?

8. How does USBE operate?

Cataloging is the process of preparing a bibliographic record by describing a work and assigning it a call number. The purpose of cataloging is to assist in communicating to library users the library's holdings and the location of each item. Therefore, the public catalog should include the information required for both identifying and locating materials—information provided by processes commonly known as "descriptive cataloging" and "subject cataloging." Descriptive cataloging establishes an item's identity through describing it, determining its "main entry," and selecting "added entries" for it. Subject cataloging consists of assigning "subject headings" and a "unique call number."

The cataloging process is by no means limited to books, as the continuing "knowledge explosion" and new forms of electronic communication present new problems and challenges to libraries. At present, a typical medium-sized library will have a collection composed of books, periodicals, newspapers, maps, music scores, microforms, motion pictures, filmstrips, sound recordings, machine-readable data files, prints, realia, and videotapes.

This text will emphasize book cataloging because the book remains the most common item in most libraries. This emphasis, however, is much less than in earlier editions, because the latest cataloging rules stress general principles of cataloging applicable to all kinds of materials. Examples of cataloging for non-book materials are included, then, as well as those for books.

The latest cataloging rules, the second edition of the *Anglo-American Cataloguing Rules* (Chicago: American Library Association, 1978), stress basic cataloging principles for all material. Earlier cataloging rules stressed books, while almost ignoring non-book material. These rules, *AACR 2*, will be discussed in later chapters.

CATALOGING—TECHNICAL AND PUBLIC SERVICES

All library staff, not just those in the cataloging department, need a basic knowledge of cataloging. The ability to identify a work and to determine its main entry is essential for acquisitions work, since without some cataloging skills, incorrect or duplicate materials may be ordered. In fact, the acquisition department often establishes main entry.

In public service work, especially at reference service points, the LMTA must know how to use the catalog, be able to show the patron how to use the catalog, and know the kinds of information that can and cannot be found in the catalog.

This requires a basic knowledge both of descriptive cataloging and of the rules for main entries, filing rules, subject heading construction, and of the classification scheme. Unless the LMTA knows this information, it will be like the "blind leading the blind." And those library patrons who realize that the "helper" knows as little as they do, perhaps will be reluctant to ask further questions.

All too often, LMTAs who want to work in public services consider technical services and cataloging as something to avoid. This is a mistake. A knowledge of *all* aspects of technical services, especially cataloging, is an asset in most public service positions. By the same token, a knowledge of public service operations is helpful in technical services.

CATALOGING TERMINOLOGY

Understanding cataloging terminology is essential for understanding the cataloging process, so the terms below should be learned before reading further. (Other important terms will be covered in later chapters.)

Access point. An entry in a library catalog that will help a user locate a particular item. Refers to the main entry, added entries, and subject entries. *See also* Entry.

Added entry. An entry made in addition to the main entry. Added entries can be made for joint authors, editors and compilers, translators, illustrators, titles, series, and subjects.
See also Main entries.

Area. A major section of a bibliographic description. Examples are the physical description area and the publication, distribution, etc. area.

Author. The person chiefly responsible for the intellectual or artistic content of a work. A *personal author* is a person responsible for the work; this can be an author, artist, cartographer, composer, or performer.
See also Corporate body.

Book number. A combination of letters and numbers assigned as part of a call number to maintain an (alphabetical) order among works with the same classification number and to insure that each item has a unique call number.

Call number. The notation used to identify and locate a particular work. The notation consists of a classification number and book number; it may also include other identifying symbols.

Catalog. A list of the holdings of a particular library or group of libraries.

Cataloging. The process of describing a work bibliographically and assigning a call number. Includes determining the main entry, describing the work, and assigning added entries, subject entries, and a call number.
See also Descriptive cataloging and Subject cataloging.

Classification number. The number assigned to a work to show its subject and to indicate its location in the collection.

Collation. The element in a bibliographic description that gives the number of its pages, volumes, illustrations, size, and accompanying materials. *See also* Physical description area.

Corporate body. A group of individuals or an organization identified by a name and acting as the entity responsible for a work.

Cutter number. A number from the *Cutter* or *Cutter-Sanborn Tables* used to create a book number.
See also Book number.

Descriptive cataloging. The cataloging process concerned with describing a work, identifying the main entry, and selecting added entries.

Dictionary catalog. A catalog in which all entries – author, title, added, and subject – are filed in one alphabet.

Divided catalog. A catalog in two or more sections. It usually consists of a separate author/title/added entry catalog and a separate subject catalog.

Entry. A record of an item in a catalog. In addition to the main entry, there are title entries, series entries, and other types of added entries and subject entries.
See also Access point.

Imprint. Place of publication, publisher's name, and date of publication for a book.

Main entry. A full catalog entry giving all the information necessary for identifying a work. The main entry includes the tracings for all other entries or access points under which a work is entered in the catalog. The main entry is usually an author entry.

Personal author. *See* Author.

Physical description area. The area in a bibliographic description used to give the physical description of a work. (For example, for a book, this area would give the number of pages, illustrative matter, and size.)

Publication, distribution, etc., area. The area in a bibliographic description used to record information about the place, name, and date of publishing, distributing, releasing, and issuing activities. (For a motion picture, for example, this area would give the place of publication or distribution; the name of the publisher, distributor or releasing agency; and the date of publication or distribution.)

Subject cataloging. The cataloging process concerned with determining the subject of a work and the selection of subject headings and a classification number.

Subject entry. An entry or access point in a catalog under a subject heading.

Subject heading. A word, name, phrase, or acronym describing the subject of a work.

Title. The name of a work.

Title proper. The chief part of a title. (For example, for a book title, *Cataloging with Copy: A Decision-Maker's Handbook*, the title proper is *Cataloging with Copy.*)

Tracings. The record, usually on the main entry and shelflist, of all additional entries for a work in a catalog.

Unit card. A basic catalog card, in the form of a main entry, with complete cataloging information. The cards can be used for all entries when the appropriate heading is typed at the top of each card.

THE CATALOG

The library catalog, the main product of the cataloging process, is the single most important reference tool in a library, since it would be difficult if not impossible to use even a moderate-sized library without a catalog. Catalogs are constructed to accomplish certain specific goals, some of which originally were stated by Charles Cutter nearly 100 years ago and are still applicable today. Cutter believed a library's catalog should:

(A)   Allow someone to locate materials if that person knows either
    (1)   The author,
    (2)   The title, or
    (3)   The subject.

(B)   Show the library's holdings
    (4)   By a given author,
    (5)   On a given subject, or
    (6)   In a given kind of literature (poetry, drama, fiction)

(C)   Assist in the choice of a work
    (7)   As to edition by describing the work adequately for easy identification (author, title, edition, etc.), and
    (8)   As to its character — topical or literary — and its location.[1]

Goals 1, 2, 4, and 7 are accomplished by the descriptive cataloging process — determining author entry, title entry, and the description of the work. Goals 3, 5, 6, and 8 are satisfied by the subject cataloging process — assigning subject headings and a call number.

A 1961 restatement of cataloging principles used in modern cataloging codes (*The Paris Principles*) practically restated Cutter's original objectives, thus testifying to the soundness of Cutter's thought.[2]

Catalog Characteristics

In addition to Cutter's principles of the function of a catalog, a catalog must possess certain other qualities. There are four basic criteria on which to judge a catalog:

1) *The catalog should be flexible.* Libraries constantly add and delete materials, and the catalog must reflect these changes. As materials are added or discarded, the catalog should reflect this. A "book catalog" is not very flexible and may quickly be out of date. The "card catalog" and "online computer catalog" are very flexible forms of a catalog; materials can be added or deleted rapidly.

2) *The entries or access points in a catalog must be easy to find.* Labeling drawers in a card catalog is an example of an aid for locating access points. Locating access points in a printed book catalog is relatively easy. Difficulties do arise when the card catalog or book catalog becomes very large.

3) *A catalog should be easy to produce and relatively inexpensive to maintain. All* catalogs, however, are expensive.

4) *The catalog should be compact or even portable.* The card catalog is neither compact nor portable compared to the book catalog or a catalog on microfilm. An online computer-based catalog may be compact (and possibly portable if terminals are located outside the library).

Card Catalog

The most widely used type of catalog in the United States, the card catalog, was developed in its modern form in the last part of the nineteenth century, and it took firm hold only in the early part of the twentieth century. The easy availability of printed catalog cards from the Library of Congress (starting in 1901) was a major reason that the card catalog became well established. With the initiation of this service, libraries were assured of the continuing availability of cards from a reliable source with high standards of cataloging. The availability of inexpensive printed cards from a number of commercial suppliers added to the popularity of the card catalog. Unless otherwise stated, then, all references to catalogs in this text will mean a card catalog.

The card catalog consists of 7.5x12.5 cm. (approximately 3x5-inch) cards filed in trays in some known order (usually alphabetical). A 15-tray (or -drawer) catalog means that there are 15 removable trays housed in one physical unit. About 800-900 cards can be filed in a tray. Each tray is labeled to show the exact sequence of cards filed therein.

Fig. 15.1
Catalog Tray Label

A - ARI

The label in Figure 15.1 means that the access points or entries in that tray start with "A" and end with a word starting with the three letters "ARI" (i.e., Aardvark to **Arizona**).

The continuing popularity of the card catalog is due to certain of its inherent qualities, the most important being:

1) Flexibility:
   a) cards can be arranged in any way suitable to a library — alphabetically or by call number
   b) the catalog can be in dictionary or divided format
   c) the catalog can be kept current by adding or removing cards
   d) drawers can be removed for easier access

2) Ease of use:
   a) the card catalog is relatively easy to use if the user understands the filing rules
   b) guide cards, cross-references, and consistency in the forms of authors' names and subject headings make the catalog an efficient tool for the experienced user
   c) printed or typed cards are easy to read

3) Cost to produce and maintain:
   a) no catalog is inexpensive, but if an up-to-date catalog is necessary, the card catalog still compares favorably with other formats[3]
   b) printed and computer-produced cards are readily available, reducing in-library card production to a minimum level
   c) in-library mechanical reproduction of catalog cards is easy and inexpensive (i.e., photocopying)
   d) cards can be added or removed as material is added or withdrawn from the collection
   e) cards can be removed for corrections
   f) maintenance consists mostly of adding and removing cards, making references, and maintaining consistency of names and subject headings

The card catalog scores positive marks on three of the four characteristics of a catalog discussed earlier. The card catalog, however, is not particularly compact and not portable, and some other disadvantages of the card catalog must be mentioned:

1) Only one entry at a time can be seen; a book catalog or computer terminal display can display a list of entries.

2) As the catalog grows, it becomes more complex and difficult to use.

3) Over time, inconsistency in names and subject headings may appear.

4) Different cataloging rules create differences in the appearance and information on the catalog cards.

5) Larger libraries have a problem with the space required by such a catalog, which may consist of thousands of trays.

6) Catalogs are relatively expensive pieces of equipment and smaller libraries have some problems in purchasing one.

7) The card catalog offers little security against vandalism or theft of cards.

All information must be copied by hand; a computer terminal display or a microformat catalog could have a printout device attached.

Changes in the cataloging process such as computer applications and the adoption of the *Anglo-American Cataloguing Rules*, second edition (*AACR 2*), will have a major impact on the card catalog. (Some of these new developments will be discussed in later chapters.) Many librarians expect the card catalog to be replaced in the next decade by a computer with CRT display terminals. The speed of these changes will depend in large measure on local financial considerations and clear evidence that the new technology will serve library needs. Consequently, since the card catalog will remain the most common type of catalog for the next few years, it will be emphasized in this text.

Other Catalog Formats

Even though the card catalog will probably remain the most popular type of catalog in the 1980s, other catalog formats are found in libraries. Several, such as COM catalogs and online computer catalogs, will become increasingly common.

The "book catalog" or printed catalog was first used in the late sixteenth century and reached its peak popularity in the late nineteenth century. Once widely accepted, it was later rejected because of its high cost and inflexibility. As collections began to grow rapidly in the twentieth century, the book catalog was difficult to update and the cost of constantly printing new editions was prohibitive. An example of a book catalog is the *National Union Catalog*. Yet, the book catalog is currently making a comeback in special situations because its cost is being reduced by the use of computers and high-speed printout units. Its advantages are several: 1) it is compact and requires little space relative to a card catalog; 2) a whole page of entries can be viewed at one time; and 3) multiple copies allow use anyplace in or even outside of the library. Disadvantages are: 1) it is too expensive to reproduce in its entirety for daily updating; 2) updating is usually accomplished by issuing supplements, which means the catalog user must look in several files; and 3) older book catalogs will not show materials removed from the collection unless they are constantly updated.

The "COM" (computer output microform) catalog is a relatively new format for general library use, although the process itself is not new. Computer output microform is produced when a computer converts electronic symbols to characters on microfilm at a rate of 10-15,000 lines a minute. The microform output is usually on 105x148 mm. microfiche or 16 mm. microfilm. The COM format is growing in popularity, and because of catalog problems created by the adoption of *AACR 2*, many libraries are considering using COM. Some advantages of the COM catalog are: 1) it is inexpensive to reproduce and can be placed in many locations inside and outside of a library; 2) there can be separate films for author entries, title entries, and subject entries; 3) several records can be viewed at one time; 4) entries can be easily copied if a microform reader/printer is available; and 5) equipment is relatively inexpensive. Some disadvantages of COM are: 1) microforms are often not very readable compared to print; 2) it is not easily updated as new materials are added; 3) updating is by supplements, which may confuse the catalog user who must look in several files; 4) the microfiche format may lead to accidental intermingling of a base catalog with supplements, etc.; 5) rearrangement of information is difficult; 6) deleted materials will remain in the file until the next update; and 7) desirable equipment, such as microform reader/printers, can require a large investment.

The "online public access catalog" is the newest, most sophisticated catalog format. Information is stored in a computer memory and displayed on a television screen called a CRT* terminal. This format has the most promise and will likely be the catalog of the future. Unfortunately, the high cost of an online catalog places it beyond the means of most libraries, at least for the next few years. One possibility that may speed up the online format is the rapidly decreasing cost of minicomputer and microprocessors, which may make local catalogs possible in the next few years. Also there needs to be more development of software to support the many demands placed on a catalog. Some advantages of an online catalog are: 1) it is easily updated; 2) it can easily provide cross-references for authors and subjects; 3) CRT terminals can be made available at many locations; 4) new access points and search capabilities can be added at any time; 5) the output can be manipulated and can be in printed format or on a CRT screen; 6) it is possible to create union catalogs among several libraries by electronic communication; and 7) studies of patron use of operating online catalogs show a high level of user satisfaction. Some disadvantages are: 1) the equipment is currently expensive and beyond the means of most libraries; 2) some costs (such as literature searches resulting in hardcopy printouts) may have to be charged to the patron; 3) failure of the equipment or loss of electricity will mean no access to the collection via the catalog; 4) there may be lines (queuing problems in computerese!) at CRT terminals at busy times; 5) catalog users may need more library staff assistance and even formal training in using the terminals; and 6) library staffs may have to receive extensive retraining.

The professional discussion about catalog formats and the role of the computer-based catalog will continue for the foreseeable future. Because of the large amount of funding needed to install them, the problem also will be political as well as professional. The next decade will see major changes in both cataloging procedures and catalog formats as profound as the changes the card catalog made nearly a century ago.

THE CATALOG CARD

The catalog card is the basic component used to enter information in a card catalog. The catalog card has been standardized at 7.5x12.5 cm. (approximately 3x5-inches) since 1901. Each card in a catalog represents an access point or entry for a work in the library. But each book or other item is represented in the catalog by a *set* of cards. The set usually consists of "unit cards"—each card is identical except for the headings on the top lines, which represent the different access points (Figure 15.3, page 151). Notice in Figure 15.3 that there is a card for each entry listed in the tracings. The "main entry card" has no heading on the top line. The components of a catalog card are shown in Figure 15.2 (page 150) and a complete set of cards is shown in Figure 15.3.[4]

(Text continues on page 153.)

---

*Also called a VDT (visual display terminal). We will use CRT in this text.

Fig. 15.2
Identification of Information Included in a Catalog Card
(Library of Congress Card)

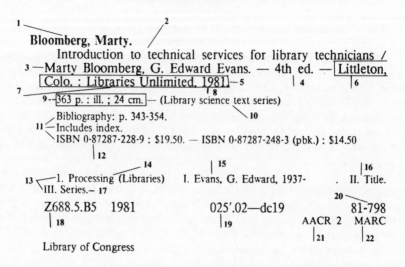

Key for Figure 15.2

1. Heading: author's name (main entry)
2. Title proper
3. Statement of responsibility
4. Edition statement
5. Publication, distribution, etc. area
6. Place of publication
7. Publisher
8. Date of publication
9. Physical description area
10. Series statement
11. Notes
12. Standard number (ISBN)
13. Tracings

14. Subject heading (Subject entries are preceded by arabic numerals.)
15. Added entry for personal name (Added entries are preceded by roman numerals.)
16. Title added entry
17. Series added entry
18. Library of Congress call number
19. Dewey classification number
20. Library of Congress card number
21. Cataloging code used (*Anglo-American Cataloguing Rules*, 2nd ed.)
22. MARC (Acronym for Machine-Readable Cataloging) indicates that the cataloging information is available in machine-readable format.

Fig. 15.3
Complete Set of Catalog Cards

Main entry

Bloomberg, Marty.
Introduction to technical services for library technicians /
Marty Bloomberg, G. Edward Evans. — 4th ed. — Littleton,
Colo. : Libraries Unlimited, 1981.

363 p. : ill. ; 24 cm. — (Library science text series)

Bibliography: p. 343-354.
Includes index.
ISBN 0-87287-228-9 : $19.50. — ISBN 0-87287-248-3 (pbk.) : $14.50

1. Processing (Libraries)   I. Evans, G. Edward, 1937-   . II. Title.
III. Series.

Z688.5.B5   1981   025'.02—dc19   81-798
                                                        AACR 2   MARC

Library of Congress

Subject entry

PROCESSING (LIBRARIES)

Bloomberg, Marty.
Introduction to technical services for library technicians /
Marty Bloomberg, G. Edward Evans. — 4th ed. — Littleton,
Colo. : Libraries Unlimited, 1981.

363 p. : ill. ; 24 cm. — (Library science text series)

Bibliography: p. 343-354.
Includes index.
ISBN 0-87287-228-9 : $19.50. — ISBN 0-87287-248-3 (pbk.) : $14.50

1. Processing (Libraries)   I. Evans, G. Edward, 1937-   . II. Title.
III. Series.

Z688.5.B5   1981   025'.02—dc19   81-798
                                                        AACR 2   MARC

Library of Congress

Added entry: Personal name

Evans, G. Edward, 1937–

Bloomberg, Marty.
 Introduction to technical services for library technicians /
Marty Bloomberg, G. Edward Evans. — 4th ed. — Littleton,
Colo. : Libraries Unlimited, 1981.

 363 p. : ill. ; 24 cm. — (Library science text series)

 Bibliography: p. 343-354.
 Includes index.
 ISBN 0-87287-228-9 : $19.50. — ISBN 0-87287-248-3 (pbk.) : $14.50

 1. Processing (Libraries)   I. Evans, G. Edward, 1937-   . II. Title.
III. Series.

Z688.5.B5   1981   025′.02—dc19   81-798
                                                       AACR 2   MARC

Library of Congress

Added entry: Title

Introduction to technical services for
 library technicians
Bloomberg, Marty.
 Introduction to technical services for library technicians /
Marty Bloomberg, G. Edward Evans. — 4th ed. — Littleton,
Colo. : Libraries Unlimited, 1981.

 363 p. : ill. ; 24 cm. — (Library science text series)

 Bibliography: p. 343-354.
 Includes index.
 ISBN 0-87287-228-9 : $19.50. — ISBN 0-87287-248-3 (pbk.) : $14.50

 1. Processing (Libraries)   I. Evans, G. Edward, 1937-   . II. Title.
III. Series.

Z688.5.B5   1981   025′.02—dc19   81-798
                                                       AACR 2   MARC

Library of Congress

Added entry: Series

Library science text series

Bloomberg, Marty.
　　Introduction to technical services for library technicians /
Marty Bloomberg, G. Edward Evans. — 4th ed. — Littleton,
Colo. : Libraries Unlimited, 1981.

　　363 p. : ill. ; 24 cm. — (Library science text series)

　　Bibliography: p. 343-354.
　　Includes index.
　　ISBN 0-87287-228-9 : $19.50. — ISBN 0-87287-248-3 (pbk.) : $14.50

　　1. Processing (Libraries)　　I. Evans, G. Edward, 1937-　　.　II. Title.
III. Series.

Z688.5.B5　1981　　　　　　　　025'.02—dc19　　　　　　81-798
　　　　　　　　　　　　　　　　　　　　　　AACR 2　MARC

Library of Congress

The cards in Figures 15.2 and 15.3 are Library of Congress cards. Libraries
also order printed or computer-produced cards from commercial sources such as
OCLC, Blackwell North America, Midwest Library Service, and RLIN (see
Figure 15.4, page 154). The commercial suppliers usually sell cards in sets, with
headings for added entries and subject entries already printed at the tops of the
cards.

Fig. 15.4
OCLC Computer-Produced Card Set*

Main entry

DS
558 Herring, George C., 1936-
H45 America's longest war : the United States and Vietnam,
1950-1975 / George C. Herring. -- New York : Wiley, 1979.
298 p. ; 22 cm. -- (America in
crisis.)
Bibliography.
Includes index.

1. Vietnamese Conflict, 1961-1975--United States. 2. Vietnam--History--1945-1975. 3. United States--History--1945- 4. United States--Foreign relations--Vietnam. 5. Vietnam--Foreign relations--United States. I. Title.

[1]03 DEC 79 [2]5126110 [3]CSBMnt [4]79-16408

Key to Note Items in Figure 15.4

1. Date card was ordered
2. OCLC Control Number
3. Holding Record (California State University, San Bernardino
4. LC card number

Subject entry

VIETNAMESE CONFLICT, 1961-1975--
UNITED STATES.

DS
558 Herring, George C., 1936-
H45 America's longest war : the United States and Vietnam,
1950-1975 / George C. Herring. -- New York: Wiley, 1979.
298 p. ; 22 cm. -- (America in
crisis.)

*Reproduced with the permission of OCLC.

Fig. 15.4 (cont'd)

Subject entry

VIETNAM--HISTORY--1945-1975.

DS
558   Herring, George C., 1936-
H45   America's longest war : the United States and Vietnam,
        1950-1975 / George C. Herring. -- New York : Wiley, 1979.
            298 p. ; 22 cm. -- (America in
        crisis.)

Subject entry

UNITED STATES--HISTORY--1945-

DS
558   Herring, George C., 1936-
H45   America's longest war : the United States and Vietnam,
        1950-1975 / George C. Herring. -- New York : Wiley, 1979.
            298 p. ; 22 cm. -- (America in
        crisis.)

Subject entry

UNITED STATES--FOREIGN RELATIONS--
        VIETNAM.

DS
558   Herring, George C., 1936-
H45   America's longest war : the United States and Vietnam,
        1950-1975 / George C. Herring. -- New York : Wiley, 1979.
            298 p. ; 22 cm. -- (America in
        crisis.)

Fig. 15.4 (cont'd)

Subject entry

VIETNAM--FOREIGN RELATIONS--UNITED
STATES.

DS
558   Herring, George C., 1936-
H45   America's longet war : the United States and Vietnam,
             1950-1975 / George C. Herring. -- New York : Wiley, 1979.
             298 p. ; 22 cm. -- (America in
             crisis.)

Title entry

America's longest war

DS
558   Herring, George C., 1936-
H45   America's longet war : the United States and Vietnam,
             1950-1975 / George C. Herring. -- New York : Wiley, 1979.
             298 p. ; 22 cm. -- (America in
             crisis.)

ROLE OF THE PARAPROFESSIONAL IN CATALOGING

The role of the paraprofessional in a cataloging department varies among libraries. Some libraries allow paraprofessionals only to type, file, and do very simple cataloging routines. In other libraries, after a suitable period of training, paraprofessionals do descriptive and subject cataloging in addition to the more routine clerical duties. The tasks assigned paraprofessionals in a cataloging department are based primarily on the attitudes and philosophy of the librarians. Other secondary factors may include the abilities of paraprofessionals on the staff, institutional policies, collective bargaining agreements, and the personnel budget.

Although the paraprofessionals may have little opportunity to be directly involved in the formulation of professional outlook, they should be aware of the basis for the division of duties in a library. Recognition that libraries differ in the roles they allow paraprofessionals to fill is important in obtaining job satisfaction. Before accepting a job in a library, the paraprofessional should be aware both of the librarians' expectations and of the responsibilities assigned to paraprofessionals.

An example of division of labor in a cataloging department is given in Figure 15.5. The example shows the broad divisions of cataloging activities, but it does not attempt to cover every duty in a cataloging department.

Fig. 15.5
Cataloging Activities

CATALOGING ACTIVITIES	PERSONNEL			
	Librarian	LMTA	Library Clerk	Part-Time Help (Students)
1. Establishes policies and procedures	X			
2. Supervision	X	X		
3. Performs bibliographic checking for main entries		X	X	X
4. Solves difficult bibliographic checking problems	X	X		
5. Catalogs material with cataloging information available		X	X	
6. Operates computer-based cataloging service terminal (e.g., OCLC)	X	X	X	
7. Original cataloging	X	X		
8. Does descriptive and subject cataloging of problem material	X	X		
9. Revises cataloging	X	X		
10. Catalogs by comparing printed cards to books			X	X
11. Revised cataloging using printed cards		X		
12. Types catalog cards			X	X
13. Revises typing of catalog cards		X		
14. Files in catalogs			X	X
15. Revises filing		X	X	
16. Files in shelflist			X	
17. Revises shelflist filing		X		
18. Supervises typing of catalog cards and regulates workload		X		
19. Prepares books for circulation			X	X
20. Supervises book preparation		X	X	
21. Performs card reproduction			X	X
22. Maintains authority files (name, series, subject)	X	X		

NOTES

[1]Charles A. Cutter, *Rules for a Dictionary Catalog*, 4th ed. (Washington: GPO, 1904), p. 12.

[2]International Conference on Cataloguing Principles. Paris, October 9th-18th, 1961, *Report* (London: International Federation of Library Association, 1963), p. 26.

³For a study of projected comparative costs for several types of catalogs, *see* S. Michael Malinconico and Paul J. Fasana, *The Future of the Catalog: The Library's Choices* (White Plains, N.Y.: Knowledge Industry Publications, 1979), pp. 84-99.

⁴Most examples of catalog cards in this text will reflect the descriptive cataloging rules in *AACR 2*.

REVIEW QUESTIONS AND EXERCISES

1. What is the main purpose of cataloging?

2. What are some of the functions of a library catalog?

3. What is a dictionary catalog? A divided catalog? What are some major differences between the two catalogs?

4. What are four characteristics on which to judge a catalog?

5. Discuss three important qualities of the card catalog.

6. Discuss negative characteristics of the card catalog that you believe are most important.

7. What catalog formats are used in addition to the card catalog? Which kind of catalog do you think will replace the card catalog, or do you think the card catalog is here to stay?

8. In Figure 15.2 what are the following:
    a) Main entry: _____
    b) Name of the publisher: _____
    c) Date of publication: _____
    d) Number of pages in the work: _____
    e) ISBN: _____
    f) Subject headings: _____, _____
        _____ .
    g) Dewey Decimal Classification number: _____
    h) Library of Congress card number: _____
    i) Library of Congress call number: _____
    j) Number of separate entries called for in the tracing: _____

9. As an LMTA responsible for supervising part-time or student help, what duties would you have part-time staff perform?

10. What kinds of duties are shared by clerks and LMTAs?

16

HOW TO READ A WORK TECHNICALLY

Before studying basic cataloging rules, the reader first should become familiar with the technique of examining a work for cataloging information. "Reading a work technically" consists of examining certain parts of it to obtain the information needed for describing the item on a catalog card, and for assigning it subject headings and a classification number.[1] It is neither possible nor necessary to read completely a book being cataloged or to view an entire film or listen to an entire recording. In most libraries, the volume of material is too great to allow for such detailed work.

In a library using printed cards or a service like OCLC or RLIN, an experienced LMTA should be able to supervise the processing of 10,000-15,000 items a year. But these figures assume a minimum of original cataloging. Reading a work technically enables a cataloger rapidly to identify the information necessary for original cataloging.

Technical reading can be separated into two steps. The first provides information for descriptive cataloging; the second step provides information for subject cataloging. Figure 16.1 (page 161) shows the various components of a catalog card. Figures 16.2-16.4 (pages 162-64) illustrate the application of a technical reading to the description of a book, and Figures 16.5-16.8 (pages 165-68) illustrate the description of a sound recording, in this example, a phonograph record.

The reader should not be too concerned if technical reading seems difficult, or if it seems unclear what information is needed or not needed. The technique is mastered only by experience, and it may require technically reading several thousand books, for example, to become proficient at descriptive cataloging of books. The best way to learn is under the direction of an experienced cataloger.

CATALOGING TERMINOLOGY[2]

Binder's title. The title imprinted on the binding of a book. This title may differ from the title on the title page if the book was rebound, or from the title on the original binding.

Blurb. A description of the contents of a book, prepared by the publisher and usually found on the book jacket. The blurb may also give information about the author.

Copyright. The exclusive right granted by a government to publish a work for a specified number of years. The copyright protects the author and publisher by preventing others from copying the work or significant parts of it without permission.

Copyright date. The date a copyright is issued. This is usually found on the verso of the title page.

Cover title. The title printed on the cover of a book or pamphlet.

Edition. All the *impressions* (copies) of a book printed at any time from one setting of type. For non-book materials, all of the impressions made from a master copy by one company or agency.

Half-title page. A brief or shortened title on the leaf preceding the title page.

Illustrative matter. Pictorial matter appearing in a work. Includes pictures, portraits, charts, graphs, maps, and facsimiles.

Impression. All of the copies of an edition produced at one time.

Index. A list of names and subjects in a book, each followed by the page number(s) where it appears. A guide to the contents.

Introduction. A preliminary part of a book that tells what the book is about and how the author intends to cover the subject.
See also Preface.

Label. The permanently affixed paper or plastic on an audiodisc describing the contents.

Leaf. A single sheet of paper in a bound book; i.e., two pages.

Pagination. A system of numbers or letters used to indicate the order of pages in a book. The part of the Physical Description Area indicating the number of pages in a book.

Preface. A section preceding the body of a book which may state the origin, purpose, and scope of the book.
See also Introduction.

Preliminaries. In a book this refers to the pages preceding the body of the book, such as the half-title page, the added title page, the verso of the title page, the cover title, and the spine.

Printer. A person or firm that prints books.

Publisher. A person or firm that issues and distributes a work.

Recto. The right-hand page in an open book. Usually odd-numbered.
See also Verso.

Series. A number of separate works, usually issued in succession, and usually related to one another in subject or form, issued by the same publisher in uniform style. The collective series title may appear at the head of the title page, on the half-title page, or on the cover.

Spine. The part of the book binding that joins the front and back covers together. Usually has the author and title of the book printed on it.

Spine title. The title that appears on the spine; also called a back title. *See also* Binder's title.

Title page. A page at the beginning of a book with the title, author's name, and publishing information.

Verso. The left-hand page in an open book. Usually even-numbered. *See also* Recto.

INFORMATION ON A CATALOG CARD

The catalog card includes only selective information about the work being cataloged. Therefore, it is necessary to know the kinds of information to look for when reading a work technically. The outline in Figure 16.1 describes the information found on the catalog card.[3] Since every work is different, different information will be needed; but the format and punctuation of the catalog card remains the same.

Fig. 16.1
Components of a Catalog Card

[10]Call
No.
    [1]Main entry (Author's name)
        [2]Title proper [GMD] : other title information / [3]statement of responsibility. -- [4]Edition statement. -- [5]Place of publication : publisher, date of publication.
        [6]Extent of item : other physical details ; dimensions. -- [7](Title proper of series; series numbering)

    [8]Notes as required
    Standard number : price

    [9]Tracings

TECHNICAL READING FOR DESCRIPTIVE CATALOGING: BOOK

Descriptive cataloging consists of describing a work and establishing its main entry. In Figure 16.1, items 1 through 8 and the added entries in 9 are established by descriptive cataloging. The subject headings in item 9 and item 10 are established by subject cataloging.

Much of the information needed for descriptive cataloging is found on the "title page" and the "verso of the title page." Descriptive information, however, is taken from all parts of a book and is *not* limited to the title page. Figure 16.2

shows a title page and verso of a title page, followed by a card containing the descriptive information found on those two pages.

Fig. 16.2
Descriptive Cataloging Information Taken from the Title Page
and Verso of the Title Page

Bohdan S. Wynar **Introduction to** **CATALOGING** **and** **CLASSIFICATION** 6th Edition with the assistance of Arlene Taylor Dowell and Jeanne Osborn 1980 Libraries Unlimited, Inc. • Littleton, Colorado	Copyright © 1980, 1976, 1972, 1971, 1967, 1966, 1964 Bohdan S. Wynar All Rights Reserved Printed in the United States of America No part of this publication may be reproduced, stored in a retrieval system, or transmitted, in any form or by any means, electronic, mechanical, photocopying, recording, or otherwise, without the prior written permission of the publisher. LIBRARIES UNLIMITED, INC. P.O. Box 263 Littleton, Colorado 80160 **Library of Congress Cataloging in Publication Data** Wynar, Bohdan S Introduction to cataloging and classification. Bibliography: p. 641 Includes indexes. 1. Cataloging. 2. Classification--Books. I. Dowell, Arlene Taylor, 1941- joint author. II. Osborn, Jeanne, joint author. III. Title. Z693.W94 1980 025.3 80-16462 ISBN 0-87287-220-3 ISBN 0-87287-221-1 (pbk.) Libraries Unlimited books are bound with Type II nonwoven material that meets and exceeds National Association of State Textbook Administrators' Type II nonwoven material specifications Class A through E.

Wynar, Bohdan S
    Introduction to cataloging and classification / Bohdan S. Wynar. -- 6th ed. / with the assistance of Arlene Taylor Dowell and Jeanne Osborn. -- Littleton, Colo. : Libraries Unlimited, 1980.

    ISBN 0-87287-220-3
    ISBN 0-87287-221-1 pbk.

While most of the descriptive information is on the two pages shown in Figure 16.2, several important items of information are lacking: the extent of the item (number of pages), other physical details (illustrations), dimensions (size), and "notes of interest." The number of pages (pagination) is determined from the *last numbered* page in the book. Sometimes books have preliminary sections numbered in roman numerals. These special pagings are usually given in the extent of item description—for example, "xv, 426p" means that there are 15 pages of text with roman numerals, followed by 426 pages of text with arabic numerals. Other physical details (illustrations, in our example) are found by examining the book. Dimensions are determined for a book by measuring the height in *centimeters*, not inches. Next, the book should be examined to see if there is any special information that should be noted on the card. The example in Figure 16.3 notes a bibliography.

Checking the book for elements of the physical description and notes of interest, we will add the following information:

Fig. 16.3
Descriptive Cataloging Information

```
Wynar, Bohdan S
    Introduction to cataloging and classification / Bohdan S.
Wynar. -- 6th ed. / with the assistance of Arlene Taylor
Dowell and Jeanne Osborn. -- Littleton, Colo. -- Libraries
Unlimited, 1980.
    xvii, 657 p. : ill. ; 24 cm. -- (Library science text
series)

    Bibliography: p. 641-643.
    ISBN 0-87287-220-3
    ISBN 0-87287-221-1 (pbk.)
```

All of the information in Figure 16.3 was obtained by reading the work technically. It was clearly not necessary to read the book.

Since many libraries have their own particular requirements as to what information is included in the catalog, technical reading may vary from one library to another. One of the more difficult decisions in technical reading is when to make notes and what kinds of information to include. The "bibliography" note in Figure 16.3 is easy, but the ability to discern other types of important notes comes only with experience. Also, the addition of notes depends on the guidelines of a specific library.

TECHNICAL READING FOR SUBJECT CATALOGING: BOOK

Subject cataloging consists of selecting subject headings and assigning a work a unique call number. It is possible to determine the subject or subjects of most books without reading the text extensively. The "blurb," which usually appears on the "book jacket," may give information about the subject of the book. However, such information must not be accepted uncritically, since the blurb is usually meant to help sell the book.

The "title" may or may not state the subject. A title such as *An Introduction to Algebra* leaves little doubt of the subject matter. The title *America's Concentration Camps*, however, gives no clue that the book is about the treatment of Japanese-Americans during World War II.

The "preface" and "introduction" may discuss the subject of the book. The "table of contents" gives the title of each chapter, which may give clues about the subject. The "index" is seldom used to determine the subject, but it may be helpful in some cases.

For most books, one or more of the above sources will provide the information necessary for subject cataloging. Only in a few cases will it be necessary to read extensively from the text.

Continuing our example, the title of Wynar's book, *Introduction to Cataloging and Classification*, states the subject of the book. The preface and table of contents confirm that the book does indeed cover the subject stated in the title.

The cataloger now has enough information to consult a standard list of subject headings and a classification schedule, so as to assign subject headings and a classification number (Figure 16.4).

Fig. 16.4
Completed Catalog Card for a Book

---

[1]Z   Wynar, Bohdan S
693   Introduction to cataloging and classification / Bohdan S.
W94   Wynar. -- 6th ed. / with the assistance of Arlene Taylor
1980   Dowell and Jeanne Osborn. -- Littleton, Colo. : Libraries
             Unlimited, 1980.
[2]025.3   xvii, 657 p. : ill. ; 24 cm. -- (Library science text
             series)

                                                          (Continued on next card)

Z   Wynar, Bohdan S
693   Introduction to cataloging and classification ... 1980 (Card 2)
W94
1980   Bibliography: p. 641-643.
                ISBN 0-87287-220-3
025.3   ISBN 0-87287-221-1 pbk.

                [3]1. Cataloging. 2. Classification--Books. I. Dowell,
             Arlene Taylor, 1941-   joint author. II. Osborn,
             Jeanne, joint author. III. Title.

Key to Note Items in Figure 15.4

[1]Library of Congress Classification   [3]Library of Congress Subject Headings
[2]Dewey Decimal Classification   (arabic numbers)

TECHNICAL READING FOR DESCRIPTIVE AND SUBJECT CATALOGING: SOUND RECORDING

AACR 2 instructs the cataloger to use the label of a disc sound recording as the chief source of information (Rule 6.0B1). Only if the information required is not found on the label can the record sleeve or container be used as a secondary source.

Below (Figure 16.5) is the label of a record we want to catalog. Refer to Figure 16.1 to refresh your memory of the information needed on a catalog card. Remember that not every work will have the same amount of information. (For example, the sound recording in our example has no series.) From the information on the label, we have the descriptive information seen in Figure 16.6 (page 166).

Fig. 16.5
Label on a Sound Recording: Disc*

REPRISE RECORDS

DON QUIXOTE
GORDON LIGHTFOOT
Produced by Lenny Waronker

MS 2056
(31,336)

SIDE
1

1. DON QUIXOTE 3:38
   (Gordon Lightfoot) Moose Music CAPAC
2. CHRISTIAN ISLAND (Georgian Bay) 4:02
   (Gordon Lightfoot) Moose Music CAPAC
3. ALBERTA BOUND 3:19
   (Gordon Lightfoot) Early Morning Music CAPAC
4. LOOKING AT THE RAIN 3:40
   (Gordon Lightfoot) Early Morning Music CAPAC
5. ORDINARY MAN 3:00
   (Gordon Lightfoot) Moose Music CAPAC
6. BRAVE MOUNTAINEERS 3:30
   (Gordon Lightfoot) Moose Music CAPAC
   (P) 1972
   Warner Bros. Records Inc.

REPRISE RECORDS. A DIVISION OF WARNER BROS RECORDS INC.
STEREO
MADE IN U.S.A.

---

*Reproduced by permission of Warner Brothers Records, Inc.

Fig. 16.5 (cont'd)

REPRISE RECORDS

DON QUIXOTE
GORDON LIGHTFOOT
Produced by Lenny Waronker

MS 2056
(31,337)

SIDE
2

1. ODE TO BIG BLUE 4:45
   (Gordon Lightfoot) Moose Music CAPAC
2. SECOND CUP OF COFFEE 3:00
   (GordonLightfoot) Moose Music CAPAC
3. BEAUTIFUL 3:14
   (Gordon Lightfoot) Moose Music CAPAC
4. ON SUSAN'S FLOOR 3:55
   (Shel Silverstein-Vince Matthews) Jack
   Music, Inc. BMI
5. THE PATRIOT'S DREAM 6:05
   (Gordon Lightfoot) Moose Music CAPAC
   ℗ 1972
   Warner Bros. Records Inc.

REPRISE RECORDS, A DIVISION OF WARNER BROS. RECORDS INC. MADE IN U.S.A.

STEREO

Fig. 16.6
Descriptive Cataloging Information from the Disc Label

Lightfoot, Gordon
  Don Quixote / Gordon Lightfoot ; produced by Lenny
Waronker. --
                    Reprise, 1972.
  1 sound disc (42 min.)
stereo
  Contents: Don Quixote -- Christian island -- Alberta
bound -- Looking at the rain -- Ordinary man -- Brave
mountaineers -- Ode to big blue -- Second cup of coffee --
Beautiful -- On Susan's floor / Shel Silverstein [and]
Vincent Matthews -- The patriot's dream.
  Reprise : MS 2056

From the chief source (the label), we have the main entry, title proper, statement of responsibility, publisher, date of publication, part of the physical description, the contents (required on sound recordings, *AACR 2* rule 6.7B18), and the publisher's number.

From other sources, such as the container and actually measuring the record, we can complete the physical description (see Figures 16.7 and 16.8, page 168).

Fig. 16.7
Completed Catalog Card for a Sound Recording

      Lightfoot, Gordon
        Don Quixote [sound recording] / Gordon Lightfoot. --
Burbank, Calif. : Reprise, 1972.
        1 sound disc (42 min.) : 33 1/3 rpm, stereo; 12 in.
        Contents: Don Quixote -- Christian island -- Alberta
bound -- Looking at the rain -- Ordinary man -- Brave
mountaineers -- Ode to big blue -- Second cup of coffee --
Beautiful -- On Susan's floor / Shel Silverstein [and]
Vincent Matthews -- The patriot's dream.
        Reprise : MS 2056

Notice that a "general material designation" is inserted after the title — [sound recording]. A general material designation can be used optionally for all materials except books.* Indicating that the material is a sound recording (or in other than book format) will be useful to anyone using the catalog.

The subject cataloging for sound recordings varies among libraries much more than books. A subject heading would probably be assigned. A classification number might be assigned, but more likely, only an acquisitions number would be used. A sample of the completed card is shown on page 168.

The next four chapters will cover in more detail the rules for descriptive cataloging, determining a main entry, selecting subject headings, and classification.

---

*The Library of Congress plans to use the General Material Designation (GMD) selectively. At the time this text was being revised LC applied the GMD to sound recordings, motion pictures and video-recordings, graphic materials, three-dimensional artifacts and realia, and microforms.

Fig. 16.8
Completed Catalog Card for a Sound Recording: Disc

M
1627   Lightfoot, Gordon
               Don Quixote [sound recording] / Gordon Lightfoot. --
            Burbank, Calif. : Reprise, 1972.
               1 sound disc (42 min.) : 33 1/3 rpm,
            stereo ; 12 in.
               Contents: Don Quixote -- Christian island -- Alberta
            bound -- Looking at the rain -- Ordinary man -- Brave
            mountaineers -- Ode to big blue -- Second cup of coffee --
            Beautiful -- On Susan's floor / Shel Silverstein [and]
            Vincent Matthews -- The patriot's dream.

                                            (Continued on next card)

            Lightfoot, Gordon
               Don Quixote ... 1972 (Card 2)

            Reprise : MS 2056

               1. Music, Popular (Songs, etc.).   I. Title.

            [M1627]

NOTES

[1]The techniques described in this chapter stress information for catalog cards. These techniques are also applicable for obtaining information for a worksheet so information can be sent on a computer terminal to a service such as OCLC, although the format differs. OCLC will be discussed in a later chapter.

[2]These terms emphasize parts of the book. Terms for other kinds of materials are not necessarily so standardized. For cataloging non-book materials *AACR 2* offers guidance on where to obtain descriptive cataloging information.

[3]Chapters 17 and 18 go into more detail on descriptive cataloging. The examples in this chapter are to introduce the reader to the technical reading procedures.

REVIEW QUESTIONS AND EXERCISES

1. What are the two basic steps in technical reading?

2. Using the outline in Figure 16.1, try to read technically a book in a library's collection for descriptive cataloging information. Then check the cataloging in the library catalog to compare your description. Select a book published after 1980, so *AACR 2* descriptive cataloging rules will have been used.

3. How are the following items determined?
   a) Title proper _____
   b) Publisher _____
   c) Extent of item _____
   d) International Standard Book Number _____
   e) Notes _____

4. What is the blurb? Can the information in the blurb be used for cataloging?

5. In Figure 16.6, how does the physical description for the sound disc differ from the physical description for the book in Figure 16.3?

17

DESCRIPTIVE CATALOGING – PHYSICAL DESCRIPTION

Cataloging consists of two processes: descriptive cataloging and subject cataloging. Descriptive cataloging consists of two elements: describing the physical work, and determining the main entry and added entries. The physical description of the work starts with the title and ends with the notes. The purpose of this description is to establish the work's unique identity. In this and the following chapter we will discuss only the basic rules of descriptive cataloging. No attempt is made to cover the more esoteric or difficult rules as they may only confuse the LMTA seeking a basic introduction. The rules discussed below should serve as a base for expanding a person's skills as cataloging experience is acquired.

The latest cataloging rules, *AACR 2*, establish general rules and guidelines for all materials – books and non-book – and give specific rules for the various media. Earlier cataloging rules stressed book cataloging while relegating non-book materials to a secondary status, but this bias has been eliminated in *AACR 2*. The format for describing materials has been standardized for card catalog form and for other formats, such as computer printouts.

This chapter concentrates on the basic rules for descriptive cataloging of books; and chapter 18 covers descriptive cataloging of non-book materials. This is an artificial separation, but it has been done to keep the size of the chapters reasonable, as well as to simplify the presentation of a rather complex set of rules. All of the examples will be in card catalog format, as this is the most common format. Because of their special nature, cataloging of serials is covered in chapter 23.

CATALOGING TERMINOLOGY

Analytical entry. An entry for a part of a work for which a comprehensive entry is made.

Area. A major section of the bibliographic description (e.g., the Title and statement of responsibility area).

Chief source of information. The source of bibliographic information given first preference in describing a work. The chief source varies for different types of materials.
See also Prescribed source of information.

Colophon. An inscription or identifying device sometimes found at the end of a book; it often includes such publication information as typeface or printer.

Data element. *See* Element.

Element. A part or subsection of an *area* in a bibliographic description (e.g., the title is an element in the Title and statement of responsibility area).

Parallel title. The title proper in another language or printed in another script (e.g., *Thumbelina — Tommelise*).

Prescribed source of information. The source recommended for describing different areas. The prescribed source varies for different areas and different materials.
See also Chief source of information.

CATALOGING RULES

The second edition of the *Anglo-American Cataloguing Rules* is the latest cataloging code used by most American libraries. *AACR 2* was officially adopted in January 1981 by the Library of Congress, commercial cataloging services, and most libraries, and is used by all but the smallest libraries. The cataloging rules and examples used in this text are based on *AACR 2*. The Library of Congress is constantly interpreting the new rules, so changes are inevitable. Therefore, it is possible, but unavoidable, that some examples in the text will have to be modified according to later interpretations of *AACR 2*.

AACR 2 is the latest result of a series of cataloging rules starting with the publication in 1841 of the British Museum's *Rules for the Compiling of the Catalogue*. More direct antecedents of *AACR 2* used by American libraries include the Library of Congress *Rules on Printed Cards* (1903 through the 1930s), the *ALA Cataloging Rules of Author and Title Entries* (1908, 1941, 1949), the Library of Congress *Rules for Descriptive Cataloging in the Library of Congress* (1949), and the *Anglo-American Cataloging Rules* (*AACR 1*) (1967).[1]

Cataloging rules give guidance to catalogers and provide consistency in cataloging practices within a library and among different libraries. This consistency means that a work will receive the same descriptive cataloging and the same main entry in different libraries. If libraries use dissimilar rules, library users would have to learn new rules each time they used a different library.

AACR 2

Development

By the early 1970s *AACR 1* had undergone many changes and modifications, and progress on standardized descriptions of all types of library materials was far advanced. Also, a number of publications suggesting alternative descriptive cataloging rules for non-book materials reflected widespread dissatisfaction with *AACR 1*. In 1974 an international conference was held to develop a new cataloging code.

AACR 2 was the result of four years' work, yet it is not a *new* set of rules; rather it is considered a continuation of *AACR 1*: "for, in spite of the changes in presentation and content which it introduces, there are still the *Anglo-American Cataloguing Rules*, having the same principles and underlying objectives as the first edition, and being firmly based on the achievement of those who created the work, first published in 1967" (*AACR 2*, Preface).

Special Features

AACR 2 calls for the cataloging of materials in the following order: 1) describe the physical item (*AACR 2* chapters 1-12); 2) select a main entry and any necessary added entries (chapter 21); 3) determine the correct form of names used as the main entry or as added entries (chapters 22-25); and 4) make any necessary references for different forms of a name (chapter 26).

The format and order of information required by *AACR 2* is based on the International Standard Bibliographic Description (ISBD). The ISBD format and rules are used with all kinds of materials—book and non-book alike. The ISBD is highly structured and calls for specific kinds of descriptive information in a specific order in the description. Figure 17.1 (page 175) illustrates the kinds of descriptive information required, the order of the information, and the required punctuation. The main purpose of ISBD is to create an international standard of description suitable for a machine-readable format to enable rapid transfer of information via computer. Another feature of *AACR 2* is that many rules are prescriptive, not mandatory. Options and alternatives are given for some rules. This feature allows latitude for catalogers to tailor descriptive cataloging for a specific library. In contrast, earlier cataloging rules were far more prescriptive, allowing little or no room for alternatives. Alternatives and options are noted in the rules. And finally, another general principle used in *AACR 2* is that ISBD is used throughout to describe all types of materials. The information and framework is the same except for certain specialized information unique to a particular medium, the format of the description remains the same.

The features discussed above represent some of the more important concepts for the beginning LMTA. Some of the more sophisticated changes, such as limited authorship, authorship compared to responsibility, and changes in corporate authorship, should be studied only after acquiring cataloging experience.

Some Criticisms and Problems

A major criticism of *AACR 2* is that it is too complex and is meant primarily for the large research or academic library. For a small public library, as an example, the rules are overwhelming and would never be used. Indeed, *AACR 2* is designed in part to accommodate the needs of larger libraries; the same criticism was made of *AACR 1*. However, it does allow flexibility and options, which in part mitigates the problem of complex rules. For example, the rules provide for more than one acceptable level of detail in a bibliographic description: a small library may use level one description while a larger library will find a level two or three description more meaningful (*AACR 2*, pp. 14-15). The rules state that they are "designed for use in the construction of catalogues and other lists in general libraries of all sizes. They are not specifically intended for specialist and archival libraries...."[2] Furthermore, the accessibility of cataloging information and printed catalog cards lifts the cataloging burden from small libraries. The rules may be complex, but outside agencies can do the cataloging. Small libraries also have the option to use Michael Gorman's *The Concise AACR2, Being a Rewritten and Simplified Version of Anglo-American Cataloguing Rules, Second*

Edition (Chicago: American Library Association, 1981). This work covers only basic cataloging rules.

Another problem created by *AACR 2* involves major changes in the form of names for main entries and added entries. New rules for selecting the form of the name used will be discussed in chapter 19. Below are several examples of name changes imposed by *AACR 2*.

Old Form of Name	*AACR 2* Form
Clemens, Samuel Langhorne, 1835-1910	Twain, Mark, 1835-1910
Arizona, University	University of Arizona
Bentley, Eric Russell, 1916-	Bentley, Eric, 1916-
Brown University. John Carter Brown Library	John Carter Brown Library
Paris	Paris (France)
United Nations. Children's Fund	UNICEF
Wells, Herbert George, 1866-1946	Wells, H. G. (Herbert George), 1866-1946
Wyoming. Geological Survey	Geological Survey of Wyoming
Dallas. Southern Methodist University	Southern Methodist University

These few examples show the complex filing and cross-reference problems libraries have encountered. These and hundreds of similar changes are forcing librarians to take a critical look at the card catalog and possible alternative formats. The Library of Congress froze its card catalog of January 2, 1981 and will rely on automated computer-based catalogs to access its collections for new cataloged materials.

Many libraries are currently evaluating alterations or alternatives to the traditional card catalog. Some of the more common alternatives are: 1) to close the card catalog and create a new card catalog based on *AACR 2*; 2) to close the card catalog and create a new catalog in microformat or a computer-based format using *AACR 2*; and 3) to retain the card catalog and make cross-references and corrections as needed, using *AACR 2* for all new works cataloged. The discussion of alternatives will intensify in the next few years, but at this time the future of the card catalog is uncertain. It is likely, however, that the card catalog will remain the prominent format for the next four to ten years.

Many libraries modify some cataloging rules and ignore others. This practice is common and acceptable and is recognized by the flexibility of *AACR 2*. Rules must often be modified to fit local needs, but not vice versa. Conversely, with the expansion of commercially produced catalog cards and centralized processing centers and with increased utilization of large central data bases via computer to transmit cataloging information, pressure has increased for standardization of cataloging rules. It is likely that the coming decade will see all but the smallest libraries using the same cataloging rules.

Contents

The rules for descriptive material are covered in *AACR 2* chapters 1 to 13.* Chapter 1 gives the general rules for describing all materials, chapters 2-12 give the rules in greater detail for specific types of materials, and chapter 13 gives special rules for preparing bibliographic entries for part of a larger work. There are no chapters 14 to 20, as the space is reserved for future expansion. The rules for selecting the main entry and added entries are covered in *AACR 2* chapter 21. Chapters 22-24 give the rules for determining the proper form of a name. Chapter 25 covers "uniform titles" and chapter 26, the form of references for alternative forms of names. (Chapters 21-26 will be covered in a later chapter in this text.)

Four appendices supplement the main body of the rules: Appendix A—Capitalization; Appendix B—Abbreviations; Appendix C—Numerals; and Appendix D—Glossary.

The reader should have a copy of *AACR 2* at hand in order to refer to the rules while reading the following chapters on descriptive cataloging. *Reference to AACR 2 is required to understand the rules fully. Do not try to catalog using the rules as they are presented in this text; always refer to AACR 2.**

Notice the mnemonic feature of *AACR 2* rule numbering. The general rule for recording a title proper is 1.1B1. The rule for recording the title proper of a book is 2.1B1; of a map, 3.1B1; and of a microform, 11.1B1.

Always refer first to the general rules in chapter 1 that govern all materials. Next, refer to chapters 2-12 for the application of the general rule to a specific kind of material.

Arrangement of Bibliographic Information

The physical description of a work is presented in eight "areas" (Figure 17.1)—Rule 1.0B:[3]

Area 1: **Title and statement of responsibility.** Included here are the title proper, general material designation, any alternative or parallel title, other title information, and information about responsibility for the work. (The general material designation will be discussed in the next chapter.) (Rule 1.1)

Area 2: **Edition.** Included here is information about the edition, and a responsibility statement relating to the edition. (Rule 1.2)

Area 3: **Material (or type of publication) specific details.** This area is used *only* for some cartographic materials and serials. For serials, it includes information about the first issue [Vol. 1, no. 1 (Nov. 1947)]; for maps, it presents mathematical data (Scale: 1:63,360). (Rule 1.3)

Area 4: **Publication, distribution, etc.** This area includes information on the place of publication, the publisher or issuing agency, and the date of publication, distribution, or release. (Rule 1.4)

---

*Rules quoted or paraphrased in this text are reprinted by permission of the American Library Association from *Anglo-American Cataloguing Rules*, 2d ed., edited by Michael Gorman and Paul W. Winkler, copyright © 1978 by the American Library Association, Canadian Library Association, and The Library Association.

Area 5: **Physical description.** This area gives a physical description of the work. For a book, this would include the number of pages, illustrations, size, and separate items. This area is where many of the differences between cataloging book and non-book materials will be most pronounced (*see* Figures 16.4, page 164, and 16.7, page 167). (Rule 1.5)

Area 6: **Series.** The name of the series is given in this area. Other information (such as editorial responsibility or series numbering) is also cited here. (Rule 1.6)

Area 7: **Note(s).** Included here are notes with information not provided elsewhere in the description. There can be more than one note. (Rule 1.7)

Area 8: **Standard number and terms of availability.** The information here includes the International Standard Book Number (ISBN), International Standard Serial Number (ISSN), or any other standard international number for the material being cataloged, and the price (ISBN 0-87287-115-0 : $12.50). (Rule 1.8)

Fig. 17.1
Arrangement of Areas on a Catalog Card[4]

---

[1]Title proper [general material designation] : other title information / statement of responsibility ; subsequent statements of responsibility. --[2]Edition statement / statement of responsibility relating to the edition. -- [3]*See key.* -- [4]Place of publication : publisher, date of publication.
[5]Extent of the item : other physical details ; dimensions. -- [6](Title proper of series / statement of responsibility, ISSN ; numbering of series.)
[7]Notes.
[8]Standard number : price

Key to Note Items in Figure 17.1

[1]Title and statement of responsibility area

[2]Edition area

[3]Material (or type of publication) specific details area. *Not shown in figure.*

[4]Publication, distribution, etc. area

[5]Physical description area

[6]Series area

[7]Note area

[8]Standard number and terms of availability area

Levels of Description

AACR 2, Rules 1.0D1, 1.0D2, and 1.0D3 present three levels of bibliographic description available to libraries. Whichever level is selected must include all the elements applicable to that level. Of course, all items cataloged will not have every element. For example, an item may not have a series; or if it does have a series, it may not be numbered. The level of description used is a professional decision based on a library's needs and the staff's skills. Most libraries will probably use the level two description, as illustrated in Figure 17.3. Examples in this text will be based on the level two description. Figures 17.2 and 17.3 show differences between level one and level two descriptions.

Fig. 17.2
Level One Description

Chan, Lois Mai
  Library of Congress subject headings. -- Libraries Unlimited, 1978.
    347 p.

  Bibliography: p. 333-339.
  Includes index.

Fig. 17.3
Level Two Description

Chan, Lois Mai
  Library of Congress subject headings : principles and application / Lois Mai Chan. -- Littleton, Colo. : Libraries Unlimited, 1978.
    347 p. : ill. ; 24 cm. -- (Research studies in library science ; no. 15)

  Bibliography: p. 333-339.
  Includes index.
  ISBN 0-87287-187-8.

Punctuation and Spacing

AACR 2 requires specialized punctuation and spacing. The example in Figure 17.1 shows the punctuation and spacing required after each area. In general, areas 1, 2, and 4 are followed by a period-space-dash-space. Area 3 ends in a full stop of period. The elements in areas 5 and 6 are separated by slashes and semicolons. The punctuation for each area is discussed below in more detail.

The requirements for such precise punctuation and spacing relate to the need for a standard format acceptable to computer input and machine-readable data bases. Strict adherence to spacing and punctuation is essential if cataloging information is to be entered into a computer information file. There is also a movement toward international standardization of cataloging formats to enable international exchange of bibliographic information.

If cataloging information is not going into a computer file, a library can be more flexible in its adherence to these rules. In any case, many libraries have their own rules and idiosyncrasies for spacing and punctuation.

Sources of Descriptive Information

The actual item being cataloged is the usual source of descriptive information. The information for each area is taken from the prescribed or "chief" source of information for that area. The source will vary for different types of materials. Information *not* found in a chief or prescribed source is placed in brackets (Figure 17.4).

Fig. 17.4
Bracketed Information from a Non-prescribed Source

Gardner, John E
  The return of Moriarty / John Gardner. -- New York : Putnam, [1974]

The chief sources or prescribed sources of information for a *book* are (Rule 2.0B):

Area	Chief Source
Area 1 (Title and statement of responsibility)	Title page
Area 2 (Edition)	Title page, preliminaries, colophon
Area 4 (Publication, distribution, etc.)	Title page, preliminaries, colophon
Area 5 (Physical Description)	Whole publication
Area 6 (Series)	Whole publication
Area 7 (Note[s])	Any source
Area 8 (Standard number)	Any source

Title and Statement of Responsibility Area

The title is the first information after the main entry (if author entry). The title is transcribed exactly as it appears in the book—wording, order, and spelling—even if there are misspellings or other errors (Rule 1.1B1). An exceptionally long title can be abridged if the meaning and essential information are retained. The first *five* words of the title are *always* retained (Rule 1.1B4). An omission is always noted by the use of an omission mark (...): "The conduct of war, 1789-1961 ..."

If the title is taken from a source other than the title page (which is the prescribed source for the title), this should be indicated in a note (Rules 1.7B3 and 2.7B3):

---

387 p. : ill. ; 27 cm.

Spine title.

When other title information is available, it is separated from the title proper by a space-colon-space (:), regardless of the punctuation on the title page or other source of the title (Figure 17.5):

Fig. 17.5
Title and Other Title Information

Dowell, Arlene Taylor
  Cataloging with copy : a decision-maker's
handbook /

A parallel title is the title in another language. Not many books have parallel titles, but a medium-sized library will have enough for the cataloging staff to be aware of the special punctuation. The title proper is separated from the parallel title by a space-equal sign-space (Rules 1.1D and 2.1D) (Figure 17.6):

Fig. 17.6
Parallel Title

Agricultural machinery in Europe = Les machines agricoles en Europe = Landwirtschaftsmaschinen in Europa.

Following the title and parallel title if there is one, and separated by a space-slash-space is the statement of responsibility. Included in this element, as needed, would be an author, editor, compiler, illustrator, or translator (Rule 1.1F1). The prescribed source for this information is the title page, so if the information is taken from another source it is placed in brackets. The responsibility statement (Figures 17.7-17.13) is sometimes deleted if the author's name is included in the title proper (*See* Figure 17.10). Names of persons who perform different functions are separated in the statement of responsibility by a space-semicolon-space (Figures 17.9 and 17.11). And, when *more than three* persons are cited, only the first name is given in the responsibility statement, followed by an omission mark and the term "et al." in brackets (... [et al.]). *See* Figures 17.9 and 17.13. ("Et al." is an abbreviation of the Latin "et alii" meaning "and others.") Titles, degrees, initials, or statements of position following an author's name are usually omitted; the title page statement " ... by Arthur Maltby, B.A., F.L.A., F.R.S.A., Senior Lecturer in Classification ..." would be transcribed as " / by Arthur Maltby." There are infrequent exceptions to this rule.

Fig. 17.7
Responsibility Statement – Single Author

Showalter, Dennis E
    Railroads and rifles : soldiers, technology, and the unification of Germany / Dennis E. Showalter. --

Fig. 17.8
Responsibility Statement – Two Authors and an Editor

Bloomberg, Marty
    An introduction to classification and number building in Dewey / Marty Bloomberg and Hans Weber ; edited by John Phillip Immroth. --

Fig. 17.9
Responsibility Statement — More Than Three Authors and
Persons Performing Different Functions

Institut für Zeitgeschichte, (Munich, Germany)
    Anatomy of the SS state / Helmut Krausnick ... [et al.] ;
translated from the German by Richard Barry, Marian Jackson, Dorothy Lang ; introduction by Elizabeth Wiskemann. --

In the item described in Figure 17.9 the title page listed four co-equal authors; Helmut Krausnick was the first name listed.

Fig. 17.10
Responsibility Statement — Editor

Joyce, James, 1882-1941.
    Selected letters of James Joyce / edited by Richard Ellmann. --

Fig. 17.11
Responsibility Statement — Persons Performing Different Functions:
Author and Introduction Writer

Swift, Jonathan, 1667-1745.
    Miscellanies in prose and verse, 1711 / Jonathan Swift ; introductory note by C.P. Daw. --

Fig. 17.12
Responsibility Statement — Persons Performing Different Functions:
Author and Translator

Perrault, Gilles.
    The red orchestra / by Gilles Perrault ; translated by Peter Wiles. --

Fig. 17.13
Responsibility Statement — More Than Three Authors

Medical-surgical nursing / Kathleen Newton Shafer ...
    [et al.]. --

The title page of the item described in Figure 17.13 listed four coequal authors; Kathleen Newton Shafer was the first cited.

Edition Area

The edition statement follows the statement of responsibility and is separated from it by a period-space-dash-space (Figure 17.14) (Rule 1.2A1). The prescribed sources of information for the edition are the title page, preliminaries, and colophon. If the edition information comes from any other source, it is placed in brackets.

The edition is an important element in establishing the unique identity of a work. In academic and research libraries, the library user may be interested only in a specific edition of a work.

The edition is usually given on the title page or verso of the title page and is recorded as it appears in the book, with abbreviations where permitted:[5]

Statement in Book	Abbreviation in Edition Area
Third edition	3rd ed.
Second edition	2nd ed.
7th Edition, Revised and Enlarged	7th ed., rev. and enl.
First American Edition	1st American ed.

(*See* Figures 17.14 and 17.15.)

Sometimes on the verso of the title page there will be a statement such as "Fifth Printing," "11th impression," "First Dell Printing," or similar wording. Publishers often use "impression," "printing," or "edition" to refer to a printing run and not necessarily to a new edition. A printing statement can usually be ignored unless it is identified as a printing with corrections or revisions. Distinguishing between a printing and an edition requires cataloging experience, and even then, it is not always easy.

Fig. 17.14
Edition Area

McKinney, Wayne C
    Archery / Wayne C. McKinney. -- 3rd ed. --

Fig. 17.15
Edition Statement in Brackets: Not from the
Prescribed Source of Information

Swift, Jonathan, 1667-1745.
    Miscellanies in prose and verse, 1711 / Jonathan Swift ;
introductory note by C.P. Daw. -- [1st ed., repr.] --

Material (or Type of Publication) Specific Details Area

This area is used only for some cartographic materials and serials. Appropriate examples will be given for those materials in the following chapters.

Publication, Distribution, Etc. Area

This area follows the edition area and is separated from the edition area by a period-space-dash-space. The Publication, distribution, etc. area includes the following elements: place of publication, name of publisher, and date of publication (Rules 1.4 and 2.4). The prescribed sources of information for this area are the title page, the preliminaries, and the colophon. Information from other sources is placed in brackets. Within the area, the place of publication is separated from the publisher by a space-colon-space; and the publisher is separated from the date by a comma-space (Figure 17.16):

Fig. 17.16
Publication, Distribution, Etc. Area

Guide to the use of books and libraries / Jean Key Gates. -- 4th ed. -- New York : McGraw-Hill, 1979.

When more than one place of publication is given, these are separated by a space-semicolon-space: Place of publication ; place of publication : publisher, date: London ; New York : Macmillan.

The place of publication is the city where the publisher's office is located. If more than one city is given on the title page, and every city is in the United States, only the first city is used, unless another city is set in a more prominent position. If a foreign city is listed first or in a more prominent position followed by a city in the United States, both cities are cited: London ; New York : Macmillan. If New York appeared first, London would be omitted: New York : Macmillan.

If the city or place of publication is well known and would not be confused with other locations, it can be cited by itself: "New York." However, if the place is not well known or could be confused, the country, state, etc. should be added for clarification: "Dominguez Hills, [Calif.]," "Waco, [Tex.]," or "Renens, [Switzerland]." If the place of publication cannot be determined, the abbreviation S.l. (for the Latin *sine loco*, meaning without place) is given in brackets: "[S.l.] : Smith and Webster."

The publisher is identified by the shortest form possible for proper identification. Terms such as "Publisher," "Company," "and Sons," or "Incorporated," as well as the articles "a," "an," and "the," are usually omitted: Macmillan & Co. is transcribed as Macmillan; Frederick A. Praeger becomes Praeger; and Penguin Books becomes Penguin. A well known publisher like Alfred Knopf is transcribed as Knopf; however, H. W. Wilson & Co. is transcribed as H. W. Wilson because it is not well known outside the library field.

When the name of the publisher is unknown the abbreviation, s.n. (for the Latin *sine nomine*, meaning "without name"), is given in brackets: New York : [s.n.]. If neither the place of publication nor publisher is known, the element would be: [S.l. : s.n.].

The date of publication, the last element in this area, is the date for the edition being described. It is usually found on the title page. The date of copyright, on the verso of the title page, is always preceded by a "©". The following examples show some commonly used ways of recording the publication date:

1975	—date of publication appears in a prescribed source and is the same as the copyright date.
[1975]	—date of publication does not appear in a prescribed source, so it is in brackets.
1972, c1971	—1972 appears in a prescribed source as the date of publication; 1971, the copyright date, is given because it differs from the publication date
1970, 1972 printing	—1970 is the date of publication appearing in a prescribed source; 1972 is the date of a later printing containing textual or other important variations
[ca. 1963]	—date of publication is unknown, but 1963 is the probable date
[196-]	—exact year of publication is unknown, but the decade is certain
[19--]	—exact year of publication is unknown, but century is certain
1960-1966	—inclusive dates of publication for a completed multi-volume item published over a period of years
1970-	—an open entry for a multi-volume item still being published

Multi-volume works present a slightly different problem. If the set is complete, as in the 1960-1966 example above, the dates are for the first volume published and the last volume published (not necessarily first and last volumes in the actual series, though). An "open entry" is used for a work still being published; thus "1970-   " means the first volume was published in 1970, and more are in process (Figure 17.17):

Fig. 17.17
Open Entry

Erickson, John.
    The road to Stalingrad : Stalin's war with Germany / John Erickson. -- 1st American ed. -- New York : Harper & Row, c1975-

Physical Description Area

This area follows the publication, distribution, etc. area; and in the catalog card format it starts a new paragraph. (If the area were not a new paragraph, it would be separated from the preceding area by a period-space-dash-space.) The whole work is the prescribed source of information, hence, little material will be in brackets in this area. An example of information placed in brackets would be unnumbered pages, e.g., 364, [8]p. The elements in this area are the extent of the item, other physical details, dimensions, and accompanying materials (Rules 1.5, 2.5). For a book, these elements are usually the number of pages or volumes, illustrative matter, height in centimeters, and separate items. The number of pages or volumes is separated from the illustrations by a space-colon-space; the illustration statement is separated from the size by a space-semicolon-space; and the size is separated from the statement of accompanying materials by a space-plus sign-space; the physical description of the accompanying materials may be added in parentheses (Figures 17.18 and 17.19):

Fig. 17.18
Physical Description Area
(Pages)

267 p. : ill. ; 22 cm. -- (Series)

(A book with 267 pages, illustrated, and 22 centimeters in height.)

Fig. 17.19
Volumes + Accompanying Material

16 v. : ill. ; 26 cm. + 1 atlas (310 p. : col. maps ;
37 cm.)

(A 16-volume set, illustrated, 26 centimeters in height, and accompanied by an atlas with 310 pages, colored maps, and 37 centimeters in height.)

The number of pages is the last *numbered* page or leaf (a leaf is printed only on one side; a page is printed on both sides of the leaf). An unnumbered page following the last numbered page is usually ignored. Preliminary paging, usually in roman numerals, is cited in the extent of work element. If a work is unpaged, the pages can be counted or estimated (Rule 2.5B7). The following examples give some of the usual extent of work statements:

480 p. :	
or	
480 leaves :	the number on the last numbered page or leaf
xxx, 712 p. :	thirty pages of roman numbered text, followed by 712 arabic numbered pages
[96] p. :	a work without numbered pages; pages are *counted* and placed in brackets
ca. 300 p. :	a work without numbered pages; pages are *estimated* and preceded by "ca.", the abbreviation for *circa*, meaning "about"

412 p. in various pagings :   the work has complicated or irregular paging; the numbers of pages in the sequences are added, and the total is followed by "in various pagings"

Multi-volume works are described in terms of volumes:

5 v. :   a five-volume work; the "v." is an abbreviation for volume

6 v. in 4 :   six bibliographic volumes are bound in four physical volumes

3 v. (xxx, 1712 p.) :   three volumes paged continuously; the first volume has 30 pages of preliminary text with roman numerals. Preliminary numbering in volumes after the first is ignored. Pagination is placed in parentheses after the volume number.

Open entries are used for incomplete multi-volume sets. The space before the "v." is left blank to be filled in when the final volume is issued. Notice that the date of publication is also left open (Figure 17.20):

Fig. 17.20
Open Entry (Open Publication Date and Extent of Item)

Natural products chemistry / edited by Koji Nakanishi ... [et al.]. -- Tokyo : Kodansha ; New York : Academic Press, c1974-
    v. : ill. ; 26 cm. -- (Kodansha scientific books)

The illustrative matter is the second element in the physical description area. The abbreviation "ill." describes most illustrative matter. If a particular kind of illustration is important, it is usually cited under its name: charts, forms, genealogical tables, maps, music, or portraits.

Some examples of the illustration element are:

210 p. : ill. ;   illustrations appear in the work

312 p. : ill., maps ;   illustrations and maps both appear in the work

310 p. : maps ;   maps are the only illustrative matter in the work

376 p. : col. ill. ;   the illustrations are colored

110 p. : all ill. ;   the work consists entirely of illustrations

126 p. : chiefly ill.   the work consists predominantly of illustrations

The two final elements are the dimensions and accompanying material. Books are measured in full centimeters with fractions counted as a whole centimeter (e.g., 23.2 cm. is cited as 24 cm.). The size for books of unusual size may include height and width, but this is seldom encountered (Rule 2.5D2). Accompanying material follows the size and is preceded by a space-plus signspace; these materials are designed to be used with the book and may include answer books, atlases, sound recordings, and filmstrips.

83 p. : col. ill. ; 27 cm. + 1 atlas (20 p. : col. maps ; 27 cm.)[6]

173 p. : 23 cm. + answer book

210 p. : ill. ; 32 cm. + 1 sound disc (21 min. : 33 1/3 rpm, stereo ; 12 in.)

Series Area

The series area follows the physical description area and is preceded by a period-space-dash-space (Rules 1.6 and 2.6). The series area is enclosed in parentheses. The chief or prescribed source of information for this area is the whole book, with information from other sources placed in brackets: [The river series]. A series number is separated from the series title by a semicolon: Research studies in library science ; no. 15. Two examples of series area follow (Figures 17.21 and 17.22).

Fig. 17.21
Series Area—Series with a Subseries and Number

310 p. ; 23 cm. -- (NATO advanced study institute series. Series C, mathematical and physical sciences ; v. 13)
Bibliography.
1. Differential games--Congresses. I. Grote, J. D., ed.
II. Title. III. Series.

Fig. 17.22
Series Area—Work with Two Series

iii, 164 p. ; 21 cm. -- (Salzburg studies in English literature) (Jacobean drama studies ; 48)
Bibliography: p. 163-164.
1. Webster, John, 1580?-1625?--Religion and ethics.
2. Webster, John, 1580?-1625?--Characters. I. Title. II. Series. III. Series: Jacobean drama studies ; 48.

Note Area

The note area follows the series area and forms a new paragraph in catalog card format (Rules 1.7 and 2.7). If the area does not form a new paragraph, it is separated from the preceding area by a period-space-dash-period. Notes are used to give important information not provided in other parts of the description and can be taken from any source. Notes can be both formal and informal for greater flexibility. *AACR 2* Rules 1.7 and 2.7 list a number of different kinds of notes and the order in which they are placed in the description. Informal notes should be brief, unbiased, and nonjudgmental about the work. Examples of frequently used notes follow (Figures 17.23-17.28).

Fig. 17.23
Note—Bibliography

89 p. ; 23 cm. -- (Problems in European civilization)
Bibliography: p. 88-89.

Fig. 17.24
Note—Imperfect Work

584 p. : ill. ; 23 cm.

Imperfect copy: p. 580-581 missing.

Fig. 17.25
Note—Title Variation

308 p. ; 22 cm.

Published in England under title: The other side of the hill.

Fig. 17.26
Note—Contents Note:
Single Volume

614 p. ; 22 cm.

Contents: The persecution of the Jews / H. Krausnick -- The SS: instrument of domination / H. Buchheim -- Command and compliance / H. Buchheim -- The concentration camps, 1933-1945 / M. Brozat -- The Kommissarbefehl and mass execution of Soviet Russian prisoners of war / Hans-Adolf Jacobsen.

Fig. 17.27
Note—Contents Note:
Multi-Volume Work

3 v. : ill. ; 24 cm.

Contents: v.1. Education of a general, 1880-1939 -- v.2. Ordeal and hope, 1939-1942 -- v.3. Organizer of victory, 1943-1945.

Fig. 17.28
Note – Annotation for a Children's Book

Whittington, K   R
   Oswald, the sily goose / K. R. Whittington ; illustrated by
Tony Escott. -- 1st American ed. -- Scarsdale, N.Y.: Brad-
bury Press, 1974.

   58 p. : ill. ; 24 cm.

   SUMMARY: The fact that Oswald's various escapades don't always
have the desired result doesn't seem to bother him much.
   ISBN 0-87888-067-4 : $4.95

   [1. Humorous stories. 2. Short stories]   I. Escott, Tony,
ill. II. Title.

PZ7.W6187 Os 3   [Fic]   73-89222
                                                MARC
Library of Congress   AC

Standard Number and Terms of Availability Area

    This area follows the notes and forms a new paragraph in card catalog
format (Rules 1.8 and 2.8). Otherwise, it is separated from the notes by a period-
space-dash-space. The standard number is the International Standard Book
Number (ISBN), the International Standard Serial Number (ISSN), or any other
standard international numbering system. The terms of availability is an *optional*
element, and is usually the cost of the item. These two elements can be taken from
any source. The ISBN or ISSN will usually be found on the verso of the title page
in a book (Figures 17.29 and 17.30):

Fig. 17.29
Standard Number and Terms of Availability Area

Bibliography: p. 285-291.
ISBN 0-87287-125-8 : $12.50.

Fig. 17.30
ISBN Element for a Multi-Volume Set

ISBN 0-910608-10-5 (v.1). -- ISBN 0-910608-11 (v.2). --
ISBN 0-910608-12 (v.3).

Analysis of Works

An analytic entry is an added entry or access point for *part* of a work that has a comprehensive entry of its own (Rules 13.1-13.6). The analytic entry is made to create access points for materials otherwise difficult to locate. Rules 13.1-13.6 suggest several methods for making analytics. Figure 17.31 is a *comprehensive* entry for a book containing ten plays by George Bernard Shaw. The "note area" in Figure 17.31 is a method of analysis, since the catalog user can see exactly which plays are in the book.

Fig. 17.31
Analysis – Note Area

PR   Shaw, Bernard, 1856-1950.
5360   Ten short plays / George Bernard Shaw. -- New York :
P60a   Dodd, Mead, c1960.
                 319 p. ; 22 cm.

▶ Contents: Why she would not -- Shakes versus Shav -- The six of Calais -- Annajanska, the Bolshevik Empress - Augustus does his bit -- The Inca of Perusalem -- O'Flaherty V.C. -- The music-cure -- The shewing up of Blanco Posnet -- The admirable Bashville.

A small library might make a title added entry for each play to provide additional access points in the catalog. A larger library would probably not make ten title entries because this would take too much catalog space. Figure 17.32 shows a title analytic entry:

Fig. 17.32
Analysis – Title Added Entry from Contents Note

▶ Why she would not

PR   Shaw, Bernard, 1856-1950.
5360   Ten short plays / George Bernard Shaw. -- New York :
                 Dodd, Mead, c1960.
                 319 p. ; 22 cm.

"In" analytics are sometimes used when more bibliographic description is required (Rule 13.5). Figure 17.33 (page 190) is an "in" analytic entry. Analytics are used only in special cases when it is essential because of a work's importance.

Fig. 17.33
"In" Analytic

Seneca fiction, legends, and myths / collected by Jeremiah
 Curtis and J. N. B. Hewitt ; edited by J. N. B. Hewitt. --
 p. 37-819 ; 30 cm.

▶ *In* United States. Bureau of American Ethnology. Annual
 report, 1910-1911. -- Washington : Government Printing
 Office, 1918.

In Figure 17.33, the work on "Seneca Fiction ..." appears in the 1910-1911
Annual Report of the Bureau of American Ethnology. Unless this additional
access point were in a catalog, the casual library user might never become aware
of this item (and it is not currently used by the Library of Congress).

A third method of handling analytics, "Multilevel Description" (Rule 13.6) is
not covered in this text.

Many libraries use different formats for analytic entries. So long as the
information remains in-house and is not included in a computer data base, the
format is unimportant. But if the entry is going into a data base, a standardized
format acceptable to a computer program must be used. Analytics are used more
frequently in small public libraries and school libraries in order to bring out more
detail from a smaller collection.

Catalog Card Format for Title Entry

When a work is entered under its title as the main entry, the description is
presented in the form of a "hanging indention." In the "hanging indention," the
title is given on the first line in the position of the main entry. All other areas in
the description are indented under the title (Figure 17.34):

Fig. 17.34
Hanging Indention for Title Main Entry

Operations management : text and cases / by Paul W.
▶ Marshall ... [et al.]. -- Homewood, Ill. : R. D. Irwin,
 1975.

xii, 680 p. : ill. ; 23 cm.

Includes indexes.

1. Industrial management. I. Marshall, Paul W.

NOTES

[1]This text does not cover any of the older cataloging rules, so the beginning LMTA may not be aware of the changes from *AACR 1* to *AACR 2*. A general comparison of rules is beyond the scope of this text, and would only be confusing to a reader unfamiliar with any cataloging rules. Readers interested in these rules changes should see Ronald Hagler's *Where's That Rule? A Cross-Index of the Two Editions of the Anglo-American Cataloguing Rules, Incorporating a Commentary on the Second Edition and on Changes from Previous Cataloguing Standards* (Ottawa: Canadian Library Association, 1979), pp. 4-127, and Wesley Simonton's "An Introduction to AACR2," *Library Resources and Technical Services* 23 (Summer 1979): 321-37.

[2]*Anglo-American Cataloguing Rules*, 2nd ed. (Chicago: American Library Association, 1978), p. 1.

[3]The rule numbers cited refer to *AACR 2* rules. Rule 1.0B, for example, is found in *AACR 2*, p. 13.

[4]See *AACR 2* Rule 1.0D2 for a more detailed example of these areas. Some details have been left out in Figure 17.1 for clarity. Notice that the format in Rule 1.0D2 is *not* in card catalog format, but the same information is included.

[5]Appendix B in *AACR 2*, pp. 550-559, lists acceptable abbreviations used for all areas.

[6]The physical description of accompanying material is optional (Rule 2.5E1). Rule 1.5E gives several other options for describing accompanying materials, but these are not covered in this text.

REVIEW QUESTIONS AND EXERCISES

1. What is the difference between descriptive cataloging and subject cataloging?

2. What is an important difference between *AACR 2* and earlier cataloging rules in the way non-book materials are handled?

3. What are two purposes for cataloging rules?

4. Do all libraries follow all cataloging rules? Why?

5. What are some concerns about *AACR 2*?

6. What is an "area" in descriptive cataloging? What are the names of the areas?

7. What "elements" are included in each area?

8. What are "levels of description"? Using the examples in Figures 17.2 and 17.3, describe this text in level 1 and level 2 descriptive cataloging.

9. Why are punctuation and spacing so important in *AACR 2*?

10.   What are chief sources of information? Do they differ for each area?

11.   What does the statement of responsibility say when a work has more than three authors?

12.   In the publication element, is the publisher's name always given in full?

13.   What are the three elements in the physical description area?

14.   What is an open entry? When is it used?

15.   What are "notes" in a bibliographic description? When are notes made?

16.   Why are analytics useful? Why do you think analytics are not made for all books?

18

DESCRIPTIVE CATALOGING – PHYSICAL DESCRIPTION NON-BOOK MATERIALS

As stated earlier, the distinction made in this text between cataloging books and non-book materials is artificial. The distinction is made only to aid the learning process and keep the chapters a reasonable size. Certainly until *AACR 2*, there was little standardization in the descriptive cataloging rules for non-book materials. This always presented a problem for the computer-based exchange of information, and for the library user who could not depend on the same standardization found in book cataloging from library to library. *AACR 2* has helped resolve this problem.

The general rules in chapter 1 of *AACR 2* apply to all non-book materials. Rules for specific kinds of materials are found in chapters 3 to 12: cartographic materials (chapter 3), manuscripts (chapter 4), music (chapter 5), sound recordings (chapter 6), motion pictures and videorecordings (chapter 7), graphic materials (chapter 8), machine-readable data files (chapter 9), three-dimensional artifacts and realia (chapter 10), microforms (chapter 11), and serials (chapter 12).

Not every kind of non-book material will be covered in this chapter. Serials are discussed in chapter 23. Manuscripts, machine-readable data files, and music are excluded, because these specialized materials usually require experience to catalog; the beginning LMTA may find it too difficult for an introductory text.

Until recently, many libraries treated non-book materials like unwanted children. Non-book materials were cataloged "just like books," but they were not considered quite the equal of books. But this attitude is changing. Although the book remains the most important medium in most libraries, recognition of the importance of other media is growing rapidly.

CATALOGING TERMINOLOGY

Art original. An original work of art, as contrasted with a reproduction.

Art print. An etching, lithograph, engraving, etc. printed from a plate prepared by the artist.

Art reproduction. A mechanically reproduced copy of a work of art.

Artifact. An object made or modified by man.

Chart. Information arranged in tabular, outline, or graphic form on a sheet of paper. May also refer to a special map such as a navigation chart.

Container. A receptacle (box, folder, etc.) used to hold non-book materials.

Diorama. A three-dimensional representation of a scene.

Filmstrip. A strip of film with a series of still pictures to be viewed in sequence; usually 16mm or 35mm. with or without sound.

Flash card. A card with information to be displayed briefly as part of a teaching method.

Game. A set of materials with rules designed to be played for competition, for education, or for entertainment.

Globe. A spherical representation of the earth, universe, or other celestial body (e.g., the moon). A relief globe has raised surfaces to indicate elevations.

Kit. A collection of information in different media, usually on a specific topic, designed to be used as a unit. The media may be interdependent or used independently.

Map. A representation of a geographic area, usually on a flat surface. The geographic area can be on earth (terrestrial) or a celestial body. A *relief map* is one with raised surfaces to indicate land elevations.

Microform. A photographic miniature reproduction on film that must be magnified on special machines in order to be read; also called "micro-reproductions." Microform formats include aperture cards, microfiche, microfilm, and ultramicrofiche.

Microscope slide. A transparent mount containing an object for viewing under a microscope.

Model. A three-dimensional representation of a real object reproduced in the original size or to scale.

Motion picture. Film with a series of pictures that creates the illusion of movement when projected at the proper speed. May be with or without sound.

Multimedia kit. *See* Kit.

Picture. A two-dimensional representation on an opaque material, usually paper. May be a photograph, painting, drawing, etc.

Realia. Real objects, specimens, artifacts.

Slide. A single frame of film or other transparent material, usually in a 2x2-inch mounting. Must be used with a slide projector or viewer.

Sound recording. A recording of sound. Formats include cylinder, disc, and magnetic tape (also called phonocylinder, phonograph record, phonotape, and phonowire).

Transparency. A still image recorded on a transparent material; viewed with an overhead projector or similar device.

Videorecording. An electromagnetic recording made for playback on a television set. Various formats include electronic videorecording, videocassette, videodisc, and videotape. Videotape is currently the most common format. Almost always includes a sound track.

ABBREVIATIONS IN THE PHYSICAL DESCRIPTION AREA

The diversity of non-book materials requires great variations in the physical description of a work. All of the abbreviations listed below are commonly used to describe sound recordings, motion pictures, videorecordings, and certain graphic materials. Become familiar with this list because the terms and abbreviations are used in many of the examples in this chapter.

Abbreviation	Term
b&w	black and white
cm.	centimeter, centimeters
col.	color
diam.	diameter
fps.	frames per second
fr.	frame, frames
ft.	foot, feet
hr.	hour, hours
in.	inch, inches
ips.	inches per second
mm.	millimeter, millimeters
min.	minute, minutes
mono.	monophonic
photo(s).	photograph, photographs
quad.	quadraphonic
rpm.	revolutions per minute
sd.	sound
sec.	seconds
si.	silent
stereo.	stereophonic

ARRANGEMENT OF INFORMATION ON THE CATALOG CARD

The arrangement of cataloging information is the same for non-books and books. The material (or type of publication) specific details area, which is not used for books, is discussed under cartographic materials. In general, the greatest difference in descriptive cataloging for books and non-books is in the physical description area.

In the title and statement of responsibility area, an optional general material designation element (GMD) occurs that is not used for books. The general material designation for non-book materials will be used in the examples in this text. The GMD is not always used by the Library of Congress and other cataloging agencies. Currently the Library of Congress uses these GMDs: filmstrip, kit, microform, motion picture, slide, sound recording, transparency, and videorecording.

General Material Designation

Lightfoot, Gordon
Don Quixote [sound recording]

The general material designation follows the title proper and comes *before* other title information:

The Southwest Indians [filmstrip] : tribes of men and
desert. --

A list of recommended general material designations is given at Rule 1.1C1 in *AACR 2*. There are two lists: List 2 is to be used for North American cataloging agencies. The Library of Congress and possibly other cataloging services may not use the general materials designation for all types of non-book materials; rather, LC intends to use the GMD selectively. Many catalogers believe the physical description area to be the more important identifying element for non-book material. Since the GMD is optional, each library is free to use or not use this element.

CARTOGRAPHIC MATERIALS
(Rules 3.0-3.11)

The chief source of information and the prescribed sources of information for cartographic materials are covered in Rules 3.0B2 and 3.0B3. In general, an item itself and/or its container are the chief sources of information. The mathematical data area is unique to cartographic materials and gives the scale or projection data (Figure 18.1):

Fig. 18.1*
Map—Mathematical Data Area

United States. Geological Survey
[1]State of Nevada [2][map] : [3]base map with highways and
contours / United States Geological Survey. -- [4]Edition of 1965.
-- [5]Scale 1:500,000 ; Lambert conformal conic projection.

Key to Note Items in Figure 18.1

[1]Title proper
[2]General material designation
[3]Other title information
[4]Edition area
[5]Mathematical data area

A different type of information is given in the extent of item element.
Instead of pages, the extent of the item is indicated by the number of physical
units and the appropriate term:

1 map	1 celestial chart
1 atlas (200p.)	3 plans
1 globe	5 map sections
1 bird's-eye view	

For a complete discussion of the various designations, refer to Rule 3.5B.1.
The size for two-dimensional cartographic materials is given in terms of
height and width (Figure 18.2). For atlases, size is the same as for a book—height
in centimeters (Figure 18.4, page 198). For globes, size is diameter in centimeters
(Figure 18.3, page 198). Some examples are:

1 map : col. ; 25 x 35 cm.
1 globe : col. ; 12 cm. in diam.
1 globe : col., plastic, mounted on metal stand ; 28 cm. in diam.

Notice that the material and mounting can be specified, if it is a significant fact
(Rules 3.5C4 and 3.5C5). Other descriptive information is often given in notes,
and Rule 3.7 lists 21 different kinds of notes appropriate to use with cartographic
materials.

---

*The Library of Congress does not currently plan to use the general material designation [map] in
their cataloging.

Fig. 18.2
Map

United States. Geological Survey
[1]State of Nevada [2][map] : [3]base map with highway and contours / [4]United States Geological Survey. -- [5]Edition of 1965.
-- [6]Scale 1:500,000 ; Lambert conformal conic projection. --
-- [7]Washington : Geological Survey, 1965.
[8]1 map : col. ; 60 x 110 cm.

[9]Contour interval 500 feet.

Key to Note Items in Figure 18.2

[1]Title proper
[2]General material designation
[3]Other title information
[4]Statement of responsibility
[5]Edition area

[6]Mathematical data area: notice both scale and projection are given
[7]Publication, distribution, etc. area
[8]Physical description
[9]Note

Notice the handling of the physical description for an atlas in book format. The extent of the item is "1 atlas," followed by the number of pages, the number of maps, and the height of the atlas (Figure 18.4).

Fig. 18.3
Globe

Rand McNally world portrait globe [globe] / compiled by
Rand McNally. -- Scale 1:31,680,000. -- Chicago : Rand
McNally, 1966.
1 globe : col., plastic, mounted on metal stand ; 42 cm. in
diam.

Fig. 18.4
Atlas

Atlas of Mexico / Michael E. Bonine ... [et al.]. -- Austin :
University of Texas, Bureau of Business Research, 1970.
1 atlas (138 p.) : 191 col. maps ; 28 cm.

Scale of principal maps : 1:15,000,000.
Bibliography : p. 137-138.
ISBN 87755-004-2 : $10.00.

SOUND RECORDINGS
(Rules 6.0-6.11)

The chief source of information and the prescribed sources of information are covered in Rules 6.0B1 and 6.0B2. The general rules in chapter 1 of *AACR 2* apply. The physical description area differs from other types of material and is a critical feature. Because it is necessary to have special equipment to use sound recordings, the cataloging description must also give detailed physical and technical specifications. Playing speed, size, and special recording techniques must be known in order to match the recording with correct playback equipment. There is little use in checking out a 78 rpm disc if the turntable only plays 33 1/3 rpm discs. Sound recordings include discs, tapes (open reel to reel), tape cassettes, tape cartridges, rolls, and sound recordings on film. The general material designation [sound recording] is used for all of the above items.

In the physical description area, the extent of the item is the number of physical units followed by the appropriate term:

1 sound disc	2 piano rolls
3 sound cassettes	1 sound tape reel
1 sound track film	

The extent of the item is followed by the total playing time in minutes:

1 sound disc (27 min.)

Other physical details follow the time and are given when appropriate in this order (Rule 6.5C1):

1) type of recording (sound track films)

2) playing speed

3) groove characteristics (discs)

4) track configuration (sound track films)

5) number of tracks (tape cartridges, cassettes, and reels)

6) number of sound channels

7) recording and reproduction characteristics (tapes)

Some examples of the physical description follow:

1 sound disc (42 min.) : 33 1/3 rpm, stereo ; 12 in.
1 sound track film reel (18 min.) : magnetic, 24 fps, center track
1 sound cassette (60 min.) : 3 3/4 ips. mono.

Because there are so many possibilities and technical details that must be given, the reader should refer to Rules 6.5C1-6.5C8 and 6.5D1-6.5D7 for specific kinds of materials.

It is recommended that a summary or list of the contents of a sound recording be given (Rules 6.7B17 and 6.7B18). The publisher's number is also given in a note when it is available. The examples in Figures 18.5 and 18.6 show the areas for a sound recording.

Fig. 18.5
Sound Recording—Disc

London Symphony Orchestra.
    Classic rock [sound recording] / London Symphony Orchestra ; Royal Choral Society. -- Minntonka, Minn. : K-Tel International, 1979.
    1 sound disc (52 min.) : 33 1/3 rpm, stereo ; 12 in.
    Contents: Bohemian rhapsody--Life on Mars--A whiter shade of pale--Whole lotta love--Paint it black--Nights in white satin--Lucy in the sky with diamonds--Without you--I'm not in love--Sailing.
    K-Tel : NU9580

Fig. 18.6
Sound Recording—Cassette

Benson, George.
    Weekend in L.A. [sound recording] / George Benson. -- Burbank, Calif. : Warner Brothers, 1978.
    1 sound cassette (70 min.) : 1 7/8 ips, stereo.
    Contents: Weekend in L.A.--On Broadway--Down here on the ground--California P.M.--The greatest love of all--It's all in the game--Windsong--Ode to a Kudu--Lady blue--We all remember Wes--We as love.
    Warner Brothers : J5A3139

Notice that no dimensions are given for the cassette because it was the *standard size* (3 7/8x2 1/2-inches) and the tape was a *standard* 1/4-inch width (Rule 6.5D4).

MOTION PICTURES AND VIDEORECORDINGS
(Rules 7.1-7.10)

The chief source of information and the prescribed sources of information for these materials are covered in Rules 7.0B1 and 7.0B2. In general, the item itself and its container are the chief sources of information. Again, the main difference in describing these materials compared to a book is in the physical description area. The general material designations for these materials are [motion picture] and [videorecording].

In the physical description area, the extent of the item is the number of physical units followed by the appropriate term:

1 film cartridge	2 film loops
1 film cassette	2 videocassettes
1 film reel	1 videodisc
1 videoreel	

The playing time is indicated after the extent of item:

1 film reel (27 min.)

Other physical details follow the time and the following are given when appropriate (Rule 7.5C1):

1) aspect ratio and special projection characteristics (motion pictures only)

2) sound characteristics

3) color

4) projection speed (motion pictures only)

5) playing speed (videodiscs only)

Some examples of physical description follow:

    ' 1 film reel (52 min.) : Panavision ; sd., col., 25 fps

The above description is for 1 film reel with a playing time of 52 minutes; Panavision is the special projection characteristic; the film has sound (sd.) and is in color (col.); and the projection speed is 25 feet per second (fps).

The dimensions are the width of a film (in millimeters) and the width of a videotape (in inches). A videodisc dimension is the diameter in inches. Some examples are:

2 film reels (152 min.) : Panavision ; sd., col., 25 fps ; 35 mm.
1 film cassette (15 min.) : sd., b&w ; standard 8 mm.
1 videoreel (32 min.) : sd., col. ; 1/2 in.
1 videodisc (41 min.) : sd., col., 1500 rpm ; 8 in.

A number of special notes for motion pictures and videorecordings are discussed in Rule 7.7. Of special interest are the notes giving the cast of featured players or performers, the credits for others who contributed to the production, and a brief summary of the contents (Figures 18.7, page 202, 18.8 and 18.9, page 203):

Fig. 18.7
Motion Picture

Hailey's gift [motion picture] / Cornpepper Productions. -- New
York : Learning Corp. of America, 1978.
1 film reel (23 min.) : sd., col. ; super 8 mm + 1 teacher's
guide.

Cast: Barry Morse, Kate Parr, Simon Cooke, Sammy Snyders,
Kevin Davies.
Credits: Producer, Robert K. Vale ; director, Bruce Pitt-
man ; writer, Chris M. Worsnop ; music, Haygood Hardy.

(Continued on next card)

Fig. 18.7 (cont'd)

Hailey's gift [motion picture] 1978 (Card 2)

Summary: The children in a small village are visited by an old
man, Hailey B. McMoon, who enchants them by opening their
eyes and their hearts to the wonders of mutual understanding.

Fig. 18.8
Motion Picture

Kindergarten puppy training [motion picture] / Walter J. Kline.
-- New York : W. J. Kline, 1974.
1 film reel (15 min.) : sd., col. ; 16 mm. -- (Dog
obedience training series).

Credits: Instructors, Margaret Pearsall, Milo Pearsall.
Summary: Provides examples of obedience instruction given to
young dogs, including instruction in walking on a leash.

Fig. 18.9
Videorecording

History of United States measures [videorecording] / KQED-TV.
-- San Francisco : KQED-TV, Bay Area Educational TV,
1965.
1 videoreel (20 min.) : sd., b&w ; 2 in. -- (Math on the
move series).

Summary: A concise history of the changing units of measurements in the United States.

Notice that Figures 18.7, 18.8, and 18.9 are all in "hanging indention" format because all are title entries. Most motion pictures and videorecordings will be entered under title, which will be discussed in the chapter on main entries.

GRAPHIC MATERIALS
(Rules 8.0-8.11)

Graphic materials include a variety of two-dimensional items ranging from original works of art to wall charts. Rule 8.5 lists ways to give a physical description of nineteen different types of graphic materials. The reader must refer to *AACR 2* for guidance in describing these materials because of the diversity of needs. This text will give examples only for several types of material beause of space limitations. Also, many of these graphic materials are seldom handled by the cataloging department unless, of course, *AACR 2* changes this.

The chief source of information is the item itself, any related labels, and any container that is an integral part of the item. Other prescribed sources are the container, accompanying textual materials, and outside sources (Rules 8.0B1 and 8.0B2). Remember, the general rules in chapter 1 of *AACR 2* apply to all materials. The major difference is again in the physical description area and the notes area.

The number of general material designations for graphic materials is limited to eight different media (Rule 1.1C1). However, you are instructed to use the descriptor [picture] for any materials not covered by one of the allowed material designations. For example, a poster would have the GMD [picture] because the term "poster" is not found in Rule 1.1C1. Some examples of graphic materials follow (Figures 18.10-18.18):

Fig. 18.10
Art Print

Fowler, Mel.
    Better to walk than to ride like that [picture] / Mel Fowler.
-- [S.l. : s.n., 1975?]
    1 art print : etching ; 19 x 16 cm.

    Size when framed: 31 x 28 cm.
    Number 58 of 100.

Notice that in Figure 18.10 neither the place of publication nor publisher is known, and the date could not be verified. The general materials designation [picture] is used because "art print" is not on the list of approved designations in Rule 1.1C1. The footnote for Rule 1.1C1 tells us to use "picture" when one of the other designations does not fit. The notes give the size when framed, and indicate that the art print is copy number 58 of 100 copies.

Fig. 18.11
Art Print

Picasso, Pablo, 1881-1973.
　Côte d'azur [picture] / Picasso. -- Paris : Ministere de Travoux Publics et des Transports, Commissariat General du Tourisme, 1962.
　1 art print : lithograph, col.; 99 x 65 cm.

　Size when framed: 110 x 74 cm.

Fig. 18.12
Filmstrip

Oil [filmstrip] : from earth to you / American Petroleum Institute. -- New York : The Institute, 1954.
　1 filmstrip (38 fr.) : b&w ; 35 mm. -- (Petroleum school series)

　Summary: Captioned drawings and photographs describe the formation of petroleum, locating an oil field, drilling for oil, and refining of oil.

Notice in Figure 18.12 that the publisher is cited as "The Institute." Rule 1.4D4 allows a shortened form of a publisher's name if it appears in full in the statement of responsibility.

Fig. 18.13
Poster

Shamir
   30 years ago [picture] : Warsaw Ghetto uprising, 1943-1973 /
Shamir. -- New York : World Federation of Bergen Belsen
Survivors [197-]
   1 poster : col. ; 94 x 71 cm.

Unmounted.

Fig. 18.14
Flash Cards

Multiplication [flash card] / Milton Bradley. -- Springfield,
   Mass. : Bradley, 1963.
   50 flash cards : b&w ; 9 x 15 cm.

For grades 3 to 6.

Fig. 18.15
Kit

Developing understanding of self and others [kit] / American
   Guidance Service. -- Circle Pines, Minn. : The Service,
   1970.
   2 v., 58 flash cards, 32 posters, 8 hand puppets, 20 sound
discs, teacher's manual, in container ; 49 x 36 x 11 cm.

For grades K-3.

The example of a kit (Figure 18.15) is arbitrarily placed in this chapter. The rules for works made up of several different media, none of which predominates, are covered in Rules 1.10A-1.10C3. The general material designation [kit] indicates that the item comprises more than two different media. (There are five different media in Figure 18.15.) Rule 1.10C2 gives three methods for handling the physical description of multi-media works.

Fig. 18.16
Slides

```
Rembrandt Hermenszoon van Rijn, 1606-1669.
    Rembrandt self portraits [slide] / Rembrandt. -- New York :
American Library Color Slides, 1968.
    50 slides : col.
```

Notice the size of the slide is not given when it is a standard 2x2-inch size (Rule 8.5D5).

Fig. 18.17
Transparencies

```
Allotropes of oxygen [transparency] / Keuffel and Esser.
    -- Hoboken, N.J. : Keuffel and Esser, 1967.
    5 transparencies (7 overlays) : col. ; 21 x 26 cm. -- (Chemis-
try series).

    Summary: Presents basic chemical theory, chemical principles
and chemical applications.
```

Fig. 18.18
Wall Chart

The modernized metric system [chart] : the international system of units (SI) and its relationship to U.S. customary units / National Bureau of Standards. -- Washington : The Bureau, 1968.
1 wall chart : col. ; 74 x 138 cm.

THREE-DIMENSIONAL ARTIFACTS AND REALIA
(Rules 10.0-10.10)

"Artifacts" covers all kinds of man-made three-dimensional objects including models, dioramas, games, puzzles, sculptures, exhibits, machines, clothing, and many naturally occurring objects. Notice that microscope slides are cataloged by these rules, as opposed to art slides, which were covered in the previous section.

The chief source of information and prescribed sources are generally the object itself and any accompanying textual materials and container. Again, the general material designations are limited to the approved list in Rule 1.1C1: diorama, game, microscope slide, model, realia. The most variation comes in the physical description area, the extent of item, and other physical details elements. Some examples follow (Figures 18.19-18.24):

Fig. 18.19
Diorama

Frogs and toads [diorama] / DCA Educational Products. -- Washington, PA. : DCA, 1970.
1 diorama (various pieces) : col. ; 33 x 22 x 9 cm.

Fig. 18.20
Game

Population [game] : a game of man and society / developed
by Urban Systems. -- Cambridge, Mass. : Urban Systems,
1971.
1 game (various pieces) : col. ; in container, 28 x 51 x 6 cm.

Contents listed on inside of container.

Fig. 18.21
Game

Scrabble [game] : a crossword game / Production and Marketing Co. -- 1953 ed. -- New York : Selchow & Righter,
1953.
1 game (106 pieces) : wood ; in box, 19 x 37 x 4 cm.

Fig. 18.22
Microscope Slides

Fern life history [microscope slide] / Ward's Natural Science
Establishment. -- Rochester, N.Y. : Ward's [1971?]
8 microscope slides : col. ; 8 x 3 cm.

For high school and college levels.
Summary: Covers life cycle of a fern, including prothallium,
sex organs, young sporophyte, vegetative organs of mature
sporophyte, and sporangia.

Fig. 18.23
Model

Brain model [model] : human / Sargent-Welch Scientific. --
Skokie, Ill. : Sargent-Welch [1974?]
1 model : plastic, col. ; 14 x 12 x 13 cm. + 1 guide sheet

Plastic replica colored to simulate actual brain.
For high school and college levels.

Fig. 18.24
Realia

Geological rock collection [realia] / Sargent-Welch Scientific.
-- Skokie, Ill. : Sargent-Welch [1967?]
32 rock specimens : col. ; in box, 28 x 41 x 6 cm.

Coded identification chart on lid of container.

MICROFORMS
(Rules 11.0-11.10)

The rules in this chapter of *AACR 2* cover all kinds of microform materials. The most common microforms are microfilm reels and microfiche. Microform materials may be reproductions of existing materials or original works. The chief source of information for microfilms and microfiche is the title frame, which gives relevant information about the publication. The container is a prescribed source and is often useful for identification of the publication. The container or other eye-readable information may be considered the chief source of information if more complete information is given there. Some examples of microform materials follow (Figures 18.25-18.27).

Fig. 18.25
Microfilm Reel

Zeitlin, Jacob Israel, 1902-
What kind of business is this [microform] : reminiscences of the book trade and book collectors / Jacob Zeitlin. -- Berkeley : University of California, Library Photographic Service, 1968.
1 microfilm reel : negative ; 35 mm. -- (The Annual public lectures on books and bibliography ; 1958) (University of Kansas Publications : Libraries series ; no. 6).

(Continued on next card)

Fig. 18.25 (cont'd)

Zeitlin, Jacob Israel. What kind of business is this, 1968 (Card 2)

Published originally as a pamphlet by the University of Kansas Libraries.

Fig. 18.26
Microfiche

Regan, Brian T   , 1938-
The Gothic word [microform] / by Brian T. Regan. -- 1st ed. -- Albany : State University of New York Press, 1972.
4 microfiches : negative ; 11 x 15 cm.

Bibliography: p. 323-336.

Fig. 18.27
Microfiche

Collier, Alan R
   The assessment of "self-concept" in early childhood education [microform] / Alan R. Collier. -- Arlington, Va. : Computer Microfilm International, 1971.
   2 microfiches : negative ; 11 x 15 cm. -- (ERIC reports ;
ED 57910).

STORAGE, EQUIPMENT, AND PROCESSING

Non-book media present storage and use problems different from those associated with books. However, storage problems are usually a concern of public services rather than technical services.

Special shelving and cabinets are required for proper storage of microscope slides, sound recordings, videorecordings, and similar materials. In addition, special equipment is necessary to use many types of non-book materials. For example, a phonodisc is useless without a turntable, amplifier, and speakers; a motion picture requires a movie projector, screen, and speakers if it is a picture with sound; and use of a reel of microfilm will require a microfilm reader. As libraries acquire more non-book media, they need to acquire hardware to use them. Some examples of equipment found in a medium-sized library are: 8mm movie projectors, Super 8mm movie projectors, turntables, amplifiers, 16mm movie projectors, slide projectors, wall screens, filmstrip previewers, speakers, television sets, videorecorders, overhead projectors, tape recorders, cassette players, headphones, microfilm readers and reader/printers, and microfiche readers and reader/printers.

Some libraries provide only the non-book media, leaving the patron to get the necessary equipment, while others provide both the material and equipment. Most libraries will at least have equipment for using sound recordings and microform materials. The availability of equipment is often indicated by an entry in the catalog (Figure 18.28).

Fig. 18.28
Catalog Card for Equipment

---

8 mm Motion Picture Projector (Equipment)

For information inquire at Reference Desk.

Care is necessary when handling non-book materials in cataloging and processing. Cataloging staff must become familiar with the requirements for handling materials to avoid accidental damage.[1] Phonodiscs, for example, must be picked up only by the edges and not exposed to any excessive or direct source of heat. Films should not be exposed to dust or jarred and should be handled only along the edges. Magnetic tapes, audio tapes, and videotapes should be handled as little as possible, and these must not be exposed to vibration or magnetic fields, such as those given off by some theft detection devices. These are only a few examples of potential problems in handling non-book materials. It is important that any special handling requirements for a particular medium be known before starting the cataloging process.

NOTES

[1]For an excellent discussion of preservation and handling of non-book materials, see Jean Riddle Weihs, Shirley Lewis, and Janet Macdonald's *Non-book Materials: The Organization of Integrated Collections*, 2nd ed. (Ottawa: Canadian Library Association, 1979).

REVIEW QUESTIONS AND EXERCISES

1. Name and define five different kinds of non-book materials.

2. What do each of the following mean in describing non-book materials:

   a. b&w   f. cm.

   b. rpm   g. col.

   c. sd.   h. si.

   d. stereo   i. sec.

   e. ft.   j. fps.

3. What is the general material designation? Can any term be used for a general material designation? Is it mandatory to use the general material designation?

4. The mathematical data area is used to describe what kind of materials?

5. What are the elements in the physical description area for a sound recording?

6. What is the chief source of information for each of the following:

   a. sound recordings   d. films

   b. motion pictures   e. transparencies

   c. atlases   f. microfilm and microfiche

7. What do the following physical descriptions tell the catalog user:

   a. 1 film reel (52 min.) : Panavision ; sd., col., 25 fps

   b. 1 globe : col., plastic, mounted on metal stand ; 42 cm. in diam.

    c. 1 art print : lithograph ; 99 x 65 cm.

    d. 1 sound disc (52 min.) : 33 1/3 rpm, stereo ; 12 in.

    e. 1 atlas (138 p.) : 191 col. maps ; 28 cm.

8. Discuss special storage and handling problems associated with the following non-book materials:

    a. phonograph record

    b. motion pictures

    c. videotapes

    d. tape cassettes

    e. microfilm

9. What kinds of equipment are needed to use the following non-book materials:

    a. motion pictures

    b. filmstrips

    c. overhead transparencies

    d. phonodiscs

    e. microfilm

19

CATALOGING—MAIN ENTRY, ADDED ENTRY, AND REFERENCES

This chapter is concerned with the second element of descriptive cataloging—selecting the main entry and added entries for a work. The main entry and added entries, also called access points, are the entries in a catalog where an item can be located.

Remember, a knowledge of rules for selecting main and added entries is important for all library staff. Reference staff will be of little help if they are unaware of how materials are entered in the catalog. And, an acquisitions staff that cannot accurately locate material by its main entry may order an unacceptable number of duplicates. Cataloging rules are not limited to use in the cataloging department, but are important in many areas of library service.

The process of determining main entry and added entries consists of three separate steps in *AACR 2*. First, the cataloger *selects* the main entry and required added entries (chapter 21). Second, the *proper form* of the entry is determined (chapters 22, 23, 24, and 25). And, finally, any required references from different forms of a name are made (chapter 26). These rules apply to all kinds of materials.

As you read this text, remember again that concurrent reference to *AACR 2* is necessary. Only a few basic rules for main and added entries will be discussed, and no overly complex rules or examples are given to help avoid confusion. Once the basic rules are learned, the more complex rules will have more meaning. The basic rules discussed in this chapter will cover most materials acquired by a medium-sized library. Remember that *AACR 2* skips from chapter 13 to chapter 21; there are *no* chapters numbered 14 to 20. These chapters are being reserved for future additions.

CATALOGING TERMINOLOGY

Anonymous work. A work of unknown authorship.

Collective title. A title proper assigned to an item that includes several works.

Compiler. A person who produces a collection by bringing together works by various persons or corporate bodies, or works by one person or corporate body.

Composer. The author of music.

Compound surname. A name formed from two or more proper names, usually connected by a hyphen, conjunction, or preposition (e.g., Liddell Hart, Scott-Moncrieff).

Corporate body. An organization or group of persons that is identified by a name and that acts as an entity. Corporate bodies include associations, conferences, institutions, business firms, and government agencies.

Editor. A person who prepares for publication or supervises the publication of a work or collection of works that are not his or her own. Responsibility may extend to revising and providing commentaries, introductory matter, etc.

Explanatory reference. A detailed *see* or *see also* reference used to guide the catalog user to information in the catalog.

Joint author. A person who collaborates with one or more associates to produce a work. The contributions of the various joint authors often cannot be distinguished.

Mixed responsibility. When more than one person or corporate body performs different activities in the creation of a work (e.g., one person writes a work, and a second person illustrates it).

Name authority file. A file of the proper form for names in a catalog. It records the *see* and *see also* references made from other forms of the name. May cite the source used to establish the name.

Name-title reference. A reference in which both a name and title are included in the reference, as opposed to a name or title alone.

See also **reference.** A guiding device in a catalog that directs the user from a name or subject to related names or subjects.

See **reference.** A guiding device in a catalog that directs the user from the form of a name or subject not used in the catalog to the form that is used.

Shared responsibility. Two or more persons or corporate bodies perform the same activity in the creation of a work. The contributions may be distinct or inseparable.

Translator. A person who translates a work from one language into another language.

Uniform title. The title chosen for cataloging purposes when a work has appeared under varying titles.

BASIC RULES FOR DETERMINING MAIN AND ADDED ENTRIES

Sources for Entries

The main entry and added entries should be determined from the chief source of information for the item. The chief source of information is discussed in Rule 1.0B1 and in the rules for specific kinds of material. The main entry for a book, for example, is taken from the title page, the chief source of information for a book. The main entry for a motion picture is taken from the title frames of the film, the chief source of information for a film.

Works by a Single Personal Author
(Rules 21.1A and 21.4)

A work that is the responsibility of a single author is entered under the name of that person (Figures 19.1 and 19.2). It can be a collection or selection of works by the author, or a single work.

Fig. 19.1
Work of a Personal Author—Single Work

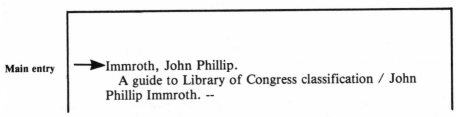

In Figure 19.1, the author was named on the title page, and no question of responsibility is raised.

Fig. 19.2
Work by a Single Author—Collection of Works
with Editorial Involvement

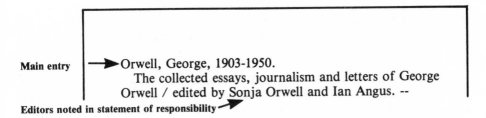

The main entry in Figure 19.2 is George Orwell, because he is the person *responsible for the content* of the work. The editors are only responsible for assembling the material; they did not write the essays. Added entries are made for the editors, so their names will be additional access points for the work (Rule 21.30D).

Works by a Corporate Body
(Rules 21.1B and 21.4B)

Rule 21.1B2 lists five categories of works issued by corporate bodies that must be entered under the name of the corporate body. The reader should refer to *AACR 2* for the complete list of categories. (These categories may be a little confusing to the beginning LMTA, so this text will not go into great detail about them.) In general, if a work or collection of works is produced by a corporate body and the work is about the corporate body, the main entry is the name of the corporate body.

The corporate entry is useful for locating material, in spite of any initial concerns of the beginning cataloger. For example, assume one person working for Texas Utilities compiled the annual stockholders report (Figure 19.3). A main entry under that person's name would be useless. The important concept is that the report is the *company's* report, *not the person's* report.

Fig. 19.3
Work Issued by a Single Corporate Body

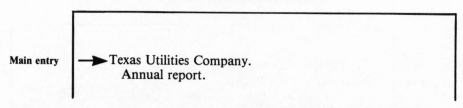

Main entry   ➤ Texas Utilities Company.
              Annual report.

This report deals with the internal policies and finances of a company and is entered under the name of the corporate body according to Rule 21.1B2.

Fig. 19.4
Work Issued by a Government Agency—Single Corporate Body

Main entry   ➤ Library of Congress.
              Annual report of the Librarian of Congress /

Rule 21.1B1 includes governments and government agencies in the definition of corporate bodies. Thus, the Library of Congress' *Annual Report* is entered under the governmental agency name, not the name of a particular librarian (Figure 19.4).

Fig. 19.5
Corporate Entry—Work Issued by a Conference

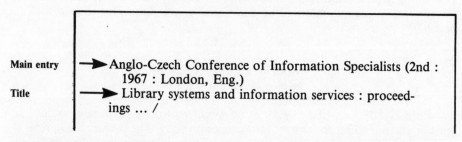

Main entry   ➤ Anglo-Czech Conference of Information Specialists (2nd :
              1967 : London, Eng.)
Title   ➤ Library systems and information services : proceed-
              ings ... /

A conference is considered a corporate body, since many persons are usually involved and individual responsibility is difficult to determine. The title page of the conference proceedings in Figure 19.5 listed three editors responsible for gathering the materials and writing introductory remarks. Added entries are made for the editors (Rule 21.30D), but the main entry is the name of the conference.

Works of Shared Responsibility
(Rule 21.6)

When a work has two or three personal or corporate body authors, the main entry is usually the first one named in the chief source of information. An exception to the first named author rule occurs when another name appears in a more prominent position or is set apart by larger type.

Fig. 19.6
Shared Responsibility – Principal Author Indicated

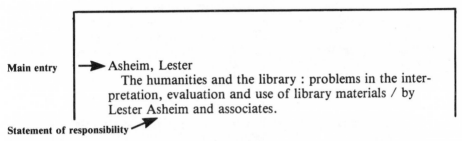

The title page of the item described in Figure 19.6 reads "The Humanities and the Library ... by Lester Asheim and associates." The main entry is Asheim because he is indicated as the principal author, the others being associates.

Fig. 19.7
Shared Responsibility – No Principal Author

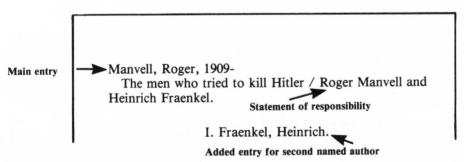

Roger Manvell was the first author named on the title page of the item described in Figure 19.7. The type size was the same and neither author was designated as a principal author, so an added entry is made for Heinrich Fraenkel (Rule 21.30B).

When *more than three* persons or corporate bodies are responsible for the creation of a work, the entry is under the title if no principal author is indicated. An added entry is made for the first person or corporate body named (Rule 21.6C2).

Fig. 19.8
Shared Responsibility—More Than Three Authors

Operations management : text and cases / by Paul
Marshall ... [et al.]. --

I. Marshall, Paul

Added entry for first named author

In Figure 19.8, the chief source of information—the title page—gave the
following information: *"Operations Management* ... by Paul Marshall, William
J. Abernathy, Jeffrey G. Miller, Richard P. Olsen, Richard S. Rosenbloom, D.
Daryl Wyckoff." Because more than three coequal authors are listed, the main
entry is the title and an added entry is made for the first named author. Notice the
"hanging indention" format used for a title main entry.

Collections and Works Produced under Editorial Direction
(Rule 21.7)

When a work is produced under editorial direction, it is entered under its title
if it has a "collective title." A work produced by editors or compilers is usually a
collection of independent works written by different authors. Rule 21.7A
establishes four categories of works produced by editors that are entered
under title. Added entries are made for the editors or compilers if there are not
more than three. For more than three editors, make an added entry for the principal compiler if identified, or for the first one named.

Fig. 19.9
A Collection Produced under Editorial Direction
with a Collective Title

Title
main entry

Readings in the history of American marketing : settle-
ment to Civil War / compiled by Stanley J. Shapiro
and Alton F. Dooley. --

Statement of responsibility

I. Shapiro, Stanley J. II. Dooley, Alton F.

Added entries for editors

In Figure 19.9, the work is a collection of articles brought together by the
compilers. Added entries can be made for both compilers.

Another example of a work produced by editors is Figure 19.10. The seminar had numerous participants, and the papers were assembled by two editors. Entry is under title, with added entries for the editors.

Fig. 19.10
Work Produced under Editorial Direction with a
Collective Title

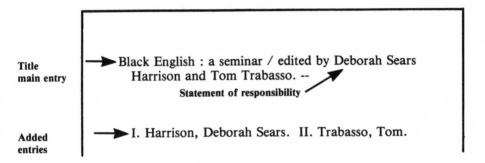

Title
main entry

Added
entries

When a work is produced under editorial direction *without a collective title*, it is entered under the main entry appropriate for the *first* work in the collection named in the chief source of information. If there is no chief source—e.g., a title page for a book—enter under the appropriate heading for the first work (Rule 21.7C).

Fig. 19.11
Work Produced under Editorial Direction with
No Collective Title

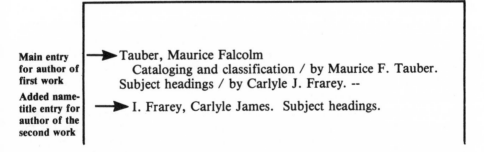

Main entry
for author of
first work
Added name-
title entry for
author of the
second work

In Figure 19.11, notice the added entry for Frarey is a "name-title" entry. When entered in a catalog, the name-title access point allows the catalog user to see immediately that Frarey is the author of a work titled *Subject Headings*. No editor was named for this work, but it was clearly an editorial responsibility to place the two separate works together.

Translations
(Rule 21.14)

The main entry for a translated work is the same as for the *original* work. The main entry is *not* the translator. The author is the person responsible for the content of the work, *regardless of the language* of the text. A translator may be creative but is not responsible for the intellectual content of the work. An added entry is made for a translator if appropriate under Rule 21.30K1 (Figure 19.12):

Fig. 19.12
A Translation

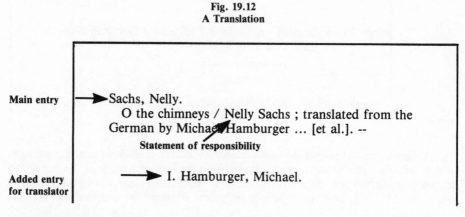

Main entry ➤Sachs, Nelly.
　　　　O the chimneys / Nelly Sachs ; translated from the German by Michael Hamburger ... [et al.]. --
　　　　Statement of responsibility

Added entry ➤ I. Hamburger, Michael.
for translator

An added entry is made for the translator, because the work is in verse.

Entry of Sound Recordings
(Rule 21.23)

Main and added entries for sound recordings are generally handled like other materials. A sound recording of *one* work is entered under the heading for the work recorded. For example, a recording by Henry Madden and Manu Tupon of Dee Brown's book, *Bury My Heart at Wounded Knee*, is entered under the heading for Dee Brown. Added entries are made for the two principal performers, Madden and Tupon (rule 21.23A).

In a second instance, a sound recording of *two or more* works by the same person is entered under the entry for that person, with an added entry for the principal performers. If there are more than three principal performers, make an added entry only for the first one named (Rule 21.23B) (Figure 19.13).

And last, a sound recording of works by *different* persons is entered under the principal performer (Rule 21.23C) (Figure 19.14). If there are two or three other principal performers, make added entries for them. The phonograph record described in Figure 19.14, included twelve songs, all by different composers, with one principal performer.

Fig. 19.13
Sound Recording of Works by One Author and One Principal Performer

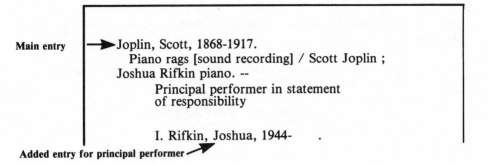

Main entry → Joplin, Scott, 1868-1917.
    Piano rags [sound recording] / Scott Joplin ;
Joshua Rifkin piano. --
        Principal performer in statement
        of responsibility

        I. Rifkin, Joshua, 1944-   .
Added entry for principal performer →

Fig. 19.14
**Sound Recording of Works by Several Composers and
One Principal Performer**

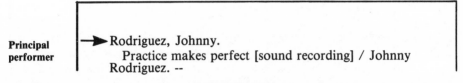

Principal → Rodriguez, Johnny.
performer   Practice makes perfect [sound recording] / Johnny
Rodriguez. --

Added Entries
(Rules 21.29-21.30)

Added entries are those entries, other than subject entries, made in addition
to the main entry. Many examples earlier in this chapter illustrated some of the
instances when added entries are made (Figures 19.7-19.13). These additional
access points help increase opportunities for the catalog user to locate desired
materials. Added entries are especially useful when the main entry is not known.
In general, an added entry can be made for a person, corporate body, or title if
the entry might be helpful to a catalog user. This requires the judgment of the
cataloger. A complete listing of possible added entries is given in Rules 21.29A
through 21.30M. Below are examples of three common types of added entries
(Figures 19.15, 19.16, and 19.17):

Fig. 19.15
Added Entry for Shared Responsibility by Two Authors

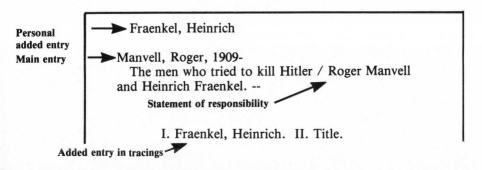

Personal → Fraenkel, Heinrich
added entry
Main entry → Manvell, Roger, 1909-
        The men who tried to kill Hitler / Roger Manvell
and Heinrich Fraenkel. --
        Statement of responsibility

        I. Fraenkel, Heinrich. II. Title.
Added entry in tracings →

Fig. 19.16
Added Entry for a Title

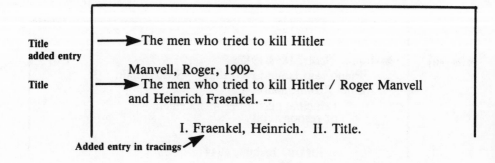

Fig. 19.17
Added Entry for a Series

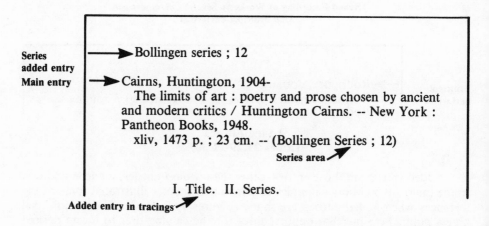

Always refer to *AACR 2* when making added entries. While a title entry is usually made, Rule 21.30 cites four instances where a title entry is not made. For example, if the title proper of a work is *Algebra* and the subject entry is "1. Algebra," it would be redundant to make the title added entry in a dictionary catalog, since the title and subject entries would file very close together. No useful access point would be created.

Laws of Modern Jurisdictions
(Rule 21.31B)

The main entry rules for modern laws are important. Library patrons often need to locate laws of a city, state, or other jurisdiction (see Figures 19.18-19.21). Laws governing a single jurisdiction—a city for example—are entered under the heading for the jurisdiction (Figure 19.18):

Fig. 19.18
Laws of a City

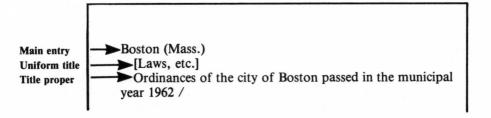

Main entry	→Boston (Mass.)
Uniform title	→[Laws, etc.]
Title proper	→Ordinances of the city of Boston passed in the municipal year 1962 /

Rule 21.31B1 instructs the cataloger to add a "uniform title," as instructed in Rule 25.15A (uniform titles are discussed below). The addition of the uniform title has the effect of bringing together these materials in the catalog. It also instructs the cataloger to make added entries for persons responsible for compiling the laws (there was no compiler in our example). The purpose of the uniform title is to aid the catalog user in locating materials. The catalog user can look up Boston (Mass.) [Laws, etc.] in the alphabetical sequence, then look for specific laws on the line for the title proper.[1] Without a uniform title, the various works on laws of the city of Boston would be skewed in a larger alphabetical array.

Fig. 19.19
Laws of a State

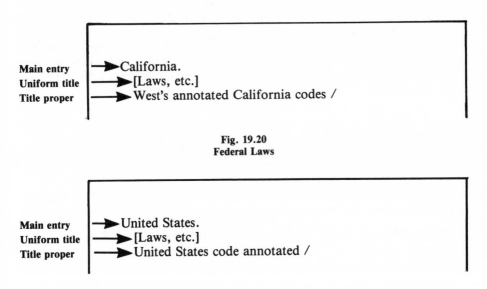

Main entry	→California.
Uniform title	→[Laws, etc.]
Title proper	→West's annotated California codes /

Fig. 19.20
Federal Laws

Main entry	→United States.
Uniform title	→[Laws, etc.]
Title proper	→United States code annotated /

Not all laws use the uniform title [Laws, etc.]. Again, the cataloger must refer to Rule 25.15A for special uniform titles. The example in Figure 19.21 (page 226) is an example of a law with added entries for the person who prepared the work and a government department involved with enforcing the laws. Notice that the compiler *did not* write the laws and is, therefore, *not* the main entry.

Fig. 19.21
Added Entries for a Law Entered under a Uniform Title

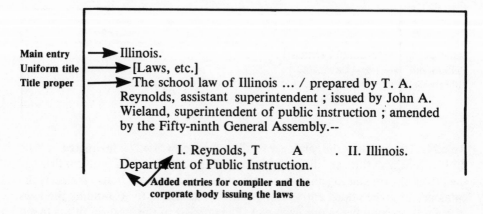

Main entry ➤ Illinois.
Uniform title ➤ [Laws, etc.]
Title proper ➤ The school law of Illinois ... / prepared by T. A.
Reynolds, assistant superintendent ; issued by John A.
Wieland, superintendent of public instruction ; amended
by the Fifty-ninth General Assembly.--

I. Reynolds, T   A   . II. Illinois.
Department of Public Instruction.
Added entries for compiler and the
corporate body issuing the laws

BASIC RULES FOR DETERMINING
THE PROPER FORM OF A HEADING

AACR 2 rules discussed in this section are concerned with determining the *proper form* of an entry. For example, you determine that a sound recording should have a main entry for the principal performer, say, Elvis Presley. Elvis Presley's full name is Elvis Aron Presley, so which is the proper form for cataloging? The rules discussed below tell the cataloger to use the form of a name by which a person is most commonly known; thus the main entry is Elvis Presley, *not* Elvis Aron Presley.

The materials in this section will cover the proper form of heading for personal names, geographic names, corporate names, and the use of uniform titles. *The form of a name is always the same*, whether the name is a main entry, an added entry, or a subject heading.

Choice of Name General Rule
(Rule 22.1)

The form of name used for a personal author is the form by which that person is *most commonly known*. Some examples are:

Name Used	Name Not Used
Carter, Jimmy	Carter, James Earl
Griffith, D. W.	Griffith, David Wark
Lawrence, D. H.	Lawrence, David Herbert
France, Anatole	Thibault, Jacques Anatole
Ruth, Babe	Ruth, George Herman
Twain, Mark	Clemens, Samuel Langhorne
Cummings, E. E.	Cummings, Edward Estlin

The commonly known form of a name is usually determined from the chief source of information in the work or from reference sources.

Choice among Different Names
(Rule 22.2)

If a person is known by more than one name, choose the most commonly used form of the name. If there is more than one other choice, select in this order: 1) the name that appears most frequently in the person's works; 2) the name that appears most frequently in the reference sources; or 3) the latest name form (Rule 22.2A). For example, the cataloger would use Jacqueline Onassis as the proper form, because it is both the latest name and the name by which she is commonly known. *Neither* Jacqueline Bouvier *nor* Jacqueline Kennedy would be used. Also, the proper form would be Muhammad Ali *not* Cassius Clay for the same reasons. A *see* reference is made from the form of name not used to the form of name used.

Pseudonyms
(Rule 22.2C)

If a person uses *one* pseudonym, the pseudonym is the proper form of the name (Rule 22.2C1). A reference is made from the real name, if known, to the pseudonym. Frederick Hardenberg, for example, wrote only under the pseudonym Novalis. Therefore the proper form of the entry is Novalis, 1772-1801; and a reference would be made from Frederick Hardenberg to the form of the name used.

When an author produces works under *several* pseudonyms, but one name (either real or pseudonymous) has become predominant, that name is used (Rule 22.2C2). For instance, Erle Stanley Gardner is the proper form of the author's name because it is predominant. References are made from other names under which Erle Stanley Gardner has written—A. A. Fair and Charles J. Kenny (Figure 19.22):

Fig. 19.22
See **References from Pseudonyms Not Used to**
Proper Form of Name

Fair, A. A.

   see Gardner, Erle Stanley

Kenny, Charles J

   see Gardner, Erle Stanley

If a person uses several pseudonyms but is *not predominantly* known by any one name, enter any work under the name appearing in that work (Rule 22.2C3). John Creasey writes under at least five different names—Gordon Ashe, Michael Halliday, J. J. Marric, Anthony Morton, and Jeremy York. In this situation, explanatory references to and among the various names would be made as required (Figure 19.23, page 228).

Fig. 19.23
Explanatory References for Author with Several Proper Entries

Creasey, John
    For works of this author written under pseudonyms, *see*
Ashe, Gordon
Halliday, Michael
Marric, J. J.
Morton, Anthony
York, Jeremy

Ashe, Gordon
    For works written under his real name, *see*
Creasey, John
    For works written under his other pseudonyms, *see*
Halliday, Michael
(etc.)

Similar *see also* references can be made for other pseudonyms as required.

Fullness of Name
(Rule 22.3A)

If a person's name varies in fullness in different works, select the *most common form*. If necessary, *see* references are made from the forms not used (Figure 19.24). The author Morris West is on occasion cited as Morris L. West. Morris West is used because it is the most common form.

Fig. 19.24
See **Reference from Form of Name Not Used**

West, Morris L.

    see West, Morris

Entry under Surname
(Rule 22.5)

For most persons, an entry is made under the *surname*, followed by other parts of the name: Smith, H. Allen; Twain, Mark. There are numerous variations of this basic rule in *AACR 2* Rules 22.5B-22.5E. For most personal authors, the surname is easily determined, but a cataloger must be aware of some exceptions and possible problems in determining surnames, even though only a small percentage of names will be problems.

"Compound surnames" are a common type of name often not easily recognized. A compound surname is entered under the element by which a person wants to be known (Rule 22.5C2). References can be made from the part of a compound name not entered first (Figure 19.25):

Fig. 19.25
Entry for Compound Surname

Liddell Hart, Basil Henry, 1895-1970.
   The German generals talk /

See **Reference from Element of Surname Not Used**

Hart, Basil Henry Liddell

   see Liddell Hart, Basil Henry, 1895-1970

A "hyphenated surname" is entered under the first element (Rule 22.5C3). Harold Boswell-Taylor is entered as Boswell-Taylor, Harold. A *see* reference is made from Taylor, Harold Boswell to the proper form, Boswell-Taylor, Harold.

Names with prefixes are generally entered under the element most usual for the person's language or country of residence (Rule 22.5D1). Examples of names with prefixes are Van Buren, Le Rouge, and De La Mare. Below are the rules for entering names with prefixes in four common languages—English, French, German, and Spanish. The reader should refer to *AACR 2* for rules governing other languages (Rule 21.5D1).

To determine the proper form of a name in French, German, or Spanish, it is necessary to know the articles and prepositions used to form prefixes. If an LMTA works with foreign-language materials or translations, it is useful to compile a list of common prefixes for those languages. It is necessary, at the least, to be aware that if a name has a prefix, the entry *could* be under the prefix.

In English, the name is entered under the prefix:

De la Mare, Walter   *not*   Mare, Walter De la, or La Mare, Walter De
Le Gallienne, Richard *not*   Gallienne, Richard Le
Van Buren, Martin   *not*   Buren, Martin Van

In French, the entry is under the prefix if the prefix consists of an article, or a contraction of an article and preposition:

Le Rouge, Gustave	*not*	Rouge, Gustave Le
Du Méril, Edélestand Pontas	*not*	Méril, Edélestand Pontas Du
Cars, Guy	*not*	Cars, Guy Des

If the prefix consists of a preposition followed by an article, enter the part followed by the article:

La Fontaine, Jean de   *not*   Fontaine, Jean de la

For German names, the entry is under the prefix when the prefix consists of an article, or a contraction of an article and preposition:

Vom Ende, Erich	*not*	Ende, Erich Vom
Zum Busch, Josef Paul	*not*	Busch, Josef Paul Zum
Zur Linde, Otto	*not*	Linde, Otto Zur

If the surname is preceded by a preposition, or by a preposition followed by an article, enter under the part of the name following the prefix:

Goethe, Johann Wolfgang von	*not*	Von Goethe, Johann Wolfgang
Mühll, Peter von der	*not*	Von Der Mühll, Peter

In Spanish, the name is entered under the article if the prefix consists *only* of an article. If the prefix is more than an article, enter under the part following the prefix:

Figueroa, Francisco de	*not*	De Figueroa, Francisco
Casa, Juan de la	*not*	De la Casa, Juan
Las Heras, Manuel Antonia	*not*	Heras, Manual Antonia las
Cervantes Saavedra, Miguel de	*not*	De Cervantes Saavedra, Miguel

In cases of names with prefixes, references can be made from those forms of a name not used to the proper form:

De la Casa, Juan

see Casa, Juan de la

Titles of Nobility
(Rule 22.6)

Many foreign authors, especially British, have and use titles of nobility. In general, the rule is to enter a person under the proper name in the title of nobility if the person commonly uses the title. Verification of the title of nobility can be difficult at times, and it is usually necessary to refer to a bibliographical reference source, such as the *National Union Catalog*. Figure 19.26 illustrates the proper entry for a title of nobility:

Fig. 19.26
Entry for a Title of Nobility

Beaverbrook, William Maxwell Aitken,
    Baron, 1879-1964.
The abdication of King Edward VIII /

See **Reference from Proper Surname**

Aitken, William Maxwell

see Beaverbrook, William Maxwell Aitken,
    Baron, 1879-1964

A *see* reference is made from the form of the name not used.

Additions to Names Consisting of or Containing Initials
(Rule 22.16)

If a part of a name consists of an initial and the full name is available, the name is entered with the initials and the full name is given in parentheses to distinguish between similar names:

Lawrence, D. H. (David Herbert)

Wells, H. G. (Herbert George)

Lawrence, T. E. (Thomas Edward)

References are generally made from the complete form of the name to the entry actually used:

Lawrence, David Herbert

see Lawrence, D. H. (David Herbert)

Distinguishing Identical Names
(Rules 22.18 and 22.19)

Sometimes names are identical even after spelling out all given names. To distinguish among identical names, the birth and death dates can be added (Rule 22.18), or a distinguishing term can be used (Rule 22.19B):

Smith, John, 1924-	(A living person)
Smith, John, 1837-1896	(Birth and death dates)
Smith, John, b. 1825	(Birth date only, year of death unknown)

or

Brown, George, *Captain*

Brown, George, *Rev.*

The rules discussed above all apply to personal names. The rules that follow relate to the proper form for geographic names and corporate bodies.

Geographic Names: General Rule
(Rule 23.2)

When a geographical name is used as a heading, the English form of the name is generally preferred. The form may have to be determined by reference to a gazetteer or other source. Some examples are:

Austria	*not*	Österreich
Florence	*not*	Firenze
Soviet Union	*not*	Russia

The form in the language of the country is used if there is no established form in English.

Geographic Names: Additions to Place Names
(Rule 23.4)

Occasionally it will be necessary to distinguish between different geographic places with the same name. Rule 23.4C is the basic rule for geographic places located in a state in the United States. In general the name of the state is added in parentheses after the geographic name:

Kansas City (Mo.)
Riverside County (Ca.)
Philadelphia (Pa.)

Corporate Bodies: General Rule
(Rule 24.1)

A corporate body is entered under the name by which it is generally known. The corporate entry, like an entry for a personal author, must be unique or distinguished in a way so that it will not be confused with similar entries. The proper name of a corporate body is determined from the publications it issues. Corporate bodies include businesses, institutions, nonprofit enterprises, governments, religious bodies, and conferences. Some examples of corporate entries are:

E. I. DuPont de Nemours & Company—Business corporation
California State University, San Bernardino—Institution
Museum of American Folk Art—Institution
United States. Commission on Civil Rights—Government agency
Catholic Church. Diocese of Ely—Religious body
Conference on Pediatric Pharmacology (1967: Washington, D. C.)—
    Conference

Corporate Bodies: Changes of Name
(Rule 24.1B)

Corporate bodies often change names during their existence. Entries are made under both earlier and later names; a work is entered under the name used at the time of publication. References from the different forms of the name can be made as necessary (Figure 19.27):

Fig. 19.27
Reference from New Form of a Corporate Name

California State University, San Bernardino

For other works by this body see also the earlier heading:

California State College, San Bernardino

Reference from Old Form of a Corporate Name

California State College, San Bernardino

For other works by this body see also the later heading:

California State University, San Bernardino

Conferences, Congresses, Meetings, Etc.
(Rule 24.7)

A conference is entered under its commonly known name. In addition to the name, the number of the conference, the year it was held, and the location are added if information is available. Some examples of conference entries are given in Figure 19.28:

Fig. 19.28
Headings for Conferences

Conference on Pediatric Pharmacology
(1967: Washington, D. C.)
▲   ▲
Date   Location

Yad Vashem International Historical Conference (2nd : 1974 : Jerusalem)
▲   ▲   ▲
Location   No.   Date

Subordinate Corporate Bodies
(Rules 24.12, 24.13)

A subordinate body is entered under its own name, with some exceptions for government bodies and some names that would not make sense alone. Some examples of subordinate bodies entered under their own name are:

- Harvard Law School (This school is a subordinate part of a larger institution, Harvard University; it can stand alone and retain its meaning.)
- Association of Research Libraries (This association is a subordinate body of the American Library Association; it too can stand alone and retain its meaning.)

References would be made from the form of the name as a subheading of the parent body:

Harvard University. Law School

see Harvard Law School

Rule 24.13 lists five types of subordinate bodies, that must be entered subordinate to the parent body. Generally, these rules apply to names that would not make much sense alone. For example, the subordinate body, "Dept. of History," makes no sense standing alone. However, it does make sense as a subordinate body: Texas Christian University. Dept. of History. Now the subordinate heading is identified as the department of history at a specific university. Study the five kinds of subordinate bodies cited in Rule 24.13 to get a sense of how to develop subordinate entries.

Government Bodies and Subordinate Government Bodies (Rules 24.3E, 24.18, 24.19, 24.21, and 24.23)

A government is entered under the name in common use, which is usually the geographic area under its jurisdiction. Figure 19.20 is an example of a government name. The heading "United States" is the common name of both our governmental jurisdiction and the geographic area under its jurisdiction. The heading for the "City of Chicago" is "Chicago (Ill.)"; the "State of California" is "California."

Rule 24.18 lists ten types of government agencies entered subordinately under the parent government. For example, the Department of State is a major executive agency of the United States government (Rule 24.18, Type 4) and is entered subordinately: United States. Dept. of State. The federal Commission on Civil Rights is another example of a subordinate agency, one that requires a government name for proper identification (Rule 24.18, Type 2): United States. Commission on Civil Rights. Many states also have agencies named Commission on Civil Rights, so without being subordinated to a particular government, the Commission's name alone is not meaningful.

Another example of a subordinate entry is for courts (Rule 24.18, Type 6). A court is entered subordinately under the name of its governmental jurisdiction:

United States. Supreme Court

California. Supreme Court

California. Superior Court (San Bernardino County)

Without being subordinated to a parent body, the terms "Supreme Court" or "Superior Court" are of no use as access points.

A final example is the subordinate entry used for legislative bodies (Rule 24.18, Type 5). The legislative body is entered subordinately under the name of the government. If there are two separate parts of the legislative body, enter each part subordinately to the name of the legislature:

United States. Congress

United States. Congress. House

United States. Congress. Senate

United States. Congress. Joint Committee on the Library

United States. Congress. Senate. Committee on Foreign Relations

Uniform Titles
(Rules 25.1, 25.2A, 25.4, 25.17, and 25.28)

The concept of a uniform title allows different editions of a work to be filed together in a catalog when the title of those editions varies. Earlier in this chapter, we gave examples of a uniform title for laws (Figures 19.18-19.21). We will limit our examples here to a work with varying titles, a classical work, and sacred literature.

Shakespeare's *Hamlet* is an example of a work that has been issued in many editions with varying titles. In order to bring these editions together in a catalog, a uniform title is placed in brackets and entered above the title proper (Figure 19.29):

Fig. 19.29
Uniform Title for Editions of a Work

	Shakespeare, William
Uniform title	➤ [Hamlet]
Title proper	➤ Hamlet, prince of Denmark

Shakespeare, William
[Hamlet]
Shakespeare's Hamlet

Shakespeare, William
[Hamlet]
The tragedy of Hamlet, prince of Denmark

The *Arabian Nights* is an example of a classical work issued with many different titles. These entries are brought together by a uniform title (Figure 19.30):

Fig. 19.30
Uniform Title for a Classical Work

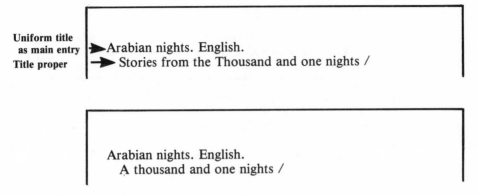

Uniform title
as main entry ▶Arabian nights. English.

Title proper   ➤ Stories from the Thousand and one nights /

Arabian nights. English.
A thousand and one nights /

Notice that in Figure 19.30, the uniform title is the main entry.

The *Bible* is an example of a work of sacred literature in which the uniform title brings together thousands of works with varying titles. Without a uniform title, entries for the *Bible* would be difficult or impossible to locate in a catalog unless the exact title was known. Several examples of uniform titles for the *Bible* are given in Figure 19.31:

Fig. 19.31
Uniform Title for the Bible

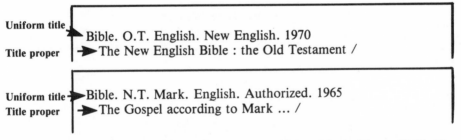

Uniform title ▶Bible. O.T. English. New English. 1970

Title proper ➤The New English Bible : the Old Testament /

Uniform title ▶Bible. N.T. Mark. English. Authorized. 1965
Title proper ➤The Gospel according to Mark ... /

Notice the order of the information in the two uniform titles in Figure 19.31. The order of information is: Bible. Testament. Language. Version. Date. The first example is the Old Testament, in English, the New English version published in 1970. The second example is the New Testament, the book of Mark, in English, authorized, published in 1965. Rule 25.18 covers the parts of the *Bible* in the uniform title.

REFERENCES
(Rule 26)

Four kinds of references are used to guide catalog users to the correct form of an entry or to related entries. The four references are *see* references, *see also* references, "name-title" references, and "explanatory" references. Rule 26 goes into detail about the specific instances when references may be needed. Generally, a reference is made when the cataloger believes it may be useful. Rules for making references vary among libraries, both as to format and when they are made. Below are examples of the four standard kinds of references.

A *see* reference directs the catalog user from the form of a heading *not* used to the form that is used (Figure 19.32):

Fig. 19.32
See **Reference for an Author with a Compound Surname**

Moncrieff, Charles Kenneth Scott

see Scott-Moncrieff, Charles Kenneth, 1899-1930

See **Reference for a Different Form of an Author's Name**

Moses ben Maimon, 1135-1204

see Maimonides, 1135-1204

See **Reference for a Pseudonym Not Used as an Entry**

Saint-Aubin, Horace de

see Balzac, Honoré de, 1799-1850

See **Reference for a Different Name Used for a Corporate Body**

Quakers

see Society of Friends

A *see also* reference is a guiding device that directs the catalog user to a related entry or name. The *see also* is normally used when a person or corporate body is entered under only two different names (Figures 19.33 and 19.34).

Fig. 19.33
See Also **References for an Author with Two Possible Entries**

Wright, Williard Huntington

see also Van Dine, S. S.

Van Dine, S. S.

see also Wright, Williard Huntington

Fig. 19.34
See Also **Reference for a Name Change for a Corporate Body**

National Education Association of the United States. Dept. of Audiovisual Instruction.

see also

National Education Association of the United States. Division of Audiovisual Instructional Service.

National Education Association of the United States. Division of Audiovisual Instructional Service.

see also

National Education Association of the United States. Department of Audiovisual Instruction.

Notice that the *see also* entry goes in both directions. However, a *see* or *see also* reference should *not* be made unless it refers to something. In the example above, if a library had works only by S. S. Van Dine and nothing by Williard Huntington Wright, no *see also* reference is needed. The same rule applies to *see* references. If a library has no works by Maimonides, there is no need for a *see* reference from a form of his name not used. A reference that leads to no other information is a "blind" reference—they are incorrect and confusing to a catalog user.

A "name-title" reference directs the catalog user from a name-title not used to the proper entry (Figure 19.35):

Fig. 19.35
"Name-Title" Reference for Name Not Used with an Edition of a Work

Halliday, Michael
The edge of terror

see York, Jeremy

The proper main entry for this work is Jeremy York, which is one of several pseudonyms used by John Creasey. (*See also* Figure 19.23.)

The "explanatory" reference is a device that gives the catalog user more detailed information than a *see* or *see also* reference (Figure 19.36):

Fig. 19.36
"Explanatory" Reference

Idaho. Division of Instructional Improvement.

In 1966 the Idaho Division of Instruction's name was changed to Instructional Services, and in 1969, to Division of Instructional Improvement.
Works by these bodies are found under the following headings according to the name used at the time of publication:
Idaho. Division of Instruction.
Idaho. Instructional Services.
Idaho. Division of Instructional Improvement.

SUBJECT ENTRY: Works about this body are entered under the name used during the latest period covered.

The authority files required to keep track of the various headings used as entries and the references made for the catalog are covered in chapter 25. Sources of information to help establish the proper form of a name are also discussed in chapter 24.

Remember that the *AACR 2* rules discussed in this chapter present *only* a basic introduction. No attempt was even made, for example, to cover every part of some of the rules included in this chapter. These rules selected form a foundation on which to develop skills in determining main entries and making necessary references. *Always use AACR 2* when cataloging.

NOTES

[1]So far, comparisons between *AACR 1* and *AACR 2* rules have been avoided so as not to confuse the beginner. This rule, however, is a good example of a problem caused by *AACR 2*. The entry in *AACR 1* is under: "Boston. Ordinances, local laws, etc." Clearly, the catalog user must be led to entries for the laws of Boston through references, changing main entries for older materials, or a combination of methods.

REVIEW QUESTIONS AND EXERCISES

1. What are the two elements of descriptive cataloging?

2. What are the three steps in *AACR 2* to determine main entries and added entries?

3. Give definitions for the following terms:

   a. compiler
   b. joint author
   c. *see also* reference
   d. uniform title
   e. corporate body
   f. editor

4. Give three examples of a corporate entry.

5. What is the main entry for a work with two authors when neither is named as the principal author?

6. What is the main entry for a work with four coequal authors?

7. If a work is a collection of different works by different authors with a collective title and a principal editor, what is the main entry?

8. What is the main entry for a translation of a work?

9. What is an added entry? Name five possible kinds of added entries.

10. Why is a uniform title used for main entries for laws of jurisdictions?

11. What form of a name is preferred for a personal author—the person's legal name or the commonly known name?

12. If a person uses several names, what are the three possible choices?

13. What is a compound surname? Are *see* references necessary for compound names? Why?

14. What is the purpose of birth and death dates following an author's name?

15. What is the general rule for the form of name for a corporate body? For a geographical name?

16. What three possible elements used to identify a conference follow the name of that conference?

17. What is a subordinate entry for a government body? Why are subordinate entries used?

18. Define and explain the need for *see* references and *see also* references. Give examples of these types of references.

19. Discuss the concept of "uniform title" as it relates to the function of a catalog as discussed in chapter 15.

20

SUBJECT CATALOGING – SUBJECT HEADINGS

Subject cataloging consists of two components: selection of subject headings and assignment of a classification number. This chapter covers the selection of subject headings, while the following chapter will cover classification.

A subject entry in a catalog creates a point of access for a work *in addition to* the main entry and any added entries. As many subject headings as necessary may be assigned to describe the contents of a work. As a practical matter, a maximum of four headings is usually assigned to any one work.[1]

Many catalog users locate works only by a subject heading approach. This is especially true for catalog users who may not know the authors who write in a particular field or any of the standard works in the field. Subject entries are vital in communicating the holdings of the library.

CATALOGING TERMINOLOGY

Subject. The topic or topics of a work.

Subject authority file. A record of the subject headings used in a catalog. It is also a record of the *see, see also*, and "explanatory" references made for each subject heading.

Subject catalog. A catalog of subject entries. Usually one part of a two-part divided catalog.

Subject entry. An access point in a catalog under a subject heading.

Subject heading. A word, phrase, or acronym describing the subject of a work.

Subject subdivision. A word, group of words, date, or geographical name added to a subject heading to limit it to a more specific meaning.

BASIC CONCEPTS OF SUBJECT HEADINGS

A subject heading can be the name of a person, group, place, object or work, a phrase, or an acronym that identifies the subject of a work. A personal name or name of a corporate body can be used as a subject heading if that is the subject of a work. When a personal name or corporate body name is used as a subject heading, the form is exactly the same as the name in a main or added entry. For instance, the subject heading for a work about the Texas Utilities Company is exactly the same as the name in the main entry (see Figures 19.3 and Figure 20.1).

Fig. 20.1
Subject Heading: Corporate Body

	63 p. : ill. ; 28 cm.
Subject heading	➤1. Texas Utilities Company. I. Title.

A book about a person is assigned a subject heading in the form of a personal name, and the form is exactly the same as the name when used as a main or added entry. A work by Pablo Picasso would have the main entry: Picasso, Pablo, 1881-1973; a book *about* Pablo Picasso would have a subject entry in exactly the same form (Figure 20.2):

Fig. 20.2
Subject Heading: Personal Name

Subject entry	➤ PICASSO, PABLO, 1881-1973

	O'Brian, Patrick
	  Pablo Ruiz Picasso : a biography / by Patrick O'Brian. --
	New York : Putnam, 1976.
	    511 p. ; geneal. tables ; 23 cm.
	    ISBN 399-11639-7

Subject heading	➤1. Picasso, Pablo, 1881-1973.

A subject heading can also be the name of an object such as a ship (Figure 20.3):

Fig. 20.3
Subject Heading: Object

Subject entry	➤ TITANIC (STEAMSHIP)

	Lord, Walter, 1917-
	  A night to remember / Walter Lord. -- 1st ed. -- New
	York : Holt, c1955.
	    200 p. : ill. ; 22 cm.

Subject heading	➤1. Titanic (Steamship). I. Title.

In a card catalog, the subject is usually typed on the top of the card in capital letters, or in red, or both. The use of capital letters or letters in a different color helps to distinguish subject entries from other entries in a catalog. In a divided catalog, of course, subject entries are filed separate from other entries. Even in a divided catalog, it is usually customary to capitalize subject headings so that cards are not accidentally filed in the author/title part of the catalog.

The basic principles used to develop the largest standard list of subject headings, *Library of Congress Subject Headings*,[2] were stated by David J. Haykin in 1951; they remain important guidelines:

1) **The reader as focus.** Subject headings should be selected with the catalog user in mind. The heading should be one the user will look for. One problem for librarians has been the diversity of library users. The catalog user may be a college freshman or a senior research-oriented professor using the same catalog.

2) **Unity.** All material on a subject should be brought together in a catalog under the same subject entry.

3) **Usage.** The subject heading must represent common modern usage so as not to confuse the catalog user.

4) **Specificity.** The subject heading(s) selected for a work should be specific, unambiguous, and cover only the topic of the work. A subject heading should not be broader than the subject of the work, since this would be misleading. Rather than an overly broad subject heading, several more specific headings could be used. For example, a work on the American Civil War would have the subject heading UNITED STATES – HISTORY – CIVIL WAR, 1861-1865 – a specific heading. It would *not* have the subject heading UNITED STATES – HISTORY because it is too comprehensive; the work is not a general history of the United States.

A subject heading may be expressed in several forms:

1) a proper name or object – RUBIK'S CUBE.

2) a single noun – ECONOMICS.

3) a noun preceded by a noun used adjectively – COUNTRY LIFE; COMPUTER GAMES.

4) two nouns connected by "and" – FERTILIZERS AND MANURES; ADVERTISING AND CHILDREN.

5) prepositional phrases – SUCCESS IN BUSINESS.

6) inverted phrases – ERRORS AND BLUNDERS, LITERARY; CHEMISTRY, ORGANIC.

7) phrases – FEDERAL AID TO LIBRARIES; FIREARMS INDUSTRY AND TRADE.

The form of subject headings and the number of subject headings used for a work have been the subject of much discussion in professional literature. The impact of computer-based cataloging systems and computer-based catalogs should allow greatly expanded subject access compared to manual systems.

Subject Subdivisions

Subject headings can be made more specific and useful by adding a subdivision. When a subject is presented in a special format or is limited geographically or chronologically, the subject heading is modified to help the catalog user. For example, a work on the American Civil War is assigned the subject heading UNITED STATES—HISTORY—CIVIL WAR, 1861-1865. UNITED STATES is the basic subject. The first subdivision, HISTORY, limits the scope of the work to American history; and the subdivision CIVIL WAR, 1861-1865 further limits the scope of the work to a specific period in American history. If the subject heading UNITED STATES—HISTORY were assigned, it would mislead the catalog user into thinking the work was a general history of the United States.

There are four types of subdivisions in general use:

1) **Topical subdivisions.** This subdivision is used to limit the scope of a subject heading to a more specific topic. It is always separated from the main heading by a dash:

PLANTS—EXTINCTION

CONSTRUCTION INDUSTRY—FINANCE

In the first example, the topical subdivision EXTINCTION limits the topic to extinction of plants. The second example clearly limits the scope of the broad heading CONSTRUCTION INDUSTRY to one specific aspect, that of financing in the construction industry.

2) **Form subdivisions.** This type of subdivision is used to show that information on a subject may be in a special format or arrangement:

Subject Heading	Form Subdivision
ACCOUNTING	ABSTRACTS
ACCOUNTING	DICTIONARIES
ACCOUNTING	HANDBOOKS, MANUALS, ETC.
ACCOUNTING	PERIODICALS

To locate a dictionary of accounting terms, the catalog user should look for the entry ACCOUNTING—DICTIONARIES. Similarly, the subject heading ACCOUNTING—PERIODICALS would be assigned to periodicals on accounting, and the catalog user would find the entries together in the catalog.

A form subdivision may also refer to a type of *approach* to a subject such as:

ACCOUNTING – STUDY AND TEACHING

ACCOUNTING – HISTORY

These form subdivisions tell the reader an author's approach to the subject.

3) **Geographic subdivisions.** These subdivisions limit the scope of a subject heading to a geographical or political area.[3] Geographic subdivisions are used when the work is clearly limited in scope:

BANKS AND BANKING – UNITED STATES

AGRICULTURE – TEXAS

ETHNIC THEATER – CALIFORNIA

The geographical subdivisions effectively limit the scope of the work. At the same time, they give the catalog user more specific information.

4) **Period or chronological subdivisions.** These subdivisions are used to denote the chronological period covered by a work and are most often used in history, literature, and art:

UNITED STATES – HISTORY – BLACK HAWK WAR, 1832

UNITED STATES – HISTORY – CIVIL WAR, 1861-1865

UNITED STATES – HISTORY – WAR OF 1898

UNITED STATES – HISTORY-20TH CENTURY

UNITED STATES – HISTORY – 1933-1945

UNITED STATES – HISTORY – 1945-

    or

ART, ANCIENT

ART, MEDIEVAL

ART, ROMANESQUE

The ART subdivisions are adjectival; nonetheless, they clearly give the chronological scope of the subject.

The information above should provide a general awareness of subject headings and how they can be subdivided. Learning to select subject headings and subdivisions requires cataloging experience. The material below on the two standard lists of subject headings further explains the use of subject headings. The reader should locate subject entries in a catalog and look through the entries to get a feel for the structure. Then look at entries that have numerous subdivisions, such as UNITED STATES, AMERICAN LITERATURE, and ENGLISH LITERATURE to get an idea of the complexity of a catalog.

STANDARD LISTS OF SUBJECT HEADINGS

Thousands of subject headings are needed to describe the materials in a medium-sized library. To help maintain consistency in the form of a heading, most libraries use standardized lists of subject headings. The English language can often be confusing and many words are ambiguous, so different catalogers will often assign different subject headings to the same work. This will happen even with standardized lists, but they at least create a fair amount of consistency among catalogers. Cataloging is still almost as much art as science.

Most libraries use one of two standard lists, *Library of Congress Subject Headings* or *Sears List of Subject Headings*. Once a standard list is selected, the library usually uses only that one list to avoid conflicting headings.

Library of Congress Subject Headings

Library of Congress Subject Headings, 9th ed. (Washington: Library of Congress, 1980. 2 vols. with supplements) is the most comprehensive and scholarly list of subject headings used in the United States. *LCSH* is available in book format, with quarterly supplements and annual cumulations. *LCSH* is also available on microfiche and cumulates quarterly. Starting in 1984 a weekly update in print format of new and revised subject headings became available: *LC Subject Headings Weekly Lists* (Washington: Library of Congress, 1984-). *LCSH* and its supplements list subject headings used in the Library of Congress from 1897 to the present. *LCSH* was developed for a large collection, so it is most often used by larger libraries. Many small public libraries, school libraries, and nontechnical special libraries would probably not use *LCSH*.

Library of Congress subject headings can be used with the Library of Congress Classification, Dewey Decimal Classification, and with other classification schemes. Many libraries use the *LCSH* list with the Dewey Decimal Classification, as the two are compatible. The subject headings can be used with both book and non-book materials.

The introductions to the eighth and ninth edition of *LCSH* give the information needed to use the list.* It is impossible to use the list properly without reading and studying the introductory materials in both editions and the supplements. Following the introduction is a section titled "Annotated Card Program: Subject Headings for Children's Literature," listing special headings for juvenile works. (This is discussed later in this chapter.)

Several sections of the introduction must be studied carefully in order to save time in learning to use the *LCSH*. The filing arrangement is *not* the same as for card catalogs. The filing rules are for efficient arrangement of entries by a computer. Therefore, the alphabetical order of headings in *LCSH* may not be in the same sequence as the subject entries in a card catalog. The supplements have information on filing rules in addition to the information in the main volume.

Another important part of the introduction is the list of headings omitted from *LCSH*. It is important to know what is *not* in the list; otherwise, time may be wasted looking for headings not included. Headings omitted from the main volumes unless established after January 1976 are:

---

*Some relevant introductory materials to the ninth edition were omitted and the reader is referred to the eighth edition. (See introductory material in the ninth edition.)

1) Individual persons. However, Thomas Aquinas, Shakespeare, Wagner, Lincoln, Washington, and Napoleon have been included to show by example the subdivisions appropriate for use under names of individual philosophers, literary authors, musicians, and statesmen.

2) Family names.

3) Gods and goddesses; legendary characters

4) Most corporate bodies, including governments and their agencies, religious bodies, societies, institutions, or firms.

5) Places and regions, except when they form an integral part of other headings; when subdivisions under them must be shown, as in the case of historical periods; or when the scope of the heading is indicated in a scope note.

6) Archaeological sites.

7) Natural features such as bays, capes, deserts, lakes, mountains, rivers, and volcanoes.

8) Structures such as aqueducts, bridges, canals, dams, reservoirs, buildings, castles, historic houses, and forts.

9) Metropolitan areas; parkways, roads, squares, streets; city quarters.

10) Parks, forests and forest preserves, and wildlife refuges.

11) Most sacred books, anonymous religious classics, or special prayers.

12) Works of art, motion pictures, and television programs.

13) Systematic names of families, genera, and species in botany and zoology; references from scientific to popular names. However, when English names of biological taxa present no ambiguity, they are preferred for use and are consequently printed in the list.

14) Chemical compounds.

Commencing with the January-March 1976 *Supplement to Library of Congress Subject Headings*, many of the headings omitted are now included.[4]

Categories of Former Non-print Headings Now Included:
1) Sacred books.
2) Names of families, dynasties, royal houses.
3) Gods, legendary and fictitious characters.
4) Geographic regions and features, city sections. (Political jurisdictions for which the Subject Cataloging Division uses its own form of name, or has made a special decision, will also be included.)
5) Archaeological sites, ancient cities, empires.
6) Structures, buildings, roads, parks and reserves, squares, etc.
7) Works of art (both movable and permanently located).
8) Biological names.
9) Chemicals.

Categories of Headings Still Omitted:

1) Most author headings, including anonymous classics in general, motion pictures, radio and television programs, etc. Certain personal and corporate headings are included, but only for illustration.

2) Individually named art collections based on a personal name.

3) Regions of cities (e.g., Chicago region, Ill.) and Metropolitan areas (e.g., Chicago metropolitan area).

And last, the section "Headings Serving as Patterns for Sets of Subdivisions" is useful for showing how subdivisions are used (1977 supplement; omitted from ninth edition preface).[5] The 1982 annual supplement includes lists of the most often used subdivisions.

The subject headings authorized by *LCSH* are printed in boldface type, followed by suggested references in medium type. There may also be "scope notes" explaining a subject heading and when it should be used. Many subject headings also have a Library of Congress class number for help in assigning classification numbers (Figures 20.4 and 20.5):

Fig. 20.4
Library of Congress Subject Heading Entry with
Suggested References and Class Numbers

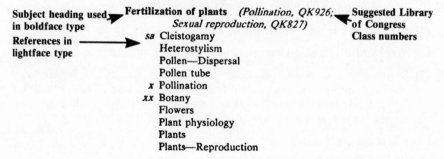

The Library of Congress class numbers in Figure 20.4 are only suggestions, and they must not be used without using the proper classification schedules (discussed in chapter 21).

Figures 20.4 and 20.5 give suggested references preceded by the symbols "sa," "x," and "xx." These symbols mean:

sa (see also)	indicates a reference to a related or subordinate topic
x (see from)	indicates a reference from an expression not itself used as a heading
xx (see also from)	indicates a related heading from which a *see also* reference is made

Fig. 20.5
Library of Congress Subject Heading Entry with
Reference and Scope Note

Public service employment *(Indirect)*

Scope note ⟶ Here are entered works on public sector employment as a counter-cyclical policy measure intended to provide jobs for the unemployed as well as to provide economic assistance to distressed areas and state and local governments. Works on government employment in general are entered under Civil service and the subdivision Officials and employees under names of countries, states, etc.

   sa Civil service

    subdivision Officials and employees
     under names of countries, states, etc.

   x Work relief

   xx Civil service

    Economic assistance, Domestic

    Full employment policies

    Labor supply

    Manpower policy

    Public works

    Unemployed

Note under Civil service

You may recall that these are similar to the references discussed in chapter 19 for personal and corporate names. Using these symbols as guides, the subject heading FERTILIZATION OF PLANTS in Figure 20.4 would need these references in a catalog:

sa (see also)

FERTILIZATION OF PLANTS

see also

CLEISTOGAMY
HETEROSTYLISM
POLLEN-DISPERSAL
POLLEN TUBE

A *See also* reference is filed before the first subject entry for FERTILIZATION OF PLANTS

x (see)

POLLINATION

see

FERTILIZATION OF PLANTS

See reference from a term not used as a subject heading to the term used

BOTANY

See also reference
from a related sub-
ject heading filed
see also
before the first
entry for BOTANY

xx (see also from) FERTILIZATION OF PLANTS

(Similar cards are made for all other *see also (xx)*
references: FLOWERS, PLANT PHYSIOLOGY,
PLANTS, PLANTS — REPRODUCTION)

Remember, references are made *only* if they lead to more information; *do not make "blind" references.* For example, the reference POLLINATION *see* FERTILIZATION OF PLANTS is made *only* if there are entries for FERTILIZATION OF PLANTS; otherwise the reference leads to nothing. The same logic applies to the *see also* references.

One reference not mentioned in *LCSH* is the explanatory or information reference. These references are usually made to show the history of a corporate body or a geographic area and its various names during its existence, and the primary purpose is to clarify the main entry. Subject heading information is the final item on the reference. Each library will develop a policy for making these informational references. The time, reference sources, and staff required to develop an information reference are beyond the means of many libraries. Sometimes these references are made only for subjects of local interest (Figure 20.6):[6]

Fig. 20.6
Information Reference

Papua New Guinea.

> British New Guinea, a British protectorate since 1884, became a territory of Australia in 1901. In 1906 its name was changed to the Territory of Papua, and in 1945 it was joined to the Territory of New Guinea to form the administrative unit of the Territory of Papua-New Guinea. The Papua New Guinea act of 1949 provided for the administration by Australia of the United Nations Trust Territory of New Guinea in an administrative union with the Territory of Papua under the name of Papua New Guinea. On Dec. 1, 1973 Papua New Guinea became self-governing.
> Works by these jurisdictions published before 1945 are found under

> New Guinea (Ter.)
> Papua.

(Continued on next card)

Papua New Guinea. (Card 2)

> Works published after 1945 are found under

> Papua New Guinea.

Subject Information ➤ SUBJECT ENTRY: Works about these jurisdictions, regardless of period covered, are entered under Papua New Guinea. Works limited in subject coverage to historical, political or cultural aspects of Papua New Guinea for the pre-1945 period are entered under Papua and/or New Guinea (Ter.) Works on other subjects relating to Papua and/or New Guinea (Ter.) for the pre-1945 period are entered under the name of the present jurisdiction, Papua New Guinea.

Throughout *LCSH*, you will see subdivisions listed with one, two, and three dashes. These represent subdivisions and sub-subdivisions of the main subject heading (Figure 20.7):

Fig. 20.7
Library of Congress Subject Heading with Subdivisions

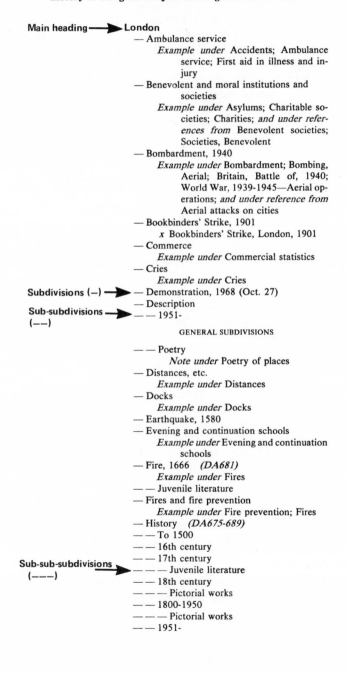

These dashes are, in effect, instructions as to how to subdivide the main heading:

LONDON—AMBULANCE SERVICE

LONDON—DESCRIPTION—1951-

LONDON—HISTORY—17TH CENTURY—JUVENILE LITERATURE

In the list, 1951 is preceded by two dashes, indicating it is a sub-subdivision (LONDON—1951- is *not* a valid heading). In the last example, HISTORY is preceded by one dash, indicating a subdivision. 17TH CENTURY is preceded by two dashes, indicating a sub-subdivision; and JUVENILE LITERATURE is preceded by three dashes, indicating a sub-sub-subdivision.

A work can be assigned more than one subject heading, and headings are assigned in order of importance: the first usually represents the class number. Headings after the first usually elaborate special aspects of the work (Figure 20.8):

Fig. 20.8
Multiple Subject Headings in Order of Importance

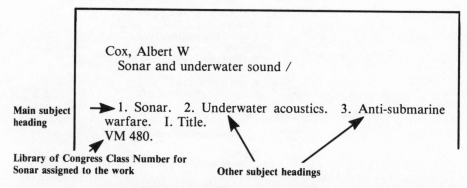

The "Subject Headings for Children's Literature" section precedes the main body of subject headings in the main volumes and supplements of *LCSH*. In 1965, the Library of Congress started its Annotated Card Program to provide "a more appropriate in-depth subject access" to children's literature (Figure 20.9). Hundreds of special headings have been established for use when cataloging children's literature. These headings are used only for juvenile literature, and on LC cards, the headings are placed in brackets. The use of these headings is explained in *LCSH*. The list of subject headings used for children's literature is cumulated in the quarterly supplements to *LCSH*.

The Library of Congress system of subject headings and accompanying cross-references serves to integrate and correlate the subject entries in a catalog. The system is complex, and it suffers from the difficulty of operating in a manual system. The LMTA must understand the basics of subject headings and references to do cataloging or give reference assistance. Subject heading work requires skill and accuracy, because mistakes can cause a chain reaction affecting many parts of the catalog.

Fig. 20.9
Library of Congress Children's Literature Annotated Card

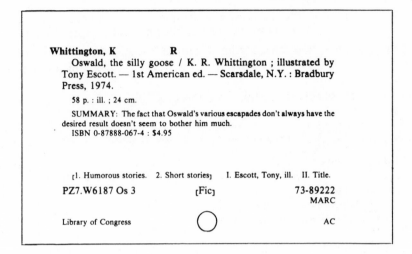

Whittington, K   **R**
Oswald, the silly goose / K. R. Whittington ; illustrated by
Tony Escott. — 1st American ed. — Scarsdale, N.Y. : Bradbury
Press, 1974.

58 p. : ill. ; 24 cm.

SUMMARY: The fact that Oswald's various escapades don't always have the
desired result doesn't seem to bother him much.
ISBN 0-87888-067-4 : $4.95

[1. Humorous stories.   2. Short stories]   I. Escott, Tony, ill.   II. Title.

PZ7.W6187 Os 3   [Fic]   73-89222
                                           MARC

Library of Congress   AC

Sears List of Subject Headings

The *Sears List of Subject Headings* (12th ed., New York: H. W. Wilson, 1982) was first published in 1923 under the title *List of Subject Headings for Small Libraries*. Minnie Earl Sears originally compiled the list in response to the need of smaller libraries for a standardized list less comprehensive than *LCSH*. *Sears* is used mostly by small public libraries and nearly all school libraries. No supplements are issued to update *Sears*; instead, a new edition is planned for every fifth year.

The subject headings in *Sears* are based on Library of Congress form, and in many instances, the subject headings in *Sears* and *LCSH* are the same. Also, the Library of Congress "Subject Headings for Children's Literature" are incorporated into *Sears* with a few exceptions. Where Library of Congress headings are changed in *Sears*, it is toward a simpler form such as "City planning" (*Sears*) rather than "Cities and towns – Planning" (*LCSH*).

It is necessary to read the preliminary materials in *Sears*, especially "Principles of Sears List of Subject Headings." This preliminary article is an excellent general introduction to subject headings. Other materials include "Checking and Adding Headings," "Headings to be Added by the Cataloger," "Key Headings," and "List of Subdivisions." *Do not* use *Sears* until you have read all the preliminary materials.

The format of *Sears* is similar to that of *LCSH*. Subject headings are in boldface type, and terms not used in medium type. The large right-hand margin in *Sears* is for checking entries used in the catalog, as described in the section on "Checking and Adding Headings." The reference symbols *see also, x,* and *xx* work the same as in *LCSH*:

See also	indicates a reference to a related or subordinate subject heading
x	indicates a reference from an expression not used as a subject heading to the subject heading under which it is placed
xx	indicates a related subject heading from which a *see also* reference is made to the heading under which it is placed

An entry in *Sears* appears as follows (Figure 20.10):

Fig. 20.10*
Entry in *Sears List of Subject Headings*

Library finance   025.1
　　　　　See also **Federal aid to libraries; State aid to libraries**
　x Libraries—Finance
　xx **Library administration**

These symbols for suggested references are interpreted as follows for the above example:

LIBRARY FINANCE *see also* FEDERAL AID TO LIBRARIES
LIBRARY FINANCE *see also* STATE AID TO LIBRARIES
LIBRARIES—FINANCE *see* LIBRARY FINANCE
LIBRARY ADMINISTRATION *see also* LIBRARY FINANCE

The following reference cards are made for the subject heading LIBRARY FINANCE:

LIBRARY FINANCE *See also* FEDERAL AID TO LIBRARIES STATE AID TO LIBRARIES	*See also* reference filed *before* the first subject entry for LIBRARY FINANCE

LIBRARIES—FINANCE *See* LIBRARY FINANCE	*See* reference from a term not used as a subject to the form used.

LIBRARY ADMINISTRATION	*See also* reference from a related subject heading filed *before* the first entry for LIBRARY ADMINISTRA-TION.
See also	
LIBRARY FINANCE	

Notice in Figure 20.10 that the *see also* reference is read *down*—LIBRARY FINANCE *see also* FEDERAL AID TO LIBRARIES—while the *see (x)* and *see also from (xx)* are read *up*—as in LIBRARIES FINANCE *see* LIBRARY FINANCE and in LIBRARY ADMINISTRATION *see also* LIBRARY FINANCE. This is the same as in the *LCSH*.

When using *Sears*, "blind" references should be avoided, just as discussed earlier in the chapter. For example, the *see also* reference "LIBRARY ADMINISTRATION *see also* LIBRARY FINANCE" is not made *unless* subject entries exist in the catalog for LIBRARY FINANCE. The authority file discussed in chapter 25 is a means to help avoid incorrect references.

NOTES

[1]The economics of the card catalog mitigates against too many subject entries. With a computer-based catalog it may be possible to assign as many subject entries as may be desirable.

[2]David Judson Haykin, *Subject Headings: A Practical Guide* (Washington: GPO, 1951), pp. 7-11.

[3]Until November 1976, the Library of Congress used both "direct" and "indirect" geographical subdivisions. A "direct" entry would be AGRICULTURE—TARRANT COUNTY (TEX.); "indirect" entry would be AGRICULTURE—TEXAS—TARRANT COUNTY. Since November 1976, only *indirect* entries are being made.

[4]*Supplement to the Library of Congress Subject Headings, 1974-76* (Washington: Library of Congress, 1977), p. v.

[5]Sources for finding the proper form of subjects and proper names not listed in *LCSH* will be covered in chapter 24. Also, the *supplements* should be checked for the latest changes in headings used for patterns.

[6]"Subject Entry Information on Information References," *Cataloging Service* 125 (Spring 1978): 10-19.

REVIEW QUESTIONS AND EXERCISES

1. Define the following terms:
   a. subject
   b. subject authority file
   c. subject heading
   d. subject catalog
   e. subject entry

2. What are the purposes of subject headings?

3. Is it true that only a proper name can be used as a subject heading? If not, what else can be used?

4. Does the form of a name used as a main entry vary from the form used for a subject heading? Why?

5. How is a subject heading distinguished on the catalog card?

6. Explain the meaning of the terms "reader as focus," "unity," "usage," and "specificity" as they apply to subject headings.

7. Why should a subject heading assigned to a work be as specific as possible?

8. Define and give examples of the following subject subdivisions:
   a. topical
   b. form
   c. geographic
   d. chronological

9. Name two standard lists of subject headings. What are the main differences in these two lists? What kinds of libraries would use each list?

10. Explain the *sa, x,* and *xx* used to make LC subject heading references.

11. What is a blind reference? How is one avoided?

12. How is the *LCSH* list updated? How is *Sears* updated?

21

SUBJECT CATALOGING—CLASSIFICATION

The second element of subject cataloging is the assignment of a classification number. These numbers are generally already predetermined and available for most works cataloged in a medium-sized library (the sources are covered in chapter 24). This chapter covers the two classification schemes used by most libraries in the United States: Library of Congress Classification and Dewey Decimal Classification.

Both the LC Classification and the Dewey Decimal Classification can be used with all kinds of library materials. Because of the special nature and shelving requirements for some non-book media, many local classification schemes have been developed for those materials. Some non-book works, such as sound recordings, often are given only an accession number and shelved in numerical order. Whether to select one of the standard classification schemes or to develop an in-house scheme for special materials is a professional decision. Elements involved in deciding how to classify non-book materials may include: the librarians' attitudes about non-book materials; the number of non-book items being acquired or already in the collection; the librarians' judgment on the best way for a patron to locate materials; the number of staff available to catalog materials and the staff's skill levels; and, the librarian's attitude toward an integrated multimedia collection. As libraries acquire more non-book materials, the question of uniform classification of all materials is a matter of importance.

A thorough knowledge of a library's classification scheme is essential for a librarian or LMTA to serve the library user. A knowledge of classification is essential in *both* cataloging and reference services.

CATALOGING TERMINOLOGY

Classification schedule. The printed scheme of a classification system.

Notation. A system of numbers and/or letters used to represent a classification scheme. *Mixed notation* uses two or more symbols (i.e., letters and numbers). *Pure notation* uses only one kind of symbol—either letters or numbers. Dewey Decimal Classification, which uses only numbers, is a pure notation; Library of Congress Classification, which uses letters and numbers, is a mixed notation.

PURPOSE OF CLASSIFICATION

The importance of classification varies among libraries, depending on their function, the size of the collection, and the components of the collection. Classification is more important in a 500,000-volume collection than in a

5,000-volume collection simply because of the need to control the larger collection. A small special library serving a select clientele, however, may be more concerned with the details of classification than would a larger general library serving non-specialist users. Many such elements go into deciding how seriously a given library approaches classification of its collection.

Given the often conflicting demands of collection size and library function, it is possible to generalize only about those purposes of classification that are true for any library. First, classification arranges a collection in a known order, which facilitates use of the collection. Second, classification places materials on the same subject together and places related materials nearby. No classification scheme is entirely successful in this function, but LC and DDC are good enough to satisfy most demands.

It is important to remember that no classification system places *all* materials on a subject together (Figure 21.1). This is important in both cataloging work and in reference work.

Fig. 21.1
Scattering of Materials on Railroads in
Two Classification Systems

Subject	DDC	LC
Engineering of building a railroad	625.1	TF200
Economic aspects of railroad transportation	385.12	HE1613
Model railroads and trains	625.19	TF197
Rail transportation law	343.095	KF2271

And third, classification allows materials to be reshelved in their proper locations. This seemingly mundane function is of great practical importance in libraries where large numbers of works must be reshelved quickly and efficiently—and where a misshelved work may be lost for years.

DEWEY DECIMAL CLASSIFICATION

Melvil Dewey first developed the Dewey Decimal Classification (DDC) in simple outline form in 1873, while a student at Amherst College. He hoped to devise a simple classification scheme that could be used by any library. The first published edition of the DDC came out anonymously in 1876 with the title, *A Classification and Subject Index for Cataloging and Arranging the Books and Pamphlets of a Library*. It was 44 pages long, with 11 pages of classification schedules, and was criticized for being too long and too detailed. The nineteenth edition is in three volumes with 3,273 pages. *Dewey Decimal Classification and Relative Index*, 19th edition (Albany, N.Y.: Forest Press, 1979. 3 vols.) has been used by the Library of Congress and other major cataloging agencies since January 1, 1980.

There is an *Abridged Dewey Decimal Classification and Relative Index,* 11th edition (Albany, NY: Forest Press, 1979) with 618 pages. The *Abridged DDC* is for use in small general libraries with 20,000 or fewer titles that have no expectation of growth much beyond that size. The eleventh edition is a true abridgement of the nineteenth edition. The tenth edition was an adaptation of the eighteenth edition, but not a true abridgement. The abridgement seldom gives more than five-digit numbers—two places to the right of the decimal.

The success of the DDC was immediate. Today, over 100 years since the first edition, no other classification scheme has been found sufficiently superior to justify the costs of reclassification in most libraries. Its success has been credited to its "cardinal virtues [which] are universality and hospitality, a simple expansive notation, which is now almost an international classification vocabulary, excellent mnemonic features, first class machinery for its perpetuation, and an admirable index."[1]

Features of the DDC that account for its success are: 1) it allows materials to be shelved in *relative locations* as a collection expands (before the DDC was introduced, libraries used a *fixed location,* each item was assigned to a certain location on numbered shelves set aside for a subject); 2) the notation is simple and easily understood; 3) the scheme is easily expanded to accept new areas of knowledge; and, 4) its schedules provide clear directions for use and for number building.

In addition to the above reasons for the DDC's initial success, several other reasons account for its continuing popularity. First, it is used by many libraries throughout the world. In the United States, the DDC is used by 98% of public libraries, nearly all school libraries, and over 50% of academic and special libraries. Second, the DDC is continuously revised, by a permanent office established in the Library of Congress in 1933—the Decimal Classification Division. This division has been responsible for editing new DDC editions since 1958. Between editions, DDC is updated by *Dewey Decimal Classification Additions, Notes and Decisions* (Washington: Library of Congress, 1959-), issued on an irregular basis as needed. Some current changes in DDC also are reported in the *Cataloging Service Bulletin* (Washington: Library of Congress, 1978-).

Third, most centralized cataloging services provide DDC numbers on catalog cards or in their information data base, and most Library of Congress catalog cards and MARC tapes provide a DDC number. And, fourth, as mentioned above, "there is a continuing lack of a general classification scheme sufficiently excellent to convince librarians of the need for reclassifying...."[2] "Thus the DDC survives and thrives because," according to one scholar of classification, "despite the agreements of its critics concerning real or imaginary faults, it is still the best classification for public and probably for college libraries. No other system has been able, in practice, to offer a decisive challenge or prove its theoretical superiority for the arrangement of such collections."[3]

Outline of the Dewey Decimal Classification*

The DDC is composed of 10 *main* classes:

000 — Generalities
100 — Philosophy and related
disciplines
200 — Religion
300 — Social sciences
400 — Language

500 — Pure sciences
600 — Technology (Applied
sciences)
700 — The arts
800 — Literature (Belles-lettres)
900 — General geography and history
and their auxiliaries

Each main class is divided into 10 *divisions*. Thus, there are 100 divisions in the 10 main classes. For instance, the main class 300 (Social sciences) is divided into divisions as follows:*

300 — Social sciences
310 — Statistics
320 — Political science
330 — Economics
340 — Law

350 — Public administration
360 — Social problems & services
370 — Education
380 — Commerce (Trade)
390 — Customs, etiquette, folklore

Each of the divisions is further divided into 10 *sections*. There are 1,000 sections in the 10 main classes. From the example in social sciences, the 370 division (Education) is subdivided as follows:*

370 — Education
371 — Generalities of education
372 — Elementary education
373 — Secondary education
374 — Adult education

375 — Curriculums
376 — Education of women
377 — Schools & religion
378 — Higher education
379 — Education & the state

Each section can be further subdivided *decimally* to build more specific numbers for a subject. The DDC progresses hierarchically *from the general to the specific*, and this concept is incorporated in the *notation*, which is lengthened by one digit for each successive division:*

600	Technology (Applied sciences)
640	Home economics and family living
646	Sewing, clothing, management of personal and family living
646.7	Management of personal and family living. Grooming.
646.72	Personal appearance
646.724	Care of hair
646.7242	Hairdressing

---

*Reproduced from Edition 19 of the *Dewey Decimal Classification*, published in 1979, by permission of the Forest Press Division, Lake Placid Education Foundation, owner of copyright.

The DDC uses a decimal notation, so the order of progression for DDC classification is:

612
612.001
612.01
612.0142
612.3
612.31
612.4

Notice that .31 comes *before* .4 because the decimal .31 is the smaller number. Works assigned these classification numbers will stand on the shelves in ascending order, as shown above. A DDC number *always has three digits to the left* of the decimal—never more and never fewer. The number of digits to the *right* of the decimal varies from 1 to as many as 17 or 18.

Two important features of the DDC are the "memory aids" and the "relative index." In the DDC, memory aids involve using a combination of numbers that represent the same subject or that have the same meaning when used anyplace in the schedules (with only occasional exceptions). The "standard subdivisions" are an example of a memory aid:*

01 — Philosophy and theory

02 — Miscellany

03 — Dictionaries, encyclopedias, concordances

04 — Special topics of general applicability

05 — Serial publications

06 — Organizations and management

07 — Study and teaching

08 — History and description of the subject among groups of persons

09 — Historical and geographical treatment

When a standard subdivision is added to *base numbers* as directed in the schedules, it shows the treatment of a topic:

109 — historical treatment of philosophy

328.309 — historical and geographical treatment of legislative branches of government

103 — a dictionary or encyclopedia of philosophy

530.03 — a dictionary or encyclopedia of physics

532.007 — the study and teaching of mechanics of fluids

591.07 — the study and teaching of zoology

There are six other "Tables" in DDC in addition to standard subdivisions, with similar memory aid features for such things as languages and geographic areas.

---

*Reproduced from Edition 19 of the *Dewey Decimal Classification*, published in 1979, by permission of the Forest Press Division, Lake Placid Education Foundation, owner of copyright.

The relative index brings together the various aspects and relationships of a topic. Arranged alphabetically, it includes all "main headings" in the DDC schedules. While the DDC schedules scatter different aspects of a topic, the relative index brings these aspects together.*

Children
art representation	704.9425
as cooks	641.5123
ethics	170.20222
etiquette	395.122
hygiene	613.0432
psychology	155.4
World War 2	940.53161

A DDC number can have 17 or 18 digits, but no number should be built longer than is appropriate for a particular library. A small library with five books on the Jewish Holocaust might use 940.53 for every book. However, a library with a large collection on World War II that included a large number of works on the Holocaust might use a more specific number, such as 940.531503924.

Since 1967, DDC numbers have been *segmented* by the Library of Congress, and these segmented numbers are available from many sources. (Sources of DDC numbers are discussed in chapter 24.) Segmenting is shown by "prime marks," which are *not* part of the actual DDC number (see Figures 21.2 and 21.3). Thus, a DDC number can be divided at each prime mark without losing meaning. A library, depending on its needs, then can select any one of three numbers for the work in Figure 21.2 (940.53, 940.531503, or 940.531503924):

Fig. 21.2
Prime Marks on a Segmented DDC Number

Rubenstein, Richard L
   The cunning of history : mass death and the American future / Richard L. Rubenstein. -- 1st ed. -- New York : Harper & Row, 1975.
   x, 113 p. ; 21 cm.

Includes bibliographical references.
ISBN 0-06-067013-4 : $6.95.

1. Holocaust, Jewish (1939-1945). 2. Civilization, Modern. 3. United States—Politics and government—1969-   . I. Title.
940.53'1503'924

prime marks

---

*Reproduced from Edition 19 of the *Dewey Decimal Classification*, published in 1979, by permission of the Forest Press Division, Lake Placid Education Foundation, owner of copyright.

Checking the DDC schedules for 940.531503924, you will find the number can be analyzed as:

940.53 — World War 2
940.531503 — Relations of specific classes of persons to the war
940.531503924 — Jews in World War 2

The number was "built" by following the directions in the DDC schedules. The relative index entry for World War 2 directs the reader to 940.53, the base number for World War 2. Looking down the schedule, 940.5315 is the number for specific classes of persons during that war. Directions in the schedule at 940.531503-.531587 tell the cataloger to add a "Persons" notation from table 7 to the base number (940.5315). Table 7 is a memory aid much like the standard subdivisions discussed above.

In table 7, -03 is the notation for persons by racial, ethnic, or national background. Adding -03 to the base, the number is 940.531503. Directions in table 7 under the -03 tell the cataloger to add from table 5 a notation for specific "Racial, Ethnic, National Groups." In table 5, the notation -924 is used for Hebrews, Israelis, and Jews. So adding -924, the completed number is 940.531503924.[4]

It is essential to read the introductory materials in the first volume of the nineteenth edition or in the eleventh abridged edition of DDC in order to understand how to use the schedules and build DDC numbers. You should also carefully examine the schedules, the tables, and the relative index. The DDC may appear to be overwhelmingly complex, but this is not really the case. Classification is not always easy, but with some practice, most LMTAs can develop a "feel" for selecting and building simple DDC numbers.

Fig. 21.3
Library of Congress Card with DDC Number and Prime Marks

Bailey, Dickson H.
    Directory of cities, towns, villages, and hamlets / ₍Dickson H. Bailey₎. — ₍Regina₎ : Chief Electoral Officer of Saskatchewan, 1981.

    37, 39 leaves ; 28 cm.

    At head of title: Province of Saskatchewan.

    1. Election districts—Saskatchewan—Directories. 2. Saskatchewan—Administrative and political divisions—Directories. I. Title.

JL313.B34   1981   82-103827
                328.7124'07345'025—dc19
                 ▲   ▲ AACR 2   MARC
Library of Congress
                 prime marks

Book Numbers

A DDC classification number by itself is not sufficient to identify a work for all library purposes. A book number, also called an author number or cutter number, is added to the classification number to create a unique "call number" for each work in a library.

The call number is composed of a "classification number" and a "book number":

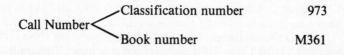

It is possible—indeed, very likely—that several works in a library will be classified in the same DDC number. Consequently, a book number must be used to create a *unique* call number:

973	973	973	973	973	973
D888	D971	E581	J842	M959	R974

The book number is a *decimal*. The initial letter in the book number is usually the first letter of the author's surname or the first letter of the main entry if the author is not the main entry. Works by different authors with the same last name would stand on the shelves as follows:

973	973	973	973
D888	D8881	D889	D921

The most obvious function of a book number is to create a unique call number for each work. But some other functions have been pointed out by Bertha Barden in her work, *Book Numbers*: "(1) To arrange books in order on the shelves; (2) To provide a brief and accurate call number for each book; (3) To locate a particular book on the shelves; (4) To provide a symbol for charging out books to borrowers; (5) To facilitate the return of books to the shelves; and (6) To assist in quick identification of a book when inventories are taken."[5]

The book number scheme most commonly used with the DDC was devised by Charles Ammi Cutter. The notations are called "cutter numbers," and assigning them is often referred to as "cuttering." The most commonly used version of the Cutter scheme is the *Cutter-Sanborn Three-Figure Author Table* (exclusively distributed by Libraries Unlimited, Littleton, Colo.), altered and fitted with three figures by Kate E. Sanborn. Cutter's original table had only two figures. Two other editions are *Cutter's Two-Figure Author Table* and *Cutter's Three-Figure Author Table* (exclusively distributed by Libraries Unlimited, Littleton, Colo.).

The *Cutter Table* consists of three or more initial letters from a surname, or else a surname and a three-digit number. Letters J, K, E, I, O, and U are followed by two-digit numbers. The order is somewhat alphabetical, *except* that S and the vowels are found at the end of the tables after all the consonants. The table is arranged as follows:

Bem	455	Chandl
Ben	456	Chandler, M.
Benc	457	Chanl
Bend	458	Chann
Bendo	459	Chant

The numbers in the center column apply to the letters in each adjoining column. The cutter number includes the initial letter of the author's name or other main entry, and then the number. Simply find the letter group nearest to the author's surname and combine the initial letter with the numbers. If the name "fits" between two cutter numbers, use the first listed in the schedule: Bendix is B458 not B459—because it falls between Bend and Bendo, the first of these is used. Thus:

Bemis	B455	or	Chandler, L.	C455
Benat	B456	or	Chandler, M.	C456
Bendix	B458	or	Channing	C458

"Work marks" or "work letters" are commonly used with cutter numbers both to help maintain alphabetical order on the shelves and to create a unique call number for each work. The work mark is usually the first letter of the title of the work, excluding initial articles. The work mark comes *after* the book or cutter number. Thus, the call number for James Michener's *Hawaii* would be:

813.5   813.5—DDC number
M682h   M682—book or cutter number
          h—work mark (Hawaii)

To maintain alphabetical order, it is sometimes necessary to use two letters from the title. Thus, Michener's *Caravans* and *Centennial* would have these work marks:

813.5   813.5
M623c   M623ce
 or
M623ca
(*Caravans*)   (*Centennial*)

Many libraries have a policy of classifying the works *by* an author along with books *about* that author. In such arrangements, works *by* an author are generally placed *before* the books *about* that author and his or her works. To accomplish this, a letter from the end of the alphabet is placed after the cutter or author number, followed by the initial of the author of the biography or criticism. Thus, Arthur Day's *James A. Michener*, a critical study of Michener's work, could be classified:

813.5
M623zD

Using the "z" ensures that the criticism will always stand after all works by Michener.

Another commonly used work mark identifies different editions of a work. For this purpose, either the date can be placed in the call number or a number can be placed after the work mark. Thus, if a library happened to have three different editions of Michener's *Hawaii*, they would be distinguished as follows:

813.5	813.5	813.5
M682h	M682h2	M682h3
	or	*or*
813.5	813.5	813.5
M682h	M682h	M682h
	1970	1978

The use of work marks is a matter of cataloging policy in each library. Their use and application vary from library to library, depending on the size of the collection and the patrons served. In all cases, work marks should be kept as simple as possible.

LIBRARY OF CONGRESS CLASSIFICATION

The Library of Congress Classification is the second most commonly used classification system in the United States. The Library of Congress decided to develop its own new classification scheme in 1897, as its collection approached one million works and still was rapidly growing. The LC Classification was developed over a period of years through the work of many subject specialists, and the various parts of the classification were basically completed between 1899 and 1920 (except for law, which is still only partially complete). Each part of the classification undergoes continuous development and revision, and each schedule or part of the LC Classification is independent of other schedules.

Unlike the DDC, LC Classification was not originally intended for use by other libraries, so it did not attempt to cover all areas of knowledge. Consequently, the subject detail in the various schedules varies, depending on the number of volumes in the Library of Congress on a particular subject. Yet because LC's collection is so large, and because the Library collects materials on every subject imaginable, the classification based on its collection is a comprehensive scheme. The LC Classification, therefore, can be used by any library. In addition the LC Classification can be expanded as necessary.

The LC Classification is used mostly by college and university libraries—almost no public library or school library uses the classification. It is best suited to larger collections of at least 100-200,000 volumes. However, collection size is only one factor to consider when selecting a classification system. Other factors are the library user, cataloging efficiency, available personnel, and the type of collection in the library.

Outline of the Library of Congress Classification

The LC Classification is issued in 38 (as of 1984) separate schedules comprising over 10,000 pages. Each schedule covers a particular subject area and is used independently of the other schedules. Twenty-one letters are used to indicate main divisions—I, O, W, X, and Y are not currently used. The main divisions, and some important subdivisions are:

A   General Works.

AE	Encyclopedias (General)
AG	Dictionaries and other general reference works
AI	Indexes (General)
AP	Periodicals (General)
AY	Yearbooks. Almanacs. Directories (General Works Only)

B   Philosophy. Psychology. Religion

B	Philosophy (General)
BF	Psychology
BJ	Ethics
BL	Religions. Mythology. Rationalism.
BM	Judaism
BP	Islam. Bahaism. Theosophy, etc.
BR	Christianity (General)
BX	Religious denominations and sects

C   Auxiliary Sciences of History

C	Auxiliary sciences of history (General)
CB	History of civilization and culture (General)
CC	Archaeology (General)
CR	Heraldry
CS	Genealogy
CT	Biography

D   History: General and Old World

D	History (General)
DA	Great Britain
DB	Austria. Czechoslovakia. Hungary
DC	France
DD	Germany
DE	The Mediterranean region. Greco-Roman world
DK	Russia
DR	Eastern Europe. Balkan Peninsula. Turkey
DS	Asia
DT	Africa
DU	Oceania (South Seas)

E   History: America (General). United States (General)

(51-99)	Indians. Indians of North America
(186-199)	Colonial History
(456-655)	Civil War
(740-)	Twentieth Century

(Outline continues on page 270.)

F	(1-975)	United States local history
	(1001-1140)	British America. Canada
	(1201-1392)	Mexico
	(1401-1419)	Latin America (General)

G Geography. Anthropology.

G	Geography (General)
GB	Physical geography
GC	Oceanography
GN	Anthropology
GR	Folklore
GT	Manners and customs (General)
GV	Recreation

H Social Sciences

H	Social sciences (General)
HA	Statistics
HB	Economic theory
HC	Economic history and conditions: National production
HD	Land. Agriculture. Industry
HE	Transportation and communications
HF	Commerce
HG	Finance
HM	Sociology (General and theoretical)
HQ	Family. Marriage. Women
HV	Social pathology. Social and public welfare. Criminology
HX	Socialism. Communism. Anarchism

J Political Science

J	Official documents
JA	Collections and general works
JC	Political theory. Theory of the state
JF	Constitutional history and administration (General works)
JX	International law. International relations

K Law

K	Law (General)
KD	Law of the United Kingdom and Ireland
KE	Law of Canada
KF	Law of the United States
KFA-KFW	Law of individual states
KG-KH	Law of Latin America
KK-KKC	Law of Germany

L   Education
    L   Education (General)
    LA   History of education
    LB   Theory and practice of education
    LC   Special aspects of education
    LD-LT   Individual institutions

M   Music and books on music
    M   Music
    ML   Literature of music
    MT   Music instruction and study

N   Fine arts
    N   Visual arts (General)
    NA   Architecture
    NB   Sculpture
    NC   Drawing. Design. Illustration
    ND   Painting
    NE   Print media
    NK   Decorative arts. Applied arts. Decoration and ornament
    NX   Art in general

P   Language and Literature
    P   Philology and linguistics (General)
    PA   Classical languages and literatures
    PB   Modern European languages
    PC   Romance languages
    PD   Germanic languages
    PE   English
    PG   Slavic. Baltic. Albanian languages and literature
    PJ   Oriental languages and literature
    PM   American Indian languages
    PN   Literary history and collections
    PQ   Romance literatures
    PR   English literature
    PS   American literature
    PT   Germanic literatures
    PZ   Fiction and juvenile literature*

(Outline continues on page 272.)

---

*As of June 30, 1980, the Library of Congress stopped classing fiction in English in PZ1, PZ3, and PZ4. American fiction is now classed in PS; English fiction in PR; and translations into English, with the original national literature [*Cataloging Service Bulletin* 6 (Fall 1979): 55.]

Q   Science

Q	Science (General)
QA	Mathematics
QB	Astronomy
QC	Physics
QD	Chemistry
QE	Geology
QH	Natural history
QK	Botany
QL	Zoology
QM	Human anatomy
QP	Physiology
QR	Microbiology

R   Medicine

R	Medicine (General)
RA	Public aspects of medicine
RB	Pathology
RC	Internal medicine. Practice of medicine
RD	Surgery
RS	Pharmacy and materia medica
RT	Nursing

S   Agriculture

S	Agriculture (General)
SB	Plant culture
SD	Forestry
SF	Animal culture
SH	Fish culture and fisheries
SK	Hunting

T   Technology

T	Technology (General)
TA	Engineering (General). Civil engineering (General)
TC	Hydraulic engineering
TD	Environmental technology. Sanitary engineering
TE	Highway engineering. Roads and pavements
TF	Railroad engineering and operation
TH	Building construction
TJ	Mechanical engineering and machinery
TK	Electrical engineering. Electronics. Nuclear engineering
TL	Motor vehicles. Aeronautics. Astronautics
TP	Chemical technology
TS	Manufactures
TX	Home economics

U	Military Science	
	U	Military science (General)
	UA	Armies: Organization, description, facilities, etc.
	UD	Infantry
	UF	Artillery
	UG	Military engineering
	UH	Other services

V	Naval Science	
	V	Naval science (General)
	VA	Navies: Organization, description, facilities, etc.
	VD	Naval seamen
	VE	Marines
	VK	Navigation. Merchant marine
	VM	Naval architecture. Shipbuilding

Z	Bibliography and Library Science	
	(4-8)	History of books and bookmaking
	(662-1000)	Libraries and library science
	(1001-8999)	Bibliography

Each main class has major subdivisions that use *two* letters. (Some subdivisions use three letters, but they are not too common—KFA-KFZ and DJK.) For example, the N schedule (Fine Arts) has the following major subdivisions:

N	Visual arts (General)
NA	Architecture
NB	Sculpture
NC	Drawing. Design. Illustration.
ND	Painting
NE	Print media
NK	Decorative arts. Applied arts. Decoration and ornament
NX	Art in general

Each of these major subdivisions is further subdivided into more specific subjects. Subdivision NK is assigned numbers NK1 to NK9990. Not every number is used, and some numbers are divided decimally. Part of the NK schedule follows:

(Outline continues on page 274.)

NK   DECORATIVE ARTS. APPLIED ARTS. DECORATION AND ORNAMENT

	Religious art (Decorative and applied)
	Including ceremonial art
	Cf. NK2190, Interior decoration
	NK4850, Ecclesiastical vestments
	NK7215, Ecclesiastical plate
	NK9310, Ecclesiastical embroidery
1648	General
	Christian
1650	General works
1652	History
.1	Early Christian
.2	Medieval
.3	Renaissance. 16th century
.4	17th-18th centuries
.5	19th century
.6	20th century
1653	Special countries, A—Z
	e.g. .S7 Spain
1655	Special, by city, A—Z
	e.g. .B34 Barcelona
1656	Special, by denomination, A—Z
	e.g. .M4 Methodist
1657	Trade catalogs, etc,
	Non-Christian
1670	General works
	Special religions
1672	Jewish
1674	Islamic
1676	Buddhist
1678	Other, A—Z

Using this schedule, a work on the history of medieval Christian art is assigned the LC class number NK 1652.2; a work on Jewish religious art, NK 1672; and Christian art in Spain, NK 1653 S7. This last number, NK 1653 S7, is an example of using both numbers and letters to form a classification number. The *S7* is a part of the classification number, *not* a book number. Similarly, in Z 696 U4, *U4* is part of the classification number, not a book number. To determine the extent of a classification number, it is necessary to check the LC Classification schedules.

LC Classification Schedules

Since each schedule in the LC Classification is developed independently of the others, the application and use of each one is different. There is no comprehensive index or set of instructions for the entire LC Classification, unlike the instructions and index for the DDC. *Library of Congress Subject Headings* is a kind of index, since most of the subject headings have a suggested classification. The format of each schedule is similar: 1) a prefatory note describing its scope and historical development; 2) a synopsis giving the broad outline of the schedule; 3) a detailed outline of the schedule; 4) the actual classification schedule; and 5) special tables, an index, and supplementary additions and changes not in the body of the schedule.

As noted, the Library of Congress continually updates and revises its schedules; some schedules in relatively sable subject areas *are* seldom revised, but a schedule such as Science (Q) is now in its sixth edition. Between new editions, the classification is updated through a quarterly publication, *LC Classification—Additions and Changes* (Washington: Library of Congress, Subject Cataloging Division, 1928-). The changes are incorporated as new editions of the schedules are published.

LC Classification Numbers

An LC Classification number consists of two elements: a class number and a book number. A single letter indicates a main class—*P* is the single-letter designation for literature. A double letter indicates a subclass—*PS* is the double-letter designation for American literature. Schedules E-F and Z currently use only single letters. Schedule D uses some triple letters (DJK), and schedule K uses triple letters frequently. The class number usually consists of two or three elements: a letter designation for the main class or subclass, and a number representing a special aspect of the class or subclass:

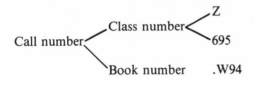

	Z	the class letter for bibliography and library science
Call number — Class number	695	a subdivision number for cataloging of books
Book number	.W94	the book number derived from special LC tables (see below)

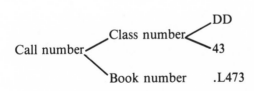

	DD	the class letter subdivision for German history
Call number — Class number	43	the subdivision number for description and travel
Book number	.L473	the book number (see below)

Some classification numbers consist of three elements:

N	the class letter for Fine Arts
72	a subdivision number for art in relation to other topics
.P5	a letter sub-subdivision for photography
D4	book number (see below)

LC Book Numbers

The book numbers used with LC Classification consist of the initial letter of an author's name or main entry, followed by a number derived according to the directions given in the tables that follow. The *Cutter Tables* are almost never used with LC Classification; conversely, the LC method of developing author numbers is seldom used with DDC. The numbers are used decimally:

1. After the initial letter *S*

for the second letter:	a	ch	e	hi	mop	t	u
use number:	2	3	4	5	6	7-8	9

2. After the initial letters *Qu*

for the third letter:	a	e	i	o	r	y
use number:	3	4	5	6	7	8

3. After other initial consonants

for the second letter:	a	e	i	o	r	u	y
use number:	3	4	5	6	7	8	9

4. After initial vowels

for the second letter:	b	d	lm	n	p	r	st	uy
use number:	2	3	4	5	6	7	8	9

Because each classification schedule is independent, the same name can have a different author number in different schedules, for the purposes of maintaining a unique number. The following examples illustrate the application of these tables:

1) Names beginning with vowels

Abernathy	.A2	Ames	.A45	Astor	.A84
Adams	.A3	Appleby	.A6	Atwater	.A87
Aldrich	.A4	Archer	.A7	Austin	.A9

2) Names beginning with the letter S

Saint	.S2	Simmons	.S5	Steel	.S7
Schaefer	.S3	Smith	.S6	Storch	.S75
Seaton	.S4	Southerland	.S64	Sturges	.S8
Shank	.S45	Springer	.S66	Sullivan	.S9

3) Names beginning with the letters Qu

Qadriri	.Q2	Quick	.Q5	Qureshi	.Q7
Quabbe	.Q3	Quoist	.Q6	Quynn	.Q9
Queener	.Q4				

4) Names beginning with other consonants

Carter	.C3(7)	Cinelli	.C5(6)	Cullen	.C8(4)
Cecil	.C4(2)	Corbett	.C6(7)	Cyprus	.C9(6)
Childs	.C45	Croft	.C7(6)		
	( ) = if using two numbers				

5) When there are no existing conflicting entries in the shelflist, the use of a third letter book number may be preferred:

Cabot	.C3	Callahan	.C34	Carter	.C37
Cadmus	.C32	Campbell	.C35	Cavelli	.C38
Daffrey	.C33	Cannon	.C36	Cazalas	.C39

If the sequence of letters in a name does not appear in the tables, the closest letters are used. A library may add to an author number derived from the LC table to create a unique call number. For example, if three books with LC classification number DD 43 have authors with the names Frank Steel, James Steel, and Roger Steel, the base number for Steel (S7) is modified to keep alphabetical sequence and to create a unique call number:

DD	DD	DD
43	43	43
S7	S75	S78

The LC Classification is not as formidable as it appears. Each schedule has directions for use, although at times the directions are minimal. Often it is relatively easy to find a classification number for a specific topic because the schedules are so detailed and numbers are given for specific topics. The booklet, *LC Classification Outline*, 4th ed. (Washington: Library of Congress, 1978), lists the major classes and subclasses. And general familiarity with the outline of the LC Classification is useful in cataloging and reference work.

As in many other aspects of library work, experience is necessary for learning to use the LC Classification. Even librarians who have taken several cataloging courses require considerable on-the-job experience to master the various intricacies of classification.

NOTES

[1]W. C. Berwick Sayers, *A Manual of Classification for Librarians*, 4th ed. (London: Andre Deutsch, 1967), p. 151.

[2]C. D. Needham, *Organizing Knowledge in Libraries: An Introduction to Classification and Cataloging*, 2nd rev. ed. (London: Andre Deutsch, 1971), p. 95.

[3]Sayers, *A Manual of Classification for Librarians*, 163.

[4]For information on number building in DDC, see *Manual on the Use of the Dewey Decimal Classification: Edition 19* (Albany, N.Y.: Forest Press, 1982).

[5]Bertha R. Barden, *Book Numbers: A Manual for Students with a Basic Code of Rules* (Chicago: American Library Association, 1937), p. 9.

REVIEW QUESTIONS AND EXERCISES

1. What factors are considered in classifying non-book materials?

2. Define the following terms:
   a. notation
   b. classification schedule

3. What are the main purposes of classification?

4. Is a knowledge of classification useful only to staff working in a catalog department? Explain.

5. Why do most small- and medium-sized libraries do little or no original classification?

6. Discuss several important reasons that the Dewey Decimal Classification has not been replaced by another system.

7. Where do you obtain a cutter number? What is the purpose of this number?

8. What are the 10 main classes of the Dewey Decimal Classification?

9. What are "memory aids" in the Dewey Decimal Classification?

10. Define the following and give an example:
    a. call number
    b. classification number
    c. book number

11. Was the LC classification scheme originally intended for general use? Why is it suitable for use in most libraries?

12. What kind of library is least likely to use LC classification?

13. What letters are *not* used in Library of Congress notation?

14. Are book numbers used with LC classification? Where do you get book numbers?

Serials often represent a significant portion of a library's collection, so they also require a large segment of the operating budget. A great range of material is included under the term "serial" — popular magazines (such as *Newsweek, Time, The New Yorker*), daily newspapers, scholarly reports published only once or twice a year, and proceedings of learned societies and conferences (issued in parts). Perhaps the simplest definition is as follows: a serial is any publication issued in successive parts at either regular or irregular intervals and, as a rule, intended to be continued for an extended period of time. One may say that any item subject to serials checking procedures in a library qualifies as a serial. Serials are very important to the library because, from the patron's point of view, they provide the most concise, up-to-date information about current problems and events. Thus, libraries try to acquire a large number of serials titles.

Because of the volume of and the complexity involved in controlling serials, libraries expend considerable staff time handling these materials. So, while this chapter will not teach you how to determine what is or is not a serial, it will discuss the procedures used to control these materials.

MAJOR CHARACTERISTICS

The very nature of serials — that is, their being issued in successive parts, none of which is completely independent of a preceding or succeeding part — creates some fundamental control problems for a library. When buying a monograph, the efforts of verifying, invoicing, and checking-in are complete when the book is received. In the case of a serial, however, these routines are a continuous process. Because serial parts are interrelated, individual parts are less useful if all are not available. This is particularly true of current periodicals in which people wish to check a specific piece of information about a specific issue. If the required issue has not been received or has disappeared, the library cannot carry out one of its primary functions.

Cost is another problem. The price of many periodical subscriptions is considerably higher than that of a single monograph, and the loss of a single number of a quarterly publication means that the library's investment in time and money is (in part) wasted. Consequently, much time is spent establishing reasonably tight control over serials publications. For example, a single issue of a serial needed for replacement purposes costs $4.25 — not including actual labor costs (according to the January 1984 figures from USBE, Inc., a *nonprofit* organization). Thus, one can understand the need for tight control over serials that are to be bound or kept for any length of time.

A significant part of controlling serials relates to the constant changes that serials undergo. New serial titles appear at the rate of about 1,000 a month, and the life span of many serials is very short. The so-called little magazines begin and cease publication with great frequency, and they very often fail to notify subscribers of changes. Delays in publication—often as long as four and five years between the appearances of consecutive numbers—are not uncommon.

The most frequent change is a change in title, which is a constant headache for everyone who deals with serials. A journal appears with one volume and issue number; the next issue continues the same volume number and the succeeding issue number, but it has a new title. One may find numerous examples of this type of change in the *Union List of Serials* and *New Serial Titles*. If title change is the number one problem in serials control, the second most common is a change in the volume or issue numbering sequence without notification to the subscribers. For example, say that the library subscribes to a bimonthly title (six issues per volume year). Suddenly, after four issues have been received, the fifth arrives with a *new* volume number; one cannot be certain what the situation is without contacting the publisher—perhaps policy changed with no notice to the subscriber, perhaps the library failed to receive issues, or perhaps, as sometimes happens, the printer made a mistake.

Those working with serials face the same problems encountered by anyone working in a library—an increasing number of publications, rising costs, poor bibliographic control, lack of storage space, deterioration of paper, problems with binding, and locating replacement items for lost, missing, or damaged issues. Only tight record keeping and constant attention to small details can provide the control needed to handle these problems for serials.

RECORD KEEPING

Patrons and librarians often want to know their library's exact holdings for a single title, from volume 1 to date. Are some items missing? When was the last issue received? When was the invoice paid? How often are issues bound? What is the publication's format? Where may one subscribe to a particular periodical? Records are kept on each of these aspects. But without careful attention to the number of files being generated and maintained, this paper work can become overwhelming. Too often, files contain needless duplication, which means wasting time in updating files unnecessarily.

Most librarians would agree that serials control constitutes one of the major record-keeping headaches in technical services. The basic controlling method is to maintain a unit control record for each title. This can be a page in a notebook, a 3x5-inch card file, a card in a visible file (Kardex®), or a computer record. A single record should contain *all* information for a given title—such as when the subscription began, the source from which it was purchased, how often it is paid for, binding information, and so forth. As files grow, it becomes exceedingly difficult to extract information quickly. If a centralized record is maintained for each title, at least in a manual system, then records can be arranged in terms of only one element of information (normally, the file is arranged alphabetically by title). The alternative is to set up several files to counteract this centralization, but then one faces all the disadvantages of a decentralized record system: a growing number of files to be handled, the need to avoid duplicating information, and an increase in searching time for both the patron and the library staff.

SERIALS BIBLIOGRAPHIES

From the number of bibliographies and guides to periodicals and serial literature, we will discuss only the five basic sources of serial information:

1) *The IMS Ayer Directory of Publications* (Philadelphia: IMS Press, 1869- . Annual.) The directory is one of the standard lists of American newspapers and periodicals. It does not claim to be a complete listing, however, it does cover a good many less commercial publications, such as religious publications, college publications, and some of the items from agricultural experiment stations in various states. It also covers Canada, the Philippines, and several other countries. It is particularly useful for newspapers and other weekly or serial publications not usually considered commercial.

2) *New Serial Titles: A Union List of Serials Commencing Publication after December 31, 1949* (Washington: Library of Congress, 1953- . Monthly.) *New Serial Titles* (*NST*) is a monthly publication that lists new serials received by a large number of cooperating libraries. There are quarterly, annual, five-year, ten-year, and twenty-year cumulations. Each monthly issue lists both title changes and those titles that have ceased publication. Sometimes the ceased publication section of *NST* is the only notification a library will receive about changes in a particular serial. *New Serial Titles — Classed Subject Arrangement*, a monthly with no cumulations, is arranged by Dewey decimal classification and indicates only Library of Congress holdings. One particularly useful cumulation is *New Serial Titles: 1950-1970* (4 vols. New York: R. R. Bowker, 1973). As of 1984 *NST* has been issued only in microfiche.

3) *Ulrich's International Periodicals Directory* (New York: R. R. Bowker, 1932- . Annual.) The scope of *Ulrich's* was expanded in 1965 to list titles open entry — its easier than updating — in the roman alphabet or those with subtitles or abstracts in English. A classified guide to 64,000 current foreign and domestic titles, it is extremely useful but by no means comprehensive. *Irregular Serials and Annuals* (also a Bowker publication) is a companion volume. Both *Irregular Serials and Annuals* and *Ulrich's* are updated by *Ulrich's Quarterly*. This notes title changes, new titles, successions, mergers, changes of address, and changes in subscription costs.

4) *Union List of Serials in Libraries of the United States and Canada.* 3d ed. (5 vols. New York: H. W. Wilson, 1965). The third edition lists 156,499 periodical titles, with the holdings of 956 cooperating libraries. Anyone doing reference work in the area of serials/periodical publications will find this useful. Also a useful source of information about title changes and locations, the *Union List of Serials* may serve as a selection aid for the librarian. It does *not* cover government publications, international documents, newspapers, law reports, publications of agricultural and other experimental stations, religious, business, fraternal organizations, chambers of commerce, house organs, alumni magazines, fraternal newsletters, or almanacs.

The *Union List of Serials* is an essential item for both the public service and technical service departments.

ORDER AND VERIFICATION PROCEDURES

The procedures for ordering and verifying serials or periodicals are very much the same as those used to order books (covered in detail in preceding chapters). There are, however, a few differences. It is important that the verification processes establish both an accurate price and frequency of publication. The usual verification sources are the bibliographies previously discussed or vendors' catalogs.

A number of specialized vendors or jobbers deal exclusively or extensively with library periodical and serial needs—among these are Faxon Company, McGregor, EBSCO, and Blackwell's, among others. Most of these jobber-vendors supply catalogs of the journals that they are readily able to supply, although most of them will claim to handle subscriptions for any periodical or serial. When a price is to be verified, check it in the vendor's catalog against the one listed in one of the standard bibliographies (*Ulrich's* or *New Serial Titles*). Occasionally, there is a discrepancy in price. The vendor's price may be the correct one because of a price increase; or the price listed in *Ulrich's* or in the *New Serial Titles* may be the correct one but, for some reason, the vendor might have included an extra service charge in the price.

It is extremely important to establish the correct title for any item being ordered. Check-in files, no matter what their format, are almost always based on a title entry approach. If the order is placed incorrectly, a check-in card and record will be established under a title *not the same* as that of the periodical that arrives in the mail. This will take a lot of effort to straighten out. A check-in card and other record keeping items are usually prepared and filed when the order is placed. Once the title is received, then, there will be no confusion as to whether it is a new subscription, a sample copy, or a publisher's error. The order itself, however, is almost never typed on the fanfold multiple copy order form, for two reasons: 1) since a record of each title on order is noted in the periodicals check-in file, there is no need for a separate file of slips representing outstanding orders; and 2) a public record, if this is deemed necessary, usually takes the form of a card placed in a Kardex® or a strip placed in the Linedex® file, to indicate that a particular title is on order but has not yet been received.

The amount of serials ordering varies from library to library. Usually, a library orders only a small number of new titles each year. Most orders are placed on a " 'Til forbidden" basis—that is, the jobber or publisher is to renew the subscription automatically until notified to the contrary. This eliminates the need for typing a new order each fiscal year, which is a great advantage. Some library systems, however, require that the entire list of periodicals be sent out to jobbers for bids every year. This means typing up purchase orders and multiple copies and submitting them to a number of vendors. Because this presents a number of problems, it is hoped that the practice will be discontinued.

SERIALS CONTROL

Check-In Routines

The most critical aspect of serials work is the daily checking in of received periodicals, serials, and newspapers. *This is the point at which the system succeeds or fails.* The routines must be established and rigorously followed; if a library loses a single number of a serial, it may have to spend three or four times the subscription price to secure a missing item.

After the daily mail has been opened, and items for the serials department have been sorted out, they are arranged alphabetically by title. A checker *cannot* assume that the issue in hand is the next issue that should be received. The table of contents or legal notice must be checked to determine the volume number, issue number, and date of the particular issue in hand. If there is a gap in the receipts, a claim must be made immediately for the missing issue. Since serial publishers do not print many copies of an issue beyond the number of their subscriptions, the claim for a loss must be made quickly if one hopes to receive a replacement copy.

Figure 22.1 shows one type of check-in card for different types of periodicals, and Figure 22.2 (page 284) is an example of the main entry card or central record for each periodical. The check-in card often notes any special routing instructions for a given periodical. The periodicals in the field of library science are often circulated to all professional staff before being placed in periodical stacks. In an academic library, a number of periodicals may go to departmental offices for examination before they are put out on shelves for the public.

Fig. 22.1
Check-In Card for Serials

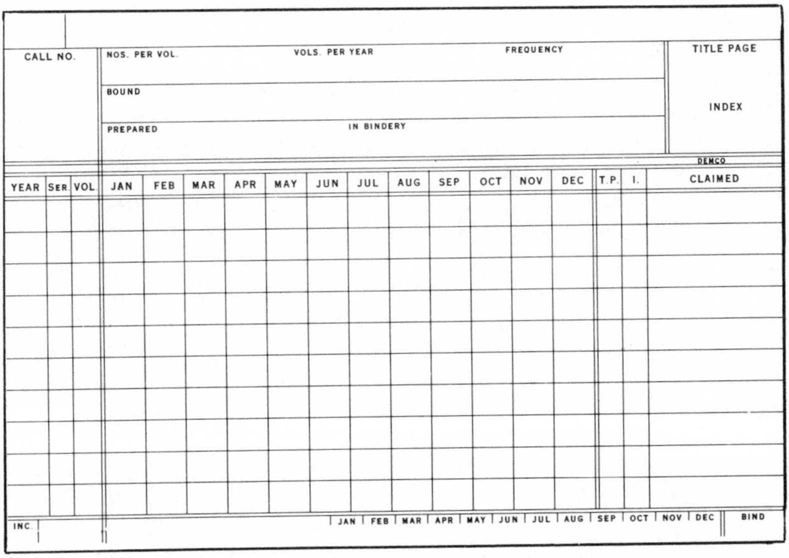
CALL NO.
NOS. PER VOL.
VOLS. PER YEAR
FREQUENCY
TITLE PAGE
BOUND
INDEX
PREPARED
IN BINDERY
DEMCO
YEAR | SER. | VOL. | JAN | FEB | MAR | APR | MAY | JUN | JUL | AUG | SEP | OCT | NOV | DEC | T.P. | I. | CLAIMED
INC.
JAN | FEB | MAR | APR | MAY | JUN | JUL | AUG | SEP | OCT | NOV | DEC | BIND

Fig. 22.2
Central Record Card

TITLE.			CALL #
HOLDINGS.			
ROUTE. LOCATION—Bound Unbd.			
BIND. in bindery ind. and t.p.	freq.	marking. color	cost
FREQUENCY. RENEWAL DATE.	price	nos. per vol.	vols. per year
TITLE CHANGES.			
CAT. ENTRY. PUBLISHER. VENDOR. NOTES.			
FUND CHARGED. BACK FILE	LANGUAGE	SUBJECT	REQUESTED BY

If periodicals are classified, the check-in person will record the class number on the periodical. All items are property stamped as part of the check-in procedure. The checking-in routine may also include noting which periodicals are ready for binding (that is, when the last number of a volume is received, attach a note to it notifying public service personnel that the issues complete a volume and can be sent to the bindery).

Claiming

An item should be claimed as soon as a gap in the sequence of issues received becomes apparent. The greater the delay between publication date and the date of claim submission for the missing issue, the less likely the library will be to receive the issue in question. The claim can be made directly to the publisher. It can also be made to the agent or vendor from whom the title was secured. The vendor in turn forwards the claim to the publisher. This delays the entire process, however, and often makes it impossible for the library to secure a copy from the publisher. Then, the library must approach a secondhand dealer and pay an extremely high premium for a single issue. Some vendors provide claim forms to be filled in by the library and sent directly to the publisher. The form alerts the publisher that the subscription in question was placed by the agent for a particular library, thus facilitating the publisher's search, with the result that there is less delay.

The first step in claiming is to check the shelves where the item should be located. (An issue will occasionally slip through the check-in procedure without being recorded.) The time, energy, and money spent on claiming should be kept to a minimum, although it accounts for much of the personnel's activity in serials—whether claiming missing issues or trying to obtain issues from second-hand dealers.

It is important to provide the publisher with information about the particular title, volume, issue number and date. But it is equally vital to indicate on what date the subscription was placed, what date the invoice was paid, and the term for which the records show the subscription was to run. If this information is not provided, the library will receive a note from the publisher saying, "Sorry, unable to process this item until the following information is received" — all of which creates a greater delay, and again reduces the chances of receiving the missing item. Figure 22.3 provides an example of a claiming form.

Fig. 22.3
Form Letter for Claiming Serials

Date:

Gentlemen:
According to our records, the following periodical(s) that were ordered from you on our order no._____
dated _____ have not been received:

Invoices

As the above paragraph implies, a careful recording of invoice information is also important in controlling periodicals. When a publisher or jobber sends an invoice, it must be carefully examined both as to price and date on which the subscription is to begin (or to continue, if a renewal) to avoid a gap of one or two issues. This is particularly important in the case of weekly or monthly publications.

In the spring or at the beginning of a new fiscal year, the serials jobber often sends an extremely long invoice. Someone must examine this invoice *item by item*, verifying that *every* element is correct. It is very unusual that an invoice of several hundred titles is error-free — either in terms of unwanted titles appearing on the list, incorrect prices, an inaccurate beginning date or continuation date (which would result in the loss of one or two issues), etc. Correction of these matters involves some delay.

Libraries often have a policy of not approving payment of an invoice until all of the problems relating to the invoice are cleared up. If the library is dealing with a jobber, who must in turn check with the publisher, that delay could jeopardize the receipt of issues of all titles on the invoice. Therefore, the invoice must be checked and corrected *very quickly and very accurately*, and errors must be listed and sent to the appropriate agency immediately in order to rectify the situation.

Automated Serials Control

There have been rapid developments in automated serials systems in the past five years. Some bibliographic utilities have added subsystems that assist in serial control work. A few commercial hardware/software vendors offer serial control packages. And, as might be expected, serial jobbers offer systems. While these systems are rapidly developing and will continue to do so, we feel the most complete serials control programs as of 1984 are those offered by the serial vendors. They have been automating their own business and therefore have the most experience in the field. Of course, there are interface problems between such systems and the utility systems, but these should be solved. We will describe two systems (OCLC and EBSCO) in some detail, only as examples *not* as endorsements.

The OCLC Serials Control Subsystem provides for three aspects of inventory control of serials of which check-in and claiming are operational; its binding module is still under development. Used in conjunction with the Acquisition and Cataloging Subsystems, this Subsystem provides virtually complete control of serials.

Libraries using the system increase the availability and timeliness of serials information. Staff and patrons have online access to up-to-date, detailed, copy-specific holdings and location information for serials in the library. Using the OCLC On-Line Union Catalog, libraries can access the bibliographic information for serials input by any library. The CONSER (CONversion of SERials) project has contributed to building a serials data base of over 600,000 titles. Through this project, the Library of Congress and the National Library of Canada have authenticated bibliographic information for over 72,000 titles.

The system enables each library to build its own online file of complete, detailed holdings statements for each copy. In addition, the library may enter receipt dates for the last 1-99 issues. When an issue is received and checked in, the system automatically updates holdings information. Based on the title's frequency, the system predicts and displays the next four expected issue numbers and dates of receipt. The system identifies a missing issue if a gap occurs in the issues checked in.

A claim cycle is set by each library for each serial. The claim cycle specifies the number of days after which an issue is considered to be overdue. The system allows each library to customize its claiming activity. Claiming may be:

Automatic   System produces claim notices according to the library's established claim cycle.

Semiautomatic System produces terminal messages and prints claim notices on command of the user.

Manual   System prints claim notices only on command of the user.

The Serials Control Subsystem supports interlibrary loan activities for serials. Although check-in records are designed primarily for local use, holdings data for support of interlibrary loan activity is accessible to other libraries through a union list capability.

A serials union listing capability provides a cost-effective means for creating, maintaining, and distributing serials union list information. Libraries enter summary holdings information into union list or serial local data records. Holdings statements conform to the American National Standards Institute standard.

- Increased availability of library resources. Processing time for serial issues is reduced.

- Reduced rate of rise of library per-unit costs. Libraries use bibliographic information in the On-line Union Catalog, reducing overall processing time, and decreasing the need for manual files.

- On-line access to detailed, up-to-date information about a library's serial holdings and about the serial collections of other OCLC participating libraries.

- Ability to monitor and control serials activities. Bibliographic and holdings information is available in a single file, easily accessed and updated.

- Printed Products.*

AUTOMATED SERIALS

EBSCO has supplied libraries with serials for many years and is well respected by serials librarians. Like other major serial vendors, EBSCO has been automating its internal operations for some time and has combined its experience with a library developed serials system (UCLA's Biomedical Library system). The automated system (called EBSCONET) consists of two separate but related serials management systems: Serials Control System and Online Subscription Service. (Note: a reminder that the system described is used as an example only and is *not* intended as a recommendation.)**

The Serial Control System (SCS) is made up of these elements: check-in, claiming, binding, full-record display, reference display, routing, invoicing, and union list. The three basic types of records in SCS are an active title, an inactive title, and a cross-reference. The cross-references provide links to other records. Cross-references usually contain only two or three lines of data. An active record is a title currently being received or on order. An inactive record is for a title no longer received or which has ceased publication but holdings are still maintained in the collection. Each serial record contains a minimum of four fields of information, but it can have

---

*Quoted by permission of OCLC.
**The following EBSCO material and figures are quoted by permission.

more than thirty fields if all functions and all comment lines are used. Certain fields contain information unique to a library; others contain common bibliographic information, such as ISSN. The fields are both fixed and variable with one or several subfields. Generally, subfields are mnemonic. The most frequently used fields are shown in Figure 22.4.

Fig. 22.4
SCS Code Fields

LISTING OF CODING FIELDS

TAG	DESCRIPTION
* SN	SERIAL NUMBER
905	BIBLIOGRAPHIC AND INVOICE INFORMATION. STATUS, *LANGUAGE, *COUNTRY OF ORIGIN, *MEDIA, COPY NUMBER, ACQUISITION SOURCE FOR JOURNAL, WHY DEAD, CODEN.
907	INVOICE.
910	CURRENT SERIAL INFORMATION. YEAR, VOLUME, ISSUE, DATE, FREQUENCY, TIMES PER YEAR, ROUTING, LOCATION, PATTERN, FIRST ISSUE, LAST ISSUE, ISSUE PER VOLUME, BOUND VOLUMES PER VOLUME, AGENCY, TITLE PAGE INDEX, CLAIM, BINDING ACTION, MONTH TO CLAIM, RETENTION.
*915	TITLE OF JOURNAL.
*916	CORPORATE NAME.
*917	SEARCH CODES {TREATED AS TITLE WORDS}.
919	PLACE OF PUBLICATION.
920	CALL NUMBER.
921	PUBLISHER.
*922	ISSN {INTERNATIONAL STANDARD SERIAL NUMBER} OR ISBN {INTERNATIONAL STANDARD BIBLIOGRAPHIC NUMBER}.
925	BINDERY INFORMATION
930	HOLDINGS OF JOURNAL TITLES. {B=BOUND/U=UNBOUND/,=MISSING ISSUE/.=INCOMPLETE VOLUME}.
935	SUPPLEMENT HOLDINGS AND CUMULATED INDEXES.
940	HISTORY STATEMENTS.
945	CHECK-IN NOTES.
950	BINDERY INTERNAL NOTES.
955	BINDERY EXTERNAL NOTES.
960	CLAIMING HISTORY.
961	CLAIM INTERNAL NOTES.
*963	EBSCO TITLE NUMBER, ACCESS CODE, SHIP-TO CODE.
964	CLAIM EXTERNAL NOTES.
965	BINDERY HISTORY.
970	CLAIM ADDRESS IF NOT TO VENDOR.
*975	ALTERNATIVE ACCESS POINTS.
980	CROSS REFERENCE TITLE.
985	BEGINNING AND ENDING DATES.
990	BINDERY TITLE {IF IT DIFFERS FROM 915 TITLE OF JOURNAL}.
995	ROUTING NAMES.

*INDICATES RETRIEVAL POSSIBILITIES

___INDICATES FIXED FIELDS

Two unique fields that should be noted are 917, an abbreviated search code, and 975, which allows for subject searching by access points chosen by the library/information center. These access points for field 975 can be alpha or numeric or a combination. For example, a library which has cataloged serials can include the subject headings already assigned. These terms can then be used as access points. In another library/information center the specialist may choose to enter personal names, a department or accounting code, project codes, or other specialized access terms. This field is highly versatile. Field 917 is also noted for flexibility in searching where a library assigned search code can be added. This flexibility facilitates recalling records for check-in for complex or frequently received titles.

The serials record can be developed in several ways. Existing MARC format records can be used to create the SCS data base. A record can be keyed online by the user or EBSCO following a completed worksheet. The record can then be reviewed online or in hard copy and online modifications can be made by the user. Brief records can be entered initially with selected fields and required fields input. Then, after the check-in process is underway, a user can add more information such as complete holdings, additional subject headings, search keys, or history notes.

The record can be retrieved by key title words, an exact title, a serial number, ISSN, a search code and original subject terms or access points. Title words can be truncated for faster searching. Rolling forward and backward can also facilitate searching.

"*Check-in*" is based on the predictive method where the 910 field includes a pattern code and other key elements to generate the expected issue line of information. A user matches the issue in hand and keys in the appropriate commands. The issue is recorded in the holdings and the expected issue line is updated (see Figure 22.5, page 290).

The *claiming function* is integrated with the check-in activity or may be handled as a separate online activity for later routine review. A missed issue can be flagged in two ways. First, there is a month to claim (MTC) value assigned to the record in field 910, the current journal information field. If an issue fails to arrive in the specific time, its absence is noted in a review file as an overdue issue for user review and action. In the review task the user may see online all items flagged as overdue as well as all previous claims which are still outstanding. Second, a skipped issue may be noted at check-in, then the current journal information field 910 can be adjusted and check-in can progress to an immediate decision to claim now or later (see Figure 22.6, page 290). This claim, placed either now or later, is automatically recorded in the claim log file. Printing is accomplished off-line in a batch mode for claims on EBSCO-ordered and any other titles received.

Fig. 22.5
Check-in Function

```
TI//US WORLD
 PV                                       S 2628 T 0200   {8075200}
CHECK-IN:    YEAR 80, VOL  89, ISS        9, ISS DATE AU25, THIS YR 34, BOUND NO
960 . . K1N IST098080 89 7AU11 AUG 18;
930 . . B1-88{1935-80}U89N1-6,8; AU18; {1980}
915 . . US NEWS AND WORLD REPORT.
922 . . 0041-5537
920 . . 031
905 . . ST1, L275, C950, MP, AJNA.
910 . . Y80, V89, I9, DAU25, FQ52, TY34, RTJK, LOCRR, P1, 1S0001, LS0026, I/V26, VBV02,
TP11, AGES, MTC01, RETP.
LAST REC'D 18/08/80              S     RR
 PV
CHECK-IN:YES


 PV                                       S 2628 T 0200   {8075200}
CHECK-IN: YEAR 80, VOL  89, ISS  10, ISS DATE SE01, THIS YR 35, BOUND NO
960 . . K1N IST098080 89 7AU11
930 . .B1-88{1935-80}U89N1-6, 8-9; AUG 25; {1980}
915 . . US NEWS AND WORLD REPORT
922 . . 0041-5537
920 . . 031
905 . . ST1, L275, C950, MP, AJNA.
910 . . Y80, V89, I10, DES01, FQ52, TY35, RTJK, LOCRR, P1, 1S0001, LS0026,
I/V26, VBV02, TP11, AGES, MTC01, RETP.
LAST REC'D 29/08/80              S     RR
OK
8075200 UPDATED.
```

Fig. 22.6
Claiming of a Skipped Issue

```
8075200 UPDATED
 PV                                       S 2628 T 0200 {8075200}
CLAIM:CODES        , YEAR:80 , VOL:89, ISS:4 DATE:JA25  CLAIM DATE:0280
915 . . US NEWS AND WORLD REPORT.
930 . . B86-88{1977-79}U89N1-3,5 ;FEB01;{1980}
910 . . Y80,V89,IS5,DFE08,FQ52,TY6,LOCR,P1,1S0001,LS0026,I/V26,VBV02,TP11,
AGES,MTC01,RETP.
STATUS:1, FREQ:52 CL:1, MTC: 1,AGES,RETP
LAST REC'D: 01/02/80
**CLAIM NOW OR LATER**
UP
YES :



 PV                                       S 2628 T 0200 {8075200}
CHECKIN: YEAR 80 , VOL: 89, ISS:  6,ISS DATE: FE 8, THIS YR: 6, BOUND: NO
960 . . K1N 1ST028080 89 4 ;JAN25;
930 . . B86-88{1977-79}U89N1-3,5;FEB01;{1980}
915 . . US NEWS AND WORLD REPORT
STATUS:1, FREQ:52 CL:1, MTC: 1, AGES,RETP
910 . . Y80,V89,I6,DFE08,FQ52,TY6,LOCR,P1,1S0001,LS0026,I/V26,VBV02,TPI1,AGES,
MTC01,RETP.
LAST REC'D 02/01/80             S     RR
OK
8075200 UPDATED
```

No activity can be performed in reference — it is a "view only" screen. Figure 22.7*a* illustrates a basic reference display from a list of titles. Coded data is translated into natural language. Figure 22.7*b* (page 292) shows a more complex search involving first a country, then modified by subject, which results in the retrieval of one active record.

Fig. 22.7
Basic Reference Displays

(*a*) **List of Titles**

```
              -REFERENCE DISPLAY-LAST REC'D 08/16/81  1056900

    XX          READING ROOM    QUARTERLY        ACTIVE
ANNALS OF HUMAN GENETICS.
B26-40{1962-77}U41N1-4{1977/8}B42-43{1978/79-1980/81}U44N1 {1980/81}
CUM. INDEX B20-34{1965-71}.
CONTINUES ANNALS OF EUGENICS.
OPTIONS:  1.  'XX' RESET PROGRAM

          2.  ANY INITIAL DISPLAY OPTION, AND:

              'RF', 'RB', {ROLL FORWARD OF BACK ONE RECORD}

              'FL' FULL RECORD DISPLAY {NOTE:  OPTIONS LIST NOT
              REPEATED}

              'PR' {OFFLINE PRINTOUT REQUEST}.


    ?FL

    :PV              S:2537      T:0122       {1056900}
    905 . . ST1,L275,C940,MP,AJNA,CDNANHGA.
    910 . . Y78,V42,L2,F04,LOCRR,P1,1S0001,LS004,I/V04,VBV01,AGES
    MTC03,RETP
    915 . . ANNALS OF HUMAN GENETICS.
    917 . . HUMGE
    919 . . {LONDON}.
    920 . . 500
    922 . . 0032-4800.
    930 . . B26-40{1962-77}041N1-4{1977/8}B42-43{1978/9-1980/1}U44N1{1980/1}
    935 . . CUM. INDEX B20-34{1956-71}.
    940 . . CONTINUES ANNALS OF EUGENICS
    975 . . GENETICS.003254800.500.JK.GENERESEARCH.RA524A267
    985 . . {19,1954+}.
```

Fig. 22.7
Basic Reference Display

(b) Search by Country and Subject

```
CT//FRANCE
          - THE SEARCH FOUND 69 TITLES -
RESULTS INCLUDE ONLY CURRENT JOURNALS.
1.  $C320 {FRANCE} COUNTRY OF 69 JOURNALS
OPTIONS:
1.  XX RESET PROGRAM 2.  TI// AND ADDED TITLE WORD
3.  SJ, LG, CT, MD OPTIONS FOR ADDED SUBJ
          LANG, COUNTRY AND MEDIA SEARCH
4.  DT DISPLAY THE TITLES OF THE SELECTED JOURNALS
5.  PR  PRINT A SEARCH LIST

SJ//GENETICS

GENETICS HAS BEEN SELECTED TO FURTHER REFINE OR EXTEND THE SEARCH,
RELATIVE TO THE PROCEEDING TERM{S} DO YOU WANT - -

          1.  AND          GENETICS
          2.  OR           GENETICS
          3.  AND NOT       GENETICS
KEY BL1, BL2, OR BL3 {BOOLEAN LOGIC 1, 2, 3 ABOVE}


BL1
          - REFERENCE DISPLAY - LAST REC'D 08/20/80
NO CALL NUMBER          STACKS      QUARTERLY CURRENT
ANNALES DE GENETIQUE.
C1-17{1958-74} U18N1, 3-4{1975}.  B19-22{1976-79}
          U23N1-4{1980}
V18N2{1975} {O.P.}
PUBLISHED AS SUPPLEMENT TO SEMAINE DES HOSPITAUX DE PARIS.
OPTIONS:
          1.  XX RESET PROGRAM   2.  ANY INITIAL DISPLAY OPTION
                    RF, RB  ROLL FORWARD OR BACK ONE RECORD
                    FL,   FULL RECORD DISPLAY
                    PR,   {OFF-LINE PRINTOUT REQUEST}
THE SEARCH YIELDED THIS TITLE ONLY.
```

The routing function provides a field for the recording of reader's names. A maximum of 14 names may be listed per title. At the time of check-in, a routing slip is produced. By using various search keys, a listing of titles sent to each reader may be produced.

Invoice information may be stored in the record and is entered in several ways. Repetitive data, such as invoice number or date, may be input using a global "add" command. For those titles ordered through EBSCO, some invoice data is automatically added to the records. The invoice function is flexible, since titles from all sources (order directs, memberships, etc.) can be included in the SCS data base, and these have a variety of invoice requirements.

The binding function includes the production of a bindery pickup list, the creation of bindery notes in the record, the printing of packing lists, and both online user input and off-line batch programs. At established times, or upon request, the bindery pickup list is printed and sent to the library. The system has predicted which titles need to be sent to the bindery based on issues and volumes completed and on coding. Once the bindery command is given, it creates a bindery history note, such as "At bindery-V34 and V34 11/82." A packing list is then produced in batch mode. After being printed, the packing list is sent to the library for shipment to the bindery with the journals. When the volumes are returned from the bindery, the program merges the holdings and deletes the bindery note (see Figure 22.8).

Fig. 22.8
Bindery Action

```
?XX//TC//2//3

KEY A FOUR-DIGIT SHIPMENT DATE {E.G., '0208' FOR FEBRUARY 8}.
OPTIONAL: FOLLOW THE DATE WITH A COLON & A 7-DIGIT SERIAL NUMBER TO START.
{TO EXIT, KEY 'XX'.}

?0823

PV                              S:3061 T:0119 {1000500}@
BIND: YEAR:80, VOL:23, ISS:1- 4.
930 . . B1-17{1958-74}U18N1,3-4{1975}.B19-22{1976-79}U23N1-4{1980}U24N1,3{1981}
935 . . V18N2{1975} O.P.
915 . . ANNALES DE GENETIQUE
LAST REC'D:04/08/82   S                    S

?PV
?YES

PV                              S:3036 T:0119 {1000500}@
930 . . B1-17{1958-74}U18N1,3-4{1975}.B19-22{1976-79}U23N1-4{1980}U24N1,3{1981}
935 . . V18N2{1975} O.P.
965 . . H1N80 23 1-  4A0823,                  "AT BINDERY V 23N1-40882"
915 . . ANNALES DE GENETIQUE.
```

Union listing is both online and batch function. The batch mode includes an off-line report which lists titles, location, and holdings for serials titles from two or more participating libraries or organizations. The Union List function requires some standardization among participants, such as title form of entry and cross referencing (see Figure 22.9, page 294).

Online Subscription Service (OSS) is intended to aid in the complex task of placing and renewing subscriptions. Figures 22.10-22.22 (beginning on page 294) illustrate some of the features of this system. Menu selection is an optional feature for those preferring menus, for less experienced users, or for infrequent users (see Figure 22.12, page 295).

Fig. 22.9
Union List Entries Showing Location and Holdings

```
PHL,CMR = CODES FOR LIBRARIES    . OR , = MISSING ISSUE OR VOLUME    B=BOUND  U=UNBOUND

BIOCHEMICAL AND BIOPHYSICAL RESEARCH COMMUNICATIONS.
CMR
 HOLDINGS: B49-76{1972-77}.B78-100{1977-81}U101-103N1-4{1981}
PHL
 HOLDINGS: B1-13{1959-63}B14N1-2,4-6{1963-64}B15-96{1964-80}B97N1-2{1980}B97N3-4{1980}
 B98{1981}B99N1-4{1981}B100N1-2{1981}B100N3-4{1981}B101N1-4{1981}B102N1-4{1981}B103N1-4
 {1981}B104N1-4{1982}B105N1{1982}U106N1-3{1982}

BIOCHEMICAL CLINICS.
PHL
 HOLDINGS: B1-4{1963-64}

BIOCHEMICAL GENETICS.
PHL
 HOLDINGS: B1-18{1967-80}B19N1-12{1981}B20N1-4{1982}
```

Fig. 22.10
Sign On

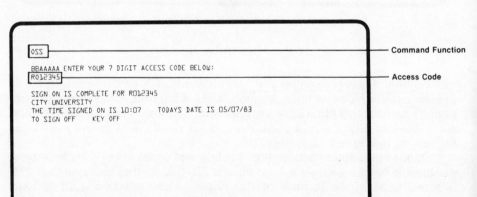

```
OSS                                                          ———— Command Function

BBAAAAA ENTER YOUR 7 DIGIT ACCESS CODE BELOW:
R012345                                                      ———— Access Code

SIGN ON IS COMPLETE FOR R012345
CITY UNIVERSITY
THE TIME SIGNED ON IS 10:07    TODAYS DATE IS 05/07/83
TO SIGN OFF   KEY OFF
```

You can access "how to" instructions for the computer functions available to you in the EBSCONET OSS system.

Fig. 22.11
Online Help

```
HELP

            EBSCO SUBSCRIPTION SERVICES AVAILABLE FUNCTIONS

    FUNCTION CODE                   PURPOSE

        OSS                         SIGN ON
        OFF                         SIGN OFF
        TITL                        TITLE FILE LIST BY TITLE NAME
        PRIC                        TITLE AND PRICE FILE INQUIRY BY TITLE NUMBER
        MCBL                        MISSING COPY BANK INQUIRY/REQUEST
        SUMM                        SUMMARY OF PUBLICATIONS ORDERED
        CLAI                        CLAIM ENTRY
        ORDE                        ORDER ENTRY

    YOU MAY NOW PROCEED BY ENTERING ONE OF THE ABOVE FUNCTIONS IN ITS REQUIRED
    FORMAT.  SHOULD YOU NEED ASSISTANCE IN DETERMINING THE PROPER FORMAT FOR
    THE FUNCTION, YOU MAY EITHER CONSULT YOUR EBSCONET USERS MANUAL OR USE
    THE HELP COMMAND.

    TO USE HELP, TYPE THE SELECTED FUNCTION CODE OVER THE DOTS BELOW,
    BEGINNING ON THE FIRST DOT, AND SEND THE COMMAND.

    HELP.  . . .
```

Fig. 22.12
Online Subscription Service Menu

```
MENU                                                                    Command

                    EBSCO SUBSCRIPTION SERVICES MENU
    COMMAND    DESCRIPTION                 DATA ITEMS
    TITL    TITLE NAME LOOKUP           ...........................................
    TITP    TITLE NAME WITH PUBL N/A    ...........................................
    PUBT    TITLES BY PUBLISHER         NNNNNNN
    PUBL    PUBLISHER NAME LOOKUP       ...........................................
    PRIC    PUBLICATION PRICE LIST      NNN-NNN-NNN
    CLAI    CLAIM ENTRY                 . {X OR TITLE NUMBER}
    ORDE    ORDER ENTRY                 .
    MCBL    MISSING COPY BANK           NNN-NNN-NNN MM-DD-YY
    SUMM    SUMMARY OF PUBLICATIONS     . {X OR TITLE NUMBER}
    MAIL    EBSCO TELMAIL               .
    EBSS    EBSCO/SEARCH                .
    ROUT    ROUTING                     .
    HELP    COMMAND INSTRUCTIONS        .
    USER    NEW ACCOUNT                 .
    OFF     SIGN-OFF                    .

    ENTER THE DATA INFORMATION TO SELECT A COMMAND YOU WISH TO EXECUTE
    THEN POSITION THE CURSOR AT THE END OF THE LINE AND SEND LINE.



        ENTER COMMAND
```

Title file inquiry allows the review of a list of titles, bibliographic information, and prices in EBSCO's title file. The title file includes title number, title, edition, publisher, publisher's billing address, and prices. Often there are several editions of each title, such as surface mail, airmail, or microform edition. You can scan forward or backward to locate the title and edition you want. Pricing information can then be reviewed. (Note the first entries in Figure 22.13, page 296.)

Fig. 22.13
Title File Inquiry by Title Name

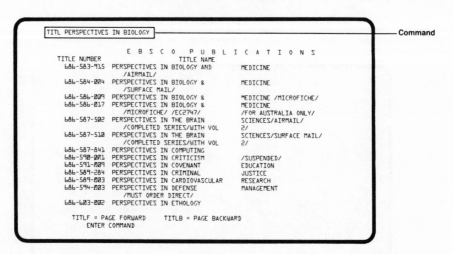

Another useful function (see Figure 22.14) lets you review bibliographic information and prices in the title file when you know the title number of the serial you want.

The summary of publications function lets you review your order file information (see Figures 22.15, 22.16, and 22.17). This order file, updated weekly, is a complete listing of the serials you subscribe to. It includes your EBSCO title numbers, titles ordered, subscriber names and ship-to addresses, quantities, terms, start dates, EBSCO order numbers, prices, and customer identification or HEGIS numbers. Your order file can be searched by subscriber name, department name, title number, HEGIS number, subscriber code, or union list code if you participate in a cooperative union group. If a title number is not known, your search can be made by title name, and the title number and name will be displayed for verification. You may include all your subscriptions, regardless of their source.

Fig. 22.14
Title File Inquiry by Title Number/Price List

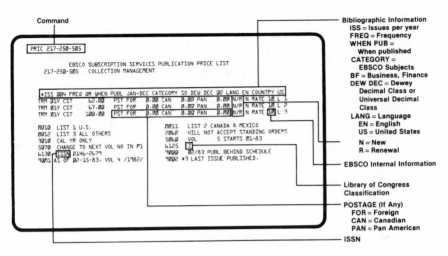

Fig. 22.15
Summary of Publications Ordered

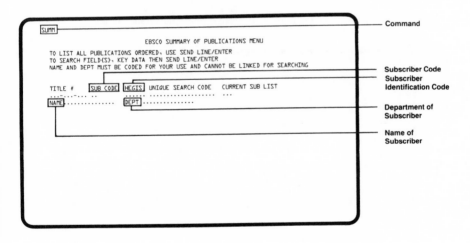

Fig. 22.16
Summary of Publications Ordered—Displayed by Title Number

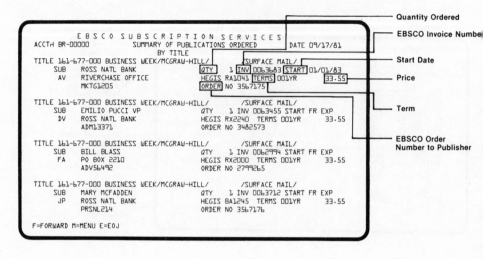

Fig. 22.17
Summary of Publications Ordered—Displayed by Subscriber

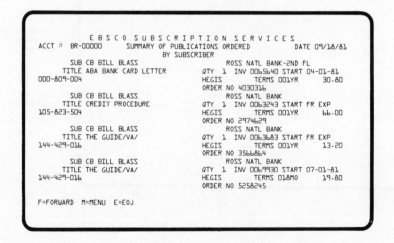

A claim entry (see Figure 22.18) is used when you want to enter claims for titles ordered through EBSCO. The screen will request the title number, type of claim, claim number, and the subscriber code. Two "comment lines" are available.

Fig. 22.18
Claim Entry

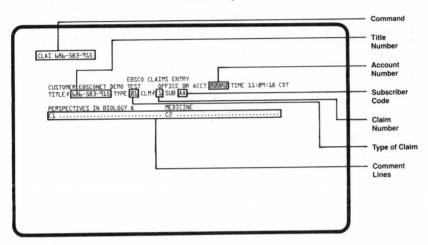

An order entry (see Figure 22.19, page 300) allows you to place an interim order for a subscription. You enter the title name, start date, quantity, subscriber address, and any miscellaneous information or instructions for your Regional Office. This order is transmitted instantaneously to your EBSCO Regional Office for final processing.

EBSCO/SEARCH is a powerful information storage and retrieval system (see Figures 22.20a, page 300, and b, page 301). This function allows you to search EBSCO's title, publisher, and price files for needed information simply by entering English-language commands with keywords or other search terms. You can access information by subject category, frequency, language, country of origin, price, Universal Decimal Code, and more, and get an exact match. Almost any word or phrase in a record can be used as a search term to locate the information you are looking for.

Fig. 22.19
Order Entry

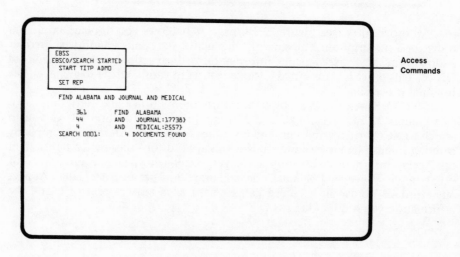

```
ORDE ──────────────────────────────────────────────────────────────── Command

                        EBSCO ORDER PROCESSING

        EBSCONET DEMO TEST              ØØØØ? BR
        TITLE NAME  PERSPECTIVES IN BIOLOGY & MEDICINE..................

        TERM  1 YR.......  QUANTITY Ø1 START DATE Ø6/Ø1/83 N/R R

        PURCHASE ORDER NUMBER NONE...............E-Ø9/12/83

        SUBSCRIBER N/A AA....................................................

        SPECIAL INSTRUCTION TO THE EBSCO BIRMINGHAM OFFICE
        SECOND ORDER TO FOLLOW..........................................

        ***.................................................................

        ORDER ACCEPTED
```

Fig. 22.20
EBSCO/SEARCH

(a)

```
        EBSS
        EBSCO/SEARCH STARTED
         START TITP ADMO ──────────────────────────────── Access
                                                          Commands
        SET REP

        FIND ALABAMA AND JOURNAL AND MEDICAL

            361       FIND  ALABAMA
             44       AND   JOURNAL:17738}
              4       AND   MEDICAL:2557}
        SEARCH ØØØ1:     4 DOCUMENTS FOUND
```

Fig. 22.20
EBSCO/SEARCH

(*b*)

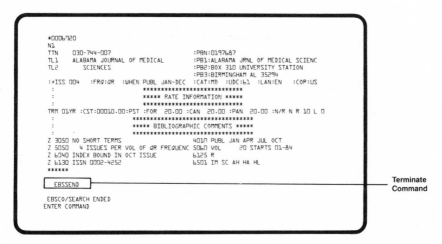

ROUTING is an automated system for building, maintaining, and printing routing lists. Using the ROUTING system, you may instantaneously change title or reader information; add titles or additional copies of a particular title; display a title and readers by delivery location; or display a reader and titles by delivery location. You are also able to print any or all routing slips at any time. All together, you may perform eight separate functions to simplify your serials routing.

Fig. 22.21
Routing

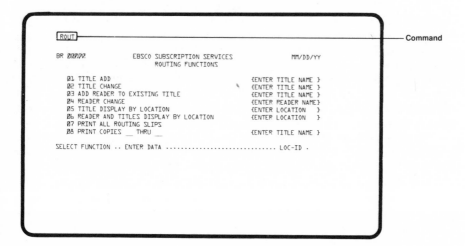

The sign off function disconnects your terminal from the system. This function also displays a summary of the activities you have performed.

Fig. 22.22
Sign Off

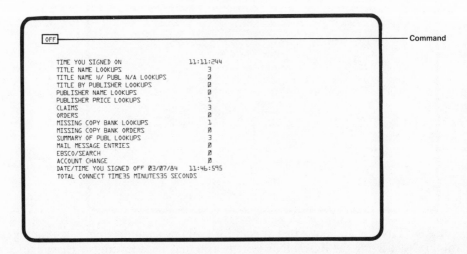

```
OFF                                                              Command

  TIME YOU SIGNED ON                    11:11:244
  TITLE NAME LOOKUPS                     3
  TITLE NAME W/ PUBL N/A LOOKUPS        0
  TITLE BY PUBLISHER LOOKUPS            0
  PUBLISHER NAME LOOKUPS                0
  PUBLISHER PRICE LOOKUPS               1
  CLAIMS                                3
  ORDERS                                0
  MISSING COPY BANK LOOKUPS            1
  MISSING COPY BANK ORDERS             0
  SUMMARY OF PUBL LOOKUPS               3
  MAIL MESSAGE ENTRIES                  0
  EBSCO/SEARCH                          0
  ACCOUNT CHANGE                        0
  DATE/TIME YOU SIGNED OFF 03/07/84  11:46:595
  TOTAL CONNECT TIME 35 MINUTES 35 SECONDS
```

The EBSCO system is a good, easy-to-use automated serials system. (Again we remind the reader that we are not endorsing the system; we are describing the system in detail because of the many features it contains and because it represents a commercial system rather than a utility system. In other chapters other automated systems are highlighted.)

BINDING

Binding library materials is usually the responsibility of the serials department. Some temporary or minor types of binding are handled by other departments (as in book preparation or mending work), but the serials department is concerned with permanent binding. Some large libraries actually do the binding in-house, but most use commercial binderies. Our discussion in this section will be limited to the preparation of materials to be sent to the bindery, and will not deal with the actual binding procedures. Since binding itself is a complicated fascinating operation, however, the technician should make an effort to visit a bindery to see the actual process.

Although periodicals provide the bulk of materials sent to the bindery, some books are also sent. The records to be kept and instructions required for sending books to the bindery are very simple, so books will be discussed first.

Except for paperbacks, most books purchased by a library are already bound. Books sent to the bindery are those that have been so heavily used that they must be rebound. Books sent for a first binding are usually paperbacks, which are "permabound" — a laminating process allowing the original covers to be used and displayed. This inexpensive process produces covers strong enough to withstand a lot of use. Many libraries purchase their paperbacks from special jobbers who bind all paperbacks automatically before sending them to the library.

The information sent to the bindery with a paperback is usually only the call number that is to be placed on the spine.

The bindery usually needs more information for books to be rebound. This is often supplied on a form that gives: 1) the exact title to be placed on the spine, 2) the author's last name, also on the spine, 3) the call number, for the spine, and 4) the desired color of binding. Each bindery has its own special requirements and ways of handling material. The technician supervising the preparation of bindery material definitely should become familiar with the routines of the bindery used by the library.

Serials, particularly periodicals, are a little more difficult to prepare for binding. The check-in file for serials usually contains the necessary binding information. Because serials are bound at regular intervals and over a period of many years, efforts must be made to keep the binding uniform for a title.

The library should have for *each* serial title the following information: 1) frequency of binding and how many issues of a periodical are to be in a volume (weekly, quarterly, monthly, annually, etc.); 2) whether the serial has a separate index that must be included in the volume; 3) the exact form of the title and the volume numbers as they should be printed on the spine; and 4) the color of the binding. (Figure 22.23 illustrates the information needed for binding.) Exactly where this information is kept varies depending on the library, but once this procedure is established, it becomes a simple matter to ensure that the binding will be handled correctly.

Fig. 22.23
Binding Information Card

	Library Quarterly	
Nos. Per Vol.	Vols. Per Yr.	Separate Index
4	1	No

Color: Red

Title on Spine: Library
                  Quarterly
                  (Yr. of Publication)

Classification No.: None

The card in Figure 22.23 tells us that four issues form one volume, the color of the binding is red, and the spine title consists of three lines (Library/Quarterly/Year). There is no separate index: the volume is complete in four quarterly issues. The bindery form giving the binder information is shown in Figure 22.24.

Fig. 22.24
Bindery Form

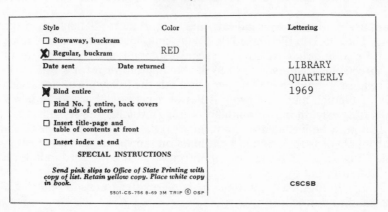

As it is very important to the library, serials work requires great accuracy. Although the work includes a lot of routine, serials work is nevertheless very interesting. One cannot escape being apprised of what is going on in the world as a result of checking in newspapers, news magazines, and periodicals of all types. If bindery work is included in the serials department's responsibilities, as is often the case, it provides a continuing variation in the type of work being performed. One never feels confined in a job that is not lacking in variety. All in all, serials work, because of the variations and flexibilities that occur in the work routine, can be one of the most interesting areas of technical services.

REVIEW QUESTIONS

1. Define serial.

2. What are the primary characteristics of a serial?

3. Name one significant control problem of serials.

4. Name two serials bibliographies.

5. How do serial order and verification procedures differ from book orderings?

6. What is the most critical aspect of serials work?

7. Are all serials property stamped as part of the check-in procedure? If not, explain.

8. List the methods of claiming missing periodicals.

9. Discuss the use and problems of invoices in serials processing and handling.

10. How does serials work change as a result of automation?

11. What information is required for serials binding?

12. What is a permabound book?

23

The basic rules and principles of descriptive cataloging and subject cataloging discussed in earlier chapters apply to the cataloging of serials. Serials cataloging is often complex and even experienced catalogers have occasional problems. Problems usually arise because of frequent name changes, difficulties in determining publication dates, and changes of main entries. There is probably more variation among libraries in handling and cataloging serials than most kinds of print materials.

CATALOGING TERMINOLOGY

Open entry. A catalog entry for a serial, series, or set not yet completed. The numeric/chronological designation and extent of item are left incomplete on the catalog card or bibliographic record to indicate the work is not yet complete.

Serial. A publication issued in successive parts at regular or irregular intervals. Usually it is intended to be continued indefinitely. Includes periodicals, newspapers, proceedings, reports, annuals, and numbered monographic series.

RULES AND PROBLEMS

The most vexing problem in cataloging serials is unquestionably the name changes that are a never ending aspect of working with serials. The problem is usually resolved by establishing a new entry for each title change, a practice called "entry under successive title." This will be discussed below.

Several unique features of serials cataloging should be kept in mind: 1) a new set of catalog cards is made when a serial changes title or when the main entry is changed; 2) most serials are entered under title, and this is especially true for periodicals; 3) a serial is cataloged from the first volume or issue, but can be cataloged from the earliest available volume or issue; 4) the holdings in a catalog are usually cited on a "holdings card" following the main entry, or in a separately issued list such as a periodicals holding list; and 5) adequate references for title variations must be made to enable the library patron to locate materials.

Information on the catalog card for a serial is arranged in the same order and format using the eight areas as for other types of material. The major difference is the use of the Material (or type of publication) Specific Details Area. You will recall that area is used only for serials and cartographic materials. The Physical Description Area will differ depending on the type of material being cataloged.

Again you will recall that the physical description for a printed volume is different from the description for a film or microfilm. The examples below use level two *AACR 2* descriptive cataloging (Rule 1.0D2). The examples will be limited to printed materials; because of the complexities of serials it seems best to keep the examples to the fundamentals.

The chief source of information for a printed serial is the title page or title page substitute (e.g., the cover) of the first available issue or volume (Rule 12.0B1). The prescribed sources of information for each area are also given in Rule 12.0B1.

The title and statement of responsibility are recorded as explained in the basic Rule 1.1B and amplified by Rule 12.1B. The statement of responsibility for most serials is given in a note rather than after the title. This is because most statements of responsibility in serials, especially periodicals, do not appear in a prominent place. The basic rules for the statement of responsibility, 1.1F, state that unless a statement of responsibility appears prominently in the item it should not be included (Rule 1.1F2). Any necessary statement is given in a note (Figure 23.1).

Fig. 23.1
Responsibility Statement of a Serial in a Note

Title	➤The Unabashed librarian: a letter for innovators. -- No. 1 (Nov. 1971) = . --
Note	➤ Founded, edited, and published by Marvin H. Scilken.

In serials where a statement of responsibility is given prominently it is given in the usual place after the title (Figure 23.2).

Fig. 23.2
Responsibility Statement of a Serial after Title

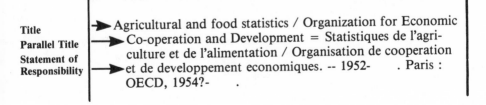

Title	➤Agricultural and food statistics / Organization for Economic
Parallel Title	➤Co-operation and Development = Statistiques de l'agri-
Statement of	culture et de l'alimentation / Organisation de cooperation
Responsibility	➤et de developpement economiques. -- 1952- . Paris : OECD, 1954?- .

Many serials, especially periodicals and newspapers, have special geographic or language editions and these are cited in the Edition Area (Figures 23.3 and 23.4).

Fig. 23.3
Edition for Language

Title
Edition
Language

Sputnik : digest of the Soviet press. -- English ed. --

Fig. 23.4
Edition for Geographic Area

Cambridgeshire farmers journal. -- Northern ed. --

The next area, Numeric and/or Alphabetic, Chronological, or Other Designation Area, is unique to serials (Rule 12.3). You will recall this area is used for mathematic data with cartographic materials. In practice, this area usually follows the title because most serials do not have a statement of responsibility or edition. The first element in this area is a numeric, alphabetic, and/or chronological designation of the first issue or volume of a serial. If the serial is still being published the designation is followed by a hyphen and four spaces (Figure 23.5):

Fig. 23.5
Numeric/Chronological Designation for the
First Issue of a Serial

Title

American libraries: bulletin of the American Library Association. -- Vol. 1, no. 1 (Jan. 1970)-   . --
Numeric/chronological designation

American Library Association.
ALA handbook of organization. -- 1971/72-   .
Chronological designation

More complex designations occur, but these are best encountered after some experience! Remember, there are four spaces after the designation for *continuing* serials so later a closing date can be entered. If a serial is no longer published the date of both the first and last issue are entered in the designation (Figure 23.6):

Fig. 23.6
Closed Designation Area for Completed Serial

> Weekly Review. -- Vol. 1 (Sept. 1936)-v.8 (July 6, 1943). --

The Publication, Distribution, Etc., Area includes the same information as in descriptions of the materials discussed in earlier chapters—place of publication, publisher, and date of publication. The date of publication is given even if it is the same as the first issue or volume in the designation area (Figures 23.7, 23.8, and 23.9).

Fig. 23.7
Publication Date and Designation Date for
First Volume Are Different

> United Nations Conference on Trade and
>   Development.
>   Review of international trade and development. -- 1967-   .
> New York : United Nations, 1968-   .   ▲
>   v. : ill.   ▲

Fig. 23.8
Publication Date and Designation Date for
First Volume Are the Same

> Weekly record. -- Vol. 1, no. 1 (Sept. 2, 1974)-   . -- New
>   York : Bowker, 1974-   .   ▲
>   ▲

Fig. 23.9
Open Entry—Publication Date and Extent of Item Are Not Complete

```
Ref     Annual review of immunology.--Vol. 1
QR         (1983)-    -- Palo Alto, Calif. :
180        Annual Reviews Inc., c1983-v.: ill.; 23 cm.
AS8        Annual.
           ISSN 0732-0582 = Annual review of
        immunology




           1. Immunology--Periodicals.
```

The Physical Description Area includes the information apropriate to the type of material comprising the serial: wall charts, filmstrips, microfilm reels, etc. (Rule 12.5-12.5E). Printed materials are indicated by v., the abbreviation for volume. Three spaces precede the type of material designation in the physical description to indicate the serial is still being published. If the serial is complete the number of volumes or parts is indicated:

22 microfilm reels (Completed serial: microform)

75 v.　　(Completed serial: print format)

v.　　(Serial still being published: print format)

Following the extent of the item are other relevant physical details, such as illustrations and size. Of course, the information will depend on the kind of materials. Examples for printed materials follow:

27 v. : ill. ; 26 cm.

v. : 26 cm.

Refer to chapter 17 on descriptive cataloging for examples of other kinds of materials.

The Note Area is used to give information not given in the other areas. Rules 12.7B-12.7B22 discuss notes used for serials including several unique to serials. Several of the more frequently used types of notes for serials are:

1) **Frequency.** The frequency the serial is issued is given unless it is apparent from the title (e.g., *The Library Quarterly, American Reference Books Annual*). Some samples of frequency notes are:
   Annual
   Quarterly
   Irregular
   Issued every month except August
   Frequency varies

2) **Variation in title.** If a serial has any title variation from the title proper, it should be noted. For example:

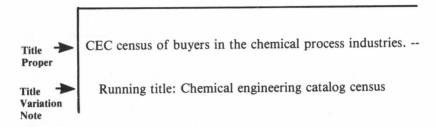

Title Proper → CEC census of buyers in the chemical process industries. --

Title Variation Note → Running title: Chemical engineering catalog census

3) **Relationships with other serials.** If the serial being cataloged has any relationship to any other serial it should be noted. Rule 12.7B7 lists numerous examples of this type of note. Other examples are:

Absorbed: Adult education and the library

Continued by Pakistan new digest

Continued by American libraries: bulletin of the American Library Association

4) **Numbering and Chronological Designation.** A note should be made for irregular or complex numbering not already given in the designation area:

Numbering begins every other year with v. 1.

Issues for Jan. 1980-July 1980 called also v. 3, no. 1-v. 2, no. 3.

The last area, Standard Number and Terms of Availability, is covered by Rule 12.8. Two unique elements given here are the ISSN (International Standard Serial Number) and the *key title*. The ISSN can be taken from any source, but is usually found in the serial. The key title can also be taken from any source and is pre-assigned. The key title is usually in the serial. *Do not make up your own key title.* The key title is separated from the ISSN by an equal sign:

ISSN 0002-9769 = American libraries

ISSN 9479-7469 = Volunteer (Washington)

In general, the rules used to select main entries and determine the proper form of main entries apply to serial publications. Several special rules from the *AACR 2* chapter on choice of access points often apply to serials and should be reviewed. Rule 21.2A discusses the definition for what is considered a change in the title proper. As mentioned earlier serials frequently change title. A title proper is considered changed if: 1) there is a change in the first five words other than an initial article; 2) any important word is added or deleted any place in the title; and 3) the order of words in the title is changed. Rule 21.2C directs the cataloger to establish a new main entry for a serial when the title proper is changed. This in effect is the rule for "successive entry."

Rule 21.3 covers those cases in which the persons or corporate body responsible for a serial is changed. This rule cites two circumstances when a new entry is established: 1) when the *name* of the person or corporate body responsible for the serial changes, and 2) when the *person or corporate body* itself changes. *This rule only applies when the serial in question is entered under the heading for the personal author or corporate body.* The new entry is made even if the title proper remains the same.

Figures 23.10 and 23.11 are examples of completed catalog cards for serials—both are periodicals and notice the notes relating the serials to each other.

Refer to chapter 24 for sources of cataloging information. In addition to the sources cited in that chapter two publications are useful for locating information about serials: *New Serial Titles: A Union List of Serials Commencing Publication After December 31, 1949* (Washington: Library of Congress; New York: R. R. Bowker, 1953-) and *Irregular Serials & Annuals: An International Directory* (New York: R. R. Bowker, 1967-).

Fig. 23.10
Completed Catalog Card for a Serial

ALA bulletin. -- Vol. 1, no. 1 (Jan. 1907)-v.63 (Dec. 1969). --
   Chicago : ALA, 1907-69.
   63v. : ill., port. ; 26 cm.

   Frequency varies.
   Title varies: 1907-38, Bulletin.
   Continued by American libraries.
   Absorbed Adult education and the library, Jan. 1931 ; Public
libraries, Mar. 1957.

 (Continued on card 2)

Fig. 23.10 (cont'd)

ALA Bulletin. (Card 2)

Official journal of the American Library Association.
Proceedings of the association's annual conference issued as a regular number of the bulletin, 1907-48; ALA handbook issued as a regular number, 1907-47.
ISSN 0364-4006 = ALA bulletin.

1. Library science—Periodicals. I. American Library Association. Bulletin. II. Title.

Fig. 23.11
Completed Catalog Card för a Related Serial

American libraries: bulletin of the American Library Association.
-- Vol. 1, no. 1 (Jan. 1970)-   . -- Chicago : American
Library Association, 1970-   .
v. : ill., port. ; 28 cm.

Issued monthly except bimonthly July-August.
Continues the ALA bulletin.
Official journal of the American Library Association.
ISSN 0002-9769 = American libraries.

1. Library science—Periodicals. I. American
Library Association.

REVIEW QUESTIONS

1. Which *AACR 2* rules cover cataloging of serials?

2. In what significant ways does serials cataloging differ from book cataloging?

3. What is the biggest problem for serials catalogers and how can it be handled?

4. How does a serials collation statement differ from books?

5. What is "successive entry" in serials cataloging?

6. What kind of title changes require a serial to be cataloged as a new title?

7. What is an open entry? Why is it used?

8. How is a statement of responsibility usually handled in cataloging a serial?

24

SOURCES OF CATALOGING INFORMATION

Nearly every library has access to cataloging information for a high percentage of works it catalogs. This *original cataloging* data is generated mostly by the Library of Congress and large academic research libraries. Most medium-sized libraries do little original cataloging because of reliance on outside sources of cataloging data.

Why, then, should the LMTA bother to learn cataloging rules if cataloging information is readily available? The situation is similar to not letting a student use a computer to solve a math problem until he or she understands the mathematical principles involved in the process. The LMTA who understands the basic principles and rules used to generate cataloging information will understand how to use the information and the kinds of information he or she is looking at. For example, if the LMTA does not understand the concept of main entry, he or she cannot effectively catalog or use a library catalog. The use of computers in cataloging has actually increased the need for skilled paraprofessional staff. It is incorrect to assume that the use of computers lessens the need to understand cataloging rules; the opposite is true because the computer is unforgiving of input errors.

The sources from which libraries obtain cataloging information have undergone major changes in the past few years. The ultimate impact of computer-based information sources such as OCLC (Online Computer Library Center), RLIN (Research Libraries Information Network), WLN (Washington Library Network), and the Library of Congress MARC (*machine readable cataloging*) is still incomplete. It seems apparent that these large "bibliographic utilities" are imposing national standards that affect all libraries and are providing wide access to massive data bases of cataloging information. The impact of these new bibliographic utilities such as OCLC can be seen in the following statistics. In 1971 the Library of Congress sold 74,474,002 printed catalog cards; by 1983 sales dropped to 13,098,980 cards.[1] During the same time, sales of OCLC computer-produced cards grew from zero in 1967 to over 130,000,000 cards in 1984. However, sales of Library of Congress catalogs such as the *National Union Catalog* have increased in recent years.

LIBRARY OF CONGRESS CATALOGS

The Library of Congress publishes eight catalogs that together comprise the *National Union Catalog*. These catalogs collectively called the *NUC* comprise the most comprehensive source of cataloging information currently available. The *NUC* catalogs are: 1) *National Union Catalog. Audiovisual Materials;*

2) *National Union Catalog. Books;* 3) *National Union Catalog. U.S. Books;* 4) *National Union Catalog. Cartographic Materials;* 5) *Music, Books on Music, and Sound Recordings;* 6) *National Union Catalog of Manuscript Collections;* 7) *National Union Catalog. Register of Additional Locations;* and 8) *New Serial Titles.* We will discuss items 1-5 in this section since those parts of *NUC* include the bulk of cataloging information.

Each part of the *NUC* has a specific function and scope and includes only certain types of material. The scope and content of *NUC* catalogs has changed over the years; it is necessary to read the introductory materials in each catalog in order to use it properly.

Starting in January 1983 *NUC* made major changes in the format and content of its major catalogs. Five of the *NUC* catalogs are now issued only in microfiche and three will continue in print format. The Library of Congress plans to convert all parts of the *NUC* to microfiche in the future. The following descriptions are brief summaries of the *NUC* catalogs:

1) *National Union Catalog* (Washington: Library of Congress, 1956-82). This catalog lists materials cataloged by the Library of Congress and 1,100 contributing North American libraries. It contains cataloging records for books, pamphlets, maps, atlases, periodicals, and other serials. The *NUC* is the successor to several earlier Library of Congress catalogs: *A Catalog of Books Represented by Library of Congress Printed Cards, Supplement to a Catalog of Books Represented by Library of Congress Printed Cards, The Library of Congress Author Catalog,* and *Library of Congress Catalog—Books: Authors.* Another set not published by the Library of Congress takes *NUC* back to 1901, *National Union Catalog, Pre-1956 Imprints* (London: Mansell, 1968-81). The *National Union Catalog* has been succeeded by *NUC Books* and *NUC U.S. Books* (Figure 24.1).

2) *National Union Catalog. Audiovisual Materials* (Washington: Library of Congress, 1979-). Issued quarterly. This catalog has been issued only in microfiche since 1983. *Audiovisual Materials* includes cataloging records for motion pictures, filmstrips, transparency sets, slide sets, and videorecordings. Only materials cataloged by the Library of Congress are included; however, cataloging records created by other libraries will be included in the near future. The catalog is issued in a register/index format: the register section includes full bibliographic information and there are name, title, subject, and series indexes (Figures 24.2, page 318, and 24.4, page 319). *Audiovisual Materials* continues two earlier Library of Congress catalogs, *Motion Pictures and Filmstrips* (Washington: Library of Congress, 1953-72), and *Films and Other Materials for Projection* (Washington: Library of Congress, 1973-78).

(Text continues on page 320.)

Fig. 24.1
Entries in the *National Union Catalog* (Print Format)

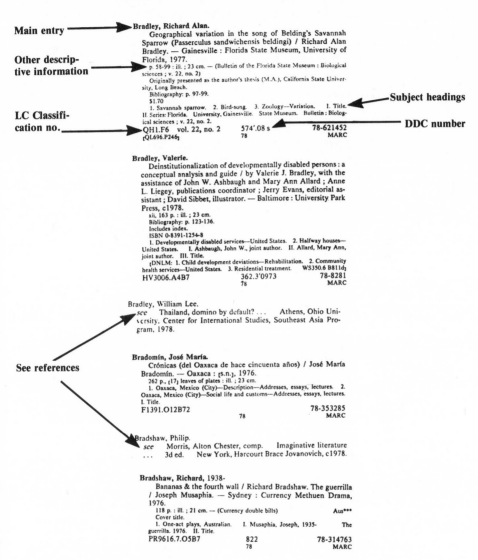

Main entry

Bradley, Richard Alan.
　　Geographical variation in the song of Belding's Savannah
Sparrow (Passerculus sandwichensis beldingi) / Richard Alan
Bradley. — Gainesville : Florida State Museum, University of
Florida, 1977.

Other descriptive information

　　p. 58-99 : ill. ; 23 cm. — (Bulletin of the Florida State Museum : Biological
sciences ; v. 22, no. 2)
　　　Originally presented as the author's thesis (M.A.), California State University, Long Beach.
　　　Bibliography: p. 97-99.
　　　$1.70
　　　1. Savannah sparrow.　2. Bird-song.　3. Zoology—Variation.　I. Title.
II. Series: Florida. University, Gainesville. State Museum. Bulletin : Biological sciences ; v. 22, no. 2.

Subject headings

LC Classification no.

QH1.F6　vol. 22, no. 2　　574'.08 s　　　　78-621452
₍QL696.P246₎　　　　　　　　　78　　　　　　　　MARC

DDC number

Bradley, Valerie.
　　Deinstitutionalization of developmentally disabled persons : a
conceptual analysis and guide / by Valerie J. Bradley, with the
assistance of John W. Ashbaugh and Mary Ann Allard ; Anne
L. Liegey, publications coordinator ; Jerry Evans, editorial assistant ; David Sibbet, illustrator. — Baltimore : University Park
Press, c1978.
　　　xii, 163 p. : ill. ; 23 cm.
　　　Bibliography: p. 123-136.
　　　Includes index.
　　　ISBN 0-8391-1254-8
　　　1. Developmentally disabled services—United States.　2. Halfway houses—
United States.　I. Ashbaugh, John W., joint author.　II. Allard, Mary Ann,
joint author.　III. Title.
　　　₍DNLM: 1. Child development deviations—Rehabilitation.　2. Community
health services—United States.　3. Residential treatment.　　WS350.6 B811d₎
　　HV3006.A4B7　　　　362.3'0973　　　　78-8281
　　　　　　　　　　　　　　78　　　　　　　　MARC

Bradley, William Lee.
　see　　Thailand, domino by default? ...　　Athens, Ohio University. Center for International Studies, Southeast Asia Program, 1978.

See references

Bradomín, José María.
　　Crónicas (del Oaxaca de hace cincuenta años) / José María
Bradomín. — Oaxaca : ₍s.n.₎, 1976.
　　　262 p., ₍17₎ leaves of plates : ill. ; 23 cm.
　　　1. Oaxaca, Mexico (City)—Description—Addresses, essays, lectures.　2.
Oaxaca, Mexico (City)—Social life and customs—Addresses, essays, lectures.
I. Title.
　　F1391.O12B72　　　　　　　　　　78-353285
　　　　　　　　　　　　　　78　　　　　　　　MARC

Bradshaw, Philip.
　see　　Morris, Alton Chester, comp.　　Imaginative literature
　...　　3d ed.　　New York, Harcourt Brace Jovanovich, c1978.

Bradshaw, Richard, 1938-
　　Bananas & the fourth wall / Richard Bradshaw. The guerrilla
/ Joseph Musaphia. — Sydney : Currency Methuen Drama,
1976.
　　　118 p. : ill. ; 21 cm. — (Currency double bills)　　　　　　Aus***
　　　Cover title.
　　　1. One-act plays, Australian.　I. Musaphia, Joseph, 1935-　　　The
guerrilla. 1976.　II. Title.
　　PR9616.7.O5B7　　　　822　　　　　78-314763
　　　　　　　　　　　　　　78　　　　　　　　MARC

Fig. 24.2
Entries in *Audiovisual Catalog*
(Print Format)

The Limits of water. ₁Filmstrip₁ / Denoyer-Geppert Audio-Visuals ; made by Michael Hardy Productions. — New York : Denoyer-Geppert Audio-Visuals, 1978.
2 rolls : col. ; 35 mm. & 2 cassettes (25 min.) and program guide. — (Water resources, the deepening crisis ; set 3)
CREDITS: Photography, Michael Hardy.
SUMMARY: Explains why water resources are limited, and explores the implications of these limits for agriculture and a growing population.
CONTENTS: pt. 1. Running out. 82 fr.—pt. 2. Too many chairs at the water table. 84 fr.
1. Water-supply.   I. Denoyer-Geppert Audio-Visuals.
II. Series: Water resources, the deepening crisis. ₁Filmstrip₁ ; set 3.
₁TD345₁   333.9   78-730772
Denoyer-Geppert Audio-Visuals
                    78

Lindisfarne Gospels
    see Bible. Manuscripts, Anglo-Saxon. N.T. Gospels. (Lindisfarne Gospels)

Linear language. ₁Filmstrip₁ RMI Film Productions. Made by Coleman Film Enterprises. Released by RMI Educational Films, 1975.
38 fr. color. 35 mm.   and disc (33 1/3 rpm. 12 in. 10 min. (Metric measurements)
Also issued with sound recording in cassette.
SUMMARY: Provides concepts, examples, and projects for developing familiarity with the language and length of the most common metric linear units. For elementary grades.
1. Meter (Unit)—Juvenile films.   2. Length measurement—Juvenile films.   3. Metric system—Juvenile films.   ₁1. Meter (Unit)   2. Length measurement.   3. Metric system₁
I. RMI Film Productions.   II. RMI Educational Films.   III. Series: Metric measurements. ₁Filmstrip₁.
₁QC102₁   389   75-736465
RMI Film Productions   76₁7811₁

Lionni, Leo, 1910-   Biggest house in the world
see
    The Biggest house in the world.

Lionni, Leo, 1910-   Frederick
see
    Frederick.

Listen to this. ₁Motion picture₁ / American Telephone and Telegraph Company ; made by Larry Keating Productions. — New York : The Co., 1978.
1 reel. 15 min. : sd., col. ; 16 mm.
SUMMARY: Shows the production of a film which traces the history of the sound motion picture and the role of the Bell System within this development.
1. Moving-pictures, Talking.   I. American Telephone and Telegraph Company.
₁TR897₁   791.43   78-701374
CINE   78

Fig. 24.3
Entries in the *Subject Catalog*
(Print Format)

CHEMICAL LITERATURE ◄——— Subject headings

Antony, Arthur.
    Guide to basic information sources in chemistry / by Arthur Antony. — New York : J. Norton Publishers : distributed by Halsted Press, c1979.
    vii, 219 p. ; 22 cm. — (Information resources series)
    Includes index.
    ISBN 0-400-26587-6
    1. Chemical literature.   I. Title.
    QD8.5.A57 1979   540'.7   79-330
                    79   MARC

CHEMICAL OCEANOGRAPHY ◄———

Riley, John Price, ed.
    Chemical oceanography / edited by J. P. Riley and G. Skirrow. — 2d ed. — London ; New York : Academic Press, 1975-
    v. : ill. ; 24 cm.   GB***
    V. 5-   edited by J. P. Riley and R. Chester.
    Includes bibliographies and indexes.
    ISBN 0-12-588601-2 (v. 1)
    1. Chemical oceanography.   I. Skirrow, Geoffrey, joint ed.   II. Chester, Roy, 1936-   joint ed.
    GC111.2.R542 1975   551.4'601   74-5679
                    75₁79₁rev2   MARC

CHEMICAL PLANTS ◄———

—AUTOMATION

Golubíátnikov, Vladimir Alekseevich.
    (Avtomatízafsíi͡a proizvodstvennykh proísessov i ASUP v khimícheskoĭ promyshlennosti)
    Автоматизация производственных процессов и АСУП в химической промышленности : ₁Учебник для хим.-технол. техникумов₁ / В. А. Голубятников, В. В. Шувалов. — Москва : Химия, 1978.
    375 p. : ill. ; 22 cm. — (Автоматизация химических производств)
                        USSR 78
    Series romanized: Avtomatízafsíi͡a khimícheskikh proizvodstv.
    Bibliography: p. 366-369.
    Includes index.
    1.10rub
    1. Chemical process control.   2. Chemical plants—Automation.
    I. Shuvalov, Valeriĭ   Vasil'evich, joint author.   II. Title.
    TP155.75.G649   79-410924

—DESIGN AND CONSTRUCTION—
CONGRESSES

Symposium on Chemical Process Hazards with Special Reference to Plant Design, 6th, University of Manchester, 1977.
    Papers of the Symposium on Chemical Process Hazards with Special Reference to Plant Design, VI : a symposium organised by the North Western Branch of the Institution of Chemical Engineers at the University of Manchester Institute of Science and Technology, 5-7 April 1977, symposium organisers, J. H. Burgoyne ... ₁et al.₁. — Rugby : I. Chem. E. Services for the Institution of Chemical Engineers, 1977.
    ₁8₁, 152 p. : ill. ; 30 cm. — (Institution of Chemical Engineers symposium series ; no. 49 ISSN 0307-0492)   GB77-19507
    Includes bibliographical references.
    ISBN 0-8429-5100-0 : £12.50
    1. Chemicals—Manufacture and industry—Safety measures—Congresses.
    2. Chemical plants—Design and construction—Congresses.   I. Institution of Chemical Engineers, London.   North-Western Branch.   II. Series: Institution of Chemical Engineers, London.   I. Chem. E. symposium series ; no. 49.
    TP149.S97 1977   660.2'804   77-377550
                    78₁79₁rev   MARC

---

*The careful reader will notice that the punctuation and general material designation differ from the examples in chapter 17. The entries in Figure 24.3 are examples of *AACR 1* descriptive cataloging.

Fig. 24.4
Entries in *National Union Catalog. Books* **(Microfiche)**

NUC BOOKS. REGISTER

[1]a-001-875
Worden, J. William (James William), 1932-
   Grief counseling and grief therapy : a handbook
for the mental health practitioner / J. William Worden.
--New York : Springer, c1982.
   x, 146p. : 24 cm.
   Bibliography : p.131-141.
   Includes index.
   ISBN 0-8261-4160-9 : $14.95

[2] 1. Grief. 2. Bereavement--Psychological aspects.
3. Mental illness. 4. Psychotherapy. I. Title.
RC455.4.L67W67 1982   616.89'14--dc19
  DCL   82-10594
                      AACR 2

NUC BOOKS. NAME INDEX

[3]Worden, J. William (James William), 1932-   .
   Grief counseling and grief therapy ... --
New York : Springer, c1982.
RC455.4.L67W67 1982   82-10594   a-001-875

NUC BOOKS. TITLE INDEX

[3]Grief counseling and grief therapy.
   Worden, J. William (James William), 1932-   .
-- New York : Springer, c1982.
RC455.4.L67W67 1982   82-10594   a-001-875

NUC BOOKS. SUBJECT INDEX

[3]GRIEF
   Worden, J. William (James William), 1932-   .
   Grief counseling and grief therapy ... c1982.
RC455.4.L67W67 1982   82-10594   a-001-875

Key to Note Items in Figure 24.4

[1]Register number. Entries are in random numerical order in the Register; it is necessary to locate an item through one of the indexes. Notice that the Register entry gives full bibliographic information.

[2]Tracings. Note that there are four subject entries and a title added entry. The Subject Index therefore has an entry for each subject (only one for GRIEF is shown in this example). The Title Index has an entry for the title. The Name Index has an entry for the author. Since this work has no series, there is no entry in the Series Index.

[3]Entries in the Name Index, Title Index, and Subject Index. Notice that the bibliographic information is given in abbreviated format.

3) *National Union Catalog. Books* (Washington: Library of Congress, 1983-). Issued monthly in microfiche. This publication is a continuation of the *National Union Catalog* and the *Subject Catalog* discussed below. *NUC Books* contains bibliographic records for books, pamphlets, printed sheets, and some microforms. It includes materials in English and foreign languages cataloged by the Library of Congress and 1,500 contributing institutions. Material is in a register/index format with full bibliographic information in the register and name, title, subject, and series indexes (Figure 24.4).

4) *National Union Catalog. U.S. Books* (Washington: Library of Congress, 1983-). Issued monthly in microfiche. The *NUC U.S. Books* is a new publication that includes books, pamphlets, printed sheets, as well as some microforms and atlases published in the United States. This catalog is intended for small and medium-sized libraries. Issued in a register/index format with name, title, subject, and series indexes.

5) *National Union Catalog. Cartographic Materials* (Washington: Library of Congress, 1983-). Issued quarterly in microfiche. *Cartographic Materials* is a new publication that includes single and multi-sheet maps, atlases, and maps treated as serials. The March 1983 Register contains the entire Library of Congress map data base. The format includes a register with full cataloging records and five indexes: name, title, subject, series, and geographic classification code. At this time only Library of Congress cataloging records are included. Records of other institutions will be included in the future.

6) *Music, Books on Music, and Sound Recordings* (Washington: Library of Congress, 1973-). Issued semi-annually with an annual cumulation in print format. This specialized catalog includes music scores, sheet music, libretti, books about music and musicians, and sound recordings. The sound recordings are of all kinds and *not* limited to music. Entries are cataloged by the Library of Congress and libraries selected by the Music Library Association. This catalog succeeded the earlier *Library of Congress Catalog: Music and Phonorecords* (Washington: Library of Congress, 1953-72).

7) *Subject Catalog* (Washington: Library of Congress, 1975-82). Since January 1983 the *Subject Catalog* is incorporated in the subject index of the *National Union Catalog. Books*. The *Subject Catalog*, prior to 1983, was issued in print format and included books, pamphlets, periodicals and other serials, maps, and atlases cataloged by the Library of Congress and that have printed cards. The entries are alphabetical by subject heading. This work is a continuation of two earlier catalogs: *Library of Congress Subject Catalog* (Washington: Library of Congress, 1950-52) and *Library of Congress Catalog Books: Subjects* (Washington: Library of Congress, 1953-74). See Figure 24.3, page 318.

MACHINE READABLE CATALOGING
(MARC)

Most Library of Congress cataloging information is available in MARC format. This service is described in the publication *Machine Readable Cataloging: MARC Tapes* (Washington: Library of Congress, Processing Department, 1977). Few libraries use MARC directly, but many use it indirectly. MARC tapes are used primarily by commercial cataloging services, network services (such as OCLC, RLIN, and WLN), and book jobbers to produce catalog cards. If a work is available on MARC, this is indicated on the LC card (Figure 24.5). Over 3,000,000 records are currently available in MARC format and nearly 400,000 new records were added in 1983.

Fig. 24.5
MARC Indicator on LC Catalog Card

Kagan, Jerome.
    Psychological research on the human infant : an evaluative summary / Jerome Kagan. — New York, N.Y. (919 3rd Ave., New York 10022) : W.T. Grant Foundation, c1982.

    53 p. : ill. ; 23 cm.
    Bibliography: p. 45-53.

    1. Infant psychology—Research.   I. Title.
    BF719.5.K33   1982   155.4'22—dc19   82-140271
       AACR 2   MARC

    Library of Congress

BIBLIOGRAPHIC SERVICES

The concept of bibliographic services supplying cataloging information was discussed in chapters 3 and 6. In this section three of the major services will be covered in more detail.

OCLC

OCLC (Online Computer Library Center) is the largest cooperative online cataloging support system in the United States. In late 1984 the OCLC data base contained nearly 11 million bibliographic records including over one million MARC cataloging records. Cataloging information is displayed on the CRT with a typewriter keyboard used to transmit information (Figure 24.6, page 322).

Fig. 24.6
OCLC CRT/Keyboard Terminal
M300 Workstation*

*Reproduced with the permission of OCLC.

Cataloging information is displayed by calling up information by means of one of the following kinds of searches: author's name, title, a combination of author's name and title, Library of Congress Card Number (LCCN), International Standard Book Number (ISBN), International Standard Serial Number (ISSN), OCLC Control Number, or Government Document Number.[2] In addition, searches using the author's name or the title may be qualified by type of material (books, serials, soundrecordings, scores, audiovisual media, maps, or manuscripts) or by publication date or a range of dates.

With a specific book in hand the cataloger has available the following information:

Author: George C. Herring

Title: *America's Longest War: the United States and Vietnam, 1950-1975*

LC Card Number: 79-16408

ISBN: 0471-015466; 0471-015474 (pbk.)

With that information the following kinds of searches can be performed.

Kind of Search	Search Method/Search Key Entered via Keyboard
Author's name: George C. Herring	herr, geo, c (first 4 letters of the surname, first 3 letters of the first name, and the initial: 4,3,1)
Title: *America's Longest War: the United States and Vietnam, 1950-1975*	ame, lo, wa, t (first 3 letters of the first word of the title, first 2 letters of the next two words, first letter of the next word: 3,2,2,1)
Author/Title	herr, amer (first 4 letters of the author's surname and title: 4,4)
LC Card Number: 79-16408	79-16408 (insert hyphen)
ISBN: 0-471-015466, or 0-471-015474 (pbk.)	0471015466 or 0471015474 (do not insert hyphens—there are always ten digits in an ISBN)

The cataloging information found from performing one of the searches listed above will be displayed on the CRT (see Figure 24.8, page 325) or printed out by a printer (see Figure 24.7, page 324).

Fig. 24.7
Printronix® P300 Printer*

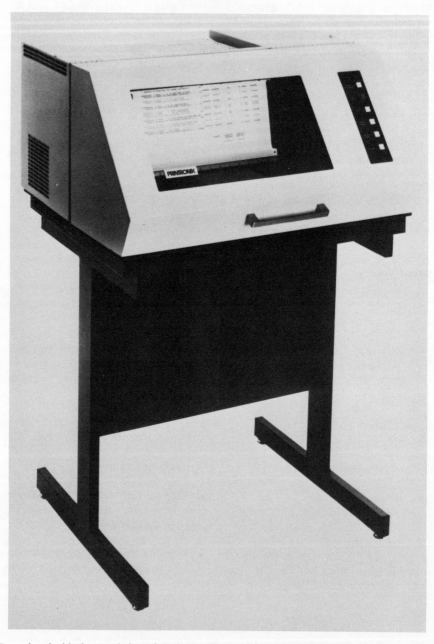

*Reproduced with the permission of Cochrane Chase, Livingstone & Company, Inc.

Fig. 24.8
CRT Display of OCLC Cataloging Information*

Screen 1 of 2

CSB - FOR OTHER HOLDINGS, ENTER dh DEPRESS DISPLAY RECD SEND

[1]OCLC: 5126110   Rec stat: p [2]Entrd: 790613   [3]Used: 840703
[4]Type: a [5]Bib lvl: m [6]Govt pub: [7]Lang: eng [8]Source: [9]Illus: b
[10]Repr: [11]Enc lvl: [12]Conf pub:[13]O Ctry: nyu[14]Dat tp: s[15]M/F/B: 10
[16] Indx: 1 [17]Mod rec: [18]Festschr: 0[19]Cont: b
[20]Desc: i [21]Int lvl: [22]Dates: 1979,
[23] 1 010   79-16408
[24] 2 040   DLC c DLC d m.c.
[25] 3 020   0471015466
[26] 4 020   0471015474 (pbk.)
[27] 5 043   a-vt--- a n-us---
[28] 6 050 0   DS558 b .H45
[29] 7 082   959.704
[30] 8 090   b
[31] 9 049   CSBM
[32] 10 100 10 Herring, George C., d 1936- w cn
[33] 11 245 10 America's longest war : b the United States and Vietnam, 1950-
1975 / c George C. Herring.
[34] 12 260 0   New York : b Wiley, c c1979.
[35] 13 300   xiii, 298 p. : b map ; c 22 cm.
[36] 14 440 0   America in crisis
[37] 15 504   Bibliography: p. 273-288.
[38] 16 500   Includes index.
[39] 17 650 0   Vietnamese Conflict, 1961-1975 z United States.

Screen 2 of 2

[40] 18 651 0   Vietnam x History y 1945-1975.
[41] 19 651 0   United States x History y 1945-
[42] 20 651 0   United States x Foreign relations z Vietnam.
[43] 21 651 0   Vietnam x Foreign relations z United States.

(Key to Figure 24.8 is on page 326.)

*Reproduced with the permission of OCLC.

Key to Note Items in Figure 24.8

[1]OCLC Control Number.

[2]Date entered in OCLC data base (June 13, 1979).

[3]Date record was last used (July 3, 1984)

[4]Type of material – "a" means printed material.

[5]Bibliographic level – "m" means monograph.

[6]Government publication – the blanks mean this is not a government publication.

[7]Language of the work – English.

[8]Source of original cataloging data – the blank means the Library of Congress.

[9]Illustrations – "b" means maps.

[10]Form of reproduction – the blank means the book is not reproduced in a format unreadable to the unaided eye (i.e., microfilm).

[11]Encoding level – indicates degree of completeness of information. The blank means this is full cataloging by the Library of Congress.

[12]Conference publication – the "0" means it is not a conference publication.

[13]Country of publication – "nyu" is New York, United States.

[14]Date code – "s" means date of publication is a single known date, i.e., 1980.

[15]Main entry indicator – the "M," "F," and "B" all indicate different information. Here the M/F/B:10 means the main entry is in the body of the card and the work is not fiction.

[16]Index indicator – the "1" means an index is present.

[17]Modified record indicator – the blank means the information in the record is the same as appears on the corresponding LC printed card.

[18]Festschrift indication – the "0" means the book is not a Festschrift, which is a collection of essays honoring a person.

[19]Form of content – the "b" indicates the work includes a bibliography.

[20]Descriptive cataloging form – the "i" indicates that AACR cataloging was used.

[21]Intellectual level – the blank means this information is not applicable to this work.

[22]Date – date work was published.

[23]LC card number.

[24]Cataloging source – DLC is the Library of Congress; "m.c." means that at least one heading in the record was verified during the machine conversion of the data base to AACR 2.

[25]International Standard Book Number.

[26]International Standard Book Number for paperback edition.

[27]Geographic Area Code – does not print on cards.

[28]Library of Congress Call Number – the "0" means the book is in the Library of Congress (the call number is DS 558 H45).

[29]Dewey Decimal Classification Number.

[30]A local call number appears in this field if desired.

[31]Holding library – "CSB" means the book is in the library at California State University, San Bernardino; the "M" means the entry appears in the main catalog.

[32]Main entry—personal name—the "1" and "0" mean it is a single surname (Herring) and the main entry is not the subject of the book.

[33]Title statement—title proper, subtitle, and statement of responsibility.

[34]Imprint or publication information.

[35]Collation or physical description area.

[36]Series statement—the "0" means there is no added entry for the series.

[37]Bibliography note.

[38]General note citing the index.

[39]Subject entry with a topical heading.

[40-43]Subject entries with geographical headings.

The numbers 1 through 21 in the first "column" (i.e., *1* 010, *2* 040, etc.) are line numbers. The numbers 010 through 651 in the second "column" are variable field tags; a discussion of these tags is beyond the scope of this text.[3]

To order a set of cards, the "produce" key on the keyboard is punched, and the OCLC computer produces a set of cards (Figure 24.9). Compare the information in the CRT display format (Figure 24.8) with the cards. It is the same information in a different format, although some information is not printed on the OCLC cards.

Fig. 24.9
OCLC Produced Catalog Card*

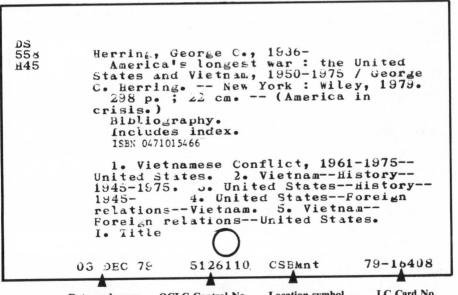

Date cards were produced   OCLC Control No.   Location symbol   LC Card No.
Cal. State University, San Bernardino

*Reproduced with the permission of OCLC.

Fig. 24.9 (cont'd)

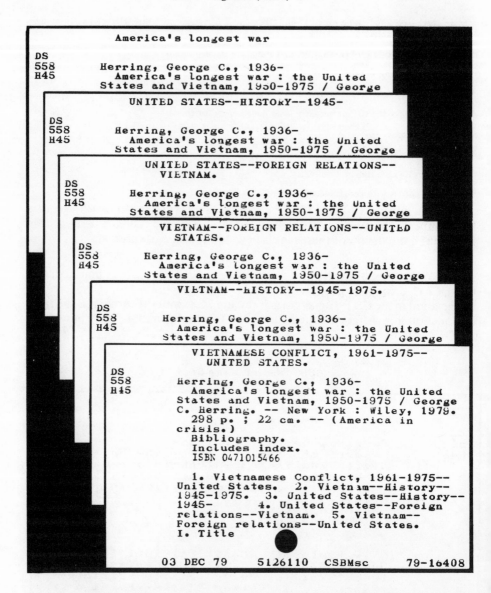

```
                    America's longest war

DS
558        Herring, George C., 1936-
H45             America's longest war : the United
           States and Vietnam, 1950-1975 / George
```

```
              UNITED STATES--HISTORY--1945-

DS
558        Herring, George C., 1936-
H45             America's longest war : the United
           States and Vietnam, 1950-1975 / George
```

```
              UNITED STATES--FOREIGN RELATIONS--
                    VIETNAM.
DS
558        Herring, George C., 1936-
H45             America's longest war : the United
           States and Vietnam, 1950-1975 / George
```

```
              VIETNAM--FOREIGN RELATIONS--UNITED
                    STATES.
DS
558        Herring, George C., 1936-
H45             America's longest war : the United
           States and Vietnam, 1950-1975 / George
```

```
              VIETNAM--HISTORY--1945-1975.

DS
558        Herring, George C., 1936-
H45             America's longest war : the United
           States and Vietnam, 1950-1975 / George
```

```
              VIETNAMESE CONFLICT, 1961-1975--
                    UNITED STATES.
DS
558        Herring, George C., 1936-
H45             America's longest war : the United
           States and Vietnam, 1950-1975 / George
           C. Herring. -- New York : Wiley, 1979.
           298 p. ; 22 cm. -- (America in
           crisis.)
           Bibliography.
           Includes index.
           ISBN 0471015466

           1. Vietnamese Conflict, 1961-1975--
           United States.  2. Vietnam--History--
           1945-1975.  3. United States--History--
           1945-    4. United States--Foreign
           relations--Vietnam.  5. Vietnam--
           Foreign relations--United States.
           I. Title

           03 DEC 79      5126110    CSBMsc      79-16408
```

The training necessary to interpret the information in Figure 24.8, and the training to find and enter information in OCLC, are beyond the scope of this text. When cataloging information is not in the data base, a library can catalog the work *originally* and enter it in the system. *AACR 2* rules are used, but the methods for entering the data are unique to OCLC, so they require special training. OCLC conducts extensive training programs and provides operations manuals to participating libraries. Two basic manuals are *OCLC Basics: An Introduction to Searching and Terminal Use* (Dublin, Ohio: OCLC, 1983) and *Cataloging: User Manual.* 2nd ed. (Dublin, Ohio: OCLC, 1984). Other manuals for scores, sound recordings, serials, audiovisuals, maps, and manuscripts are also available.

RLIN

A second national computer-based cataloging service is RLIN (Research Libraries Information Network). RLIN is a part of RLG (Research Libraries Group), which is a partnership of major academic research libraries. RLIN became available nationally in 1978. Currently RLIN has cataloging information for about 12 million items in seven different files: archival control, books, films, maps, recordings, scores, and serials. RLIN's cataloging products include catalog cards, machine-readable tapes with cataloging information, and online displays of cataloging information.

The input of information, display of information, and requests to produce catalog cards are handled on a CRT keyboard similar to the one described for OCLC. RLIN allows access to data base information through more than twenty search methods including: personal name, corporate or conference name, title, LC card number, RLIN record identification number, local call number, subject headings, ISBN and ISSN, and Superintendent of Document numbers. An especially useful feature of RLIN is its capacity to conduct a subject search to locate cataloging information. For example, a search request for a subject could be entered to locate maps for the Paris subway — "select file maps/find subject phrase subway # and subject subdivision paris." All maps of the Paris subway in the RLIN data base would be displayed on the CRT. In practice, the search commands would be abbreviated. A search to find films by Jean Cocteau would be entered — "sel fil flm/fin pn cocteau,jean" ("select film file/find personal name cocteau, jean").

Cataloging information can be displayed in either card catalog format or in "full display," which breaks down the data into its component input fields (Figures 24.10, page 330, and 24.11, page 331).

WLN

WLN (Washington Library Network) was established in 1976 and is the newest and smallest of the major bibliographic services. In 1984 WLN served about 140 members in the Pacific Northwest and other areas of the west; WLN currently has no plans to expand nationally. WLN offers an online cataloging system with authority control for the form of personal names and subject headings. A variety of cataloging products are available to members: catalog cards, pre-printed spine labels and book pocket labels, and COM (computer-output-microfilm) and book catalogs.

(Text continues on page 332.)

Fig. 24.10
RLIN Cataloging in "Long" Display
Catalog Card Format*

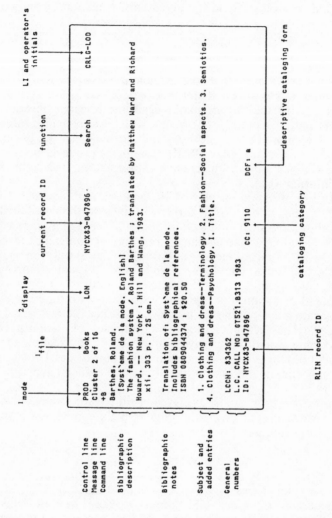

Key to Note Items in Figure 24.10

[1]Mode, File—Indicates information came from the bibliographic data base for books.

[2]LON—Long bibliographic display format.

*Reproduced from *Searching in RLIN II: User's Manual* by permission of the Research Libraries Group, Inc.

Fig. 24.11
RLIN Cataloging in "Full" Display
Data Entry Format*

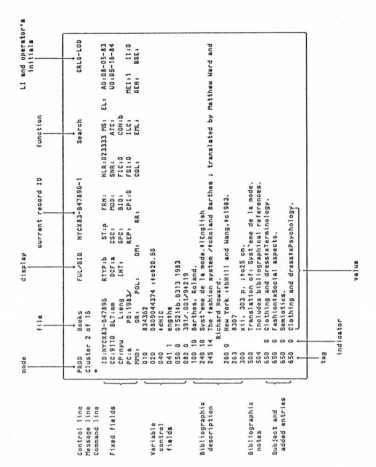

*Reproduced from *Searching in RLIN II: User's Manual* by permission of The Research Libraries Group, Inc.

Input, display of information, and requests for products are performed on a CRT with a keyboard. WLN's data base can be searched in several ways including: author, title, ISBN, ISSN, corporate or conference name, series, subjects, WLN record number and LC card number. An inquiry into the data base requires four commands: 1) a command telling the computer what file to search, 2) a "key ID" identifying the desired access point (e.g., author, title, subject), 3) a search key consisting of an author's name, title, and so forth, and 4) a command telling the computer how you want the information displayed. For example, the following search entry instructs the computer to search the bibliographic data base for the title keywords "pelicans" and "poems" and to display the results in title order:

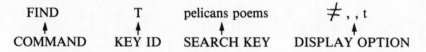

FIND	T	pelicans poems	$\neq$, , t
↑	↑	↑	↑
COMMAND	KEY ID	SEARCH KEY	DISPLAY OPTION

Cataloging information is displayed in either "full display," which is in catalog card format, or "complete display," which breaks down the data into its component input fields (Figures 24.12, 24.13, and 24.14 on page 334).

Fig. 24.12
Cataloging Information in Full Bibliographic Display*

```
F R wln82-47984  . F


                                        BIBLIOGRAPHIC DISPLAY

    COLLECTION ID.  1          a m
    Chui, Tai Wik David'.
    Highway runoff in the state of Washington : model validation and
statistical analysis / by Tai Wik David Chui'. 1981'.
    vii', 121 leaves : ill. : 28 cm.
    Thesis (M.S'.)--University of Washington', 1981'.
    Bibliography: p'. [95]-96'.
       1. Runoff--Washington (State)    2'. Water quality--Washington
(State)--Measurement--Mathematical models.    3. Water quality--
Washington (State)--Statistics.    4'. Road drainage--Environmental
aspects--Washington (State)    I. Title.
       625.79/09.797 19
    WaOT wln82-047984
```

---

*Reproduced with the permission of the Washington Library Network.

Fig. 24.13
Cataloging Information in Complete Bibliographic Display*

```
F R wln82-47984  ', C


                                          BIBLIOGRAPHIC DISPLAY

COLLECTION ID: 1

am     wln82-47984    db   03/31/82  03/31/82  08/06/83  WLN       WaOT
   LCDN       abcde   2 3 3 2 3
   MEPS       a       Chui', Tai Wik David.
   TILAO      abc     Highway runoff in the state of Washington : model
                     validation and statistical analysis / by Tai Wik David
                     Chui'.
   IMPX       c       1981'.
   COL        abc     vii, 121 leaves : ill'. ; 28 cm'.
   NOD        a       Thesis (M'.S'.)--University of Washington, 1981'.
   NOB        a       Bibliography: p'. [95]-96'.
   SUT-L      az      Runoff Washington (State)
   SUT-L      azxx    Water quality Washington (State) Measurement
                     Mathematical models.
   SUT-L      azx     Water quality Washington (State) Statistics.
   SUT-L      axz     Road drainage Environmental aspects Washington
                     (State)
   GAC        a       n-us-wa
   DDCF       a2      625.79/09797 19
   CAS        ac      WaOT WaOT
   LON        a       (WaOLN)2335032
   FFD        CONF=        FEST=        INDEX=      ME IN B= x
         INTEL LV=          FIC=         BIOG=      DAT KY= s       LAN= eng
            DATE1= 1981  DATE2=         CNTRY= wau   ILLUS= a      REPRO=
         CONTENTS= b      MODRC=         CAT S= d   GOV PUB=     CAT FORM= a
```

*Reproduced with the permission of the Washington Library Network.

(Text continues on page 336.)

Fig. 24.14
Catalog Cards

```
625.7909
CHUI       Chui, Tai Wik David.
1981          Highway runoff in the state of
           Washington : model validation and
           statistical analysis / by Tai Wik
           David Chui. 1981.
              vii, 121 leaves : ill. ; 28 cm.
        Thesis (M.S.)--University of Washington,
       1981.
          Bibliography: p. [95]-96.

          1. Runoff--Washington (State) 2. Water
       quality--Washington (State)--Measurement--
       Mathematical models. 3. Water quality--
       Washington (State)--Statistics. 4. Road
       drainage--Environmental aspects--Washington
       (State) I. Title.
                            O    625.79'09797  [19]
                        WaOT              wln82-47984
```

```
                 RUNOFF--WASHINGTON (STATE)

625.7909
CHUI       Chui, Tai Wik David.
1981          Highway runoff in the state of
           Washington : model validation and
           statistical analysis / by Tai Wik
           David Chui. 1981.
              vii, 121 leaves : ill. ; 28 cm.
        Thesis (M.S.)--University of Washington,
       1981.
          Bibliography: p. [95]-96.

          1. Runoff--Washington (State) 2. Water
       quality--Washington (State)--Measurement--
       Mathematical models. 3. Water quality--
       Washington (State)--Statistics. 4. Road
       drainage--Environmental aspects--Washington
       (State) I. Title.
                            O    625.79'09797  [19]
                        WaOT              wln82-47984
```

```
                 WATER QUALITY--WASHINGTON (STATE)--
                 MEASUREMENT--MATHEMATICAL MODELS
625.7909
CHUI       Chui, Tai Wik David.
1981          Highway runoff in the state of
           Washington : model validation and
           statistical analysis / by Tai Wik
           David Chui. 1981.
              vii, 121 leaves : ill. ; 28 cm.
        Thesis (M.S.)--University of Washington,
       1981.
          Bibliography: p. [95]-96.

          1. Runoff--Washington (State) 2. Water
       quality--Washington (State)--Measurement--
       Mathematical models. 3. Water quality--
       Washington (State)--Statistics. 4. Road
       drainage--Environmental aspects--Washington
       (State) I. Title.
                            O    625.79'09797  [19]
                        WaOT              wln82-47984
```

Fig. 24.14 (cont'd)

```
              WATER QUALITY--WASHINGTON (STATE)--
                 STATISTICS
 625.7909
 CHUI       Chui, Tai Wik David.
 1981          Highway runoff in the state of
           Washington : model validation and
           statistical analysis / by Tai Wik
           David Chui. 1981.
               vii, 121 leaves : ill. ; 28 cm.
        Thesis (M.S.)--University of Washington,
        1981.
           Bibliography: p. [95]-96.

           1. Runoff--Washington (State) 2. Water
        quality--Washington (State)--Measurement--
        Mathematical models. 3. Water quality--
        Washington (State)--Statistics. 4. Road
        drainage--Environmental aspects--Washington
        (State) I. Title.
                            O   625.79'09797  [19]
                            WaOT              wln82-47984
```

```
              ROAD DRAINAGE--ENVIRONMENTAL
                 ASPECTS--WASHINGTON (STATE)
 625.7909
 CHUI       Chui, Tai Wik David.
 1981          Highway runoff in the state of
           Washington : model validation and
           statistical analysis / by Tai Wik
           David Chui. 1981.
               vii, 121 leaves : ill. ; 28 cm.
        Thesis (M.S.)--University of Washington,
        1981.
           Bibliography: p. [95]-96.

           1. Runoff--Washington (State) 2. Water
        quality--Washington (State)--Measurement--
        Mathematical models. 3. Water quality--
        Washington (State)--Statistics. 4. Road
        drainage--Environmental aspects--Washington
        (State) I. Title.
                            O   625.79'09797  [19]
                            WaOT              wln82-47984
```

```
              Highway runoff in the state of
                 Washington
 625.7909
 CHUI       Chui, Tai Wik David.
 1981          Highway runoff in the state of
           Washington : model validation and
           statistical analysis / by Tai Wik
           David Chui. 1981.
               vii, 121 leaves : ill. ; 28 cm.
        Thesis (M.S.)--University of Washington,
        1981.
           Bibliography: p. [95]-96.

           1. Runoff--Washington (State) 2. Water
        quality--Washington (State)--Measurement--
        Mathematical models. 3. Water quality--
        Washington (State)--Statistics. 4. Road
        drainage--Environmental aspects--Washington
        (State) I. Title.
                            O   625.79'09797  [19]
                            WaOT              wln82-47984
```

COMMERCIAL CATALOGING SERVICES

A variety of services and cataloging information can be obtained from commercial processing and cataloging services. These companies can supply one or more of the following types of services: 1) sets of catalog cards, 2) microform catalogs, 3) book catalogs, 4) fully processed ready-to-circulate materials with sets of catalog cards, 5) Library of Congress cataloging copy for non-book materials, and 6) various combinations of the services listed above. Some well-known companies include Brodart; Baker & Taylor; Midwest Library Services; Blackwell North America; and Catalog Corporation of America. Each of these companies offers a range of products and services including purchasing materials, processing materials, and supplying catalog cards or COM catalogs (Figure 24.15).

Fig. 24.15
Commercially Produced Catalog Cards

Brodart*

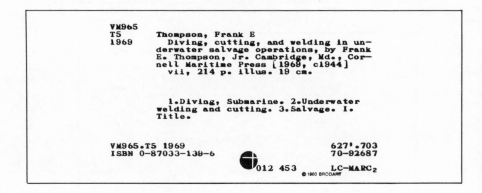

Baker & Taylor**

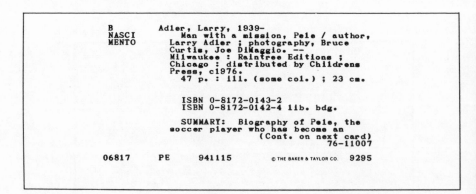

(Text continues on page 339.)

---

*Reproduced with the permission of Brodart Co.

**Reproduced with the permission of Baker & Taylor.

Fig. 24.15 (cont'd)

Baker & Taylor*

```
B            Adler, Larry, 1939-      Man with a
NASCI            mission... c1976.  (Card 2)
MENTO
             international celebrity.


                 1. Nascimento, Edson Arantes do,
             1940-        —Juvenile literature.
             2. Soccer--Juvenile litera-
             ture.  [1. Pele, 1940-        2.
             Soccer players]  I. Curtis, Bruce.
             II. DiMaggio, Joe.  III. Title.

    GV942.7.N3A65                 796.33'4'0924 [B]
                                      [ 92 ]
                                          76-11007
                                          MARC
                                          AC
     Library of Congress
     06817      PE      941115    © THE BAKER & TAYLOR CO.   9295
```

Blackwell North America**

```
 DS         BenDasan, Isaiah, 1918-
 821            The Japanese and the Jews.
 B44713         Translated from the Japanese by
 1972           Richard L. Gage.  [1st English ed.]
             New York, Weatherhill [1972]
                xi, 193 p. 24 cm.
                Translation of the author's
             Nihonjin to Yudayajin.
                ISBN 0-8348-0068-3

                 1. National characteristics,
             Japanese.  2. Jews.
             3. Ethnopsychology.  I. Title.



    DS821.B44713 1972            915.2/C3/4
                                 72-78591

    LSBO         B/NA A BS-587705 ACC        09/13/78
```

---

*Reproduced with the permission of Baker & Taylor.
**Reproduced with the permission of Blackwell North America.

Fig. 24.15 (cont'd)

Catalog Card Corporation of America*

```
TX
361        Haas, Robert, 1948-
.A8           Eat to win : the sports nutrition bi-
H3         ble / Robert Haas ; recipes by Hilarie
1983       Porter. -- 1st ed. -- New York : Rawson
           Associates, c1983.
              xiii, 267 p. ; 22 cm.

              Bibliography: p. [243]-256.
              Includes index.
              ISBN 0-89256-228-5 : $14.95


              1.Athletes--Nutrition. I.Porter, Hilar-
           ie. II.Title.
        TX361.A8H3 1983              613.2'024796
                                     dc19
                                                 82-42687
              CATALOG CARD CORPORATION OF AMERICA   AACR2      MARC
```

Midwest Library Service**

```
DS         Bennett, Paul Jerome, 1934-
485           Conference under the tamarind tree; three
.B86       essays in Burmese history [by] Paul J.
B45        Bennett. [New Haven, Conn.] Yale University
           Southeast Asia Studies [1971]
              vii, 153 p. map. 23 cm.
              Bibliography: p. [143]-153.




           1. BURMA--HISTORY.  I. Ya    le University. Southeast
        Asia Studies Monograph ser    ies, no. 15  II. Title.

        #211870      77-137999              MLSA
```

*Reproduced with the permission of Catalog Card Corporation of America.
**Reproduced with the permission of Midwest Library Service (MATSS—Midwest Automated Technical Services System).

Library of Congress Cataloging
Distribution Service

The Cataloging Distribution Service (CDS) section of the Library of Congress is responsible for the sales of all *NUC* catalogs and printed catalog cards. In addition to the *NUC* catalogs discussed above, the CDS sells printed catalog cards produced by the Library of Congress. LC cards have been available for purchase since 1901. Currently cards are available for over 7 million bibliographic records including books, maps, atlases, music, documents, audiovisual materials, and serials. In recent years sales of LC cards have fallen because of the impact of the major bibliographic services (OCLC, RLIN, WLN) and other sources of cataloging information. Complete information for ordering LC cards is found in the booklet, *Catalog Cards* (Washington: Library of Congress, Cataloging Distribution Service, 1984). CDS supplies both complete catalog cards from MARC records and CIP (cataloging-in-publication; see the following section) cards when full MARC cataloging is not available (Figures 24.16 and 24.17 on page 340).

Fig. 24.16
Order Form for Library of Congress Cards

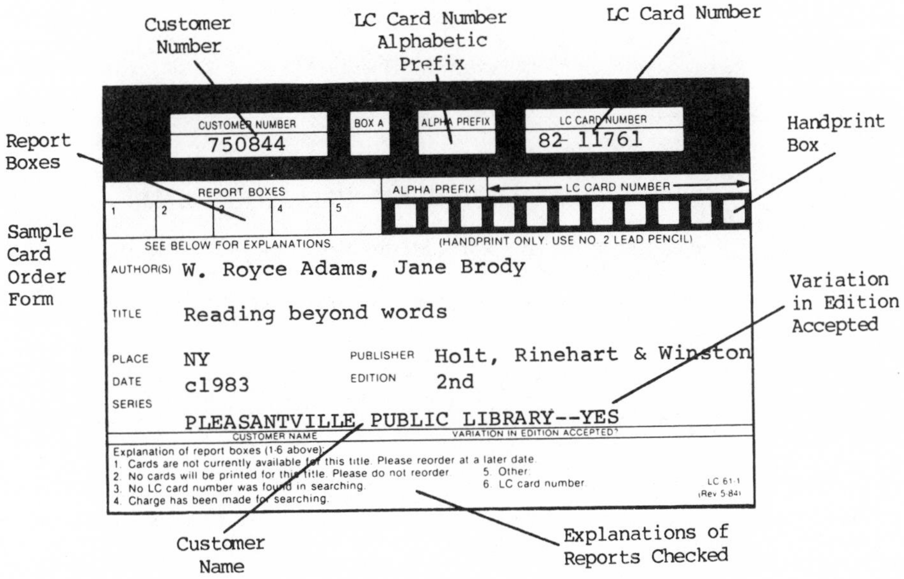

Fig. 24.17
Library of Congress Catalog Cards

Full MARC

Bedford, Richard.
 Perceptions, past & present, of a future for Melanesia / Richard Bedford. — Christchurch, N.Z. : Dept. of Geography, University of Canterbury, c1980.

 73 p. : ill., maps ; 21 cm. — (Macmillan Brown lectures, ISSN 0464-2767 ; 1979)

 Bibliography: p. 66-73.
 $5.00 (pbk.)

 1. Melanesia—Politics and government—Addresses, essays, lectures. 2. Melanesia—Economic conditions—Addresses, essays, lectures. 3. Melanesia —Social conditions—Addresses, essays, lectures. 4. Melanesia—Population— Addresses, essays, lectures. I. Title. II. Title: Perceptions, past and present, of a future for Melanesia. III. Series.
 DU490.B43 1980   993—dc19   81-196414
                   AACR 2 MARC

 Library of Congress

Cataloging-in-Publication (CIP)

           CATALOGING IN PUBLICATION 07/83
McCauley, Martin.
 The origins of the cold war / Martin McCauley. — London ; New York : Longman, 1983.

 p. cm. — (Seminar studies in history)

 Bibliography: p.
 Includes index.
 Summary: Analyzes events of 1941 through 1948 resulting in an acrimonious relationship between the United States and the Soviet Union which gradually affected Europe and the rest of the world.
 ISBN 0-582-35388-2

          (Continued on next card)

                82-18665
        AACR 2 MARC CIP
                AC

Cataloging-in-Publication
(CIP)

Cataloging-in-Publication (CIP) was started by the Library of Congress in July 1974 in cooperation with over 1,000 publishers. Today, most trade and university press publications in the United States provide CIP data. CIP consists of printing essential cataloging information in the actual work — usually on the verso of the title page in a book — and usually including the main entry, title proper, some notes, subject headings, LC call number, and a DDC classification number. Note that on all sources of LC cataloging data, the *LC call number is usually complete*; the *DDC is only a class number* and must be assigned a book number to become a call number. The incomplete descriptive cataloging information must be completed by the library (Figures 24.18, 24.19 and 24.20 on page 342). Cataloging is usually done from galley proofs submitted to the Library of Congress, which is the reason for incomplete descriptive information.

Fig. 24.18
Cataloging-in-Publication: Personal Name Main Entry

Library of Congress Cataloging in Publication Data

Showalter, Dennis E.
　Railroads and rifles

　Bibliography: p.
　Includes index.
　1. Germany--History, Military--19th century.
2. Prussia--History, Military. 3. Railroads--
Germany. 4. Germany--Defenses--History. 5. Krupp,
Alfred, 1812-1887. I. Title.
DD103.S54　　　335'.00943　　　75-17710
ISBN 0-208-01505-1

Fig. 24.19
Cataloging-in-Publication: Title Main Entry

Library of Congress Cataloging in Publication Data

Main entry under title:

Management principles for nonprofit agencies and
organizations.

Includes index.
1. Corporations, Nonprofit--United States--Management--
Addresses, essays, lectures. I. Zaltman, Gerald.
HD38.M31865 658'.04'8 79-15453
ISBN 0-8144-5518-2

Fig. 24.20
Cataloging-in-Publication: British Library

British Library Cataloguing in Publication Data

The Oxford dictionary of quotations.
-- 3rd ed.
1. Quotations, English
808.88'2 PN6081 79-40699

ISBN 0-19-211560-X

Weekly Record and *American Book Publishing Record*

The *Weekly Record* (New York: R. R. Bowker, 1974-) is a weekly listing of *books only*, American and foreign, distributed in the United States. Prior to 1974, information now in the *Weekly Record* appeared in the "Weekly Record Section" of *Publishers Weekly* (R. R. Bowker, 1872-). The entries give Library of Congress cataloging data for the work (Figure 24.21). A few entries marked with an asterisk (*) represent cataloging data prepared by the *Weekly Record* staff.

Entries in the *Weekly Record* are cumulated monthly in the *American Book Publishing Record—BPR* (New York: R. R. Bowker, 1960-). *BPR* is cumulated annually and there are several cumulations covering multi-year periods: 1876-1949 and 1950-1977, for example, and 1876-1981 in microfiche.

Fig. 24.21
Entries in the *American Book Publishing Record**

PALMER, Benjamin   347.9720973
  Whipple, 1889-
Marshall and Taney: statesmen of the law [by]
Ben W. Palmer. New York, Russell & Russell.
1966 [c.1939] viii, 281p. ports. 23cm. 66-
24745 7.50
1. *Marshall, John, 1775-1835. 2. Taney, Roger
Brooke, 1777-1864. 3. U.S. Supreme Court. I.
Title.*
Originally published by the Univ. of Minn. Pr.
in 1939.

PALMER, Benjamin   347.9720973
  Whipple, 1889-
Marshall and Taney: statesmen of the law [by]
Ben W. Palmer. New York, Russell & Russell.
1966 [c1939] viii, 281 p. ports. 23 cm. 66-
24745
1. *Marshall, John. 1775-1835. 2. Taney, Roger
Brooke, 1777-1864. 3. U.S. Supreme Court. I.
Title.*

COPE, Alfred   347.972 347.99
  Haines, 1912- ed.
*Franklin D. Roosevelt and the Supreme Court,
edited with an introd.* by Alfred Haines Cope
[and] Fred Krinsky. Boston, Heath [1952] 109
p. 24 cm. (Problems in American civilization:
readings selected in cooperation with the
Dept. of American Studies, Amherst College)
Heath new history series. 52-1656
1. *U. S. Supreme Court. 2. Judicial review—U.
S. 3. Courts—U. S. 4. U. S.—Pol. & govt.—
1933-1945. I. Title.*

The *Monthly Catalog*

The *Monthly Catalog of United States Government Publications* (Washington: Government Printing Office, 1895-) is an index and bibliography of current federal publications. The arrangement is alphabetical by issuing agency. In recent years, the entries have been presented in catalog card format. Information useful for cataloging include the main entry, other descriptive information, subject headings, and for a limited number of works, a DDC class number or LC call number. Most works are entered in the OCLC data base and can be located by the OCLC control number, which appears in the *Monthly Catalog* (Figure 24.22, page 344). The *Monthly Catalog* is a useful source of information for libraries cataloging federal documents.

H. W. Wilson Standard Catalog Series

The H. W. Wilson Company issues a series of catalogs of works recommended for smaller libraries, and a recommended DDC number is also given for most entries. The titles in this series are: *Children's Catalog, Junior High School Library Catalog, Senior High School Library Catalog*, and *Public Library Catalog*. All titles are updated by supplements. These catalogs are useful mostly for small public or school libraries.

Fig. 24.22
Sample Entry from the *Monthly Catalog**

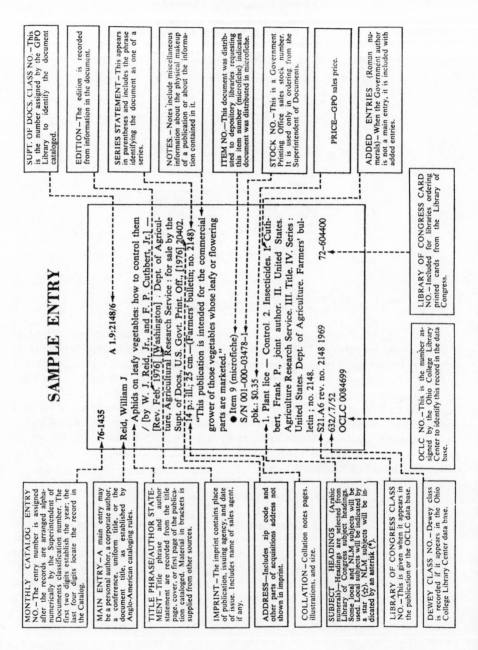

*Reproduced from the *Monthly Catalog*.

NOTES

[1]Library of Congress, *Annual Report of the Librarian of Congress, 1983* (Washington: Library of Congress, 1984), p. A-15.

[2]A search by CODEN, a specialized code for certain scientific serial titles, is possible, but is not covered in this text because of its specialized application.

[3]Information required for interpreting OCLC cataloging data is found in the various OCLC manuals. This information is best learned as part of the training for using the OCLC system.

REVIEW QUESTIONS AND EXERCISES

1. Do most libraries have access to outside cataloging information?

2. Name four catalogs published by the Library of Congress. What kinds of materials are included in each catalog?

3. What is MARC?

4. Name three bibliographic network services.

5. What is a CRT/Keyboard terminal?

6. How many methods can be used to search the OCLC data base? RLIN data base? What is one major difference?

7. What do the abbreviations RLIN and WLN mean?

8. What is CIP? Is it a complete process? If not, what information is sometimes missing?

9. What is the *Monthly Catalog*?

10. Name three titles in the H. W. Wilson standard catalog series. What kinds of libraries would use these catalogs for cataloging information?

25

The routines and procedures used to maintain accurate cataloging records are important and may, in fact, take as much time as the cataloging of a work. Without these supporting routines, however, the public catalogs and official library records would quickly be filled with errors and omissions. The routines covered here include shelflisting, authority file maintenance, catalog card production, filing, and preparation of materials for use by patrons.

CATALOGING TERMINOLOGY

Authority file. A record of the proper form of names, subjects, or series used in a catalog. The purpose of an authority file is to maintain uniform entries.

Series authority file. A file of the series represented by works in the collection. Includes the proper names of the series, instructions on whether to make a series added entry, prescriptions for *see* or *see also* references, and special instructions for classifying items in a series.

Shelflist. A record of materials in a library usually arranged in order by call number.

THE SHELFLIST

The shelflist is a record of the works in a library. Items in the shelflist are arranged in the same order as the works on the shelves—usually in call number order. *The shelflist is the most current and accurate record of a library's collection.* One card from a set of catalog cards is used for the shelflist record; it usually has "SL" or "Shelflist" stamped or typed on it for easy identification (Figure 25.1).

One of the important functions of the shelflist is to list the exact holdings for every work in the library. In Figure 25.1, the "c.1" indicates that one copy of the work is held. Examples of other holdings records are shown in Figures 25.2, 25.3 and 25.4 on page 348, and 25.5 on page 349.

(Text continues on page 349.)

Fig. 25.1
Shelflist Card
(One Copy in the Collection)

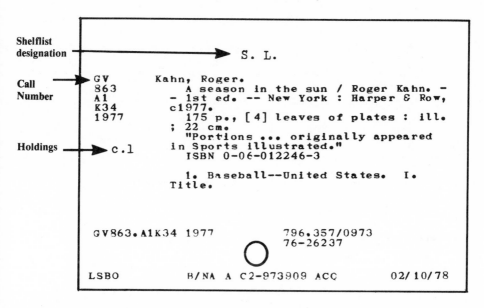

Fig. 25.2
Shelflist Card
(Three Copies in the Collection)

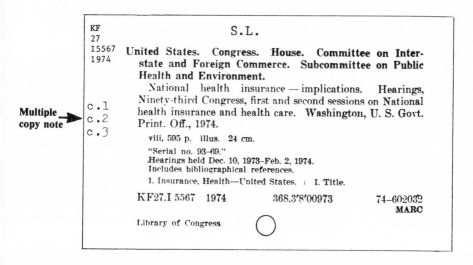

Fig. 25.3
Shelflist Card
(Holdings for an Open Entry Annual Publication)

```
                            S.L.
        Ref    United States Savings and Loan League.
        HG         Savings and loan fact book.  1954-
        2151   Chicago.
        U55
                   v. diagrs.


        1971
        1972
        1973
                   1.Building and loan associations-U.S.-
               Yearbooks.  I.Title.
```

Holdings by year ➡ (1971, 1972, 1973)

Fig. 25.4
Shelflist Card
(Holdings for an Incomplete Set)

```
                        S.L.
        QD     Natural products chemistry / edited by
        415        Koji Nakanishi ... [et al.] . --
        N35        Tokyo : Kodansha ; New York : Aca-
                   demic Press, c1974-
                       v.  : ill. ; 26 cm. -- (Kodansha
               scientific books)

                   Includes biographical references and
               index.
        v.1        ISBN 0-12-513901-2
        v.2
                   1. Biological chemistry.  I. Naka-
               nishi, Koji, 1925-     .
```

Volumes held ➡ (v.1, v.2)

Fig. 25.5
Shelflist Card
(Holdings for a Complete Set)

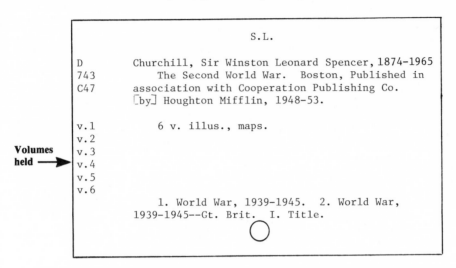

One alternative to entering holdings of multi-volume works directly on the shelflist card is the use of holding cards. For works published frequently and/or over long periods of time, the single shelflist card will quickly become filled. The holding cards in Figure 25.6 can be placed directly behind the shelflist card; the holdings are then entered on these cards:

Fig. 25.6
Holdings Card for Shelflist

Library has those that are checked:

1920/1	1930/1	1940/1	1950/1	1960/1
1921/2	1931/2	1941/2	1951/2	1961/2
1922/3	1932/3	1942/3	1952/3	1962/3
1923/4	1933/4	1943/4	1953/4	1963/4
1924/5	1934/5	1944/5	1954/5	1964/5
1925/6	1935/6	1945/6	1955/6	1965/6
1926/7	1936/7	1946/7	1956/7	1966/7
1927/8	1937/8	1947/8	1957/8	1967/8
1928/9	1938/9	1948/9	1958/9	1968/9
1929/30	1939/40	1949/50	1959/60	1969/70

(The library has volumes for the years 1920/21, 1926/27, 1967/68, 1968/69, and 1969/70, according to the shelflist holdings card shown on page 349.)

Library has those that are checked.

1910	1920	1930	1940	1950
1911	1921	1931	1941	1951
1912	1922	1932	1942	1952
1913	1923	1933	1943	1953
1914	1924	1934	1944	1954
1915	1925	1935	1945	1955
1916	1926	1936	1946	1956
1917	1927	1937	1947	1957✓
1918	1928	1938	1948	1958✓
1919	1929	1939	1949	1959✓

(This holdings card shows the library has volumes only for the years 1957, 1958, and 1959.)

Library has those that are checked:

1✓	11	21	31	41	51	61	71	81	91✓
2✓	12	22	32	42	52	62	72	82	92✓
3✓	13	23	33	43	53	63	73	83	93✓
4✓	14	24	34	44	54	64	74	84	94✓
5✓	15	25	35	45	55	65	75	85	95✓
6	16	26	36	46	56	66✓	76	86	96✓
7	17	27	37	47	57✓	67	77	87	97✓
8	18	28	38	48	58	68	78	88	98✓
9	19	29	39	49	59	69	79	89	99✓
10	20	30	40	50	60	70	80	90	100✓

(This holdings card indicates the library only has volumes 1-5, 57, 66, and 91-100.)

The "main entry card" or holdings card in a public catalog usually gives the holdings for a set or a continuing publication, but it does not give information on the number of copies. *The shelflist is not a public catalog because, for security reasons, it is not often accessible to the public.* The shelflist also includes information about lost or missing copies (Figure 25.7):

Fig. 25.7
Shelflist Card
(Missing/Lost Book Information)

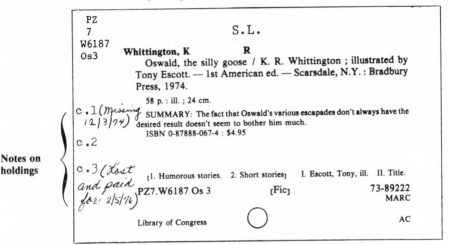

The "missing/lost" information is written in pencil so the records can be changed if items are found or replaced.

The shelflist is an essential tool for classifying and assigning call numbers. When doing original cataloging, a tentative classification number can be compared to works with the same number in the shelflist to see if similar material is classed together. When assigning book numbers, the new call number is compared to the shelflist to be certain it is not identical to a call number assigned previously. If two call numbers are found to be identical, one is changed so that each is unique.

The shelflist is the official record of *all* entries in the catalog for a work. The "tracings" on the shelflist card cite all added and subject entries, and notes are made if an entry has been deleted or if new ones are added. All cards in a set may have the tracings, but usually only the shelflist would reflect any changes. An accurate record of all entries in the catalog must be made so that entries can be deleted when materials are withdrawn.

The shelflist is used in taking inventory of the collection. Because the shelflist is arranged in shelf order, entries in the shelflist can be compared to the material on the shelf. Actual holdings are compared to "official" holdings. Inventories are more complicated than indicated here, but the shelflist is essential for conducting any inventory.

Because the shelflist is to important, it is usually housed in the cataloging department with limited public access. To ensure against its destruction or vandalism, many libraries microfilm the shelflist. If the public catalog is vandalized or destroyed, the shelflist records provide a method to help "recreate" it.

Clerks and LMTAs are usually assigned to do shelflist work, such as recording added copies or new volumes. Filing shelflist cards is usually performed by clerks or student assistants with the LMTA checking for accuracy. An up-to-date accurate shelflist is essential for a well-functioning cataloging and acquisitions department.

AUTHORITY FILES

The catalog department usually maintains three authority files: name authority, series authority, and subject authority.

A name authority file helps to maintain consistency in the form of a personal or corporate name, and to keep a record of all *see* and *see also* references made for a name. Many libraries use the main public catalog as the name authority; they keep a separate authority file only for names requiring references. Some libraries use the *NUC*, OCLC, RLIN, or similar data base as the authority for the proper form of a name, and they limit the authority file to names requiring references. Figures 25.8-25.12 are examples of name authority cards:

Fig. 25.8
Name Authority Card

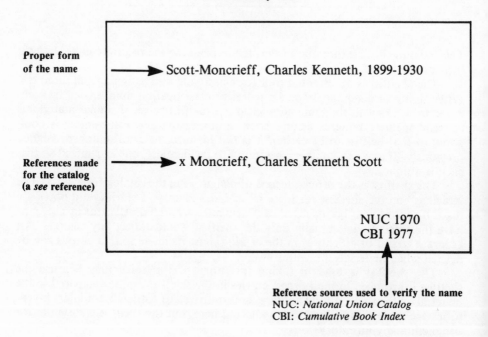

(Text continues on page 354.)

Fig. 25.9
Name Authority Card: Author Using Several Pseudonyms

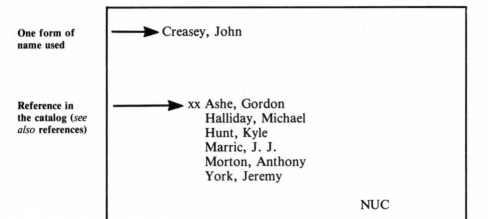

One form of
name used

Creasey, John

Reference in
the catalog (*see
also* references)

xx Ashe, Gordon
Halliday, Michael
Hunt, Kyle
Marric, J. J.
Morton, Anthony
York, Jeremy

NUC

Fig. 25.10
See Also **Reference in the Catalog**

Creasey, John

see also

Ashe, Gordon
Halliday, Michael
Hunt, Kyle
Marric, J. J.
Morton, Anthony
York, Jeremy

Fig. 25.11
Name Authority Card: Corporate Name

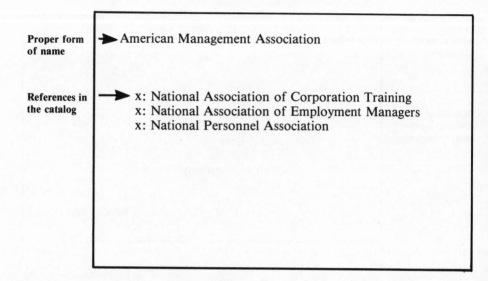

Proper form
of name

American Management Association

References in
the catalog

x: National Association of Corporation Training
x: National Association of Employment Managers
x: National Personnel Association

Fig. 25.12
See **Reference in the Catalog**

National Association of Corporation Training

see, American Management Association

The series authority file is a record of every series represented in the library, indicating whether an added entry is made. The file also indicates whether works in a series are classified together, or classified separately (Figures 25.13 and 25.14). A librarian is responsible for establishing how series are to be cataloged. Once policy is made, the LMTA can maintain this file and simply refer decisions for new series to the librarian.

Fig. 25.13
Series Authority Entry—Series Added Entry Made
and Material Classed Together

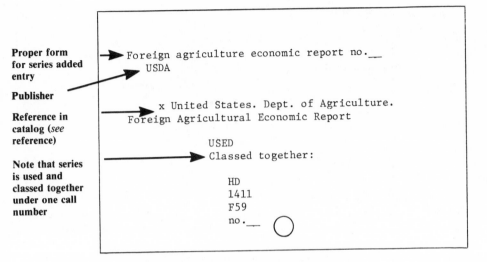

Proper form
for series added
entry

Publisher

Reference in
catalog (*see*
reference)

Note that series
is used and
classed together
under one call
number

Fig. 25.14
Series Authority Entry—No Added Entry Made
and Material Classed Individually

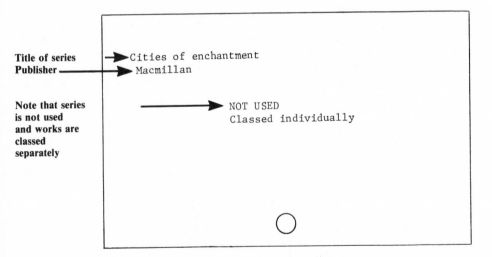

Title of series
Publisher

Note that series
is not used
and works are
classed
separately

The subject authority file is a record of the subject headings used in a catalog and of the *see* and *see also* references made for the heading. This file is usually maintained in the printed list of subject headings used by the library. The introductory materials in *Sears List of Subject Headings* suggest one widely used method of maintaining the authority file in a printed list that can also be used with the *Library of Congress Subject Headings*. If the file is maintained in card format, it might resemble Figure 25.15 (page 356):

Fig. 25.15
Subject Authority Card

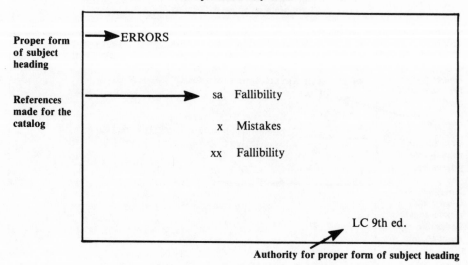

Proper form
of subject
heading

References
made for the
catalog

ERRORS

sa   Fallibility

x   Mistakes

xx   Fallibility

LC 9th ed.

Authority for proper form of subject heading

CATALOG CARD REPRODUCTION

More and more libraries are acquiring sets of catalog cards from the sources discussed earlier in this chapter. In-house production of catalog cards has dropped considerably in the past few years in many libraries. There are still about 15 methods in use to reproduce catalog cards. Only two of the most popular will be mentioned. First, photocopy machines are used by many libraries to produce sets of cards from a master copy. The dry-copy process produces permanent copy. Once cards are reproduced, headings are typed in, and the new cards are ready to file. A second method for producing cards is multilith duplication, an offset process requiring typing a stencil, or typing and photographing a master. Multilith produces a print-like permanent copy. Both in-house processes are relatively expensive and will probably be phased out of most libraries in favor of outside sources.

The LMTA is often in charge of the production of catalog cards. Thus, you must become familiar with equipment, know its capabilities, and be able to make minor adjustments. Companies selling reproduction equipment offer training courses and provide manuals on operating their machines. The quality of reproductions depends on the reproducing machine, the typewriter ribbons used to type masters, and the quality and color of the catalog card paper. Careful attention to these details will result in good quality reproductions.

The decision to purchase a certain copying machine is made by a librarian. It will be based on such factors as quality of reproduction, cost per card, cost of the copying machine, and the personnel needed to operate the machine(s).

As mentioned earlier, in-library production of catalog cards has been significantly reduced in many libraries. In the 1960s and 1970s, the copying machine revolutionized the production of catalog cards in libraries. Now, outside vendors using computers are rapidly changing libraries' sources of catalog cards as well as cataloging information.

FILING

Two sets of rules for filing in a card catalog are currently in use. The *ALA Rules for Filing Catalog Cards*. 2nd ed. (Chicago: American Library Association, 1968) is the set of rules used by most libraries. Most card catalogs are currently alphabetized on the basis of the 1968 rules. An abridged edition with 37 basic rules is available for use in small libraries. The latest rules, *ALA Filing Rules* (Chicago: American Library Association, 1980), are discussed at the end of the section on filing.

Everyone who works with the catalog must know basic filing rules. It is equally important for staff in reference, acquisitions, and cataloging to be acquainted with filing, although staff members who are regularly assigned to filing duties will be more proficient.

Some basic filing rules to build on are given below. These are the 1968 rules.

1) all entries are alphabetized **word by word,** and letter by letter within the words:

Word by Word	Letter by Letter
I met someone	Imagine a woman
Imagine a woman	I met someone
In time to run	India
India	In time to run

Alphabetizing letter-by-letter, without concern for individual words, as in the right column above, is confusing. Word-by-word arrangement illustrates the principle of "nothing before something"—that is, the space between words determines the end of each filing element.

2. any modification of letters within a name is ignored; this includes umlauts, cedillas, and other accent marks:

Mullen, Alden
Müllen, David
Mullen, George

3) names beginning with Mc and M' are filed as if they were spelled "Mac":

Mach
McHale
McHenry
Machinery

4) all punctuation marks in an entry are ignored:

Love

Love--a fleeting thing

Love, but not too much

Love! It is wonderful

5) all articles *within* an entry are *regarded* in filing, and all *initial* articles are ignored:

The man of his time	Work for a man
A man of the time	Work for the beginner

6) abbreviations are filed as if they were spelled out (Mister, Doctor, Saint, etc.), but *Mrs.* and *Ms.* are filed as written:

Doctor at sea

Dr. come quickly

Mr. Brown

Mister Jones

7) numerals in a filing entry are filed as though spelled out (1911 is filed as "Nineteen eleven," 100 as "One hundred"):

One America

100 American Poems [one hundred]

101 Best Games for Teens [one hundred and one]

100,000 watts [one hundred thousand]

1,999 laughs [one thousand, nine hundred and ninety-nine]

8) alphabetization of **subject** entries follow the same rules, with the following exception: when a subject has chronological subdivisions, *entries are filed chronologically* (the earliest date is filed first).

UNITED STATES—HISTORY—REVOLUTION, 1775-1783
—WAR OF 1812
—CIVIL WAR, 1861-1865
—20TH CENTURY
—1933-1945
—1945-

Notice also that the more inclusive period **20th century** precedes more specific period divisions in the 20th century (1933-1945 and 1945-).

9) spelling differences are ignored; words spelled more than one way are filed together as if spelled the same:

    Color

    Colour harmony

    Color harmony test

10) *see* references are filed alphabetically, and *see also* references are filed *before* the first entry under the same word:

See	*See also*
MONCRIEFF, CHARLES	ACCOUNTING, see also
MONCRIEFF, CHARLES SCOTT, see	ACCOUNTING
	ACCOUNTING--ABSTRACTS

11) in a **dictionary catalog,** works *by* a person are filed *before* works *about* a person (subject entries).

12) when a work has more than one edition, cards for the first edition are filed *first*, followed by cards for later editions. It is also acceptable to file the latest edition first, followed by cards for earlier editions. In either case, filing must be consistent.

The *ALA Filing Rules* (Chicago: American Library Association, 1980) is the latest set of filing rules. Some libraries have adopted the rules or modified the catalogs to comply with the rules. Because refiling a catalog is so expensive, it will be many years before the new rules will be widely used. Libraries relying on traditional card catalogs will not be under immediate pressure to make major changes; libraries going to computer-based public catalogs will have to make changes in filing rules more rapidly. The *ALA Filing Rules* (1980) are a *new* set of rules and *not* a revision of the 1968 rules. These new rules are suitable for filing either in a manual system (the card catalog) or for machine filing (a computer data base).

Below are some examples of the 1980 filing rules that represent major changes from earlier rules. The basic principle of the 1980 rules is "file-as-it-is" with few exceptions. Some of the rule changes are:

1) Abbreviations are filed exactly as written; *not* as if spelled out:

Doctor	Mr. Jones
Doctor Jackson	Mrs. Blue
Dr. Ames	Ms. Anderson

2) A word spelled in different ways used as an entry word is filed as spelled:

    color

    color harmony

    colour

3) An initial article is *sometimes* regarded in filing if it is an integral part of a name:

> That's life
>
> *The* Company ("the" forms part of a proper name)

4) Numbers expressed as numerals (arabic or roman) are filed according to their numerical value; this file is before the first alphabetical file (e.g., before "A"). Numbers that are spelled out as words are filed as spelled:

200	Six thousand
275	Two hundred
6,000	Two hundred seventy-five

Be alert to the different ways a number can be written because they can file in separate locations — "*a* thousand," "*one* thousand," "two hundred seventy-five," "two hundred *and* seventy-five."

The rules discussed above are meant to provide a brief introduction to filing. The LMTA responsible for filing must be familiar with the rules used in his or her library.

Experience is the only way to master filing; it is not always as easy as it appears. One or two years of filing experience will be needed to master filing rules. Filing is usually performed by clerks or student assistants under the supervision of an LMTA. The LMTA, of course, is expected to refer problems that cannot be easily resolved to a librarian.

When using tools like the *National Union Catalog* or the *Library of Congress Subject Headings*, always read the introductory materials on filing arrangement. Many reference tools are produced from computer data bases that require a filing arrangement different from the rules governing a manual system.

PREPARATION OF MATERIALS

Materials acquired by a library must be prepared for in-library use or for circulation. Materials usually need a property stamp, book pocket, book card, date due slip, and a label or lettering on the spine to give the call number. Specific requirements depend in part on the circulation system used in a library. Many libraries, especially school and public libraries, cover books with plastic book jackets, and nearly all libraries put paperback books into pamphlet binders.

Mending materials is another major responsibility of the processing department. Extensive mending is often not economical, but torn pages, split backs, damaged covers, and other minor problems can be repaired quickly. This helps to extend the useful life of materials.

Many book jobbers and commercial cataloging services offer processing kits with ready-to-use book pockets, book cards, and spine labels. This eliminates much in-library work and simplifies the preparation process.

The details of book processing and mending are beyond the scope of this text, as whole books and handbooks are devoted to these topics. Many library supply companies offer excellent handbooks explaining book mending; these are readily available. In any case, preparation and mending should be done by clerks and student assistants. The LMTA's role should be limited to supervision and consultation on difficult problems. If employees who are paid comparatively well become too involved in processing and mending, the unit cost for the department may rise to an unacceptable level.

The LMTA must become familiar with the supplies required not only for processing and mending, but for all library operations. Looking through the catalogs of major library supply companies (such as Brodart, Demco, Gaylord, Highsmith, and American Library Line) is an interesting way to learn about library supplies.

STATISTICS AND REPORTS

Libraries vary greatly in the types of statistics they maintain. Some libraries keep only a few vital statistics, while others record every conceivable technical service activity. The librarians will establish a policy defining the statistics required, and the LMTA supervising an area of the library will devise the methods for gathering those statistics.

At the simplest level, statistics show two things: 1) the quantity of work accomplished by a department, and 2) the library's collection size. *Only useful statistics should be gathered.* Most libraries keep statistical records of the following:

1) number of titles and/or volumes or items added to the collection

2) number of titles, volumes, or other items withdrawn from the collection

3) number of titles or items received

4) number of periodical volumes bound

5) number of titles and/or volumes classified in various subject areas

6) number of items repaired or mended

REVIEW QUESTIONS AND EXERCISES

1. Name four cataloging routines. Why is each one important?

2. Define the term "shelflist." Name several important functions of this tool.

3. Is the shelflist usually available to the public? Why?

4. Name three authority files found in many cataloging departments. What is the function of each file?

5. Name two popular methods for in-library production of catalog cards. Why has in-house production of catalog cards dropped off in recent years?

6. What kinds of materials are used to prepare items for circulation and use by patrons?

7. Name four major library supply companies.

8. Name five statistics likely to be maintained in a cataloging department.

GLOSSARY OF TERMS AND ACRONYMS
USED IN TECHNICAL SERVICES

AACR 2. *Anglo-American Cataloguing Rules*, 2nd edition. *AACR 1*, 1st edition.

Access point. An entry in a library catalog that will help a user locate a particular item. Refers to the main entry, added entries, and subject entries. *See also* Entry.

Accession number. A number assigned to each book or item as it is received by the library. Accession numbers can be assigned through continuous numbering or a coded system.

Account. A record of the effects of a business transaction on assets, liabilities, and proprietorship.

Acquisition work. The process of securing materials for the library's collection. Materials can be secured by purchase, as gifts, or through exchange programs.

Added entry. Any entry made in addition to the main entry. Added entries can be made for joint authors, illustrators, editors, compilers, translators, series, title, and subjects.

Analytical entry. An entry for a part of a work or for a whole work that is part of a series for which a comprehensive entry is made.

Annual. A serial work that is issued once a year.

Anonymous work. A work of unknown authorship.

Approval plan. An agreement between a library and a supplier that allows the supplier to send the library automatically one copy of each item he has on a specified subject or in a particular format. The library is then allowed a certain amount of time to examine the material, select the items it will purchase, and return unwanted items.

Area. A major section of a bibliographic description. Examples are the physical description area and the publication, distribution, etc., area.

Art original. An original work of art as contrasted with a reproduction.

Art print. An etching, lithograph, engraving, etc. made from a plate prepared by the artist.

Art reproduction. A mechanically reproduced copy of a work of art.

Artifact. An object made or modified by man.

Author. The person chiefly responsible for the intellectual or artistic content of a work. A *personal author* is a person responsible for the work; this can be an author, artist, cartographer or performer. *See also* Corporate body.

Author entry. The name of the author of a work used as an entry in the catalog. This is usually the main entry.

Authority file. A record of the proper form of names, subjects, or series used in a catalog. The purpose of an authority file is to maintain uniform entries.

Balance sheet. A statement of financial condition at a given point in time.

BALLOTS. Bibliographic Automation of Large Library Operations Using a Time-Sharing System.

Bibliography. A list of books or periodical articles, usually on a particular subject. National bibliographies may include all books published in a particular geographic area or written in a particular language.

Binder's title. The title imprinted on the binding of a book. This title may differ from the title on the title page if the book was rebound, or from the title on the original binding.

BIP. *Books in Print.*

Bit. A unit of information. The smallest unit of information in a computer memory. An abbreviation for *bi*nary digi*t*.

Blanket order. A method of acquisition very similar to the approval plan. The distinction between the two systems is that with a blanket order the library agrees to buy one copy of everything the supplier sends.

Blurb. A description of the contents of a book, prepared by the publisher and usually found on the book jacket. The blurb may also give information about the author.

Book jacket. A paper cover placed around a book to protect the binding. Sometimes called a dust jacket, dust cover, or dust wrapper.

Book number. A combination of letters and numbers assigned as part of a call number to maintain an (alphabetical) order among works with the same classification number. The book number is sometimes called an *author number* or *cutter number*. The term "cutter number" comes from the use of *Cutter Tables* to generate the numbers.

BPR. *American Book Publishing Record.*

Byte. A letter or word, usually composed of eight bits, that forms the smallest unit of information that can be accessed on a computer.

Call number. The notation used to identify and locate a particular work. The notation consists of a classification number and book number and may also include other identifying symbols.

Catalog. A list of the holdings of a particular library or group of libraries.

Cataloging. The process of describing a work bibliographically and assigning a call number. Includes determining the main entry, describing the work, and assigning added entries, subject entries, and a call number. *See also* Descriptive cataloging and Subject cataloging.

Cathode Ray Tube display unit. An electronic tube that is capable of producing a visual image much like a television set. When equipped with a typewriter keyboard it is used to input data into the computer and to view visually the output of data. Also called VDT (visual display terminal).

CBI. *Cumulative Book Index.*

Central Processing Unit. The main part or nerve center of a digital computer. Coordinates and controls all functions and activities of the computer. The CPU is composed of three elements: internal memory, arithmetic unit, and control unit.

Chart. Information arranged in tabular, outline, or graphic form on a sheet of paper. May also refer to a special map such as a navigation chart.

Chief source of information. The source of bibliographic information given first preference in describing a work. The chief source varies for different types of materials. *See also* Prescribed source of information.

CIP. Cataloging in Publication, a program sponsored by the Library of Congress. A partial bibliographic description is provided in each book produced by cooperating publishers.

Classification number. The number assigned to a work to show its subject and to indicate its location in the collection.

Classification schedule. The printed scheme of a classification system.

Collation. The element in a bibliographic description that gives the number of pages, volumes, or illustrations, the item's size, and accompanying materials. *See also* Physical description area.

Collection development. The process of identifying the strengths and weaknesses of a library's information resources with respect to patron needs and community resources, and of attempting to correct the weaknesses. It requires a continual examination and evaluation of the library's resources. Further, it requires a constant study of patron needs and changes in the community the library serves.

Collective title. A title proper assigned to a work that includes several works.

Colophon. An inscription or identifying device sometimes found at the end of a book; it often includes such publication information as typeface or printer.

Compiler. A person who produces a collection by bringing together works by various persons or corporate bodies, or works by one person or corporate body.

Composer. The author of music.

Compound surname. A name formed from two or more proper names usually connected by a hyphen, conjunction, or preposition (e.g., Liddell Hart, Scott-Moncrieff).

CONSER. Conservation of Serials Records.

Container. A receptacle (box, folder, etc.) used to contain non-book materials.

Copyright. The exclusive right granted by a government to publish a work for a specified number of years. The copyright protects the author and publisher by preventing others from copying the work or a significant part of it without permission.

Copyright date. The date a copyright is issued. This is usually found on the verso of the title page.

Corporate body. An organization or group of persons that is identified by a name and that acts as the entity responsible for a work. Corporate bodies include associations, conferences, institutions, business firms, and government agencies.

Cover title. The title printed on the cover of a book or pamphlet.

CPU. *See* Central Processing Unit.

Credit. A term used to refer to the right side of an account (liability and proprietorship).

CRT. *See* Cathode Ray Tube display unit.

Cutter number. A number from the *Cutter* or *Cutter-Sanborn* tables used to create a book number. *See also* Book number.

Data base. A file of information maintained and available for recall on a computer.

Daybook. An informal record of the day's economic activity.

DDC. Dewey Decimal Clasification.

Debit. A term used to refer to the left side of an account (assets).

Descriptive cataloging. The cataloging process concerned with describing a work, identifying the main entry, and selecting added entries.

Dictionary catalog. A catalog in which all entries — author, title, added, subject — are filed in one alphabet.

Diorama. A three-dimensional representation of a scene.

Divided catalog. A catalog in two or more sections. It usually consists of a separate author/title/added entry catalog and a separate subject catalog.

Double-entry accounting system. An accounting system in which all transactions are recorded twice — once in the *journal* and once in the *ledger*.

Dust jacket. *See* Book jacket.

Edition. All the *impressions* (copies) of a book printed at any time from one setting of type. For non-book materials all of the impressions made from a master copy by one company or agency.

Editor. A person who prepares for publication or supervises the publication of a work or collection of works that are not his or her own. Responsibility may extend to revising and providing commentaries, introductory matter, etc.

Element. A part or subsection of an *area* in a bibliographic description (e.g., the title is an element in the title and statement of responsibility area).

Encumbering. A bookkeeping procedure that commits a given amount of money to the payment of an order. Each time an order is placed, an amount of money – an encumbrance – equal to the total price of all items in that order is deducted from the free balance.

Entry. A record of an item in a catalog. In addition to the main entry, there are title entries, series entries, and other types of added entries and subject entries. *See also* Access point.

Explanatory reference. A detailed *see* or *see also* reference used to guide the catalog user to information in the catalog.

Fanfold order form. *See* Multiple order form.

Field. That part of a record used for a specific category of information in a machine-readable record.

Field, fixed. A field limited to a predetermined size, content, and position in a machine-readable record.

Field, variable. A field *not* limited to a predetermined size, content, or position in a machine-readable record.

Filmstrip. A length of film with a series of still pictures to be viewed in sequence; usually 16mm or 35mm, with or without sound.

Flash card. A card with information to be displayed briefly as part of a teaching method.

Game. A set of materials with rules designed to be played for competition, for education, or for entertainment.

Globe. A spherical representation or map of the earth, universe, or celestial bodies (e.g., the moon). A relief globe has raised surfaces to indicate elevations.

Half-title page. A brief or shortened title on the leaf preceding the title page.

Hardware. The physical units of a computer system.

Illustrative matter. Pictorial matter appearing in a work. Includes pictures, portraits, charts, graphs, maps, and facsimiles.

Impression. All of the copies of an edition produced at one time.

Imprint. Place of publication, publisher's name, and date of publication for a book.

In print. An item currently available from the producer; the term is used primarily in connection with the book trade.

Index. A list of names and subjects in a book, each followed by the page number(s) where it appears. A guide to the contents.

International Standard Book Number (ISBN). A unique ten-digit number assigned to each book published in the United States as well as in other countries. It is hoped that in time it will cover all publishers in the world.

International Standard Serial Number (ISSN). A system of assigning a unique eight-digit number to each serial title published.

Introduction. A preliminary part of a book that tells what the book is about and how the author intends to cover the subject. *See also* Preface.

Invoice symbols. NE, NEP — new edition pending
NOP — not our publication
OP — out of print
OS — out of stock
NYP — not yet published
TOP — temporarily out of print
TOS — temporarily out of stock

ISBD. International Standard Bibliographic Description. A standardized format for descriptive bibliographic information compatible for computer input.

ISBN. *See* International Standard Book Number.

ISSN. *See* International Standard Serial Number.

Jobber. A supplier, usually a wholesaler, who stocks a wide range of items. Using jobbers reduces the work load in the acquisitions department, since it then becomes possible to secure from one source items produced by many different publishers.

Joint author. A person who collaborates with one or more associates to produce a work. The contributions of the various joint authors often cannot be distinguished.

Journal. A book in which the first entry for a business transaction is made; the journal is maintained in chronological order.

Journalizing. The recording of entries in a journal.

Kardex®. A metal file that has a number of shallow drawers in which serial check-in cards are kept.

Kit. A collection of information in different media, usually on a specific topic and usually designed to be used as a unit. The media may be interdependent or used independently.

Label. The permanently affixed paper or plastic on an audiodisc describing the contents.

LC. Library of Congress.

LCC. Library of Congress Classification.

LCCN. Library of Congress Card Number.

LCSH. *Library of Congress Subject Headings.*

Leaf. A single sheet of paper in a bound book; i.e., two pages.

Ledger. A group of accounts containing data derived from a journal.

Librarian. A person who holds a fifth-year master's degree from a library school accredited by the American Library Association.

Library binding. A special strong binding designed for heavy library use.

Library clerk. A person who has the equivalent of at least a high school education and has office skills such as typing, filing, shorthand, etc. Probably has only on-the-job training experience in library service.

Library Media Technical Assistant. A person who has had some post-high school academic training and some training in library service. Also called *Library technician.*

Library technician. *See* Library Media Technical Assistant.

Linedex®. A metal file with a number of flat metal leaves. It contains single cardboard strips (lines) listing titles and holdings.

Machine-readable data file. Information encoded and stored in a format that requires a machine to retrieve the information. Includes such media as magnetic tapes, magnetic discs, punched cards, punched paper, etc.

Main entry. A full catalog entry giving all the information necessary for identifying a work. The main entry includes the tracings for all other entries or access points under which a work is entered in the catalog. The main entry is usually an author entry.

Mainframe. A large computer with a large internal memory unit.

Map. A representation of a geographic area, usually on a flat surface. The geographic area can be on earth (terrestrial) or a celestial body. A relief map is one with raised surfaces to indicate land elevations.

Memory. The component of a computer where data and programs are stored. The primary memory is in the computer, while other memory units can be stored in peripheral units.

Microform. A photographic miniature reproduction on film that must be magnified on special machines in order to be read; also called "microreproductions." Microform formats include aperture cards, microfiche, microfilm, and ultramicrofiche.

Microscope slide. A transparent mount containing an object for viewing under a microscope.

Mixed notation. *See* Notation.

Mixed responsibility. When more than one person or corporate body performs different activities in the creation of a work (e.g., one person writes a work and a second person illustrates it).

Model. A three-dimensional representation of a real object reproduced in the original size or to scale.

Monograph. A book, usually a systematic and complete study of a particular subject. Often used in libraries as a synonym for the words "book" or "title."

Monograph series. A series of monographs with a collective title, usually published by a university press or a society.

Motion picture. Film with a series of pictures that create the illusion of movement when projected at the proper speed. May be with or without sound.

Multiple order form. A form designed so that multiple copies of an order are made. Some forms use carbon paper, others use a paper that does not require carbon. Also called a fanfold order form.

Name authority file. A file of the proper form for names in a catalog. It records the *see* and *see also* references made from other forms of the name. May cite the source used to establish the name.

Name-title reference. A reference in which both a name and title are included as opposed to either a name or a title alone.

Notation. A system of numbers and/or letters used to represent a classification scheme. "Mixed notation" uses two or more symbols (i.e., letters and numbers). "Pure notation" uses one kind of symbol—either letters or numbers. Dewey Decimal Classification, which uses only numbers, is a pure notation; Library of Congress Classification, which uses letters and numbers, is a mixed notation.

NUC. *National Union Catalog.*

OCLC control number. A unique sequential number assigned to each work entered in the OCLC data base.

Open entry. A catalog entry for a serial, series, or set not yet completed. The numeric/chronological designation and extent of item are left incomplete on the catalog card or bibliographic record to indicate the work is not yet complete.

Out-of-print. A designation that a book is no longer available from the publisher.

Pagination. A system of numbers or letters used to indicate the order of the pages in a book. The part of the Physical description area indicating the number of pages in a book.

Pamphlet. In present usage a pamphlet is an independent publication of 49 pages or fewer, bound in paper covers. Many libraries use pamphlets to maintain a very current information file on topics that are subject to rapid change.

Parallel title. The title proper in another language or printed in another script.

Partial title. A secondary part of the title as given on the title page. It may be a catch-word title, subtitle, or alternative title.

Periodical. A publication issued in succeeding parts, each with the same title but with a different number. Most periodicals are issued at regular intervals and in paper covers. Libraries usually secure periodicals on a subscription basis.

Personal author. *See* Author.

Physical description area. The area in a bibliographic description used to give the physical description of a work. (For example, for a book, this area would give the number of pages, illustrative matter, and size.)

Picture. A two-dimensional representation on an opaque material, usually paper. May be a photograph, painting, drawing, etc.

Posting. The transfer of debit and credit information from a journal to the proper account in the ledger.

Preface. A section preceding the body of the book which may state the origin, purpose, and scope of the work. *See also* Introduction.

Preliminaries. In a book this refers to the pages preceding the body of the book, such as the half-title page, the added title page, the verso of the title page, the cover title, and the spine.

Prescribed source of information. The source recommended for describing different areas. The prescribed source varies for different areas and different materials. *See also* Chief source of information.

Printer. An output device that converts the electronic impulses from a computer into printed format. Also refers to person or firm that prints books.

Process record. A file maintained by the acquisition department containing a record (usually on a 3x5-inch card) of all items on order, received, or being processed in technical services.

Program. A set of instructions that tell a computer what to do and how to do it.

PTLA. *Publishers Trade List Annual.*

Public services. Library work that deals with patrons and their use of the library collection.

Publication, distribution, etc. area. The area in a bibliographic description used to record information about the place, name, and date of publishing, distributing, releasing, and issuing activities. (For a motion picture, for example, this area would give the place of publication or distribution; the name of the publisher, distributor or releasing agency; and the date of publication or distribution.)

Publisher. A person or firm that issues and distributes a work.

Publisher series. A series of books whose only link may be the collective title assigned by the publisher.

Pure notation. *See* Notation.

PW. *Publishers Weekly.*

Realia. Real objects, specimens, artifacts.

Recto. The right-hand page in an open book. Usually odd-numbered. *See also* Verso.

Replacement copy. A copy that replaces a stolen or discarded book.

Reprint. A new issue (printing) of material that has been published before. The New printing contains no textual changes except for the correction of printer's errors from the first printing. The period of time that passes between the first printing and the reprinting may be a day, several weeks, or hundreds of years.

Resources. The information materials available from a library. These materials may be books, periodicals, pamphlets, reports, manuscripts, microformats, motion pictures, video and audio tapes, sound recordings, etc. In essence, almost any physical object that conveys information, thoughts, or feelings could be included in a library collection.

RLG. Research Libraries Group.

RLIN. Research Libraries Information Network.

RLIN identification number. A unique number assigned to each work entered in the RLIN data base.

See also **reference.** A guiding device in a catalog that directs the user from a name or subject to related names or subjects.

See **reference.** A guiding device in a catalog that directs the user from the form of a name or subject not used in the catalog to the form that is used.

Serial. A publication issued in successive parts at regular or irregular intervals. Usually it is intended to be continued indefinitely. Includes periodicals, newspapers, proceedings, reports, annuals, and numbered monographic series.

Series. A number of separate works, usually issued in succession, and usually related to one another in subject or form, issued by the same publisher, and in uniform style. The collective series title may appear at the head of the title page, on the half-title page, or on the cover.

Series authority file. A file of the series represented by works in a collection. Includes the proper names of the series, instructions on whether to make a series added entry, prescriptions for *see* and *see also* references, and special instructions for classifying items in a series.

Series title. The collective title given to volumes or parts issued in a series.

Set. A work of two or more volumes.

Shared responsibility. Two or more persons or corporate bodies perform the same activity in the creation of a work. The contributions may be distinct or inseparable.

Shelflist. A record of materials in a library usually arranged in order by call number.

Slide. A single frame of film or other transparent material, usually in a 2x2-inch mounting. Must be used with a slide projector or viewer.

Software. The programs and other documentation that are used to tell the computer what to do and how to do it. *See also* Program.

Sound recording. A recording of sound. Formats include cylinder, disc, and magnetic tape (also called phonocylinder, phonograph record, phonotape, and phonowire).

Spine. The part of the book binding that joins the front and back covers together. Usually has the author and title of the book printed on it.

Spine title. The title that appears on the spine; also called a back title. *See also* Binder's title.

Standing order. A variation of the blanket order system. The supplier sends a very limited number of items to the library for purchase. Standing orders are usually used for a series of related items that are produced over a long period of time. Book producers usually welcome standing orders for succeeding parts or editions of a series.

Storage. *See* Memory.

Subject. The topic or topics of a work.

Subject authority file. A record of the subject headings used in a catalog. It is also a record of the *see, see also*, and "explanatory" references made for each subject heading.

Subject catalog. A catalog of subject entries. Usually one part of a two-part divided catalog.

Subject cataloging. The cataloging process concerned with determining the subject of a work and selection of subject entries and a classification number.

Subject entry. An access point in a catalog under a *subject heading*.

Subject heading. A word, name, phrase, or acronym describing the subject of a work.

Subject subdivision. A word, group of words, date, or geographic name, added to a subject heading to limit it to a more specific meaning.

Technical services. Work performed in or for a library to ensure that its materials are available for patron use. This work does not require direct contact with library patrons.

Terminal. A device for communicating with the computer. Data can be input or withdrawn. The CRT/keyboard terminal is a device for communicating with the computer.

'Til forbidden. A term used by jobbers to indicate that a subscription for a serial is to be placed for a library and that renewals are to be made automatically until the library cancels the subscription.

Time sharing. A method of use that allows a number of users to access a data base at one time.

Title. The name of a work.

Title entry. The record of a work in the catalog under the title.

Title page. A page at the beginning of a book with the title, author's name, and publishing information.

Title proper. The chief part of a title. (For example, a book entitled *Cataloging with Copy: A Decision Maker's Handbook* has *Cataloging with Copy* for a title proper.)

Tracings. The record, usually on the main entry card and shelflist, of all additional entries for a work in a catalog.

Trade book. A book that is considered to be of wide reader appeal. Trade books represent 95% of a bookseller's stock.

Translator. A person who translates a work from one language into another language.

Transparency. A still image recorded on a transparent material; viewed with an overhead projector or similar device.

Trial balance. A listing of ledger accounts showing *debit* and *credit* balances. The object of the trial balance is to determine whether the debits and credits are equal, or in balance.

Turnkey systems. Computer systems that have been pretested and determined trouble-free (debugged) and ready for immediate use.

Uniform title. The title chosen for cataloging purposes when a work has appeared under varying titles.

Unit card. A basic catalog card, in the form of a main entry, with complete cataloging information. The cards can be used for all entries when the appropriate heading is typed at the top of each.

Variable field. *See* Field, variable.

VDT. *See* Cathode Ray Tube display unit.

Verso. The left-hand page in an open book. Usually even-numbered. *See also* Recto.

Videorecording. An electromagnetic recording made for playback on a television set. Various formats include electronic videorecordings, videocassette, videodisc, and videotape. Videotape is currently the most common format. Almost always includes a sound track.

Volume. In the bibliographical sense, a book distinguished from other books by having its own title page and usually independent pagination, foliation, or register.

Voucher. A form that verifies a business transaction as correct, authorizes its entry into the books, and approves payment of charges.

WLN. Washington Library Network.

Work slip. A card or other form that accompanies a book throughout the cataloging and preparation processes. The cataloger and assistants note on it directions and information that are needed to prepare catalog entries, cross-references, etc.

The bibliography is intended as a guide to further reading on the topics covered in the text. With only a few exceptions, books cited or discussed in the text are not cited again. The reader should refer to *Library Literature: An Index to Library and Information Science* for a more complete listing of materials available on all aspects of librarianship.

ACQUISITIONS AND SERIALS

ACQ Scenarios. Dublin, Ohio: OCLC, 1983.

Acquisitions: Training Manual. Dublin, Ohio: OCLC, 1981.

Alley, Brian, and Jennifer Cargill. *Keeping Track of What You Spend: The Librarian's Guide to Simple Bookkeeping.* Phoenix, Ariz.: Oryx Press, 1982.

American Book Trade Directory. New York: R. R. Bowker, 1915- . (Annual).

American Library Association. Bookdealer-Library Relations Committee. *Guidelines for Handling Library Orders for In-Print Monographic Publications.* 2d ed. Chicago: American Library Association, 1984.

————. *Guidelines for Handling Library Orders for Microforms.* Chicago: American Library Association, 1977.

American Library Association. Resources and Technical Services Division. *Guidelines for Handling Library Orders for Serials and Periodicals.* Chicago: American Library Association, 1974.

American Reference Books Annual. Littleton, Colo.: Libraries Unlimited, 1970- .

Boss, Richard W. *Automating Library Acquisitions: Issues and Outlook.* White Plains, N.Y.: Knowledge Industry Publications, 1982.

Boss, Richard W., and Judy McQueen. "Serials Control in Libraries: Automated Options." *Library Technology Reports* 20 (March/April 1984): 89-282.

Bracken, James K., and John C. Calhoun. "Profiling Vendor Performance." *Library Resources & Technical Services* 28 (April/June 1984): 120-28.

Cargill, Jennifer S., and Brian Alley. *Practical Approval Plan Management.* Phoenix, Ariz.: Oryx Press, 1980.

Evans, G. Edward. *Developing Library Collections.* Littleton, Colo.: Libraries Unlimited, 1979.

Ford, Stephen. *The Acquisition of Library Materials.* rev. ed. Chicago: American Library Association, 1978.

Futas, Elizabeth, ed. *Library Acquisition Policies and Procedures.* 2d ed. Phoenix, Ariz.: Oryx Press, 1984.

Gellatly, Peter, ed. *The Management of Serials Automation: Current Technology and Strategies for Future Planning.* New York: Haworth Press, 1982.

Groot, Elizabeth H. "Comparison of Library Tools for Monograph Verification." *Library Resources & Technical Services* 25 (April 1981): 149-61.

Katz, William A. *Collection Development: The Selection of Materials for Libraries.* New York: Holt, Rinehart and Winston, 1980.

Magrill, Rose Mary, and Doralyn J. Hickey. *Acquisitions Management and Collection Development in Libraries.* Chicago: American Library Association, 1984.

Melin, Nancy Jean, ed. *The Serials Collection: Organization and Administration.* Ann Arbor, Mich.: Pirian Press, 1982.

Name-Address Directory: Training Manual. Dublin, Ohio: OCLC, 1981.

Orne, Jerrod. *The Language of the Foreign Book Trade: Abbreviations, Terms, Phrases.* 3d ed. Chicago: American Library Association, 1976.

Samore, Theodore, ed. *Acquisition of Foreign Materials for U.S. Libraries.* 2d ed. Metuchen, N.J.: Scarecrow Press, 1982.

Serials Control: Training Manual. 2d ed. Dublin, Ohio: OCLC, 1981.

Serials Format. 2d ed. Dublin, Ohio: OCLC, 1983.

Slote, Stanley J. *Weeding Library Collections—II.* 2d ed. Littleton, Colo.: Libraries Unlimited, 1982.

Smith, G. Stevenson. *Accounting for Librarians and Other Not-for-Profit Managers.* Chicago: American Library Association, 1983.

Tuttle, Marcia. *Introduction to Serials Management.* Greenwich, Conn.: JAI Press, 1983.

AUTOMATION AND TECHNICAL SERVICES

Annual Review of Information Science and Technology. White Plains, N.Y.: Knowledge Industry Publications, 1966- .

Aveney, Brian, and Brett Butler, eds. *Online Catalogs, Online Reference: Converging Trends.* Chicago: American Library Association, 1984.

Bierman, Kenneth John. *Automation and the Small Library.* Chicago: American Library Association, 1982.

Boss, Richard W. *The Library Manager's Guide to Automation.* 2d ed. White Plains, N.Y.: Knowledge Industry Publications, 1983.

Broadus, Robert N. "Online Catalogs and Their Users." *College & Research Libraries* 44 (November 1983): 458-67.

Brod, Craig. *Technostress: The Human Cost of the Computer Revolution.* Reading, Mass.: Addison-Wesley, 1984.

Carter, Ruth C. *Data Conversion.* White Plains, N.Y.: Knowledge Industry Publications, 1983.

Corbin, John. *Developing Computer-Based Library Systems.* Phoenix, Ariz.: Oryx Press, 1981.

Dowlin, Kenneth E. *The Electronic Library: The Promise and the Process.* New York: Neal-Schuman, 1984.

Fayen, Emily Gallup. *The Online Catalog: Improving Public Access to Library Materials.* White Plains, N.Y.: Knowledge Industry Publications, 1983.

Fayen, Emily Gallup. "The Online Public Access Catalog in 1984: Evaluating Needs and Choices." *Library Technology Reports* 20 (January/February 1984): 7-59.

Fosdick, Howard. *Computer Basics for Librarians and Information Scientists.* Arlington, Va.: Information Resources Press, 1981.

Freedman, Maurice J. "Automation and the Future of Technical Services." *Library Journal* 109 (June 15, 1984): 1197-1203.

Graham, Peter S. "Technology and the Online Catalog." *Library Resources & Technical Services* 27 (January/March 1983): 18-35.

Hildreth, Charles R. *Online Public Access Catalogs: The User Interface.* Dublin, Ohio: OCLC, 1982.

Jones, C. Lee. "Library Patrons in an Age of Discontinuity: Artifacts of Technology." *Journal of Academic Librarianship* 10 (July 1984): 151-54.

Kilgour, Frederick G. "The Online Catalog Revolution." *Library Journal* 109 (February 1984): 319-21.

Maciuszko, Kathleen L. *OCLC: A Decade of Development, 1967-1977.* Littleton, Colo.: Libraries Unlimited, 1984.

Malinconico, S. Michael. *The Future of the Catalog: The Library's Choices.* White Plains, N.Y.: Knowledge Industry Publications, 1979.

————. "Planning for Obsolescence." *Library Journal* 109 (February 1984): 333-35.

Matthews, Joseph R. "The Automated Library System Marketplace, 1982: Change and More Change!" *Library Journal* 108 (March 15, 1983): 547-53.

————. "Competition & Change: The 1983 Automated Library System Marketplace." *Library Journal* 109 (May 1, 1984): 853-60.

————. "The Four On-Line Bibliographic Utilities: A Comparison." *Library Technology Reports* 15 (November/December 1979): 665-838.

————. *A Reader on Choosing an Automated Library System.* Chicago: American Library Association, 1983.

————. "You're in the Chips; or, The Computer: What It Is and What It Can Do." *Drexel Library Quarterly* 17 (Fall 1981): 5-17.

Matthews, Joseph R., Gary S. Lawrence, and Douglas K. Ferguson. *Using Online Catalogs: A Nationwide Survey.* New York: Neal-Schuman, 1983.

Moore, Carole Weiss. "User Reactions to Online Catalogs: An Exploratory Study." *College & Research Libraries* 42 (July 1981): 295-302.

Reynolds, Dennis. *Library Automation: Issues and Applications.* New York: R. R. Bowker, 1984.

Rice, James. *Introduction to Library Automation.* Littleton, Colo.: Libraries Unlimited, 1984.

Richards, Timothy F. "The Online Catalog: Issues in Planning and Development." *Journal of Academic Librarianship* 10 (March 1984): 4-9.

Rorvig, Mark E. *Microcomputers and Libraries: A Guide to Technology, Products and Applications.* White Plains, N.Y.: Knowledge Industry Publications, 1981.

Saffady, William. *Introduction to Automation for Librarians.* Chicago: American Library Association, 1983.

Sager, Donald J. *Public Library Administrators Planning Guide to Automation.* Dublin, Ohio: OCLC, 1983.

Salmon, Stephen R. "Characteristics of Online Public Catalogs." *Library Resources & Technical Services* 27 (January/March 1983): 36-67.

Schabas, Ann. "Postcoordinate Retrieval: A Comparison of Two Indexing Languages (PRECIS and LC Subject Headings)." *Journal of the American Society for Information Science* 33 (January 1982): 32-37.

Steinberg, David, and Paul Metz. "User Response to and Knowledge about an Online Catalog." *College & Research Libraries* 45 (January 1984): 66-70.

Swanson, Don R. "Miracles, Microcomputers and Librarians." *Library Journal* 107 (June 1, 1982): 1055-9.

Thompson, James. *The End of Libraries.* London: Clive Bingley, 1982.

Tijerina, Louis. *Optimizing the VDT Workstation: Controlling Glare and Postural Problems.* Dublin, Ohio: OCLC, 1983.

Walton, Robert A. *Microcomputers: A Planning and Implementation Guide for Librarians and Information Professionals.* Phoenix, Ariz.: Oryx Press, 1983.

Williamson, Nancy J. "Is There a Catalog in Your Future? Access to Information in the Year 2006." *Library Resources & Technical Services* 26 (April/June 1982): 122-35.

Woods, Lawrence A., and Nolan F. Pope. *The Librarian's Guide to Microcomputer Technology and Applications.* White Plains, N.Y.: Knowledge Industry Publications, 1983.

CATALOGING

Aguilar, William. "Influence of the Card Catalog on Circulation in a Small Public Library." *Library Resources & Technical Services* 28 (April/June 1984): 175-84.

Berman, Sanford. *The Joy of Cataloging: Essays, Letters, Reviews, and Other Explosions.* Phoenix, Ariz.: Oryx Press, 1981.

Books Format. 2d ed. Dublin, Ohio: OCLC, 1984.

Burger, Robert H. *Authority Work: The Creation, Use, Maintenance, and Evaluation of Authority Records and Files.* Littleton, Colo.: Libraries Unlimited, 1985.

Carothers, Diane Foxhill. *Self-Instruction for Filing Catalog Cards.* Chicago: American Library Association, 1981.

Cataloging Service Bulletin. Washington: Library of Congress, Processing Services, 1978- . (Quarterly).

Chan, Lois Mai. *Cataloging and Classification: An Introduction*. New York: McGraw-Hill, 1981.

Cockshutt, Margaret E., C. Donald Cook, and Ann H. Schabas. "Decision Logic for Anglo-American Cataloging Rules, Chapter 21: Choice of Access Points." *Library Resources & Technical Services* 27 (October/December 1983): 371-90.

Comaromi, John P. *Book Numbers: A Historical Study and Practical Guide to Their Use*. Littleton, Colo.: Libraries Unlimited, 1981.

Cope, Gabriele E. *Coping with the OCLC Subsystems*. Lincoln, Nebr.: Ego Books, 1984.

Curley, Arthur, and J. Varlejs. *Akers' Simple Library Cataloging*. 7th ed. Metuchen, N.J.: Scarecrow Press, 1984.

Cutter, Charles A. *Cutter-Sanborn Three Figure Author Table*. Chicopee, Mass.: H. R. Hutting Co., 1969.

DDC; Dewey Decimal Classification: A Conversion Table of Substantial Number Changes from Edition 18 to Edition 19 in Edition 19 Order Based on Dewey Decimal Classification and Relative Index. Albany, N.Y.: Forest Press, 1979.

Dodd, Sue A. *Cataloging Machine-Readable Data Files: An Interpretive Manual*. Chicago: American Library Association, 1982.

Dowell, Arlene Taylor. *AACR2 Headings: A Five-Year Projection of Their Impact on Catalogs*. Littleton, Colo.: Libraries Unlimited, 1982.

Epstein, Susan Baerg. "Integrated Systems: Dream vs. Reality." *Library Journal* 109 (July 1984): 1302-3.

Estabrook, Leigh. "The Human Dimension of the Catalog: Concepts and Constraints in Information Seeking." *Library Resources & Technical Services* 27 (January/March 1983): 68-75.

Farber, Evan Ira. "Catalog Dependency." *Library Journal* 109 (February 1984): 325-28.

Fleischer, Eugene, and Helen Goodman. *Cataloguing Audiovisual Materials: A Manual Based on the Anglo-American Cataloguing Rules II*. New York: Neal-Schuman, 1980.

Foskett, Anthony Charles. *The Subject Approach to Information*. 4th ed. Hamden, Conn.: Linnet Books, 1982.

Foster, Donald L. *Managing the Catalog Department.* 2d ed. Metuchen, N.J.: Scarecrow Press, 1982.

Friedman, Maurice J. "Must We Limit the Catalog?" *Library Journal* 109 (February 1984): 322-24.

Frost, Carolyn O. *Cataloging Nonbook Materials: Problems in Theory and Practice.* Littleton, Colo.: Libraries Unlimited, 1983.

Gorman, Michael. *The Concise AACR2, Being a Rewritten and Simplified Version of Anglo-American Cataloguing Rules, Second Edition.* Chicago: American Library Association, 1981.

————. "New Rules for New Systems." *American Libraries* 13 (April 1982): 241-42.

Greenberg, Alan M., and Carole R. McIver. *LC and AACR2: An Album of Cataloging Examples Arranged by Rule Number.* Metuchen, N.J.: Scarecrow Press, 1984.

A Guide to the OCLC Database and Special Collections Therein. Dublin, Ohio: OCLC, 1984.

Guidelines for Using AACR2 Chapter 9 for Cataloging Microcomputer Software. Chicago: American Library Association, 1984.

Hoduski, Bernadine A., ed. *Cataloging Government Documents: A Manual of Interpretation for AACR2.* Chicago: American Library Association, 1984.

Holly, Robert P. "The Future of Catalogers and Cataloging." *Journal of Academic Librarianship* 7 (May 1981): 90-93.

Lawry, Martha. "A 'Word' for the Cataloger: Special Pleading or Definition of Function!" *Journal of Academic Librarianship* 10 (July 1984): 37-40.

Lehnus, Donald J. *Book Numbers: History, Principles, and Application.* Chicago: American Library Association, 1980.

Manual on the Use of the Dewey Decimal Classification: Edition 19. Albany, N.Y.: Forest Press, 1982.

Maxwell, Margaret F. *Handbook for AACR2: Explaining and Illustrating Anglo-American Cataloguing Rules, Second Edition.* Chicago: American Library Association, 1980.

Miller, Rosalind E., and Jane C. Terwillegar. *Commonsense Cataloging: A Cataloger's Manual.* 3d ed. New York: H. W. Wilson, 1983.

Name-Authority: User Manual. 3d ed. Dublin, Ohio: OCLC, 1984.

Olson, Nancy B. *Cataloging of Audiovisual Materials: A Manual Based on AACR2*. Mankato, Minn.: Minnesota Scholarly Press, 1982.

Osborn, Jeanne. *Dewey Decimal Classification, 19th Edition: A Study Manual*. Littleton, Colo.: Libraries Unlimited, 1982.

Rogers, JoAnn V. *Nonprint Cataloging for Multimedia Collections: A Guide Based on AACR2*. Littleton, Colo.: Libraries Unlimited, 1982.

Ryans, Cynthia C., ed. *The Card Catalog: Current Issues, Readings and Selected Bibliography*. Metuchen, N.J.: Scarecrow Press, 1981.

Smiraglia, Richard P. *Cataloging Music: A Manual for Use with AACR2*. Lake Crystal, Minn.: Soldier Creek Press, 1984.

Smith, Lynn S. *A Practical Approach to Serials Cataloging*. Greenwich, Conn.: JAI Press, 1978.

Stibbe, Hugo L. P., ed. *Cartographic Materials: A Manual of Interpretation for AACR2*. Chicago: American Library Association, 1982.

Tseng, Sally C., comp. *LC Rule Interpretations of AACR2, 1978-1982*. cum. ed. Metuchen, N.J.: Scarecrow Press, 1982.

Webster, James K. *The Bibliographic Utilities: A Guide for the Special Librarian*. New York: Special Libraries Association, 1980.

Wilson, Patrick. "The Catalog as Access Mechanism: Background and Concepts." *Library Resources & Technical Services* 27 (January/March 1983): 4-17.

Wynar, Bohdan S. *Introduction to Cataloging and Classification*. 6th ed. Littleton, Colo.: Libraries Unlimited, 1980.

LIBRARY MEDIA TECHNICAL ASSISTANTS

American Library Association. Library Education Division. "Library Education and Manpower: ALA Policy Proposal." *American Libraries* 1 (April 1970): 341-44.

Asheim, Lester. "Education and Manpower for Librarianship." *ALA Bulletin* 62 (October 1968): 1096-1118.

Atkinson, Hugh C. "Who Will Run and Use Libraries? How?" *Library Journal* 109 (October 15, 1984): 1905-7.

Battin, Patricia. "Developing University and Research Library Professionals." *American Libraries* 14 (January 1983): 22-25.

Braden, Sally, John D. Hall, and Helen H. Britton. "Utilization of Personnel and Bibliographic Resources for Cataloging by OCLC Participating Libraries." *Library Resources & Technical Services* 24 (Spring 1980): 135-54.

Butler, Pierce. "Librarianship as a Profession." *Library Quarterly* 21 (October 1951): 235-47.

Chergwin, F. John, and Phyllis Oldfield. *Library Assistant's Manual.* 2d rev. ed. London: Clive Bingley, 1982.

Chernik, Barbara E. *Introduction to Library Services for Library Technicians.* Littleton, Colo.: Libraries Unlimited, 1982.

_____. *Procedures for Library Media Technical Assistants.* Chicago: American Library Association, 1983.

Conant, Ralph W. *The Conant Report: A Study of the Education of Librarians.* Cambridge: MIT Press, 1980.

Davinson, Donald Edward. "Non-professional Library Staff Education: A State of the Art Report and Proposals for the Future." In *Studies in Library Management*, vol. 7, 37-60. London: Clive Bingley, 1982.

Downs, Robert B., and Robert F. Delzell. "Professional Duties in University Libraries." *College & Research Libraries* 26 (January 1965): 30-39.

Evans, Charles W. "Evolution of Paraprofessional Library Employees." In *Advances in Librarianship*, vol. 9, 63-101. New York: Academic Press, 1979.

Gill, Suzanne. "New Directions for Library Paraprofessionals?" *Wilson Library Bulletin* 55 (January 1981): 368-69.

Holly, Edward G. "The Merwine Case and the MLS: Where Was the ALA?" *American Libraries* 15 (May 1984): 327-30.

Library Human Resources: A Study of Supply and Demand. Chicago: American Library Association, 1983.

Martin, Murray S. *Issues in Personnel Management in Academic Libraries.* Greenwich, Conn.: JAI Press, 1981.

Mathews, Anne J. *Communicate! A Librarian's Guide to Interpersonal Relations.* Chicago: American Library Association, 1983.

Montgomery, Margot. "New Guidelines Developed for Library Technician Programs." *Canadian Library Journal* 39 (June 1982): 159-62.

Mugnier, Charlotte. *The Paraprofessional and the Professional Job Structure.* Chicago: American Library Association, 1980.

Ricking, Myrl, and Robert E. Booth. *Personnel Utilization in Libraries: A System Approach.* Chicago: American Library Association, 1974.

Rogers, A. Robert, and Kathryn McChesney. *The Library in Society.* Littleton, Colo.: Libraries Unlimited, 1984.

Schlessinger, Bernard S. "The Library Technical Assistant (LTA) in Perspective." *California Librarian* 39 (January 1978): 46-51.

Shaffer, Dale Eugene. *The Maturity of Librarianship as a Profession.* Metuchen, N.J.: Scarecrow Press, 1968.

United States. Office of Education. Manpower Development and Training Program. *A Suggested Two-Year Post High School Curriculum: Library Technical Assistant.* Washington: Government Printing Office, 1973.

Veaner, Allen B. "Librarians: The Next Generation." *Library Journal* 109 (April 1, 1984): 623-25.

Westin, Alan, Heather A. Schweder, Michael A. Baker, and Sheila Lehman. *The Changing Workplace: A Guide to Managing the People, Organizational, and Regulatory Aspects of Office Technology.* White Plains, N.Y.: Knowledge Industry Publications, 1984.

TECHNICAL SERVICES

Advances in Librarianship. New York: Academic Press, 1970- .

The ALA Glossary of Library and Information Science. Chicago: American Library Association, 1983.

ALA World Encyclopedia of Library and Information Services. Chicago: American Library Association, 1980.

The ALA Yearbook: A Review of Library Events. Chicago: American Library Association, 1976- .

Bernhardt, Frances Simonsen. *Introduction to Library Technical Services.* New York: H. W. Wilson, 1979.

The Bowker Annual of Library & Book Trade Information. New York: R. R. Bowker, 1956- .

Clinic on Library Applications of Data Processing: Proceedings. Urbana, Ill.: Graduate School of Library Science, University of Illinois, 1963- .

Davies, Ruth Ann. *The School Library Media Program: Instructional Force for Excellence.* 3d ed. New York: R. R. Bowker, 1979.

Encyclopedia of Library and Information Science. 36 vols. New York: Marcel Dekker, 1968-83.

Evans, G. Edward. *Management Techniques for Librarians.* 2d ed. New York: Academic Press, 1983.

Futas, Elizabeth. *The Library Forms Illustrated Handbook.* New York: Neal-Schuman, 1984.

Godden, Irene, ed. *Library Technical Services: Operations and Management.* New York: Academic Press, 1984.

Gorman, Michael. "On Doing Away with Technical Services Departments." *American Libraries* 10 (July/August 1979): 435-37.

Harrod, Leonard Montague. *Librarians' Glossary of Terms Used in Librarianship, Documentation and the Book Crafts, and Reference Book.* 5th ed. Brookfield, Vt.: Gower, 1984.

Hicks, Warren B., and Glenn E. Estes, eds. *Managing the Building-Level School Library Media Center.* Chicago: American Association of School Libraries, American Library Association, 1981.

Hicks, Warren B., and Alma M. Tillin. *Managing Multimedia Libraries.* New York: R. R. Bowker, 1977.

Library of Congress. *Annual Report of the Librarian of Congress.* Washington: Library of Congress, 1866- .

Lyle, Guy R. *The Administration of the College Library.* 4th ed. New York: H. W. Wilson, 1974.

Nickel, Mildred L. *Steps to Service: A Handbook of Procedures for the School Library Media Center.* Chicago: American Library Association, 1975.

Rogers, Rutherford D., and David C. Weber. *University Library Administration.* New York: H. W. Wilson, 1971.

Weihs, Jean. *Accessible Storage of Nonbook Materials.* Phoenix, Ariz.: Oryx Press, 1984.

GENERAL LITERATURE GUIDES

Library Literature: An Index to Library and Information Science. New York: H. W. Wilson, 1934- . (Bi-monthly).

SELECTED LIBRARY PERIODICALS
FOR PARAPROFESSIONALS

The Acquisitions Librarian.

American Libraries.

Cataloging and Classification Quarterly.

College & Research Libraries.

Information Technology and Libraries.

Journal of Academic Librarianship.

Journal of Library Automation.

LITA Newsletter.

Library Journal.

Library Quarterly.

Library Resources & Technical Services.

Library Trends.

SLJ: School Library Journal.

Special Libraries.

Unabashed Librarian.

Wilson Library Bulletin.